Psychoanalysis: Critical Conversations

Selected papers by Arnold D. Richards

Volume 1

Editor
Arthur A. Lynch

A joint imprint of:

 Contemporary Freudian Society

 and

 IPBOOKS.net
International Psychoanalytic Books

International Psychoanalytic Books (IPBooks),
New York • http://www.IPBooks.net

Copyright © 2015 New York: International Psychoanalytic Books (IPBooks),
25–79 31st Street Astoria, NY 11102
Online at: http://www.IPBooks.net

Cover Painting: *Suprematist Composition* by Kazimir Malevich (1914).

ISBN: 978-0-9965481-2-0

Dedicated to
Arlene Kramer Richards

CONTRIBUTORS

Jacob A. Arlow, M.D., Past President, American Psychoanalytic Association; former Editor-in-Chief, Psychoanalytic Quarterly. Recipient of the Inaugural Sigourney Award, esteemed as investigator, supervisor, teacher and clinician.

Janet Lee Bachant, Ph.D. is a psychologist, psychoanalyst, author and educator who has practiced for over 30 years. She is a supervising and faculty member of the Chinese American Continual Training Project for Senior Psychodynamic Psychotherapists in Wuhan, China since 2012. Dr. Bachant is the author of numerous journal articles and co-author (with Elliot Adler) of *Working in Depth: Framework and Flexibility in the Analytic Relationship.* She is in private practice in New York City.

Harold Blum, M.D. is a former Editor in Chief for the Journal of the American Psychoanalytic Association; President, Psychoanalytic Research and Development Fund and 1990 recipient of the Inaugural Sigourney Award. He is a Clinical Professor of Psychiatry and Supervising and Training Analyst at the Psychoanalytic Institute of the New York University Medical and former Executive Director of the Sigmund Freud Archives. Recognized as a Freud scholar he has been highly influential in psychoanalytic thought both in the United States and abroad.

Lawrence Friedman, M.D. is Clinical Professor of Psychiatry at the Weill-Cornell Medical College in New York City, and is on the Faculty of the Institute for Psychoanalytic Education affiliated with New York University Medical College. He has published extensively. He is an Honorary Member of the American Psychoanalytic Association, the New York Psychoanalytic Institute and Society, and the Psychoanalytic Institute of New York. He was the 2012 recipient of the Sigourney Award. He is currently in private practice of psychoanalytic psychotherapy.

Arthur A. Lynch, Ph.D is Past President, Senior Faculty member, Training and Supervising Analyst at the American Institute for Psychoanalysis. He is an Adjunct Professor at Columbia University School of Social Work, and a Visiting Professor and head of training for the Chinese American Psychoanalysis continuous training program at the Hospital for Psychotherapy in Wuhan, China. Dr. Lynch has authored and co-author numerous articles on psychoanalysis. He is co-editor of *Encounters with Loneliness, Only the Lonely* with Arlene K Richards and Lucille Spira (2013). Dr. Lynch is in private practice in New York City.

Arlene Kramer Richards, Ed.D. is a member of the Contemporary Freudian Society, the Institute for Psychoanalytic Training and Research, the American and the International Psychoanalytic Associations, A.P.A. Division 39. She has been the organizer and administrator of the Committee on Women and Psychoanalysis (COWAP) meeting in New York on International Adoption and Consequences for Psychic Development; co-organizer and administrator of COWAP's meeting in New York on Myths of Mighty Women. Currently she is the North American Representative to the IPA from 2012 to the present. Her recent publications, include: Myths of Mighty Women (with Lucille Spira); *Encounters With Loneliness: Only the Lonely* (with Lucille Spira, and Arthur Lynch), Winner Gradiva Prize; and, *Psychoanalysis: Listening to Understand* (Ed. Nancy Goodman).

Psychoanalysis: Critical Conversations

Selected papers by Arnold D. Richards

Volume 1

Contents

II: SELF PSYCHOLOGY AND THE WORK OF HEINZ KOHUT

III: THE HERMENEUTIC SCIENCE OF MERTON M. GILL AND IRWIN Z. HOFFMAN

IV: INTERPERSONAL AND RELATIONAL THEORY

V: CONTEMPORARY CONFLICT THEORY

Integrative Plurality in Psychoanalysis

Arnold Richards's psychoanalytic contributions follow the leitmotif of "integrative pluralism": how to continue the dialogue between the contributors of disparate psychoanalytic schools of thought (i.e., thought collectives) with the larger psychoanalytic knowledge base as it grows and changes with each new contribution. The chapters of the first section of this book show us the evolution of this design.

Although these chapters give us a noticeable trace of this motif, it has taken more then half a century to develop, requiring life experience from the many roles Richards has played and the posts he has held (see Friedman, 2015). He has been editor of *The American Psycho-analyst* (*TAP*), *Journal of the American Psychoanalytic Association* (*JAPA*), Festschrifts for four prominent psychoanalysts (1986, 1988, 1993, 1994), two additional collections (2001, 2010), and lately *InternationalPsychoanalysis.net.* He is also the Editor-in-Chief for the publishing company International Psychoanalytic Books (IPBooks; online as IPBooks.net). During this time, he has continued to hone his craft as teacher, supervisor, training analyst, and clinician, along the way contributing over a hundred publications to the psychoanalytic literature. As editor-in-chief of *InternationalPsychoanalysis.net,* Richards has kept its readers up to date on all things psychoanalytically fit to print. He has also organized a series of annual conferences bringing together dissimilar points of view around (a) common clinical concerns and (b) major educational and training dilemmas. It has been suggested that he be given the title "omnicompetent editor" (Friedman 2004, p. 13). Throughout these efforts, as we will see, Richards has attempted to engage, in dialogue, those who claim a new orthodoxy and would minimize the overall efforts of psychoanalysis; those who claim new theories, usually untested and unproven, that would replace the old; and those immovably complacent in the deep malaise of the status quo.

Richards begins the "critical conversations" in the introductory section by reflecting on his personal journey. In "Growing up Orthodox" he locates himself in a variety of dialectics: orthodoxy and deviance, pluralism and uniformity, free exploration and dogmatism. He explores psychoanalysis as an historical discipline that needs to come to terms with its history on "personal, intellectual and institutional levels" (1996, p. 9). In chapter two, "A.A. Brill and the Politics of Exclusion," he deepens our understanding of the "institutional level" by using as a case study Brill's life and his shepherding of psychoanalysis in New York (primarily through the New York Society) from 1911 through the end of the First World War. Exploring Brill's motives in safeguarding the profession, he highlights Brill's opposition to lay analysis. This opposition would become formalized as an institutional dynamic that Richards calls the "politics of exclusion" (p. 12). He traces the consequence of this form of segregation to its end result: not only prohibiting nonmedical personnel from training but extending it to the exclusion of dissenting ideas. The complex legacy of exclusionary policies has three main themes, all leading to the present state of fragmentation in our field. Richards, going beyond responses aimed at theoretical restoration, seeks a new politics of inclusion.

In chapter three of this section, we can see the natural development of this theme as he advocates for a measure of humility regarding the presumed supremacy of traditional theory. He cites a willingness by those who share this assumption (presumed supremacy) to implement exclusionary politics to secure their professional and personal success. In this chapter ("Psychoanalytic Discourse at the Turn of Our Century: A Plea for a Measure of Humility"), Richards proposes two variables (theoretical pluralism, and the increasing heterogeneity in the practitioner base) that have exacerbated a problem in which competing groups represent different ideas theoretically, professionally, and educationally. He finds that attempts to address this problem have led only to greater dissension and frustration between the groups. To mend these injuries, which have intergenerational sources, he suggests a spirit of transparency and a dialogue that accepts responsibility for mistakes. Although this reasonable request was attractive to those invited to respond to this paper, most had difficulty defining the problem or suggesting a solution.

Richards offers a broad historical understanding of the problem by defining the divergent paths since Freud. On one hand was the Hartmann group, who saw Freud as a cautious scientist accumulating data to frame hypotheses and confirm theories. They attempted to clarify and systematize many of the ambiguities of psychoanalytic theory and, as some believe, "to sanitize Freud" (Bergmann 2000, p. 60). Working alongside these theorists was another group who read Freud differently (Grossman 2002) and felt restricted by the incompleteness of his work. These theorists sought to advance Freud's ideas with alternative theories. This uneven and often conflicted growth led to a series of disagreements and schisms.[1]

Having traced this stormy dimension of psychoanalytic history, Richards suggests a path that gives reason for optimism. He suggests that psychoanalytic theory has evolved into an irreversible pluralism differentiated by major perspectives (e.g., contemporary Freudian, object relations, self psychology, relational and intersubjective theory, interpersonal theory, and Lacanian theory). As Lombardi (2005) notes, and as Richards is aware, not everyone agrees with his conclusion that today's pluralism is irreversible, even those with whom Richards finds major theoretical agreement (Di Chiara 2010; Rangell 2004, 2007, 2008; Brenner 2006).

Given this pluralistic landscape, Richards argues that the only reasonable course of action is to reach out in an open-minded and scientific spirit and learn from one another. If we fail to achieve this outcome, he warns, the only solution remaining—hardly salutary—is to cling to the remnants of old attachments and alliances with our professional ancestors. This solution has not worked well in the past and most likely will not work now. To make his point, Richards uses the relational perspective. His dispute with the relational theorists is not over the

---

[1]Richards distinguishes between "schisms" and "disagreements," the former leading to an official break between the parties resulting in one party developing in isolation from the larger group. This rupture rarely leads to a period of quiescent growth, on either side. More often, whatever essential differences these groups had, they tended to mirror each other, and their difficulties continued to be enacted long after the rupture. This point has been made in various ways by Eckhardt (1978), Quen and Carlos (1978), Frosch (1991), Kirsner (2000), Roazen and Swerdloff (1995), and Rangell (2004) and can easily be illustrated, in the U.S. by continuous breaches beginning with the 1941 separation of Horney and her colleagues from the New York Psychoanalytic Institute. That break led, directly or indirectly, to the creation of the Association for the Advancement of Psychoanalysis, the American Institute for Psychoanalysis, the William Alanson White Society, the National Psychological Association for Psychoanalysis, the New York University Postdoctoral Program in Psychotherapy and Psychoanalysis, the Association for Psychoanalytic Medicine, the Columbia Psychoanalytic Clinic, and the American Academy of Psychoanalysis (Frosch 1991; Gedo,1999; Levenson 2006). All of these institutions bear, in some degree, the mark of the original conflict.

important "neglected issues" they raise, nor does it involve theoretical disagreements, old or new. His main difficulty is with their consistent dismissal of the entire Freudian tradition, which is their approach to preserving the field's relevance. This movement had the potential to create a broader, more integrative psychoanalytic identity that would have provided an environment inclusive of differences, while maintaining the value of the psychoanalytic legacy. This was a moment of change that emerged out of a long and painful struggle in American psychoanalysis, with its intermittent radical shifts, all helping to redirect the field. It was an opportunity lost. Now, it is only through recognizing the diverse nature of psychoanalysis that we can see its full possibilities and make our contributions. Merton Gill saw this as well, and in his turn brought the roles of science and hermeneutics closer together.

The reactions from the discussants to this paper are an important reflection of the time and even today reflect the views of many. Although most of the commentators expressed agreement with the need for a more humble, civil, or respectful debate, there was little consensus among them regarding the nature of the problem, the context of the debate, or potential solutions. We must wonder what compelled Richards to write this when he did. Eisold (2003) thought that Richards had to know his message would be devalued—"dissected, deconstructed, and attacked" (p. 301)—and so it was. What wasn't clearly recognized, however, is that the paper is offered as an organizing framework, not simply as a plea for humility. That was merely the lesson learned from being in the fray for fifty years. What one sees in the paper and finds repeated in each of the chapters that follow, is a struggle to understand and debate the claims for territoriality, the political misuse of science, and attempts at theoretical domination, often initiated by groups who were themselves victims of exclusionary tactics. The chapters that follow, all written in the heat of debate, together offer a broad perspective on the profession's attempts to grow in an era of grand contributions and tumultuous change. This is the very hallmark of Richards's work and attests to the tireless commitment he brings to psychoanalysis. He possesses a relentless curiosity about all things human, and seeks answers from a biopsychosocial/cultural/political perspective. For Richards, our knowledge of the human condition is never static or finished. Always evolving, it requires an integrative pluralism.

PSYCHOANALYTIC THEORY

In Sections II, III, and IV, Richards examines theories from self psychology, hermeneutics and social constructivism, and the relational perspective.

Chapter four, "Self Theory, Conflict Theory, and the Problem of Hypochondriasis," is an attempt to compare self psychological and modern conflict models on clinical and theoretical grounds. Richards chose the case of a man suffering from hypochondriasis to evaluate the two models. His findings call into question any theory or technical approach relying on diagnostic categories to indicate technical interventions. Richards presents four additional concerns regarding Kohut's theory: (1) the patient's narcissistic and object-libidinal lines of development were not sharply distinct but interactive and intertwined; (2) the patient's presentation of disintegration anxiety could be described in everyday language and was never devoid of content; (3) the emerging analytic interaction did not require understanding through idealizing or mirror transferences, which may initially be useful organizers but tend to constrict the analyst's attention as greater weight is assigned them; finally, (4) the patient's and the analyst's cognitive and synthetic mental functions were as critical in attaining the necessary insight that promotes change as were introspection and empathy. Essential to Richards findings is the thesis that every case has its own uniqueness and complexity. This premise is often overlooked in the zeal of discovery.

Richards continues his exploration of Kohut's ideas in chapter five, "The Superordinate Self in Psychoanalytic Theory and in the Self Psychologies," which broadens the subject of his critique to include the theories of George Klein and John Gedo. All three theorists assign superordinate status to the self. Richards begins with Hartmann's clarification (1950) of Freud's ambiguous use of "das Ich": ego or self? Hartmann redefines narcissism as a libidinal cathexis of the self rather than of the ego, distinguishing three distinct domains of Freud's concept of das Ich: as ego (function focused), as self-experience, and as self or person (identity focused). This refinement, which led to the concept of the "representational world" (Sandler and Rosenblatt 1962), offered the analyst a new way to talk about the complex nature of wishes, fantasies, identifications, and attitudes. Hartmann's distinction, unfortunately, seemed lost on those building the new self psychologies.

Richards begins his evaluation of the three self theories with that of Klein and his collaborators. They proposed to replace metapsychology with a "self-schema" containing both systemic features and individual personal qualities. The clinical theory flowing from this self-schema emphasized the personal encounter and the importance of relating observational data to clinical theory. Richards finds Klein's overall efforts seriously flawed and spells out his reasons.

Next he turns to the contributions of Gedo, who rejects metapsychology because it loses sight of the "person" as "agent." As a corrective, Gedo (1979) suggests a self-organization emerging from an "epigenetic model." This self-organization, a developing hierarchy of personal aims and values, has autonomy as its highest goal. Gedo's model of technique includes a wide range of interventions, each aimed at difficulties specific to a particular mode of psychological functioning, typified by the early modes of psychic organization. Richards's main criticism is of Gedo's emphasis on interventions directed at contentless states. These shift the clinical unit of attention from the intrapsychic reality of the patient to his or her environment. This problem appears endemic to the other psychologies of the self.

Richards returns again to the work of Kohut, broadening his earlier critique. Of all the self psychologies, Kohut's is most clearly presented as a new theory. Kohut (1977) accords the self a superordinate status, arguing for an understanding of the self as a single content of the mind within which we can find contradictory selves and varied degrees of stability and accessibility to consciousness. Richards argues that Kohut, like Klein and Gedo, relies on a theory where mental agency is both the driving force and the entity driven.[2] Kohut's theory concludes with a view of the human condition organized around either Guilty Man or Tragic Man. Kohut acknowledges that this is a new conception of human beings, one in which self-cohesion is the highest aim and its loss the greatest danger. Richards ends by noting that all of these ideas are hypotheses in need of clinical validation.

In chapter 6, "Extenders, Modifiers, and Heretics," Richards evaluates Kohut's contribution using Martin Bergmann's taxonomy of psycho-

---

[2]As mentioned earlier, Kohut's emphasis on the underlying state of self cohesion or specific transference states leaves the analyst struggling with manifest content and no tools to discover a wealth of possible latent meanings.

analytic innovators (1993).[3] He begins by identifying three difficulties in the use of this classification: 1) an asymmetry of the terms, 2) a different definitional essence when applied to the self or another, 3) potential misapplication due to their historical variability and retrospective alteration. With these methodological weaknesses in mind, Richards tests the taxonomy by asking whether Kohut's views, especially his rejection of unconscious mental functioning, qualify him more as a modifier or as a heretic.

Richards reviews the literature of several theorists who were struggling with Kohut's theory at the time. They include Curtis (1985), Friedman (1980, 1986), Modell (1986), Treurniet (1983), Reed (1987), and Wallerstein (1983). These authors found that in an attempt to extend the description of ego development Kohut depreciated the theory of drives by perceiving them as disintegration products or symptoms. These theoretical changes diminish the technical value of conflict, transference, and defense/resistance, which are further downplayed by the inflated use of introspection and empathy. Kohut's overreliance on those concepts further reduces the significance of the unconscious. With this in mind, Richards wonders how Kohut might be classified. He furthers his inquiry by turning to the concept of "scientific research tradition" (Laudan 1977). One conclusion is that Kohut is suggesting a methodology leading to a different kind of observation, which shows him to be following a different, even separate, research tradition. He is not only listening for different issues; he is listening in a different way, using different criteria for validation. The only remaining question for Richards is: does this research tradition fall within the parameters of psychoanalysis, or is it a separate tradition? In closing, he acknowledges that different research traditions can increase the clinician's awareness of features of human experience that tend to be overlooked. Regarding this paper, Goldberg (1995) noted that Richards's "careful and tolerant evaluation, searching for a way to share the rubric of psychoanalysis, is itself a tribute to one of Bergmann's often-cited hallmarks: to

---

[3]Bergmann's taxonomy included *modifiers,* who modify theory or practice but stay within the range of acceptable practice (e.g., Ferenczi , Hartmann, Winnicott); *extenders,* who explore new areas without modifications in theory or technique (e.g., Abraham, Nunberg, Waelder, Fenichel); and *heretics,* who often make important contributions but then leave to start their own schools (e.g., Adler, Jung, Rank, Wilhelm Reich).

'embrace rather than bemoan the multiplicity of models' (p. xvi)" (pp. 860–861).

Section III covers the work of Merton Gill and Irwin Z. Hoffman. In chapter 7, "Transference Analysis: Means or End?" Richards explores Gill's belief that the transference is at the heart of the analytic process and has been overshadowed by genetic interpretation. To correct this flaw, Gill expands the definition of analysable transference and advocates for the technical centrality of transference analysis. Richards finds Gill's transference taxonomy simple yet progressive. It includes "resistance to the awareness of transference," "resistance to involvement in transference," and "resistance to the resolution of transference." Gill believed that resistance to the awareness of the transference is ubiquitous and emphasized it as the essential focus in early treatment. Not talking about any particular issue is, Gill noted, an aversion to specifically telling the analyst anything. Although this is an important possibility, it is troubling to Richards because it ignores other possibilities, such as the patient's inability to admit a painful issue even to himself. Gill believed that the patient's neurosis should be translated into the transference neurosis and that from the beginning the analyst should make active transference interpretations to root out and surmount inherent transference resistance. For Gill, this was the very essence of the analytic process.

Later, joined by Hoffman (1982), Gill attempted to empirically validate this premise. Richards points out that this effort is fraught with methodological problems that make for a less than entirely convincing demonstration of the overriding power of here-and-now transference interpretation. His greater concern, however, is the authors' effort to place the transference technically front and center. He suggests that the only technical precept one can draw from their approach is that it requires the analyst to listen for unconscious meanings and themes that concern personal wishes and fantasies. These, among other data, are often related, but not limited, to transference wishes and fantasies. Interpretation or clinical inference, Richards notes, is often fuelled by the analyst's knowledge of the entire analysis, while an insistent pursuit of transference meaning can encourage formulaic inquiries and rote responses. He acknowledges that Gill's contribution on transference analysis provides an important correction in psychoanalytic treatment, but these must now be absorbed within the broader theory.

In chapter 8, Richards (with Arthur Lynch) broadens his exposition of Gill's many contributions. Beginning as a classical analyst, Gill looked at issues from a range of perspectives during a fifty-year psychoanalytic career. He went from promoting and extending a metapsychological framework with Rapaport; to renouncing metapsychology with Klein, Holt, Schafer, and others (Gill 1976); to disclaiming first the topographical model and then the structural model (Gill 1963); to briefly exploring neurophysiology. Throughout all these efforts, he kept a focus on concerns regarding the psychoanalytic process. As a result, Richards notes, it is difficult to locate Gill theoretically. In the end, he is best seen as a "theoretical extender" (Bergmann 1993) at the center of investigation in many areas pursued in American psychoanalysis.

Richards addresses Gill's depiction of the classical analyst's perspective on the interactive nature of psychoanalysis by demonstrating how psychoanalysts have persistently struggled with the concept of interaction, the ubiquitous nature of transference, and the co-constructed perceptions that shape and move the analytic relationship. In developing these ideas, however, the authors did not neglect the deeper subtleties that Gill's work demands. Richards and Lynch discuss Gill's thoughts on one-person v. two-person psychology, transference, neutrality, alliance, and silence. Drawing special attention to the interactive spectrum, they show the travails and growth these concepts have undergone. Gill theorized from an apolitical position, maintaining that differences are best understood as the emphasis of an issue within a dialectic. This position allowed him to explore psychoanalysis well beyond Freud's realm. He repeatedly challenged the clinical frontiers, from many perspectives, but in a truly Freudian spirit.

In chapter 9, Richards outlines Hoffman's use of social constructivism in psychoanalysis. For Hoffman, analyst and analysand are unavoidably engaged in interactions, the meaning of which the analyst must continually reflect on. This process replaces the use of free association. Richards examines this premise and how these beliefs fit into three specific aspects of Hoffman's thinking: (1) the position of the dialectic in psychoanalytic practice, (2) the nature of therapeutic change, and (3) the question of a new paradigm in psychoanalysis. Like Hoffman, Richards believes that the vast rift in psychoanalysis is between dialectical and dichotomous thinkers. Yet as sensitive as Hoffman is to this, Richards points out that Hoffman takes a positivistic position on the essential nature of the dialectic in constructivism. Richards agrees with Hoffman that the analyst always influences the patient: neutrality is an ideal never strictly met. But Richards adds that the analyst can offer valuable interpretations from a "neutral-enough" stance. Richards rejects Hoffman's, or anyone's, attempt at placing a single variable (e.g., "interactive subjectivity") as the center of attention in working toward psychoanalytic change. No singular connection is robust enough to fully account for the extremely complex nature of the psychoanalytic process. Richards concludes that Hoffman's perspective may enlarge our own but that little evidence it could replace a reliance on insight and interpretation. Richards's final concern about dialectical constructivism is that despite its inability to offer empirical evidence or greater explanatory power in the real world, it claims to be a replacement for the older theory.

In chapter 10, Richards's probes further into dialectical constructivism: "How new is the 'new American psychoanalysis'?" Somewhat optimistic that contemporary psychoanalysis has entered an era of productive dialogue (Aron1996; Wallerstein1998), he nonetheless remains concerned that some proclaim a paradigm shift to a new psychoanalysis, providing no substantial evidence for the claim. Richards is convinced that paradigm shifts can be determined only in historical retrospect. To his point, he cites Hoffman's evaluation of the concept of the "blank screen," his insistence on the inevitability of interaction, and his acceptance of the constructivist perspective. These technical conclusions, Richards argues, act as self-fulfilling prophecies designed to imbue the analytic situation with countertransference in order to foster the illusion of an ordinary relationship. This in turn limits Hoffman's intervention strategies primarily to attempts at correcting complaints at the manifest content level. For Richards, acknowledging interaction and the use of the analyst as a new object leads to a different technical conclusion, one calling for greater caution and restraint rather than suggestion and active influence.

Richards extends his argument for a neutrality[4] that creates a "predictable atmosphere" allowing for openness and compassion. This is not only possible; it is essential. So how new *is* the new American psychoanalysis? The title's question, like the issues dealt with in this chapter, is offered in homage to those who would reach beyond complacency to engage in further dialogue.

---

[4]He finds a sense of "good enough" neutrality in the work of Loewald (1960), who contends that Freud's use of the term *"Indifferenz,"* is better construed as "disinterestedness" (i.e., a detached contemplation).

In Section IV (chapters 11–13) we find Richards and colleagues engaged in dialogue and debate with relational theorists, on levels both intellectual and emotional. In chapter 11, Richards (with Janet Lee Bachant) critiques Stephen Mitchell's *Relational Concepts in Psychoanalysis* (1988). From the outset, the authors wonder how Mitchell arrived at his core argument, which proposes an inherent opposition between drive and relational premises.

They consider Mitchell's relational thinking at the time and compare it with the contemporary classical position on three clinical issues: sexuality, the importance of early experience in the development of psychic structure, and transference. They note that Mitchell found the dominant meanings of sexuality in the basic patterns of search, surrender, and escape but failed to recognize that Freud's concept of infantile sexuality was deeply ingrained in the emotionally dramatic experiences the child endures as he learns to love in new ways while traveling through life in a family of significant others. The authors next focus on Mitchell's efforts to redefine developmental theory based wholly on relational considerations. This, they stress, abandoned the importance of early experience as consequential in the expression of needs that are active throughout life. This redefinition of development substantially changed psychoanalytic theory, especially with regard to the dynamic unconscious, the pleasure principle, and technique. Consequently, it significantly reduces the explanatory base of the theory. Richards and Bachant also summarize Mitchell's view of transference as resting on three relational assumptions: transference as (1) an allegory contained within relational patterns; (2) a vehicle for rewriting and broadening the analysand's narratives; and (3) as dyadic in nature, interactive in style, and egalitarian by design. They end with some thoughtful ideas on the politics of model making.

In chapter 12, Richards (with Janet Lee Bachant and Arthur Lynch) return to the relational perspective, providing a broader evaluation and identifying the particular impact it has on the psychoanalytic situation. They discuss five exponents of relational theory.

The authors argue that the antagonism between relational theory and drive theory, as posited by relational theorists, is a false dichotomy designed to elevate differences and prove superiority. They show that Greenberg and Mitchell (1983) misrepresent drive theory, conceptualize development as derived principally from the interpersonal field, thereby minimizing intrapsychic conflict, and substantially redefine the concepts of resistance, transference, and free association. As the relational perspective progressed, there was much less concurrence among relational theorists. Mitchell remained committed to the complete rejection of drive theory, recommending a purely relational model. By 1992, Greenberg (1991), Ogden (1992a, & b), and Slavin and Kriegman (1992) all argued for some form of drive theory in understanding the individual's differentiation. The authors conclude that psychoanalysis grows with careful attention to specific clinical and conceptual issues, as can be seen in the works of Ogden, Rangell, Pine, and Wallerstein, all of whom have struggled with a range of epistemologies.

In chapter 13 Richards (with Arlene Richards) comments on the work of Benjamin Wolstein, with special interest in the psychoanalytic situation and the therapeutic action of psychoanalysis. They find that Wolstein's works, before the advent of PEP, had been isolated from the broader profession. The authors discuss many of Wolstein's fundamental concepts and begin a comparative exercise by pointing to parallels between Wolstein's work and that of contemporary Freudians. These parallels include an emphasis on individuation and the uniqueness of each individual and therapeutic dyad; contributions in countertransference; and the need for the analyst to empathically experience the analysand's fear and pain. There is also some agreement that a crucial aspect of the analytic work is to attend to unexpressed affect. The authors describe three aims for the chapter: to convey what was lost in the period of isolation, to identify the areas of convergence in clinical findings, and to begin addressing ways to end theoretical estrangements. These examples, the authors find, illustrate how related clinical findings may be arrived at independently. This realization brings the authors to the question, How do theoretical differences exhibit or conceal different ways of working in the clinical situation? The authors note that clinicians draw on and/or create theory, in part, to correct for aspects of their character that would otherwise circumvent or impede the clinical process. The authors end the review with an appreciation of Wolstein's contributions, viewing him as a pioneer with the spirit of a broad-minded thinker.

USES OF CONTEMPORARY CONFLICT THEORY AND BEYOND

In Section V, (chapters 14–18), Richards and colleagues explore the theoretical core of contemporary conflict theory. In chapter14, Richards outlines Brenner's contributions. Early in his career, Brenner (1955), considered psychoanalysis a natural science in which data is gathered by a particular method and evaluated from a specific attitude.[5] This data-oriented attitude continued to guide Brenner throughout his technical works. In 1964, Brenner and Arlow revised psychoanalytic theory and argued the case for privileging the structural model. In 1982, Brenner offered a new view of the mind that considered all aspects of mental functioning to be compromise formations: complex pleasurable and unpleasurable affects; various wishes and fears[6] as unique expressions of libidinal and aggressive trends; defensive functions that deny awareness of complete or part components of unpleasurable affects; protective and self-punitive moral trends; and environmental pressures brought to bear at a given point in time. Richards points out that for Brenner, metapsychology was a mode of discourse or a way of observing no different from that in other sciences.[7] Brenner (1994) modified this view by moving to a model of functional categories and mental processes. The ego, Richards notes, becomes the person,[8] drive becomes wish, and superego becomes the moral component of compromise formation. What Brenner offers, Richards notes, is an ego that is dynamically indistinguishable from a neurotic symptom and a view of the child motivated above all by the need to win his or her parents' love. For Richards, the most important concept was Brenner's proposal of compromise formation. Brenner (2006) also advocated for a definition of psychoanalytic treatment not defined by the frequency of sessions or from the physical position the patient is in as he examines his life, but by an analytic attitude and/or the search for meaning.

The psychoanalytic situation, according to Brenner, is organized around this new model of mental functioning, which alters the goals and aims of technique. Brenner emphasized how technique follows conflict

---

[5]Richards points out that this was also Brenner's method for theory building: first a careful literature review, next an identification of assumptions not supported by clinical data, and then construction of a theory that better fits the data and points in a new direction.

[6]These wishes and fears (along with fantasies, dreams, neurotic symptoms, and associative material) express their meanings in language and gestures that make up the principal data of psychoanalysis privileged by practitioners.

[7]What Gill (1994) would later call a hermeneutic science, one where meanings are data.

[8]Richards (1986) speculates that Brenner would continue to focus on the constituents of psychic conflict while incorporating certain hermeneutic features and could eventually offer a model of the mind in which the elements of conflict replace the traditional concepts of agency. Shortly after Brenner (1994) did just that.

and warned that no single technical element or explanation attains greater prestige than its place in the theory of mental functioning. This data-oriented attitude continued to guide Brenner through his technical works, where he came to appreciate all aspects of mental functioning as compromise formations. Brenner required that all aspects of the conflict presenting in behavior, character traits, and symptoms be looked at, while interpreting the components of conflict as they emerge in the analysands's associations.[9] In treatment, compromise formations change and alter the character and strategy of defense as a new homeostasis of mind is achieved.

Richards sees Brenner's work as establishing him as a psychoanalytic extender who innovated by addressing the meaning of traditional psychoanalytic concepts (e.g., drive, defense, superego, affect, transference, countertransference, regression). In providing this new theory, he challenged alternative schools to provide a comprehensive and coherent presentation of their fundamental principles and concepts.

In chapter 15, Richards (with Jacob Arlow) describes the principles fundamental to psychoanalytic psychology: psychic determinism, dynamic psychology, conflict, and the role of unconscious mental elements. These conceptual abstractions are detectable only in time of psychic conflict. Solutions or compromise formations resolve conflicts by ensuring that all aspects of the conflict find participation of their dynamism in the solution. When these solutions ward off unpleasure, they are considered successful. When they fail, the solution will bring a greater or lesser degree of pain or may place the person in harm's way. This leaves the mind in a constant effort to adapt, integrate, and compromise. Richards and Arlow describe the different methods available to accomplish this as the child encounters the vicissitudes of life.

As the authors move into the treatment section, they note that fundamental operational principles shape the psychoanalytic situation in order to attain a dynamic record of the analysand's style of mental functioning. Treatment aims at providing insight into the nature, magnitude, and automatic actions of the unconscious, which broadens his capacity

---

[9]Brenner puts this quite succinctly: "What psychoanalysts do (of particular importance) . . . is make inferences with respect to the causes of the wishes, fears, fantasies, dreams, neurotic symptoms, and associative material that constitute their data of observation . . . psychoanalysts try to discover or, to be more precise, to infer what it is that causes the normal and pathological mental phenomena they observe" (Brenner, 1980, p. 205; quote abbreviated in Richards, 1986, p. 6).

for choosing less conflictual compromise formations. The authors demonstrate the flexibility and growth of psychoanalytic theory in its continuous revision and integration of new insights and discoveries, offering clear discussions of transference, object relations, narcissism, identification, and the role of compromise formations.

Social applications are addressed as the authors propose that advances in psychoanalytic theory have provided insight into social and group phenomena, (e.g., myths, fairy tales, literary works, religious traditions), which embody repressed wishes often based on a secret rebellion against maturation and social prohibitions. Validation of these insights is lacking. In chapter 16, Richards (with Lynch) reviews, in five sections, the theoretical roots of contemporary conflict theory in ego psychology. In an introductory section, the authors trace the emergence of ego psychology from Freud's final theoretical revision (1923b, 1926). The clinical implications now shift from an energy model to a meaning model, as Freud returns to the threatening wish that now elicits signals of danger.

In parts two, three and four, the authors review the clinical implications of ego psychology: the effect of theory change on technique and the shift of clinical observation to the ego; the analyst as participant observer (efforts to ensure that interpretation respect the unique interaction of analysand and analyst); and issues of transference and countertransference. They trace the concepts from Freud's early work through that of contemporary conflict theorists. Together, ego psychologists and object relations theorists provided the grounding for contemporary debates regarding a variety of clinical interactions, including enactment.

In the final section, the authors review contemporary conflict theorists who have critically examined such concepts as anxiety, repression, defense and symptom formation, affect, and the superego. Two issues of technique are traced: the difference in clinical emphasis between those who espouse interpretation of defense, and those who focus on interpretation of conflict and compromise formation in the context of unconscious fantasy and the technical role of the patient-analyst relationship—its active use in the treatment versus a greater emphasis on its interpretation. The paper ends with a recognition that psychoanalysis will continue to generate diverse and conflicting positions that require a firm grasp of collective history and scientific influences if partisan squabbles are to be avoided.

In chapter 17, Richards and Lynch review the work of Leo Rangell. Rangell (2007) worked to create a unified psychoanalytic theory he called "total composite psychoanalytic theory." He saw the domain of psychoanalysis as the study of unconscious intrapsychic conflict, and his efforts focused on how intrapsychic events that lead to action both affect and are affected by the varieties of human experience. The authors begin the review with Rangell's concept of "the human core" and outline the twelve sequential steps he proposed as defining "the intrapsychic process." The intrapsychic process is affected by signals of anxiety or safety that lead to active unconscious decision making and free will, to breaches of integrity, and to questions of personal responsibility and accountability as one struggles with the willingness required to live by superego values.[10]

Rangell believed that the final test of any idea is in the clinical domain. His clinical contributions fall into two areas: the psychoanalytic core (contributions made to the psychoanalytic process) and specific clinical problems in the application of technique. For Rangell, the authors note, it was the analytic process that distinguishes the method and not frequency or furniture. He rejected privileging any technical aspect of the process until it is clinically called for.

The authors conclude that for Rangell most alternative psychoanalytic schools contain important individual contributions that could be supplemental to the total theory but instead often get stuck in partisan struggles. Rangell believed that theoretical pluralism is the current problem for psychoanalysis. This has been fostered by four basic fallacies[11] that have led to a theoretical drifting with no real efforts at "consistency or intellectual unity" (Rangell 2007, p. 99). Rangell's alternative is "total composite psychoanalytic theory."[12] Both the collective and the individual decide what is accepted into this broad theory.

---

[10]The compromise of integrity falls on a range from the familiar to the ego-alien and is found in psychopathology from mild to severe. Treatment is through the analysis of the syndrome with the analytic aim of "turning out an honest man," free from both the compromise of integrity and neurosis.

[11]These fallacies are (1) replacement of a pre-existing set of observations or parts of explanatory theory by another when both new and old are both valid, (2) the pathogenic fallacy—"pars pro toto"—a selection of a part and its replacement for the whole, (3) failure to aptly apply knowledge and insight gained in one sphere to related relevant situations, (4) failure to follow up one's thought or actions with the consequences that could be expected from new discoveries or insights.

[12] It is cohesive and cumulative, aiming at "completeness with parsimony" (Rangell 2007, p. 116): "total"—containing all nonexpendable elements; "composite"—a blend of all valid discoveries; and "psychoanalytic"—fulfilling the criteria of psychoanalysis (Rangell 2007, p. 85).

The section concludes with Chapter 18, Clinical Theory and Psychoanalytic Technique. In this chapter Richards (with Arlene Richards) turns to clinical issues and the interaction of theory and technique. The Richards ask: Are there technical consequences to theory, and are theories comparable? They begin with a reflection of some important theoretical dialectics and then turn to a clinical case. Insight into unconscious fantasies arises organically in the course of the analysis, as the analyst uses key aspects of contemporary conflict theory. These concepts inform a technical stance that successfully offers the patient new knowledge of her thoughts and feelings. The authors agree with Arlow (1994, qtd. in Richards and Richards 1995) that uncovering distressing wishes and thoughts is generally a painful aspect of analysis but it is not, as some contend, a humiliating experience.

After a review of the literature, the authors identify the problem that theory is not unitary. Rather, it consists of a set of discrete yet interrelated models of the mind, development, pathogenesis and symptom formation, and the therapeutic process and cure. Additions or modifications to some of these subtheories may be more technically consequential than others. The authors ask: Do the technical modifications that follow from these new theories represent genuine advances? To answer this they review various pluralistic theories, outlining how each theory informs technique and then propose a series of technical challenges. They find that self psychology practitioners minimize the role of unconscious fantasy and focus technically on the real relationships with the parents and the analyst. The authors conclude, after reviewing the many helpful interventions, that the overall patient-analyst interaction appears to offer little more than friendly comfort. They are even less optimistic about intersubjective and relational theories, which appear to have important but deleterious effects on technique. The authors next turn to the modern Kleinians, who despite having a different subtheory in their models of mind, development, and pathogenesis resemble modern Freudian theorists in technique. Finally, the American object relations school attempts to devise treatments for patients who cannot tolerate the rigors of psychoanalysis practiced by ego psychologists. Technically, the authors find that American object relations theories and techniques fit comfortably into the ego psychology model. The authors conclude with some comparative issues. They agree with Wallerstein (1990) that differences in theory do not necessarily translate into differences in technique and follow Arlow and Brenner (1990), who note that analytic technique is best viewed as coterminous with analytic process. The authors come away from this exercise with the belief that maintaining an integrationist position is more challenging with some schools than others, but leave to the future the answer to whether or not convergence is possible with such divergent approaches.

EPILOGUE

In chapter 19, "A View from Now", Richards offers us his latest thoughts on a long and productive psychoanalytic career.

CONCLUSION

In summary, Richards's curiosity has made him a natural pantologist reflecting a new version of the old value of Bildung.[13] As a result, he has contributed to psychoanalysis on many levels. He is an organizer, advocate, publisher, editor, writer, teacher, practitioner, and student. He has taken Freud's discoveries of the organizing and disorganizing forces in the mind and applied them to the growth and development of psychoanalytic theory. His theory of psychoanalysis is broad and congruent in its' models of mind, development, pathology and technique.

This theory emerges from Freud's work, continues with the contributions from ego psychology and structural theory; eventually settling down in a core contemporary conflict theory. It is not as traditional as it might sound, as Richards requires explanations from bio/psycho/sociocultural contributions that are determined epigenetically. Having arrived at a theory with suitable explanations segued Richards into an inspired and challenging dialogue with other thought collectives.

Although not often recognized, these debates follow the spirit of Bergmann as they 'embrace rather than bemoan the multiplicity of models.' (Munter, C.H. & Pekowsky, J.C., 1995, p. xvi). So in the subtext of these included papers Richards recognizes that within each psychoanalytic thought collective the members separately and together delete, alter and enhance the theoretical concepts provided by prior members. These alterations and enhancements are multiply determined from sources of internal creativity to sources of conflict with external thought collec-

---

[13]This is a concept reflecting education and transformation. Wang (2003) applied it to psychoanalysis in "*Bildung* or The Formation of the Psychoanalyst."

tives. The overall contributions keep psychoanalytic theory vital and relevant to the times. They continue to offer the best explanations possible for the clinical problems we face everyday (Brenner, 2006). As each thought collective alters and enhances their theories, they offer further opportunities for the modification of a total composite psychoanalytic theory from an individual micro level through an international macro level (Rangell, 2004, 2007).

While musing over where he fits in the analytic world, Richards noted: "I like to think I am my own person." Like his teachers before him, Richards has influenced several generations of psychoanalysts from many quarters. He has also not sought a following or thought collective, opting instead for the works of originality and integration.

REFERENCES

ARON, L. (1996). *A Meeting of Minds: Mutuality in Psychoanalysis.* Hillsdale, NJ: Analytic Press.

—— (1994).

AHUMADA, J.L., OLAGARAY, J., RICHARDS, A.K., & RICHARDS, A.D., Eds. (1997). *The Perverse Transference & Other Matters: Essays in Honor of R. Horacio Etchegoyen.* Northvale, NJ: Jason Aronson.

AINSFELD, L. & RICHARDS, A.D. (2000). The Replacement Child: Variations on a Theme in History and Psychoanalysis. *Psychoanalytic Study of the Child* 55:301–318.

ARLOW, J.A. (1994). The Process of Validation and Hypothesis Testing in the Analytic Situation. Unpublished.

—— & BRENNER, C. (1964). *Psychoanalytic Concepts and the Structural Theory.* New York: International Universities Press.

—— —— (1990). The Psychoanalytic Process. *The Psychoanalytic Quarterly,* 59:678–692.

—— RICHARDS, A.D. (1991). Psychoanalytic Theory. *The Encyclopedia of Human Biology,* (vol 6.) Renato Dulbecco (Editor-in-Chief). The Salk Institute La Jolla, California. New York: Academic Press, pp. 305–317.

BACHANT, J.L. & RICHARDS, A.D. (1993). Review Essay: Relational Concepts in Psychoanalysis: An Integration by Stephen A. Mitchell. *Psychoanalytic Dialogues,* 3:431–460.

—— LYNCH, A.A. & RICHARDS, A.D. (1995). Relational models in psychoanalytic theory. *Psychoanalytic Psychology,* Vol. 12 (1), pp.71–88.

BERGMANN, M.S. (1993). Reflections on the History of Psychoanalysis. *Journal of the American Psychoanalytic Association* 41:929–955.

—— , ed. (2000). *The Hartmann Era.* New York: Other Press.

BLUM, H.P., KRAMER, Y., RICHARDS, A. K, & RICHARDS, A.D., eds. (1988). *Fantasy, Myth and Reality: Essays in honor of Jacob A. Arlow.* New York: International Universities Press.

BRENNER, C. (1955) *An Elementary Textbook of Psychoanalysis Revised Edition.* New York: International Universities Press, Inc., 1973.

—— (1980). Metapsychology and Psychoanalytic Theory. *Psychoanalytic Quarterly,* 49:189–214.

—— (1982). *The Mind in Conflict.* New York: International Universities Press.

—— (1994). The mind as conflict and compromise formation. *Journal of Clinical Psychoanalysis* 3:473–488.

—— (2006). *Psychoanalysis or Mind and Meaning.* New York: The Psychoanalytic Quarterly.

CURTIS H.C. (1985). Clinical perspectives on self psychology. *Psychoanalytic Quarterly* 54:339–377.

DI CHIARA, G. (2010). The Unconscious: Seemingly Gone Missing and Yet it Represses. *The Italian Psychoanalytic Annual,* 4:39–52

ECKHARDT, M.H. (1978). Organizational schisms in American psychoanalysis. In *American Psychoanalysis, Origins and Development: the Adolf Meyer Seminars,* eds., Jacques M. Quen & Eric T. Carlson. New York: Brunner/Mazel, pp. 141–161.

EISOLD, K. (2003). Toward a Psychoanalytic Politics. *Journal of the American Psychoanalytic Association,* 51S:301–321.

FREUD, S. (1923). The ego and the id. *Standard Edition* 19:1–66.

—— (1926). Inhibitions, symptoms and anxieties. *Standard Edition* 20:87–176.

FRIEDMAN, L. (1980). Kohut: A book review essay, *Psychoanalytic Quarterly,* 49: 393–423.

—— (1986). Kohut's testament. *Psychoanalytic Inquiry,* 6 (3): 321 – 347.

—— (2004). Arnold Richards: An Appreciation. *Journal of the American Psychoanalytic Association,* 52:11–13.

—— (2015). Preface. In *Psychoanalysis: Critical Conversations,* Arthur Lynch, ed.. *The selected papers of Arnold D. Richards, M.D., Volume I.* New York: IPBooks.

FROSCH, J. (1991). The New York Psychoanalytic Civil War. *Journal of the American Psychoanalytic Association,* 39:1037–1064

GEDO, J. (1979). *Beyond Interpretation.* New York: International UniversitiesPress.

—— (1999). The Evolution of Psychoanalysis. New York: Other Press. *Annual of Psychoanalysis* 29:105–116 (2001).

GILL, M. (1963). *Topography and Systems in Psychoanalytic Theory.* New York: International Universities Press.

—— (1976). Metapsychology is not psychology. In *Psychology Versus Metapsychology,* ed. M. Gill & P. Holzman. New York: International Universities Press, pp. 71–105.

—— (1982). Analysis of Transference, Vol. I: Theory and Technique. *Psychological Issues*, Monograph 53. New York: Int. Univ. Press.

—— & HOFFMAN, I.Z. (1982). Analysis of Transference, Vol. II: Studies of Nine Audio-Recorded Sessions. *Psychological Issues*, Monograph 54. New York: Int. Univ. Press.

—— (1994). *Psychoanalysis in Transition: A Personal View.* Hillsdale, NJ: The Analytic Press.

GOLDBERG D.A. (1995). Review of *The Spectrum of Psychoanalysis: Essays in Honor of Martin S. Bergmann.* eds. A.K. Richards & A.D. Richards. *International Journal of Psycho-Analysis* 76:859–862.

GREENBERG, J. (1991). *Oedipus and beyond: A clinical theory.* Cambridge, MA: Harvard University Press.

HARTMANN, H. (1950). Comments on the psychoanalytic theory of the ego. *Psychoanalytic Study of the Child* 5:74–96

HOFFMAN, I. (1996). Merton M. Gill: A Study in Theory Development in Psychoanalysis. *Psychoanalytic Dialogues*, 6:5–53

KIRSNER, D. (2000). *Unfree Associations: Inside Psychoanalytic Institutes.* London: Process Press.

KOHUT, H. (1977). *The Restoration of the Self.* New York: International Universities Press.

LAUDAN, L. (1977). *Progress and Its Problems: Towards a Theory of Scientific Growth.* Berkeley: University of California Press.

LEVENSON, E.A. (2006). Fifty Years of Evolving Interpersonal Psychoanalysis. *Contemporary Psychoanalysis,* 42:557–564.

LOMBARDI, R. (2005). Curare con la psicoanalisi. Percorsi e strategie [Curing with psychoanalysis. Routes and strategies] by Giuseppe Di Chiara Milano: Cortina. 2003. 143 pp. *International Journal of Psycho-Analysis*, 86:938–941.

LYNCH, AA. (2006). My Life in Theory by Leo Rangell [an essay review]. *The American Journal of Psychoanalysis* 66:293–312.

—— Bachant, J.L., & Richards, A.D. (2008). Erotic Transference and the Spectrum of Interaction. *International Psychoanalysis.net.* March 27, 2008 Posting of Paper.

—— Richards, AD. (2010). Leo Rangell: The Journey Of A Developed Freudian. *The Psychoanalytic Review,* Vol 97, Iss. 3. p. 361–391

—— Richards, A.D. & Bachant, J.L. (2013). "Afterword." In *The Rangell Reader*, eds. B. Kalish & C. Fisher, New York: IPBooks, pp. 243–254.

MITCHELL, S. (1988). *Relational Concepts in Psychoanalysis.* Cambridge, MA: Harvard University Press.

MODELL, A. (1986), The missing element in Kohut's cure. *Psychoanalytic Inquiry* 6:367–385.

MUNTER, C.H. & PEKOWSKY, J.C. (1995). Preface: the good hour and a half. In *The Spectrum of Psychoanalysis: Essays in Honor of Martin S. Bergmann,* eds. A.K. Richards & A.D. Richards. Madison, CT: International Universities Press.

Ogden, T.H. (1992A). THE DIALECTICALLY CONSTITUTED/DECENTRED SUBJECT OF PSYCHoanalysis. I. The Freudian subject. *International Journal of Psycho-Analysis* 73:517–526.

—— (1992b). The dialectically constituted/decentred subject of psycho-analysis. II. The contributions of Klein and Winnicott. *International Journal of Psycho-Analysis* 73: 613–626.

QUEN, J. & CARLSON, E., EDS. (1978). *American Psychoanalysis, Origins and Development: The Adolf Meyer Seminars.* New York: Brunner/ Mazel.

RANGELL, L. (1985). On the theory of theory in psychoanalysis and the relation of theory to psychoanalytic therapy. *Journal of the American Psychoanalytic Association,* 33, 59–92.

—— (2004). *My Life in Theory.* New York: Other Press.

—— (2007). *The Road to Unity in Psychoanalytic Theory.* New York: Jason Aronson.

—— (2008). Reconciliation: The Continuing Role of Theory. *Journal of American Academy of Psychoanalysis* 36:217–233

REED, G. (1987). Rules of clinical understanding in classical psychoanalysis and in self psychology: A comparison. *Journal of the American Psychoanalytic Association* 35:421–455.

RICHARDS, A.D. (1981). Self Theory, Conflict Theory, and the Problem of Hypochondriasis. *Psychoanalytic Study of the Child* 36: 319–337.

—— (1982). The Superordinate Self in Psychoanalytic Theory and in the Self Psychologies. *Journal of the American Psychoanalytic Association* 30: 939–957.

—— (1984). Transference Analysis: Means or End? *Psychoanalytic Inquiry* 4:355–366.

—— (1986). Introduction in Psychoanalysis, the Science of Mental Conflict: Essays in Honor of Charles Brenner. In *Psychoanalysis: the Science of Mental Conflict,* A.D. Richards, A.D. & M.S. Willick, M.S., eds. New York: International Universities Press.

—— (1996). 1996 Growing Up Orthodox. In *More Psychoanalysts at Work,* ed. J. Reppen. Northvale, NJ: Jason Aronson.

—— (1999a). A.A. Brill and the politics of exclusion. *Journal of the American Psychoanalytic Association* 47:9–28.

—— (1999b). Review of: *Ritual and Spontaneity in the Psychoanalytic Process: A Dialectical Constructive Point of View* by Irwin Hoffman. *Psychoanalytic Psychology* 16:288–302.

—— (2002). How New is the "New American Psychoanalysis"? The Example of Irwin Z. Hoffman. *Journal of Clinical Psychoanalysis* 11: 379–401.

—— (2003). Psychoanalytic Discourse at the Turn of Our Century: A Plea for a Measure of Humility. *Journal of the American Psychoanalytic Association* 51(Suppl.): 73–89.

—— (2007). Psychoanalysis or Mind and Meaning. by Charles Brenner.

Psychoanalytic Quarterly, 76:1029–1032.

——— Lynch, A.A. (1997). Merton Gill: A place in the psychoanalytic firmament. *The Annual of Psychoanalysis* 24:49–61.

——— ——— (1998). From Ego Psychology to Contemporary Conflict Theory: An Historical Overview. In *The Modern Freudians: Contemporary Psychoanalytic Technique, eds.* C. Ellman, S. Grand, M. Silvan & S. Ellman. Northvale, NJ: Jason Aronson.

——— ——— (2008). The Identity of Psychoanalysis and Psychoanalysts. *Psychoanalytic Psychology* 25: 203–219.

——— ——— (2010). From Ego Psychology to Contemporary Conflict Theory: An Historical Overview. In *When Theories Touch*, Steven Ellman, ed. Northvale, NJ: Jason Aronson.

RICHARDS, A.K. & RICHARDS, A.D., EDS. (1994). *The Spectrum of Psychoanalysis: Essays in Honor of Martin S. Bergmann.* New York: International Universities Press.

——— ——— (1995). Notes on psychoanalytic theory and its consequences for technique. *Journal of Clinical Psychoanalysis* 4:429–456.

RICHARDS, A.D. & WILLICK, M.S., EDS. (1986). *Psychoanalysis: the Science of Mental Conflict.* New York: International Universities Press.

RICHARDS, A.K. & RICHARDS, A.D. (2000). Benjamin Wolstein and us: Many roads lead to rome. *Contemporary Psychoanalysis*, 36: 255–265.

ROAZEN, P., & SWERDLOFF, B. (1995). *Heresy: Sando Rado and the Psychoanalytic Movement.* Northvale, NJ: Jason Aronson.

SWERDLOFF, B. (1986). A historical portrait of Sandor Rado. *Bulletin of the Association for Psychoanalytic Medicine* 25:118–124.

SANDLER, J. & ROSENBLATT, B. (1962). The concept of the representational world. *Psychoanalytic Study of the Child*, 17:128–145.

SLAVIN, M.O. & KRIEGMAN, D. (1992). Psychoanalysis as a Darwinian depth psychology: Evolutionary biology and the classical–relational dialectic in psychoanalytic theory. In *Interface of Psychoanalysis and Psychology,* eds. J.W. Barron, M.N. Eagle, & D.L. Wolitzky, pp. 37–76. Washington, DC: American Psychological Association.

TREURNIET, N. (1983). Psychoanalysis and self psychology: A metapsychological essay with a clinical illustration. *Journal of the American Psychoanalytic Association* 31: 59–98.

WANG, W. (2003). Bildung or the formation of the psychoanalyst. *Psychoanalysis and History* 5(2): 91–118.

WALLERSTEIN, R.S. (1983). Self psychology and "classical" psychoanalytic psychology: The nature of their relationship. *Psychoanalysis and Contem-porary Thought.* 6:553–593.

——— (1990). Psychoanalysis: The common ground. *International Journal of Psycho-Analysis* 71: 3–30.

——— (1998). The new American psychoanalysis: A commentary.*Journal of the American Psychoanalytic Association* 46:1021–1043.

An Appreciation of
Arnold D. Richards, M.D.

Dr. Richards needs no introduction to any reader or analytic audience.
yet his accomplishments and contributions to our field are so numerous
and multifaceted that to encompass them all would require a Richards
biography.

Dr. Richards was a Brooklynite, a brilliant student who completed
his bachelor's degree at the University of Chicago by age eighteen.
Elected AOA, the honor medical society, he received his M.D, from
Downstate medical Center. Dr. Richards went on to a residency at the
Menninger Clinic in Topeka, Kansas and to subsequent analytic training
at the New York Psychoanalytic Institute, where he became a training
and supervising analyst. He is on the faculty of the New York Psychoanalytic Institute. He is a member of numerous psychoanalytic societies including the New York Psychoanalytic Society, Psychoanalytic
Association of New York, The Contemporary Freudian Society, and
Division 39 of the American Psychological Association. Dr. Richards
is now a distinguished professor of Psychiatry at Han University in
Wuhan, China, where he has advanced a program in dynamic psychotherapy for one hundred-forty students. An esteemed psychoanalytic
scholar, author, and editor, he is the recipient of numerous honors including the Sigourney Award.

Dr. Richards began his publishing career when he was chosen to edit
the American Psychoanalytic Association Newsletter. Under his direction it became *The American Psychoanalyst,* redesigned with significant
interviews, reports, and historical accounts. Dr. Richards is renowned as
former editor-in-chief of Journal of the American Psychoanalytic
Association. In that capacity he spared no effort to maintain and advance
the journal in every respect. He recruited top editorial talent, inspired the
young and the aged, sought out the best authors and papers, arranged for
integrative book essays and embraced controversial issues. Anonymous
outside experts were regularly invited to participate in the editorial

process. The American Psychoanalytic Association is deeply indebted to Dr. Richards for altering the previous publishing arrangement. The American Psychoanalytic Association became the de facto publisher of its Journal, and consequently gained substantial revenues. He now serves on the editorial boards *of Psychoanalytic Inquiry* and *Psychoanalytic Review.*

Dr. Richards's open-mindedness, evident in the *Journal of the American Psychoanalytic Association* continued in his many subsequent activities. He has been outspoken in voicing his ideas and convictions. He has always been interested in transparency rather than opacity and in lifting censorship, not only in clinical psychoanalysis, but in our understanding of psychoanalytic history and institutions. He has presented numerous honorary lectures, including the Brill Lecture at the New York Psychoanalytic Society and the Freud Lecture at the Psychoanalytic Society of New York.

Dr. Richards is the founder and publisher of International Psychoanalytic Books (IPBooks). IPBooks is dedicated to the publication of cutting edge manuscripts by authors from all over the world with diverse viewpoints, within the entire field of psychoanalysis and related disciplines. A product of Dr. Richards's creativity and dedicated enterprise, it has become an outstanding publisher, especially valuable in a difficult climate for print media.

Dr. Richards initiated what originated as the "PEP-CD ROM Symposia" and chaired them for many years. These annual rewarding symposia are now sponsored by thirty-five psychoanalytic organizations. The most recent conference organized by Dr. Richards, 2014, "Therapeutic Action: What works in Psychoanalysis" brought together distinguished psychoanalysts drawing theoretical and technical inferences based on both clinical data and formal research. Dr. Richards soon founded another forum, his psychoanalytic blog: www.internationalpsychoanalysis.net. It provides rapid access to current analytic topics, events, and controversies.

In addition to his work as editor and publisher Dr. Richards has written numerous significant papers and books. They have encompassed such important topics as "The Seduction Hypothesis; Trauma, Fantasy and Reality Today"; "Contemporary Psychoanalytic Perspectives on Transference"; and "Empathy: Clinical and Critical Perspectives." Some of my favorites among his many writings are "The Superordinate Self in Psychoanalytic Theory and self Psychology," a critical review of self chology in relation to traditional psychoanalytic thought; "The Replacement Child" (with Leon Anisfeld); "The Many Faces of Narcissism: Theory, Therapy, and Nosology; A Personal Journey"; "The Analyst's Participation: A New Look"; "The Future of Psychoanalysis: Past, Present, and the Future of Psychoanalytic Theory," and a very moving recount of "Growing Up Orthodox."

A very important dimension of Dr. Richards's ardent commitments is closely linked to his Jewish identity. he organized two Yiddish film Festivals (1972 and 1973) and helped organize the "Center for Jewish History" which brought together five major Jewish institutions For five years he chaired the Board of Directors of YIVO Institute for Jewish Research. founded in 1924 in Vilnius, its purpose is to preserve and promote the Yiddish language and literature and cultural history of the Jews in Eastern Europe. Bridging his two long-standing interests, Dr. Richards organized the conference on Freud and Judaism. The papers of this conference, including my own "Anti-Semitism in the Freud Cast Histories" were collected in a remarkable book *The Jewish World of Sigmund Freud.*

Dr. Richards has shared his life and work with Dr. Arlene Kramer Richards, a distinguished analyst in her own right. Enjoying their three children, grandchildren, and cultural events such as concerts and theater; they have also arranged memorable meetings with fond friends. Extensive travel, including recent trips to China, has been an important and valued part of Dr. Richards's life, learning about and from many different cultures.

These multi-faceted activities exist only because Dr. Richards is a unique polymath who can plumb the depths and scan the horizons of our field with boundless energy.

REFERENCES

RICHARDS, A.D. (2010). *The Jewish world of Sigmund Freud.* Jefferson, NC: McFarland.

A One-Person
Thought Collective

As print on paper, this book can only hint at the inexhaustible creativity of its author. To be sure, the reader will glimpse the variety of Richards' interest. He will see his work on basic clinical realities, but also his abiding interest in unprejudiced but discriminating comparative psychoanalysis. What is not as visible, but the very essence of Arnold Richards, is his movement from printed page out to the world of action. It moves into the realm of psychoanalytic education in institutes and national associations, where he has fought for diversity of opinion. It builds a new institution—an annual symposium—where hitherto isolated thinkers and practitioners from the far flung archiphelago of analytic schools actually meet face to face and exchange ideas without being distorted as imagined strangers. And, Arnie seems to ask, if every institute, why not every journal to be represented? One accomplishment suggests another: If annual symposia, why not a new on-line journal with a wide catchment and independent allegiance? And if an annual journal, why not a new publishing venture so as not to relinquish paper publishing just because he was a psychoanalytic pioneer in the use of the internet? You can almost see Richards' gaze constantly moving to the horizon.

Readers of this book may have some idea of how this phenomenon shaped a central journal of their profession. Moving from the American Psychoanalytic Association's newsletter, which he transformed into a serious journal of record, he set his imagination to work on *JAPA,* where he redesigned the cover, added a semi-detached book review journal with substantive review essays, somehow conjured theme issues (which is no small trick in a non-invitational peer-reviewed journal), introduced substantive editorial introductions, brought in specialized associate editors for child analysis and research, flung a broad net for international contributions, and situated *JAPA* on the web for discussion and controversy. He used his extraordinary array of management skills to make the journal a profitable self-publishing venture.

From these papers, the reader might infer some part of the rest of Richards's activities only if he understood that Richards's never seemed to need to remove himself from one of his creations in order to tend to another. Thus he was teaching, supervising, arranging and contributing to internet education, participating in the life of three institutes and international analytic meetings, editing four festschrifts for eminent psychoanalysts, writing scientific and historical articles, sometimes with his analyst wife, Arlene, organize with her the post-9/11 New York Disaster Counseling Coalition that provided free mental health services for police, firefighters and EMS workers, conducted study groups near his summer home, started a psychoanalytic program in China where he and Arlene teach twice a year, as well as the innovations referred to above. And all of that is on one side of his life, while at the same time he has been fully invested in nourishing Jewish heritage and culture, for example, as Chair of the Board of YIVO Institute dedicated to preservation of Yiddish culture.

All of that whirlwind—and often intensely practical—activity will not be immediately evident in these scholarly pages. What will be on view, along with his technical writing, is Richards's vocation as an historian—an historian of science, of psychoanalysis, of Jewish life, and the intersection of all of these as they shaped the analytic profession in this country, though the reader may not be aware of the actual field work and process of discovery that Richards pursues with the excitement of a bloodhound, both programmatically, and opportunistically, as when seeking out information about Sabina Spielrein's fate during a visit to the USSR.

One thing the reader won't fail to note is Richards's core concern with fairness and his rejection of hierarches. That infuses his attitude to his profession and its fate. He has been extremely effective in fighting for his ideals, and willing to take the hard knocks that are a fighter's fate. That last is an understatement. Fighting for one's ideals is politics, and politics means clashing opinions. Richards is not just a chronicler of American psychoanalysis but is now a part of its famously irritable history. Whatever stake one has in its course, I think nobody can deny that Arnie Richards has shown outstanding courage.

It is a lot easier for him to maintain that spirit, I think, because he is gifted with a prodigious imagination and creativity that confirm his effectiveness. Whether it's a matter of design or publicity or public organization, Arnie is feet-on-the-ground prophetic: he can see how things will work, and—always, always—how to make them work better. What will he think of next? What won't he think of next? There are many who disagree with Arnie on many things, but nobody would deny him laurels as an impresario. It is one of the colorful paradoxes of this rebel that he could have made a bundle as an entrepreneur.

Another paradox is that, though a life-long, aggressive activist and an unsleeping planner, he is more interested in accomplishing his ends than in self-promotion. Proud of being known as a "slave driver" of his associates, driving them to their own fulfillment, he is also known for respecting their aims and giving them their freedom. He saw himself as working in a "thought collective," I think even before he discovered Ludvik Fleck.

One would expect a social and intellectual activist who is also such a canny futurologist to be a little impatient with the past. But Arnie is as proud of our heritage, both in general culture and in psychoanalysis, as he is oriented to the future. Maybe his University of Chicago background helped him fuse a rich culture with an open mind about beliefs. More likely, I think, it is the result of Arnie's deep respect – often reverence— for ancestry and roots, tradition, history in general. That is the real paradox for this radical character. I don't know whether he will appreciate my saying it, but he is more a humanist than a radical. He is a genuine historian, a hunter-down of primary sources and original testimony. It might be Russia; it might be New York. His delight in re-animating the figures and atmospheres of the past is contagious. He loves discovery and has made fascinating discoveries in psychoanalytic history. Arnie's portrayal of the multiple socio-cultural-intellectual forces at work in the formation of American—and particularly the New York—psychoanalytic movement, the interwoven motives of the various leaders, and the effect on the doctrines and organization of the field is as fascinating a model of intellectual history as it is enlightening about the history of the psychoanalytic movement. The same thing can be said about his penetrating work on Freud's Jewish world.

Everyone's different, of course, and we enjoy the specialness of all of our friends, but Arnie seems somehow a little more sui generis than most. For me, Arnie is a little like a character in a novel – maybe a Russian novel. And that is not just a sentimental impression. It has something to do with the coherence of a long life ideal that moves dramatically through many varied chapters of endeavor and learning, always translated into the action of the local context.

And it also has to do with the astonishing energy, unflagging determination, and boundless enthusiasm that seem to be part of his very being. That up-for-it-ness certainly does not arise from an easy life, unchallenged health or a wildly applauding cohort. His inner engine is, of course, his ethical and political principle, assisted by his lifelong comrade-in-arms, his wife, Arlene. But it seems to me that his larger-than-life vitality is also spurred by the fun he gets in the game. For a man who is always seriously engaged in a campaign for what he sees as basic fairness and human dignity, he is remarkably light-hearted and good-humored, and generally amused by the skirmishes as food for a supremely vital life.

I. Diversity and Unification

The papers in the first section emphasize the importance of reflection and historical context to understanding the current state of psycho-analysis and psychoanalysts. In Chapter 1, "Growing Up Orthodox," Richards begins by reflecting on his own personal journey. He asks the reader to think about where s/he draws her/his personal boundaries that address the question:

- Where do you fall on the following psychoanalytic dialectics: orthodox to radical, pluralism to uniformity, and free exploration to dogmatism?
- Where does your theory draw these boundaries?
- Where do your institutions draw these boundaries?

In Chapter 2, "A. A. Brill And The Politics Of Exclusion," Richards sharpens his focus to the institutional impact on psychoanalytic theory and practice. His purpose is to transform the debate among advocates of different perspectives to a genuine dialogue. He uses the life of A.A. Brill as a case illustration and demonstrates its consequence as the "pol-itics of exclusion". Here he considers:

- How has institutional history in psychoanalysis (in the US) con-tributed to the emergence of theoretical pluralism and the sense of professional fragmentation?
- What broad trends followed in the wake of the politics of exclusion?

In Chapter 3, "Psychoanalytic Discourse at the Turn of Our Century: A Plea for a Measure of Humility," Richards continues to explore the con-tinuous negative consequences of exclusionary politics and carefully con-siders both theoretical pluralism and the increasing heterogeneity in the practitioner base. Richards offers a broad historical understanding of the problem by defining the divergent paths since Freud and argues that psy-choanalytic theory has evolved into a state of irreversible pluralism differ-entiated by major perspectives. Given this pluralistic landscape, he asks:

- What is the reasonable course of action?
- Can we learn from one another or will we continue in splits and schisms?
- Does every new movement need a hateful object to oppose?

Richards offers a solution to this dilemma reflecting his view that our knowledge of the human condition is always evolving and requires constant revision into an integrative pluralism.

Encounters with Psychoanalytic Theories

In sections II, III, IV, and V, Richards critiques psychoanalytic theories from four main perspectives: the self psychologies; the hermeneutics and social constructivist perspectives; the interpersonal and relational perspectives; the ego psychological and contemporary conflict theories.

CHAPTER 1

Growing Up Orthodox

[Richards, A.D. (1996). In *More Psychoanalysts at Work,* ed. J. Reppen, Northvale, NJ: Jason Aronson, pp 117–131.]

My aim in this chapter is to locate myself and my work in relation to the current state of psychoanalysis. Specifically, I want to consider my relationship to orthodoxy and deviance, pluralism and uniformity, free exploration and dogmatism. Let me acknowledge at the outset that each of us who practices psychoanalysis is a product of his or her training, institute traditions, and the values and approaches of analytic teachers, supervisors, and training analyst or analysts. The influence of these factors varies with the individual. Some analysts are very much bound by tradition and influenced by authority and reluctant to question received wisdom. Other analysts are more freewheeling, free-spirited, and antiestablishment. Openly questioning, they are committed to an attitude of "show me." One would hope that in matters of science such personal differences would eventually succumb to the corrective of verifiable experience, logical demonstration, and rational proof. To be sure, even in some "hard" scientific endeavors ideology may determine differences in theory and preferred explanatory systems. Yet there probably isn't a single scientific or intellectual discipline as value-laden and colored by emotionality as psychoanalysis.

I think I can show this most vividly by relating a little bit about my own personal route to psychoanalysis. I believe that my earliest lexical memory is of seeing an article in the *Yiddish Forward* about the death of Sigmund Freud when I was 5 years old. I remember the picture of the bearded man and the announcement, which I read or which was read to me by a grandfatherly figure, also bearded, who taught me to read Yiddish and Hebrew. This may well be a screen memory, but I am certain that Sigmund Freud and psychoanalysis were subjects I knew about and was interested in during my latency years.

I know I read about him in the encyclopedia and pursued some of the subjects described as part of my broader prepubertal search for sexual knowledge. In retrospect, it is difficult to determine whether my interest in sexuality fueled my interest in literature or the other way around. But I do remember reading novels for both their literary and their titillating value, selecting from a wide range of books that included Pearl Buck's *The Good Earth* and Aldous *Huxley's Point Counter Point.* My second great childhood passion was politics, and I was exposed by a succession of leftist elementary school teachers to writers such as Lincoln Steffens, John Dos Passos, Upton Sinclair, and John Steinbeck. Theirs was the literature of rebellion, revolution, and social justice.

The first important nonfiction book that I read was Flanders Dunbar's work *Emotions and Bodily Health.* I was about 12½, and my interest in the book was fueled by my yearly bouts with hay fever when I felt as if I were drowning in a sea of secretions. Dunbar's book made the case that allergies, asthma, and hay fever were psychosomatic, somehow connected to the passions of my child's mind. Conflict, sexuality, and the unconscious were concepts that offered me the hope of mastery, a power over my membranes that came from understanding how the mind worked and how the mind in its workings affected the workings of the body. I found these explications about the mental and bodily machinery as interesting and exciting as the drawings of the mechanisms of the cars in the pages of *Popular Mechanics* or the steam engines and cotton gins in the *Encyclopedia Britannica* and the *World Book of Knowledge.* About four years after reading Dunbar I read *New Introductory Lectures of Psychoanalysis,* the yellow Permaback edition of Sigmund Freud (1933).

Freud's interlocutory style in those lectures was for me absolutely convincing. The concepts of psychic determinism, unconscious mental processes, and infantile sexuality offered a way to order the mysterious world of mind and human interaction-mind at work and mind at play, mind during the day and mind at night-that simply brooked no competition. The "Introductory Lectures" and the "Dream Book," in A. A. Brill's translation, formed a foundational pair; they represented a solid psychology that could be applied to everyday functioning and to the world of pathology. Starting from that point, psychoanalysis became a lens through which I observed a whole host of intellectual, literary, and scientific experience. It served a role similar to that of Marxism for others of my generation. Whether I was reading T. S. Eliot, e. e. cummings, Homer, Aeschylus, or Euripides in high school, Aristotle, Plato, or Kant at the University of Chicago, or works on neurophysiology and brain functioning in medical school, psychoanalysis offered relevant organizing principles. Through it, I could understand a broad range of intellectual movements that I read about during the day; it likewise helped me parse the dreams I had at night.

I relate the circumstances in which I first became exposed to psychoanalytic ideas to show how their compelling nature stems from their ability to help the individual make sense of experiences that are personally meaningful. Similarly, of course, physics appeals to us because it orders the world of physical things; literature draws its power from its relevance to the real-life personal and interpersonal dramas to which we are always exposed. And so with psychoanalysis. A person who never gives much thought to dreams, never makes slips of the tongue, and never puzzles other symptoms, inhibitions, or delusional thoughts will not be drawn to psychoanalytic explanation. But inasmuch as most everyone does, psychoanalysis continues to hold its own in the intellectual marketplace along with other powerful explanatory systems that account for important aspects of human experience.

Thirteen years elapsed from the time I began college until I started my analytic training at age 30. During that period my early wish to become a psychoanalyst was both at risk-subject to dissuasion, disenchantment, and disillusionment-and open to reinforcement. The period in question-the fifties and sixties was, it turns out, the heyday of psychoanalysis.

Psychoanalysis enjoyed a boom right after World War II when a cohort of psychiatrists returned from the service and sought analytic training. The American Psychoanalytic Association grew rapidly, training institutes had many applicants, and treatment centers had large backlogs. Psychoanalysis seemed to be a profession that provided for the intellectual, therapeutic, and socioeconomic needs of a group of physicians who were perhaps ambivalent about the choice of medicine as a profession because of its trade school aspects and its seeming lack of intellectual and humanistic excitement.

During this time my interest in psychoanalysis was challenged by the attraction of other sciences: mathematics in college, medicine and pathology in medical school, and forensic psychiatry and criminology during my psychiatric residency. But their allure was more than offset by the support and reinforcement I received from both peers and mentors during my college and professional education. Between my third and fourth years of medical school I spent a summer as an extern at the Marine Hospital in Staten Island, assigned to a medical and a psychiatric service. The doctor in charge of the psychiatric service was in analytic training, and his own rather well-known analyst, who specialized in psychosomatic illness, practiced her calling with almost religious conviction.

During my internship in Baltimore I serendipitously had as a neighbor a first-year psychiatric resident at the University of Maryland who was just starting his analytic training and had entered into the program with enthusiasm and gusto. It was then that I almost succumbed to the lure of a New York psychiatric residency program that was almost totally identified with psychoanalysis in general and the New York Psychoanalytic Institute in particular. I don't know whether there was some adaptive or self-preservative mechanism at work that made me opt for a residency in Topeka, Kansas, that, while analytically oriented, was much broader in overall outlook. There certainly was a difference between Karl Menninger's, view of psychoanalysis and that of Milton Rosenbaum, Herb Weiner, and the other Cincinnati transplants in the Bronx. And I think that I benefitted greatly from exposure in Topeka to some of the great minds of the twentieth century—Konrad Lorenz, Aldous Huxley, S. I. Hayakawa, Margaret Mead, and Ludwig von Bertalanffy, among others. In Topeka, as in Chicago during my college days, my emphasis was on trying to place psychoanalysis within the wider context of Western humanistic and scientific thought. I like to tell myself that when I began analytic training at the New York Psychoanalytic Institute in 1964 I brought to that rarefied and perhaps somewhat stultifying atmosphere a sense of the larger scientific landscape. At the same time I had the personal sense that psychoanalysis, as an investigative and explanatory tool, accounted for human behavior and human motivation in a way no other discipline or approach did. Psychoanalysis contained a set of explanatory constructs—the Oedipus complex, infantile sexuality, the dynamic unconscious—that seemed to me to be of awesome power.

My analytic class began as a group of thirteen: twelve men and one woman, twelve psychiatrists and one psychologist. Graduates of elite colleges and medical schools, we were convinced that we were the best and the brightest and that our training was going to bring us to the top of the psychiatric profession and provide us with the most effective tools for relieving psychological suffering. We were awed by our instructors, who were indeed recognized as among the greats in contemporary psychoanalysis. Several, transplanted from Vienna not so long before, could claim a direct lineage from Freud and had written the definitive works in the field. I refer of course to Heinz Hartmann, Rudolph Loewenstein, Edith Jacobson, Annie Reich, Kurt and Ruth Eissler, and George Gero. There was a group of American psychoanalysts, somewhat younger but also giants in the field: Phyllis Greenacre, Jacob Arlow, Charles Brenner, and David Beres.

With so distinguished a faculty, the institute was conductive to idealization, identification, and acceptance of theory and ideology. It was hardly a place that promoted skepticism, questioning, and argument, although several members of my class developed a sufficiently disbelieving posture that they left the program. Of course, much depends on whether the candidate's own experience in analytic treatment is positive-whether the analysis provides the sense that all the hypothetical and theoretical constructs about the way the mind works ring personally true. After all, what is taught always stands or falls not on its strength as a hypothesis or theory but on the extent to which the constructs can be personally validated. This is not to say that one can pursue a course of training in a totally objective fashion The fact is, a training analysis can never be purely for oneself, uncontaminated by the presume for advancement, success, and graduation; it is inevitably influenced by strong pushes toward conformity and acceptance. I think it is remarkable how well candidates generally come through this experience. And I have a hunch that the candidates who didn't finish training were those who tended toward total acceptance rather than toward a more questioning attitude.

Analytic training at that time mostly involved reading Freud, in depth and in detail. Since completing training, I have read all of Freud twice as part of a private seminar exercise; reading him the second and third times gave me a sense of how little I had understood in the classroom setting. Yet I am convinced that analytic training provided me with understanding and conviction about what I consider the basic principles of psychoanalysis. The fundamental tenets of my training had to do with (1) the basic principle of psychic determinism; (2) the centrality of unconscious mental functioning and its implications for the theories of motivation, symptom formation, and personality disorder and personality development; (3) the ambivalence and conflicts of childhood and the centrality of experiences with parents and siblings and of the bodily processes; and (4) the role of transference. Finally there was the overarching idea of the centrality of affect-that psycho analysis is a psychology of emotionality and not just an intellectual discipline.

I trained during the era of the psychoanalysis of plenty: there were plenty of candidates, plenty of patients, and lots of prestige for psychoanalysis and for psychoanalysts. This had an effect, I think, on the kinds of patients who were treated and on the nature of their treatments. Training analysts had full analytic practices with candidates who were patient, docile, and compliant. It was the kind of situation in which analytic neutrality, abstinence, and inflexible methodological rules were accepted without question. The candidates understood that there was always someone waiting in the wings to take their place if they did not go along with the program. Perhaps that was an exaggerated view, but I think it fostered changes on both the national and the local level. It was at this same time that people began to write about widening the scope of psychoanalysis and to look at the ways in which psychoanalysis could or could not be adapted to the treatment of the sicker patient. My own experience and that of my fellow candidates suggested that the scope had already widened and that the so-called ideal analytic patient-cooperative, neurotic, without serious psychopathology was becoming the exception.

At meetings of the affiliated staff some of the training analysts would respond to case presentations of sicker patients by readily diagnosing schizophrenia, psychosis, or worse and by dismissing such patients as unanalyzable. Others seemed to take a different approach and, operating from a continuum point of view, espoused a wider tolerance for severe illness. In New York the European group, the older analysts closer to Freud, were most willing to diagnose serious illness and take this exclusionary approach. The younger, American-trained analysts, such as Arlow, Brenner, and Beres, seemed to have a much more tolerant approach.

The debate in the International Psychoanalytical Association (IPA) Congress in 1969 among Arlow and Brenner and Freeman (1970) and Greenson and Wexler (1970) revealed these different points of view. This all influenced me because my first patient presented severe psychopathology. David Beres, my supervisor, kept my focus on analyzing and understanding, to the ultimate clinical benefit of the patient and to the benefit of my training experience. My own style has developed out of the fact that I trained at a classical institute, yet early in my career had the experience of analyzing patients with severe psychopathology.

I reported on one of these patients (Richards 1988), a woman who was a self-mutilator. I saw her in analysis four or five times a week, which resulted in a very positive therapeutic outcome. The case was dramatic because it turned out that her psychopathology was in part a response to the severe trauma of father-daughter incest. Memories of these experiences were recovered through the analysis of dreams and transference-countertransference constellations and enactments.

And so I had the interesting experience of undergoing orthodox analytic training with a group of instructors and colleagues who were committed to the analytic cause, while at the same time I honed an attitude of philosophical and intellectual questioning about theory and practice. Very early on I was drawn to alternate schools of psychoanalytic thought. I remember, sometime during my training, reading Edward Glover's (1950) *Freud or Jung*. I know I did this on my own; it was not assigned in any of my courses. The message of that book was very simple: the difference between Freud and Jung was that Freud believed in the unconscious while Jung did not. This may sound like something of an oversimplification, but I think it is one of those simple ideas that is profound in import. Even today, there is a tendency in discussions of psychoanalytic theoretical diversity to accept the position that everyone believes in the unconscious, that it is, indeed, an operative assumption across the spectrum of psychoanalytic perspectives. But my sense is that this is not. the case, and I have argued as much in publications critical of popular theories put forward by Mitchell, Greenberg, Stolorow, and others (Bachant and Richards 1993).

Recent stress on the "here and now" of the therapeutic interaction often shifts the focus away from unconscious fantasy determined by childhood experiences and revolving around libidinal and aggressive themes with the primary objects. An interactive approach to the patient in the analytic situation may also muddy the waters at times, and make it difficult to see the contribution of the unconscious to the patient's symptomatology, experience, behavior, and character. It is a foundational idea that the unconscious reveals itself in an environment of quiet contemplation and observational situation closer to dreaming than to waking. Of course the unconscious also becomes evident in the noise of interaction and in the noise of a patient's life. But it seems to me that one is on much more solid ground, when symptomatic acts and maladaptive behaviors can be understood through inferences about the material of dreams and free associations.

Although such an approach perhaps sounds old-fashioned, it remains for me the heart of the analysis, with its unique interpretive mode. The issue may be one of background versus foreground: for analysts trained in my tradition the relationship is a given, in the background; insight occupies the foreground. Insights are received by the patient in the context of a positive therapeutic relationship, which is fueled in turn by the insight and understanding that the analyst offers the patient.

One misconception is that, the centrality of insight in this approach emphasizes intellectual understanding and downplays the affective component of the treatment. Nothing could be further from the case. Affect remains central. Intellectual insight without its emotional concomitants is pallid and hardly therapeutic. I think a crucial aspect of psychoanalytic training is developing a feel for what is analytic. This doesn't necessarily involve a rigid adherence to rules of analytic conversation. It does involve learning to eschew interactions that are primarily of a counseling nature: advice-giving, reassurance, approval, and so forth. The idea that, even though patients may want to be counseled, at some level they understand that such interventions are not really what they need.

The trick in conducting this kind of analysis is to be able to maintain this posture without being, experienced as cruel, withholding, or self-serving. There is no doubt that the approach can be carried to an extreme, and it is often caricatured by critics of traditional analytic technique. It cannot be stressed enough that classical technique does not preclude common sense. At no point does the analyst deny the legitimacy of the patient's needs and wishes, which are recognized by the analyst as understandable in content and pressing in nature. The: emphasis is on helping the patient assume a stance in which short-term benefits are given up for the sake of long-term, lasting change.

The major controversy when I completed my analytic training in 1969 involved psychoanalytic metapsychology. No major alternative points of view had yet been advanced, and the main theoretical issue was the concept of identity developed by Erik Erikson and Heinz Lichtenstein. But a group of psychoanalysts, primarily students of David Rapaport, were questioning Freud's metapsychology, in particular its energic assumptions. George Klein's (1973) "Psychoanalysis: One Theory or Two?," an influential statement of the antimetapsychological position, argued that psychoanalysis was a clinical theory and that its metapsychology was at best superfluous, at worst confusing and irrelevant. The antimetapsychology movement continued until the present time and has drawn into its orbit theoreticians as different in their orientation as Roy Schafer and Charles Brenner.

The issues raised in the debate tended not to have important clinical consequences. The language of energy, libido, cathexis, and decathexis and Hartmann's language of neutralization and deneutralization were not readily translatable into strategies germane to the analytic situation. The most cogent response to the antimetapsychologists came earlier, from Robert Waelder (1936), who conceptualized the levels of psychoanalytic theory from the most clinical to the most metapsychological. His idea that people were arguing from different levels of abstraction had for me a compelling logic. But then, I have always been drawn to approaches that are dialectic rather than dichotomous.

Heinz Kohut's *The Analysis of the Self* (1971) and *The Restoration of the Self* (1977) represented the first serious challenge to classical psychoanalysis from both a theoretical and a clinical or technical point of view. His psychology of the self offered a new theory of pathogenesis and of treatment and cure. Kohut was not alone m offering the self as the rubric for a psychoanalytic paradigm. His work was in certain ways anticipated by George Klein, for whom the concept of the self was also important. John Gedo (1979), who collaborated with Kohut and then broke away, offered a concept of a superordinate self in the theoretical and clinical system that he began propounding in the 1970s.

Neither Klein nor Gedo achieved the same prominence and following as Kohut. Kohut's rhetoric was engaging, and his two books represented a serious challenge, a well-thought-out alternative to received psychoanalytic wisdom. He offered the appealing dichotomy of "guilty man," whose problems originate in interpsychic conflict, and "tragic man," whose problems result primarily from developmental arrest and disturbance in the self. According to Kohut, tragic man has to be treated according to the principles of self psychology, whereas guilty man can be treated according to the older precepts of Freud's psychoanalysis.

Beginning in the late 1970s and carrying over into the 1980s, self psychology developed into a new psychoanalytic movement with its own publications, conferences, and so forth. Nevertheless, it remained within the organizational framework of the American and International Psychoanalytic Associations. Kohut did not suffer the same fate as Jung, Adler, Horney, and Clara Thompson before him. He came out of an orthodox Freudian tradition, trained in Vienna, was analyzed there by Aichorn and in Chicago by Ruth Eissler. He taught at the Chicago Institute, where he was one of the outstanding presenters of psychoanalytic theory for successive classes. He was known as a brilliant theoretical synthesizer and systematizer who had the entire Freudian corpus at his fingertips. The response to self psychology by many of my mentors at the New York Psychoanalytic Institute, and by some of my colleagues and peers as well, was generally dismissive. It was disturbing to me that the rejection of Kohut's point of view was not always based on a careful study of his work. Exceptions at that time were two reviews by members of the institute, Martin Stein (1979) and Lester Schwartz (1978): the first critical, the second more appreciative. In discussions with colleagues and teachers, I had the sense that I was being given the task of studying self psychology and reporting back to them as to whether there was anything in Kohut worth considering seriously. The resulting study and critiques of self psychology (1981, 1982) enhanced my career and my standing with the powers that be in the orthodox New York psychoanalytic establishment.

The challenge of self psychology as an alternate theoretical, clinical, and therapeutic system is still with us today. Kohut's dichotomy of tragic man and guilty man remains a cogent alternative guide to the practice of psychoanalysis. And many of the controversies, both theoretical and therapeutic, that have become part of the psychoanalytic debate over the decades come down to this distinction. The role of insight and interpretation as opposed to the role of the therapeutic relationship has to do with whether the patient's primary psychopathology is a function of a childhood environmental failure and developmental deficit This raises questions as to the best mode of therapeutic intervention. John Gedo's (1979) ideas about working through and the needs to address consciously the cognitive deficits that are part of the patient's difficulty represent a more recent contribution to this fundamental debate.

During the past decade, self psychology has been on the wane as the flash point of psychoanalytic! controversy. It has been supplanted by the relational, intersubjective, and interpersonal schools. The prime movers of these approaches are not members of the psychoanalytic establishment; indeed, like other non-M.D.'s, they were not eligible for training and membership in the American Psychoanalytic Association until 1989. This fact may partly account for certain skewed views of contemporary Freudian psychoanalysis that appear again and again in their papers and books. Unsurprisingly, my own writing during the past ten years has involved discussions and critiques of these points of view. I have followed the same route as I did with self psychology in the 1970s, and my position within my group remains that of a contemporary Freudian analyst who interprets and critiques new approaches.

In pursuing this course I am fortunate to have had the advantage of greater opportunities for interaction with nonmedical analysts than many of my colleagues have. In part this is a result of my own interests, my training in Topeka (where there has always been a very strong nonmedical presence), and my marriage to a psychologist/psychoanalyst. My career and my approach belie the claim that the American Freudian establishment is an orthodox monolith. This position fails to recognize the revisionist trends within the ranks of the Freudian orthodox. Melanie Klein's approach exemplifies one such trend abroad, and the Arlow-Brenner group within the New York Psychoanalytic Institute exemplifies it today in this country. Arlow and Brenner have been quite outspoken in their criticism of various aspects of classical Freudian theory. Their own approaches, particularly that of Brenner, are theoretically very close to that of the antimetapsychologists. Brenner's eschewal of reification and his rejection of concepts of psychic agency and mental structures are consonant with the assumptions that underlie Roy Schafer's action language. My own commitment to Arlow and Brenner's emphasis on conflict, compromise formation, and unconscious fantasy works well for me as a personal compromise formation, enabling me to be part of the establishment while espousing what I see as an evolutionary, though not revolutionary, Freudian point of view.

What does all the foregoing have to do with how I work? I think I have come to listen with a fourth ear. The third ear, as Theodor Reik observes, listens to the patient's unconscious. The fourth ear, I believe, tries to listen from the various vantage points of competing theoretical schools. I practice this kind of listening because it holds the promise of validating clinically competing hypotheses about how the mind works. But I also do so because a receptivity to new ideas, a willingness to consider them on their own merits, follows from the therapeutic nature of the analytic situation, which 1 requires a pragmatic commitment to what works best for one's patients. I distinguish this kind of pluralism from an indiscriminate eclecticism. Pluralism involves a willingness to consider new points of view, but not an acceptance of all points of view as equally valid and clinically helpful.

My espousal of pluralism does not lead me to endorse extreme versions of the doctrine of narrative truth, in which anything goes. I think that there are more or less consensually validated facts some things really happen to our patients, and although the ultimate truth may not be knowable, patients and analysts are involved in a quest to come as close as possible to some veridical understanding of the past. Einstein maintained that an extreme relativist position and a belief in uncertainty were antithetical to the proper motivational stance of the scientist. Only some belief in truth, he held, can motivate the scientist to extend great energy studying the basic laws that govern the universe. I think that the same can be said of the psychoanalyst and the analysand.

REFERENCES

BACHANT, J.L. & RICHARDS, A.D. (1993). Review of *Relational Concepts in Psychoanalysis: An Integration*, by S. Mitchell. *Psychoanalytic Dialogues* 31:431–460.

FREEMAN, T. (1970). The psychopathology of the psychoses: A reply to Arlow and Brenner. *International journal of Psycho-Analysis* 51:407–415.

FREUD, S. (1933). *New Introductory Lectures on Psychoanalysis*, trans. W. J. H. Sprott. New York: Norton.

—— (1950). *The Interpretation of Dreams,* trans. A. A. Brill. New York: Modern Library.

GEDO, J. (1979). *Beyond Interpretation: Toward a Revised Theory for Psychoanalysis.* New York: International Universities Press.

GLOVER, E. (1950). *Freud or Jung.* London: Allen & Unwin.

GREENSON, R.R. & WEXLER M. (1970). Discussion of "the non-transference in the psychoanalytic situation." *International Journal of Psycho-Analysis* 51:143-166.

Klein, G. (1973). Psychoanalysis: One theory or two? *Bulletin of the Menninger Clinic.* 37:102–132.

KOHUT, H. (1971). *The Analysis of the Self.* New York: International Universities Press.

—— (1977). *The Restoration of the Self.* New York: International Universities Press.

RICHARDS, A.D. (1981). Self theory, conflict theory and the problem of hypochondriasis. In: *Psychoanalytic Study of the Child* 36:319-337. New Haven, CT: Yale University Press.

—— (1982). The superordinate self in psychoanalytic theories and the self psychologies. *Journal of the American Psychoanalytic Association* 30:717–736.

——— (1984). Self-mutilation and father/daughter incest. In: *Fantasy, Myth, and Reality: Essays in Honor of Jacob Arlow*, ed. H.P. Blum, Y. Kramer, A.K. Richards and A.D. Richards, Madison: CT: International Universities Press.

Schwartz, L. (1978). Review of *The Restoration of the Self* by H. Kohut. *Psychoanalytic Quarterly* 47:436–443.

Stein, M. (1979). Review of *The Restoration of the Self* by H. Kohut. *Journal of the American Psychoanalytic Association* 27 665–680.

Waelder, R. (1936). The principle of multiple function: Observations on over-determination. *Psychoanalytic Quarterly* 5:45–62.

CHAPTER 2

A. A. Brill and the
Politics of Exclusion

[Richards, A.D. (1999). *Journal of the American Psychoanalytic Association* 47:9–28.]

Both as a theory and as a therapeutic method, psychoanalysis is an historical discipline. Any attempt to assess the present state of psychoanalysis must therefore involve coming to grips with its history. As Freud originally conceived the mind as comprised of conscious, preconscious, and unconscious systems, each with its own laws yet forming an interdependent whole, so the history of psychoanalysis can be said to unfold on three distinct levels—personal, intellectual, and institutional. Although the first two continue to be sifted by both analysts and scholars, the institutional history of psychoanalysis has perhaps not received the attention it merits from clinical practitioners. Analysts of all persuasions engage in an ongoing process of self-scrutiny to test how the legacies of Freud and other pioneers can be renewed in the contemporary context. If this process inevitably exposes fault lines that cause one to be skeptical of the prospects for a complete integration, it nonetheless fosters a recognition of the diversity and distinctiveness of the views that can justly call themselves psychoanalytic—a recognition that may in turn enable us to transform the debate among partisan advocates into a genuine dialogue.

For American psychoanalysts, Abraham Arden Brill (1874–1948) is one such pioneer, whose example is singularly instructive. As historian Paula Fass (1969) has written, "If any individual helped to determine the shape of the American experience with psychoanalysis, it was Brill. He was the first practicing American psychoanalyst; it was he who established New York City as the psychoanalytic center of the United States, a position which it held for many years. Many of the young physicians who became psychoanalysts during the first decades of the twentieth century were trained and inspired by Brill. From 1911 to the close of the First World War, the New York Psychoanalytic Society was kept alive practically single-handedly by A. A. Brill" (pp. 2–3).

Originally presented at the New York Psychoanalytic Society as the 47th A. A. Brill Lecture, November 28, 1995.

Indeed, Brill's career can be regarded as our profession's Horatio Alger story. In 1889 he immigrated to this country, a fifteen-year-old from the Hapsburg Empire with less than three dollars in his pocket. He supported himself, educated himself, and eventually became a psychiatrist. Discovering Freud in the first decade of the new century, he imported psychoanalytic ideas from Europe, where he had returned to study, and interested a small group of New York psychiatrists in the new endeavor to understand nervous and mental diseases. His efforts bore organizational fruit in February 1911, with the founding of the New York Psychoanalytic Society.

Brill was the quintessential expositor and public advocate of psychoanalysis. In this role, he rivals Ernest Jones and has yet to meet his American match. Indefatigable as a lecturer and media spokesperson— that is, a radio commentator—he addressed medical, neurological, analytic, and lay audiences from coast to coast. Brill introduced psychoanalysis to social workers, the New York City Police College, and the Department of Pedagogy at New York University. He analyzed many of the leading literary figures and intellectuals in New York City, and his translations of Freud into English had a lasting influence, though they have since been superseded by the Standard Edition. As late as 1962, Bertram Lewin deemed Brill's translations to be the single most important contribution to American psychoanalytic education. "Even today," he wrote, "many future psychoanalysts begin their analytic education, perhaps while still in high school, by reading his translations" (p. 121).

Yet Brill presents us a number of paradoxes. Chief among these is that even as he dedicated himself to promoting Freud's ideas, he remained a thorn in the master's side. It is ironic that the formation of the New York Psychoanalytic Society was actually an expression of defiance aimed at Freud and Jones, who had decided that James Jackson Putnam of Boston should lead the national association that would be the institutional umbrella of American psychoanalysis. Brill refused to affiliate the New York Society with that association, and neither he nor any other New York member was in Baltimore to attend its founding meeting on May 9, 1911. At the Weimar Congress that September, Brill again resisted pressure from Freud and Jones to bring his society into the newly formed American Psychoanalytic Association.

Then, too, there was the vexed question of lay analysis. Although Brill strove to safeguard what he regarded as the core ideas of Freudian psychoanalysis, he implacably opposed Freud's judgment about who might practice it. In his celebrated defense of lay analysis, Freud (1926) argued that psychoanalysis requires less a medical education than "psychological instruction and a free human outlook" (p. 230). Brill, however, pursued an agenda diametrically opposed to Freud's. A physician himself, he not only used his medical credentials to campaign for psychoanalysis, but was convinced that it would not flourish in America unless it became a branch of the medical profession. For the same reason, Brill did not emphasize the necessity for analytic training, since this requirement tended to deter physicians from joining the ranks. But he remained adamant that psychiatrists alone could practice Freud's controversial new science. Fass contends that the intensity with which Brill proselytized for medical psychoanalysis demonstrates an ambivalent desire to rebel against Freud's authority while simultaneously identifying with an esteemed professional class: "The triple aspects of Brill's identity—his connection with psychoanalysis, his position as an American, and his role as a doctor and psychiatrist—determined his attitude towards lay analysis, which Freud espoused in the early 1920s. Although Brill presented this as an effort to protect people from quacks and impostors, he was clearly trying to guard the medical affiliation for which he had fought so long and which had now become an integral part of his personality" (pp. 83–84).

But whatever personal motives underlay it, Brill's opposition to lay analysis remains significant because of its enduring institutional effects. It would be easy from a contemporary standpoint to condemn out of hand Brill's politics of exclusion, yet his desire to safeguard psychoanalysis as a medical profession must be understood in historical context. By the mid-1920s, when the New York Society restricted both membership and attendance at its meetings to physicians, quackery had become an urgent issue to physicians, the public, and regulatory bodies alike. As Brill went about promoting the psychoanalytic cause, he had to be wary of critics such as Abraham Flexner and Morris Fishbein, who were determined to ward off encroachment on any area of treatment that might be regarded as a medical specialty. In April 1926, after some glaring abuses had come to light, the New York State legislature outlawed the practice of medicine by anyone not registered as a medical doctor. It likewise prohibited the unauthorized use of the title *Doctor* by anyone involved in public health. In 1935 the New York Psychoanalytic Society, yielding to increasing pressure from the New York County Medical Society to act against lay analysts, voted to abrogate an agreement reached in 1929 to accept lay members. The final blow against lay analysis was struck three years later, when the

American Psychoanalytic Association, following the lead of Brill's New York Society, limited membership to physicians who had completed a psychiatric residency. But Brill apparently remained of two minds about this matter. According to Nellie Thompson, historian of the New York Society, Brill sent his two children, Edwin and Joia, to lay analysts for treatment.

In *The Rise and Crisis of Psychoanalysis in the United States,* Nathan Hale (1995) discusses at length the medicalization of American psychoanalysis under Brill's aegis, and the conflicts to which this gave rise between the American and the International Psychoanalytic Associations. In Hale's view, Brill's politics of exclusion bequeathed two unfortunate legacies. First, it ensured that academic psychologists in the United States would take little interest in psychoanalysis, since those who might otherwise have gravitated to it could not receive clinical training.[1] Second, his policies, flourishing in an organizational climate that promoted the identification and exclusion of dissidents, contributed to the success of the American Psychoanalytic Association in centralizing its control over psychoanalysis. When Karl Menninger became president of the American in 1941, he appointed a committee on reorganization, chaired by Thomas French, which recommended that the American prescribe standards, evaluate institutes, and admit only graduates of its affiliates to membership.

For better and for worse, the shadow cast by Brill's politics of exclusion lingers to the present day. On the debit side, it haunts us in the unabated fragmentation of psychoanalysis and in our lack of theoretical consensus. The deplorable penchant for dichotomous thinking, with the tendency on the part of orthodox practitioners to brand interpersonalists and others outside the institutional fold as "not analysts," can be laid at Brill's door. Yet, to his credit, Brill was indubitably a force for conservatism in the best sense. In a turbulent period, he "conserved" the science and profession of psychoanalysis against external threats and helped to create an organizational structure within which like-minded people could come together, learn from one another, and advance its frontiers. As a public spokesman, he represented his community with passion and commitment. Thus, although in some respects he furnishes a negative object lesson, Brill also suggests strategies for coping with—and mitigating—the divisions and disarray for which he himself bears considerable responsibility.

---

[1]A related point is that the bar against lay analysis had for many years the unintended consequence of greatly reducing the number of women who entered the profession, since women formed a minority of the medical students and physicians in the United States, the pool from which analytic candidates could be drawn.

METATHEORETICAL CURRENTS

To draw the constructive lessons of Brill's example, I turn now from the politics of the past to those of the present, where several broad trends can be discerned. Perhaps the most prominent is a widespread rush to judgment that classical Freudian theory has become obsolete. One influential version of this position postulates a basic polarity between the drive model, which is disdained as biological, mechanistic, and insufficiently attentive to intersubjective dynamics, and the relational model, which is lauded for being empathic and concerned with human values. It is not the least of the historical ironies of Brill's legacy that this caricature of classical analysis as a wholly intrapsychic theory is a mirror image of the unwarranted condescension with which he and other defenders of orthodoxy formerly regarded interpersonalists. In order to escape this impasse, which impedes or even precludes productive discourse, I believe it is incumbent on analysts of all persuasions to adopt a dialectical outlook that makes the respectful recognition of our differences the precondition for an authentic possibility of reconciliation.

A second broad trend follows from the premature obsequies performed in some quarters over the body of classical analysis. In an era that has lost its traditional moorings, many colleagues have resorted to an eclecticism that would make a virtue of necessity by not simply tolerating but advocating the coexistence of a multiplicity of rival schools. Contemporary Freudianism, self psychology, object relations (both Kleinian and Independent), intersubjectivity, interpersonalism, relational psychoanalysis, Lacanianism, and the rest constitute a dizzying array of theories. All are bolstered to a greater or lesser extent by organizations, publications, lecture series, and conferences. We have, in short, not simply diverse but competing versions of psychoanalysis, whose adherents vie for students, patients, and public acceptance.

A third trend is the obverse of the second. Several outstanding analysts have proposed metatheories in an effort to make sense of the heterogeneity that defines the contemporary scene. They search for a road map with which to navigate the bewildering landscape. I will focus here on four major positions, each of which is associated with a prominent theorist. The first holds that all analysts share common ground as clinicians. The second contends that each of the varying standpoints should be adopted at one time or another in the clinical situation. The third seeks to subsume the divergent emphases within a composite psychoanalytic theory. The last classifies psychoanalytic theories according to the rubric of a drive/relational dichotomy and insists that mixed models are untenable. Although there is much to be learned from each of these metatheories, they are all limited in various ways and present the views with which they disagree as if from the outside. Hence, rather than look to any one of them for a definitive answer, analysts should aim to steer between the Scylla of an unduly rigid insistence on antinomies and the Charybdis of a complete blurring of distinctions, all the while striving to understand the subjective and ideological components of all psychoanalytic theorizing—including their own.

Clinical Common Ground

The idea of clinical common ground was introduced by Robert Wallerstein (1988) at the 1987 Montreal Congress. Two years later, as president of the International Psychoanalytical Association, he participated in planning the Rome Congress, which focused on this theme. To bolster his claim that psychoanalysts of various theoretical positions all share a clinical common ground, he convened a panel (Wallerstein 1990) consisting of an ego psychologist, a Kleinian, and a representative of the British Middle School. But no self psychologists or proponents of the interpersonal, intersubjective, or Lacanian schools were chosen. Had they been included, I believe, the case for common ground might well have been weakened, as the clinical practices following from the theoretical premises of these schools are far less reconcilable with Freudian ego psychology than are those of either Kleinian or Independent object relations theory.

Recently Arlene Kramer Richards and I (Richards and Richards 1995) proposed a psychoanalytic thought experiment in which we presented a clinical case interpreted first from our own contemporary Freudian perspective and then from what we took to be the perspective of other psychoanalytic schools. Two Kleinian analysts, two self psychologists, an intersubjectivist, and an American object relations theorist were asked to respond. From this exercise we concluded that modern Kleinian thought and contemporary Freudian theory indeed sustain Wallerstein's claim of common ground, probably because both positions accept the centrality of the concepts of conflict and un-conscious fantasy. However, we also found—and were supported by the responses of Paul Ornstein (1995) and James Fosshage (1995), the two self psychologists—that there is a disjunction between self psychology and contemporary Freudian and Kleinian points of view. In the terms that I have adapted (Richards 1993) from Martin Bergmann, self psychology is a modification, rather than an extension, of classical psychoanalysis. This result should not be surprising. After all, self psychology has developed its own theory of mind, development, pathogenesis, and therapeutic action. It can hardly be said to occupy common ground with its rivals if, as Arnold Goldberg (1984, 1987) has argued, it represents an alternative interpretive framework whose clinical advantages can be appreciated only from the inside—that, is by those already immersed in the system.

This example raises the possibility that still other points of view predicated on radically innovative theories of mind, development, pathogenesis, and therapeutic action likewise cannot be accommodated on clinical common ground. Wallerstein's ideal is thus perhaps best understood as an institutional response to the centrifugal pressures that continue to beset psychoanalysis—that is, as an assimilative vision designed to promote the illusion of political unity among analysts. The most critical assessment of this approach would see it as glossing over the genuine conflicts between alternative schools deemed to be marginal and the comprehensive mainstream position comprised of the Freudian and object relations currents in the International Psychoanalytical Association.

In the most recent restatement of his position, Wallerstein (1998) begins by taking for granted that "we have been engaged, over at least the past fifteen years, in a major shift—call it a paradigm shift or not—in our conceptualization of the nature of the psychoanalytic enterprise" (p. 1021). Later in the same paper, however, he pays tribute to Merton Gill for recognizing that this ostensibly new two-person psychology "should not displace the concomitant equal value of also considering our work from within the framework of a one-person psychology with its emphases and its requirements" (p. 1030). Here Wallerstein seems to have forgotten about the paradigm shift he announced at the outset, which implies an incommensurability between drive and relational models, and tries once again to find a place at the table for everyone in "the new American psychoanalysis."

Four Psychologies

The second response to pluralism is the multiple-model approach of Fred Pine (1990), a sophisticated eclecticism that attempts to give each of the principal competing theories its due. Eschewing innovations that are products of the culture and historical circumstances of their inventors, he regards the broadly gauged "psychologies" of drive, ego, object relations, and self as equally applicable to different sets of clinical phenomena. Pine presents these psychologies as models generated by particular kinds of observations that cannot be reduced to theories, although each emanates from a distinctive perspective. According to him, the psychology of the self invokes Kohut's self psychology, the psychology of drives invokes Freudian drive theory, the psychology of the ego invokes ego psychology, and the psychology of the object invokes object relations theory.

Like Wallerstein, Pine has continued to refine his initial position in light of subsequent critiques, though without, in my judgment, being able to overcome all its inherent difficulties. Indeed, in his latest work, Pine (1998) specifically takes issue with the characterization of his approach as eclectic. He does so by distinguishing between "the thoughtful integration of diverse ideas from various sources" and "a random or inconsistent or internally contradictory collection of ideas" (p. 47). But this attempt to differentiate "good" and "bad" forms of eclecticism does not gainsay the fact that because Pine believes that the proponents of each model can muster plausible arguments on their own behalf, the problem of establishing primacy among viewpoints becomes less urgent. In formulating interpretations, we are asked to use whichever model is called for by the shifting requirements of the moment. Pine does not believe that clinical common ground exists as a given. He hopes, rather, that it will be a byproduct of his approach—that is, that it will emerge as analysts work with a greater variety of models and become more sophisticated in their theoretical awareness.

Both Wallerstein's common ground and Pine's phenomenological approach can be viewed as strategies for mitigating theoretical pluralism. In the interest of promoting ecumenical peace, we are asked to foreclose theoretical disputation and to assume that there are no rational or empirical strategies for adjudicating competing claims. The problem, however, is that such eclecticism is acceptable only to eclectics. It will appeal to practitioners who do not align themselves with any major psychoanalytic school, who avoid theoretical controversies, and who prefer to remain above the fray. As Pine (1998) himself has conceded, his solution "looks eclectic only when one starts from the point of view of already developed systematic theories" (p. 48). Theorists committed to any given persuasion, that is, inevitably tend to prefer their own theories. They mount arguments in hope of persuading others and thereby establishing the primacy of their particular point of view. And this is as it should be. The proponents of Pine's four major psychologies do not consider the one that they favor to be partial, confined to a circumscribed range of clinical interests. Rather, each is held to be complete and to provide an account of motivation, personality, self-esteem, and relationships.

In a rejoinder to Pine's multiple-model approach, Charles Hanly (1994) has argued this point explicitly. He contends that contemporary Freudian theory provides the most comprehensive framework for grasping the interconnections among drive, ego, object relations, and narcissism. Indeed, for Hanly the great virtue of this model is precisely its capacity to hold the four psychologies in a productive tension in which no single component is accorded disproportionate weight. In his words, it "integrates yet allows for variable weighing and continuous clinical testing of the full range of the causalities that other models either reduce or omit or disconnect" (p. 179). Many analysts (I among them) would agree. But proponents of self psychology could make the argument that theirs is an equally comprehensive theory that encompasses and illuminates the interconnections among divergent psychologies. So, of course, could the adherents of other modifying theories. As Arnold Modell (1994) observes, Pine is recommending "not the use of particular theories that are in conflict, but four highly generalized points of view that seemingly rise above the conflict of local theories" (p. 202).

Total Composite Theory

The third response to theoretical pluralism, the total composite approach of Leo Rangell (1990), is in the spirit of Hanly's response to Pine. It holds that contemporary Freudian theory subsumes the narrower emphases of dissident models and offers a balanced presentation of drives, ego, object relations, and narcissism. This total composite theory represents for Rangell our cumulative inheritance from Freud and his successors. Theoretical diversity can be tolerated only within the parameters of a unified conglomeration, rooted in American ego psychology and culminating in modern structural conflict theory. Ego psychology, based on Freudian metapsychology as codified by David Rapaport, itself exemplifies Robert Waelder's principle of multiple function and Freud's principle of overdetermination. Rangell dimisses rival models as merely "new partial theories" that embody the logical fallacy of pars pro toto. Examples include the deficit environmentalism of Kohut, Sullivanian interpersonalism, and the object relations approach (which defines the organism as object-seeking rather than pleasure-seeking) of Fairbairn, Winnicott, and Guntrip. Each of these theories, according to Rangell, emphasizes one aspect of human experience at the expense of another: "deficit at the expense of conflict, preoedipal issues at the expense of oedipal issues, annihilation anxiety at the expense of castration anxiety, and so forth" (p. 836). The only legitimate model for theoretical change is growth by "accretion," by which Rangell means filling in the gaps in Freud's all-encompassing system. Through additions and refinements, classical psychoanalysis enlarges its domain by subsuming the valid insights of later partial theories. But such enlargement is always measured and incremental; it takes pains to preserve the fundamental dualities of mental life that are at the core of the Freudian perspective.

Although it certainly cannot be accused of glossing over genuine theoretical differences, Rangell's approach carries with it the danger of foreclosing consideration of potentially revolutionary departures that question fundamental aspects of the system, or even the system itself. However skeptical we may be about currently available alternative models, we put our scientific principles at risk if we decide in advance that we cannot accept any future paradigm shift in psychoanalysis. Indeed, there are critics from outside the contemporary Freudian perspective who contend that such a shift has already occurred and that many of us have simply missed it. The "dialectical constructivism" of Irwin Hoffman (1998) is one such recent argument to the effect that "there is a new paradigm struggling to emerge in the field," though he adds that "it has not yet fully arrived, much less been firmly established" (p. 134). For Hoffman the essential shift is not from a drive model to a relational model, but from a positivist to a constructivist model for understanding the psychoanalytic situation. A middle position would allow classical analysts to remain open to conceptual innovations more far-reaching than Rangell is preprared to contemplate, even while articulating and defending the core principles that we believe to be integral to any theory that calls itself psychoanalytic. Rangell's systematic criticism of non-Freudian models bears an affinity to Pine's multiple-model approach. Both view modern Freudian psychoanalysis as encompassing the insights of newer psychoanalytic schools. Both likewise stress the conceptual and clinical insufficiencies of any single alternative model. But whereas the multiple-model approach advocates an eclecticism that strives to give each model its due, total composite theory invokes the comprehensiveness of the Freudian model as a justification for excluding current alternative models—and perhaps the endeavor to propound alternative models altogether.

Rangell's total composite theory is the creation of a pioneer ego psychologist who is among the most persuasive proponents of modern structural theory. It is a distinctively American response to pluralism in the International Psychoanalytical Association, since it argues that contemporary Freudianism—call it ego psychology, structural theory, conflict psychology, or what you will—can subsume the contributions of Kleinianism and British (now European) object relations theory. Inevitably, therefore, Rangell's total composite theory is in part a personal response to the exigencies of his particular psychoanalytic situation. But however congenial this approach to pluralism may be to many analysts, it is likely to be perceived as dismissive by those outside the international Freudian mainstream. They may view its essentialism as undercutting their prerogative to develop and defend new models, which of course they will do in any case. Much as I admire Rangell's forthright defense of classical principles, which I regard as closest to my own, we must be wary of abandoning serious dialogue with those beyond our immediate psychoanalytic ken. What is political expedience for us may be political anathema to them.

Drive/Relational Dichotomy

At the opposite end of the spectrum from Wallerstein's search for clinical common ground is the fourth metatheoretical approach, one that posits an irremediable dichotomy between drive theories and relational theories. The foremost proponent of this position is Stephen Mitchell, who first in collaboration with Jay Greenberg (1983), later in Relational Concepts in Psychoanalysis (1988), and most recently in Hope and Dread in Psychoanalysis (1993) and Influence and Autonomy in Psychoanalysis (1997), argues that classical psychoanalysis, grounded in Freudian drive theory, and contemporary relational psychoanalysis, grounded in object relational and interpersonal theories, are alternative explanatory models that are neither complementary nor amenable to integration. They are in principle incompatible, since each is coextensive with the entire domain of human psychology. Each, that is, offers an explanatory paradigm that covers the same broad range of phenomena as the other.

Whereas Wallerstein's vision of a clinical common ground and Pine's ideal of multiple-model eclecticism are both politically assimilative, Mitchell's relational approach, like Rangell's total composite theory, draws clear lines of demarcation. For Mitchell, the various theories in the psychoanalytic marketplace collapse into antagonistic metatheories, among which one must choose. To align oneself with any variant of contemporary Freudianism is, according to Mitchell, to opt for a drive theory that is anachronistic and antihumanistic. To prefer a theory that falls under the heading of the "relational perspective," by contrast, is to evince sensitivity to the interpersonal and intersubjective wellsprings of human development, motivation, pathogenesis, and mind. In addition to attesting an awareness of the impact of culture and language on personality and psychopathology, it is to acknowledge the interactive nature of what takes place within the psychoanalytic situation.

As I have argued, the drive/relational antithesis can be explained historically as a reaction to Brill's politics of exclusion. American relational theory is largely the product of gifted psychologists who obtained their analytic training outside the American Psychoanalytic Association. It is instructive in this regard to compare Mitchell with Irwin Hoffman. Whereas Mitchell, an unabashed "outsider," depicts the choice between drive and relational theories as an either/or dichotomy, Hoffman, an "inside outsider" who trained at an institute of the American, commendably highlights the importance of dialectical thinking in psychoanalysis. The relationalists' vision of classical theory, which dwells almost exclusively on Freud's early energic concepts, does not adequately recognize that contemporary Freudianism offers a contextually grounded notion of conflict, compromise formation, and unconscious fantasy rooted in actual childhood experience and then re-created throughout the life cycle. Within this tradition there is a line of development, ranging from Roy Schafer's promulgation of an action language (1976) to Charles Brenner's revision of Freud's structural model (1982, 1994), that has progressively freed the concepts of id, ego, and superego from their putative biological "bedrock" and redefined them as constructs of mental agency in a dynamically and relationally sophisticated way. The drive/relational dichotomy presented by the relationalists tends to oversimplify contemporary Freudian psychoanalysis and to give insufficient attention to the evolution of drive concepts within it.

THE LIMITS OF METATHEORY

Each of the four responses to theoretical pluralism has both its strengths and its limitations. While exemplary in its aspiration to inclusiveness, the notion of clinical common ground seems to me to be predicated on a weak relationship between psychoanalytic theory and clinical practice. It assumes that our theories are metaphors located in what Joseph and Anne-Marie Sandler (1987) term the "present unconscious," but it has not demonstrated them to be consequential for the actual practice of psychoanalysis. The spectrum of theories that can fit comfortably under the ecumenical tent likewise proves to be much narrower than we had been led to anticipate.

From their respective vantage points, the proponents of multiple models and of total composite theory assert that modern Freudian psychoanalysis is the comprehensive psychoanalytic theory of choice. The former shares the syncretic spirit of the search for common ground, the latter sets forth its lines of demarcation with vigor and forthrightness, but neither position acknowledges that rival psychoanalytic schools have also proposed systems they deem equally comprehensive. Finally, the drive/relational dichotomy, a mirror image of total composite theory, reduces a diverse spectrum of positions to a fundamental dichotomy of incompatible global approaches. Although the equation of contemporary Freudianism with drive theory does a disservice to classical analysis, it does an even greater one to relational theory, which cannot develop to its fullest potential if it insists on sparring with a mislabeled partner.

How, then, can Brill's legacy help us formulate a more satisfactory response to the problem of pluralism, one that takes the best from all four approaches in order to facilitate rational discourse about theory and technique? What can be done to promote a program of comparative psychoanalysis and thereby lead our discipline into the twenty-first century? What do I recommend in lieu of these metatheoretical strategies?

I think it must be taken for granted that pluralism is a fact of contemporary psychoanalytic life. However great the demands it places on us, this reality must be acknowledged and not evaded. There are, not only in this country but around the world, several comprehensive psychoanalytic systems, each vying for ascendancy. One was created by Freud and has been elaborated by his closest colleagues and successors, including the generation trained by Brill. Contemporary Freudian conflict theorists, who have assumed the responsibility to continue its development, can accomplish this task only by engaging in discussion and debate with the proponents of other psychoanalytic systems.

This, then, is what Brill ultimately has to teach us: that we must be proactive in explaining and defending our viewpoint to the public, to other mental health professionals, and now, no less important, to psychoanalysts who see things differently. In the service of science, we need to sharpen our differences rather than paper them over. To this extent, an awareness of political issues is helpful. But if our goal is indeed to advance psychoanalysis as a science and not simply to defend our hegemony, the effort to represent our interests to other psychoanalysts—including self psychologists, relational psychoanalysts, and interpersonalists—must engage these colleagues constructively. If we want them to listen to us, obviously we must be prepared to listen to them. Thus, to appropriate the positive aspect of Brill's legacy we must finally disavow its obverse—the politics of exclusion sustained by its enshrinement of dogma. In a concrete way, my *JAPA* editorial, "Politics and Paradigms" (Richards 1998), attempted to chart a more inclusive course for this journal. It cannot be denied that the dark side of Brill's legacy bears no small measure of responsibility for the travails of pluralism. Without making this acknowledgment, we cannot hope to persuade colleagues that rival systems, regardless of their merits, incorporate serious misconstruals of contemporary Freudianism.

To renounce dogma is to open ourselves to an exploration of the personal and political roots of adherence to any particular psychoanalytic viewpoint. Arnold Rothstein (1980) has written about narcissistic paradigm competition. Rangell (1990) frames the issue in terms of what he calls "transference to theory." He refers to candidates' transference to their training institute, as well as to a more specific transference to theory, based on satisfaction or dissatisfaction with their personal analysis.

Consider the case of self psychology. Ernest Wolf (1994), interviewed by Virgina Hunter for *Psychoanalysts Talk,* describes his negative experience with his first analyst, Maxwell Gitelson, which doubtless contributed to his gravitating toward a theory at odds with Gitelson's approach. Indeed, we may infer the same dynamic in the case of Kohut. If Kohut himself was indeed Mr. Z in his celebrated "The Two Analyses of Mr. Z" (1979)—as is now widely believed—then perhaps we are justified in surmising that Kohut's unsatisfactory experience in his first analysis—which was classically conducted—played a role in his subsequent development of self psychology. Is it far-fetched to suspect that analysts who write about cold, authoritarian, unempathic classical analysts are telling us something about their own analytic experiences? There is evidently a self-reinforcing process at work here. A candidate or patient who has had a failed analysis in one particular school may well seek out an analyst of a different, even opposite, persuasion. This reaction promotes the candidate's or patient's acceptance of the "new" school's view of the deficiencies of the old one.

Although he emphasizes the way in which bad analysis often leads to theoretical innovation, Rangell (1990) does not exempt his own Freudian approach from such transference to theory. He speaks of transference displacements "that can be to any theory, old or new, and in any direction, positive or negative" (p. 828). I am reminded here of Kohut's provocative essay, "Creativeness, Charisma, and Group Psychology" (1976), which examines traditional analysts' idealization of Freud, left unresolved in their training analyses, as a factor in their residual narcissistic problems and concomitant insensitivity to narcissistic issues in clinical work.

THE LESSONS OF HISTORY

In "Politics and Paradigms" I adduced the strikingly different trajectories followed by the Columbia University Center for Psycho-analytic Training and Research and the William Alanson White Institute as a cardinal instance of the dynamic interplay between intellectual and institutional history. That comparison remains illuminating in the context of my present effort to assess the double-edged legacy of Brill and the New York Psychoanalytic Society and Institute in American psychoanalysis. Briefly, when Sandor Rado, the first director of the New York Institute, found himself at odds with leading members of the institute's education committee—including Brill—over his neo-Freudian "adaptational psychoanalysis," he founded the Association for Psychoanalytic Medicine in 1942 and the Psychoanalytic and Psychosomatic Clinic 1946, which he affiliated with Columbia University. Crucially, however, Rado did all he could to secure the acceptance of his new institute by the American Psychoanalytic Association.

By contrast, when Clara Thompson and Karen Horney left the New York Psychoanalytic Institute in 1941, Horney—stripped of her status as a training analyst—organized the American Institute of Psychoanalysis. Thompson, Frieda Fromm-Reichmann, and Erich Fromm soon led a split from the AIP when Fromm's own training analyst status was revoked. Joined by Harry Stack Sullivan, they formed a new institute affiliated with the Washington School of Psychiatry. In 1945 the Washington connection was severed and the institute renamed the William Alanson White. In 1952 the White abandoned its effort to affiliate with the American, though it remains unclear whether or not this was voluntary on the part of Thompson and her colleagues. In any event, after this separation the Sullivanian interpersonal point of view gained ascendancy at the White Institute and to this day remains its dominant theoretical orientation.

On the theoretical plane, Rado's adaptational approach at Columbia closely parallels the interpersonal outlook of the White Institute. Like the first generation of White analysts, Abram Kardiner and other members of the Columbia group produced vigorous critiques of libido theory (Kardiner, Karush, and Ovesey 1959a,b,c,d), which, after being rejected by official journals, were published in the *Journal of Nervous and Mental Diseases.* Yet, despite a shared culturalist heritage, the White Institute retains its autonomy as the leading center of interpersonal psychoanalysis, while the Columbia Center is an integral part of the American Psychoanalytic Association. It is, however, ironic to think that had Rado not exerted himself to keep Columbia within the American, we might find ourselves today debating adaptational psychoanalysis instead of relational theory. This is not to venture a judgment as to which historical path is to be preferred. Rather, I simply want to underscore the way in which politics and personalities affect our attitudes toward theory and even our decisions about what strategy to pursue in the face of substantive differences.

The lesson I would draw from this historical reprise is the same as that to be derived from the four more recent examples of subjectively motivated theory-building I presented earlier. This is not a brief for one psychoanalytic viewpoint over and against all others. Rather, my point is simply that we must acknowledge the inescapability of institutional pressures in the unfolding of any theory. We have reached a juncture where this lesson has special salience, for only by recognizing the overdetermined influences that sustain all ideological allegiances—again not excluding our own—can analysts cope with the pluralism of our time in a rational and judicious manner. But if we are willing to take this step, we will begin to clear a real common ground where productive work can be undertaken on the urgent problems besetting our field.

As we know all too well, there is a psychopathology of everyday psychoanalytic life. It is manifested in the power struggles and rivalries from which no analytic group is immune. It escalates into clashes with colleagues of different persuasions in which we turn a blind eye to our shared need to promote the hard-won gains of our science in an increasingly hostile environment. This acrimony hardens artificial boundaries that have little if any theoretical basis. The diversity of points of view within the American Psychoanalytic Association, for example, is no greater than that found in institutes throughout the world. Instead of uniting in response to the threats posed by our increasingly vociferous detractors—to whom, nonetheless, we should listen with an unprejudiced mind—we become embroiled in the narcissism of minor differences, wasting in internecine struggles energies and passions that could be put to better use.

As we seek at long last to put Brill's legacy of exclusion behind us, I think it fitting to conclude by reasserting that Freud's work indeed continues to provide the common foundation of psychoanalysis. I refer here not to this or that specific tenet of Freudian theory, each one of which has come under fire at some point in the past century. Rather, it is the open-ended quality of Freud's thought—his emphasis on process rather than content—that constitutes his abiding gift to posterity. On every crucial dilemma we continue to face—whether it be the choice between drives and relationships, between the epistemologies of positivism and constructivism, between insight and experience as agents of therapeutic change, or between a conception of psychoanalysis as a scientific or a hermeneutic discipline—Freud declines to come down on one side or the other. By this refusal of premature closure Freud teaches us to resist our own temptations to prefer the ready simplifications of dogmatism and dichotomies to the exacting (yet ultimately exhilarating) rigors of dialectics.

On one issue, of course, Freud did speak out unequivocally—that of lay analysis. In this matter, it is now beyond dispute, Freud was right and Brill was wrong. There is today a collective willingness to define psychoanalysis as an autonomous healing profession, so that the evaluation of a person's suitability for psychoanalytic training will be divorced once and for all from his or her profession and academic degrees. But though Brill felt constrained to oppose Freud in principle, let us not forget that he followed his lead in practice when it came to the treatment of his own children. Adoption of these enlightened policies is at once a symbolic and a real step that will place us in the best position to continue Brill's efforts to promote our scientific growth and to earn public acceptance. By transforming an outworn legacy of exclusion into a new politics of inclusion we will be able both to till a common ground with our colleagues and to advocate a distinctive vision that is—in the most vital, enduring sense of the term—Freudian.

REFERENCES

BRENNER, C. (1982). *The Mind in Conflict.* New York: International Universities Press.

—— (1994). Beyond the ego and the id. *Journal of Clinical Psycho-analysis* 3:473–488.

FASS, P. (1969). A. A. Brill: Pioneer and Prophet. Master's dissertation, Columbia University. Unpublished manuscript in the Archives collection of the Abraham A. Brill Library.

FOSSHAGE, J. (1995). How theory affects technique. *Journal of Clinical Psychoanalysis* 4:483–490.

FREUD, S. (1926). The question of lay analysis. *Standard Edition* 20:179–258.

GOLDBERG, A. (1984). Translation between psychoanalytic theories. *Annual of Psychoanalysis* 12:121–135.

—— (1987). How theory shapes technique: A self psychological perspective. *Psychoanalytic Inquiry* 7:181–188.

GREENBERG, J., & MITCHELL, S. (1983). *Object Relations in Psychoanalytic Theory.* Cambridge: Harvard University Press.

HALE, N. (1971). *Freud and the Americans: The Beginnings of Psycho-analysis in the United States.* New York: Oxford University Press.

—— (1995). *The Rise and Crisis of Psychoanalysis in the United States: Freud and the Americans, 1917–1985.* New York: Oxford University Press.

HANLY, C. (1994). Clinical advantages and disadvantages of multiple models. *Psychoanalytic Inquiry* 14:164–184.

HOFFMAN, I. (1998). *Ritual and Spontaneity in the Psychoanalytic Process: A Dialectical Constructivist Point of View.* Hillsdale, NJ: Analytic Press.

KARDINER, A., KARUSH, A., & OVESEY, L. (1959a). Libido theory. *Journal of Nervous and Mental Diseases* 129:133–143.

—— (1959b). A methodological study of Freudian theory (1) Basic concepts. *Journal of Nervous and Mental Diseases* 129:11–19.

—— (1959c). Narcissism, bisexuality, and the dual instinct theory. *Journal of Nervous and Mental Diseases* 129:207–221.

—— (1959d). The structural hypothesis, the problem of anxiety, and post-Freudian ego psychology. *Journal of Nervous and Mental Diseases* 129:341–356.

KOHUT, H. (1976). Creativeness, charisma, and group psychology. *Psychological Issues* 34:379–425.

—— (1979). The two analyses of Mr. Z. *International Journal of Psycho-Analysis* 60:3–27.

LEWIN, B. (1962). American psychoanalytic education: Historical comments. *Journal of the American Psychoanalytic Association* 10:119–138.

MITCHELL, S. (1988). *Relational Concepts in Psychoanalysis.* Cambridge:

Harvard University Press.

———— (1993). *Hope and Dread in Psychoanalysis*. New York: Basic Books.

———— (1997). *Influence and Autonomy in Psychoanalysis*. Hillsdale, NJ: Analytic Press.

MODELL, A. (1994). Common ground or divided ground? *Psychoanalytic Inquiry* 14:201–211.

ORNSTEIN, P. (1995). Self psychology is not what you think it is. *Journal of Clinical Psychoanalysis* 4:491–506.

PINE, F. (1990). *Drive, Ego, Object, Self.* New York: Basic Books.

———— (1998). *Diversity and Direction in Psychoanalytic Technique.* New Haven: Yale University Press.

RANGELL, L. (1990). *The Human Core.* Madison, CT: International Universities Press.

RICHARDS, A.D. (1993). Extenders, modifiers, heretics. In *The Spectrum of Psychoanalysis: Essays in Honor of Martin Bergmann*, ed. A.K. Richards & A.D. Richards. Madison, CT: International Universities Press, pp. 145–160.

———— (1998). Politics and paradigms. *Journal of the American Psycho-analytic Association* 46:357–360.

———— & RICHARDS, A.K. (1995). Notes on psychoanalytic theory and its consequences for technique. *Journal of Clinical Psychoanalysis* 4:429–564.

ROTHSTEIN, A. (1980). Psychoanalytic paradigms and their narcissistic investment. *Journal of the American Psychoanalytic Association* 28:385–396.

SANDLER, J., & SANDLER, A.-M. (1987). Past unconscious, present unconscious, and the vicissitudes of guilt. *International Journal of Psycho-Analysis* 68:331–342.

SCHAFER, R. (1976). *A New Language for Psychoanalysis.* New Haven: Yale University Press.

WALLERSTEIN, R. (1988). One psychoanalysis or many? *International Journal of Psycho-Analysis* 69:5–22.

———— (1990). Psychoanalysis: The common ground. *International Journal of Psycho-Analysis* 71:713–20.

———— (1998). The new American psychoanalysis: A commentary. *Journal of the American Psychoanalytic Association* 46:1021–1043.

WOLF, E. (1994). Interview. In V. Hunter, *Psychoanalysts Talk.* New York: Guilford Press, pp. 143–82.

CHAPTER 3

Psychoanalytic Discourse at the Turn of Our Century: A Plea for a Measure of Humility

[Richards, A.D. (2003). *Journal of the Amer. Psychoanalytic Assoc. 51(Suppl.) 73–89.*]

Since Freud's death in 1939, American psychoanalysis has grown from a small, homogeneous, and hierarchical community that resolved disputes primarily by ostracizing dissidents to a larger and more democratic one notable for its intellectual and cultural diversity. Theoretical pluralism and an increasingly heterogeneous population of practitioners have precipitated a renewed struggle for equilibrium between subversive energies and older traditions and have tested the civility of our discourse as perhaps never before. Although these challenges should not be underestimated, the present moment affords analysts in the United States a unique opportunity for mending fences and building bridges. To this end, I would urge adherents of the various analytic traditions to forgo a discourse of dichotomy and polarization and instead approach one another in a dialectical spirit. Just as the essence of science is to be open to evidence that might refute one's preconceptions, so too is it the essence of the psychoanalytic wisdom to which we all aspire to avoid defensiveness and to acknowledge our mistakes. Human nature being what it is, a counsel of perfection is not what I have in mind; a plea for a measure of humility on all sides, however, seems eminently worth making.

Given the long shadow cast over the psychoanalytic movement by Freud's powerful and paradoxical personality, it is an indication of how far we have come in our collective journey that few analysts today find it necessary to idealize him. If we turn back to the mid-century writings of Heinz Hartmann, whose ambition to make psychoanalysis a "general psychology" remains exemplary, it is clear that his vision of Freud requires qualification. Seeking to minimize the role played by emotional or unconscious factors in Freud's work, Hartmann (1959) wrote that Freud's "striving for scientific discipline, his patient accumulation of

Originally presented in the Distinguished Lecturer Series, Contemporary Center for Advanced Psychoanalytic Studies, Fairleigh Dickinson University, October 26, 2003.

observational data, and his seach for conceptual tools to account for them have reduced [their] importance to a stimulus factor in psychoanalytic theories" (p. 339). In a similar vein, he praised Freud's case histories "because they show the constant mutual promotion of observation and hypothesis formation, the formation of definite propositions which make our knowledge testable, and the attempts to validate or invalidate them" (p. 342).

To be sure, Freud's case histories still have much to teach us, and at his best moments Freud indeed displays the "scientific discipline" that Hartmann prized so highly. In introducing the case of Little Hans, for example, Freud (1909) warned that "it is not in the least our business to 'understand' a case at once; this is only possible at a later stage, when we have received enough impressions of it. For the present, we will suspend our judgement and give our impartial attention to everything that there is to observe" (pp. 22–23). Similarly, he advised analyst readers "not to try to understand everything at once, but to give a kind of unbiased attention to every point and to await future developments" (p. 65). These admirable precepts, however, are often contradicted in his actual clinical practice. In his single consultation with Hans, Freud informed the boy that even before his birth he "had known that a little Hans would come who would be so fond of his mother that he would be bound to feel afraid of his father because of it" (p. 42). Indeed, at the conclusion of the narrative, Freud avowed, "Strictly speaking, I learnt nothing new from this analysis" (p. 147); it simply confirmed his findings from adult treatments.

To call into question Hartmann's vision of Freud as a cautious scientist and to see him instead as a Faustian figure largely in the grip of preconceptions is not to diminish his genius. It is simply to recognize that Freud is important to us today as much because of the questions he raises—and the contradictions he embodies—as because of the answers he provides. This more nuanced, even critical, attitude toward Freud has long been taken by revisionists such as Erich Fromm, Theodor Reik, Karen Horney, and Clara Thompson. What is new is the degree to which it has of late become accepted even by analysts within the American Psychoanalytic Association. If contemporary Freudians have learned to become more iconoclastic, the converse is that relational and other analysts are willing to give Freud his due. Stephen Mitchell (1993) spoke for many when, invoking Hans Loewald, he urged that Freud be transformed from "an improperly buried ghost who haunts us into a beloved and revered ancestor" (p. 176). Analysts of all persuasions can now agree that Freud is owed an immense debt, but our loyalty is no longer (if it ever was) to a single fallible human being; rather, it is to a psychoanalytic mode of thinking and working that has undergone continuous evolution in the more than sixty years since Freud's death.

When, as fate would have it, both Melanie Klein and Anna Freud settled in London during World War II, a conflict broke out in British psychoanalysis centering on these two formidable child analysts, each claiming to be Freud's legitimate heir (King and Steiner 1990). Through the mediating influence of figures such as Ernest Jones, Sylvia Payne, and D. W. Winnicott, a compromise was worked out that established three parallel training tracks in the London Institute. Because a schism was averted, psychoanalysis in Great Britain developed more dialecti-cally than elsewhere, and the postwar period was exceptionally rich and exciting. Indeed, the "relational turn" that has exerted such a powerful hold on late-twentieth-century thinking originates in large measure with analysts in the Independent (that is, non-Kleinian) object relations tradition— Fairbairn, Winnicott, Balint, and Bowlby—who mounted a systematic challenge to the assumptions of what they took to be Freud's libido theory. Ironically, however, because no faction was excluded and thereby forced to found a separate institute, there is even today only one institute belonging to the International Psychoanalytic Association in all of Great Britain, and this lack of diversity has had adverse long-term consequences. Surely in the larger cities of the United Kingdom, it would be healthy to have greater competition for candidates and patients, which is the norm is in other European countries and the Americas.

Although some refugees from Nazi persecution came to England, by far the greatest number immigrated to the United States, where a new version of psychoanalysis began to take hold, severed from the past both by the expanse of the Atlantic Ocean and by the traumas of recent history. From the 1940s through the 1960s, American psychoanalysis was dominated by these Continental figures, most from Central Europe, who though dispersed in various cities were concentrated most heavily in New York. Some were sponsored by the New York Psychoanalytic Society's Rescue Committee, led by Lawrence Kubie and Bettina Warburg, while others came on their own. Among those brought to our shores by this wave of immigration were Hartmann, Ernst Kris, Rudolf Loewenstein, George Gero, Andrew Peto, Hermann Nunberg, Robert Bak, Edith Jacobson, and Kurt and Ruth Eissler. These and other old-world analysts established themselves as the predominant theoretical and political force at the New York Psychoanalytic Institute, whence their influence radiated to institutes across the country.

Whereas object relations theory took hold primarily in Great Britain and only later converged with the American interpersonalism of Harry Stack Sullivan, the mainstream tradition of ego psychology was forged jointly by Central European analysts in the United States and the group led by Anna Freud in London. Although Hartmann and his colleagues sought to use Freud's structural theory in a flexible and pragmatic fashion, they never questioned its metapsychological assumptions, particularly Freud's model of the drives and his view of the ego as simply one system in the personality rather than as synonymous with an overarching "self."

Strikingly, whereas most of the architects of ego psychology came from Vienna, the repudiation of metapsychology in the United States was promoted mainly by students of the Hungarian-born David Rapaport— Merton Gill, Roy Schafer, George Klein, and Robert Holt. (Trained as a psychologist, Rapaport was a brilliant theorist of psychoanalysis, but he never had an analytic practice. Nor did he become a member of the American Psychoanalytic Association.) This divergence between the legacies of Vienna and Budapest goes back to the creative tension between Freud and Ferenczi, and it underscores Ferenczi's importance as the progenitor of many of the innovative trends in contemporary psychoanalysis. More recently, though Heinz Kohut and Otto Kernberg—the two analysts who have gone furthest in recasting Freud's explanatory system—were both born in Vienna, Kernberg's analytic formation in Chile immersed him in the object relations tradition, whereas Kohut developed self psychology in the United States as a continuation of ego psychology. Not by chance, Kohut's first two references in The Analysis of the Self (1971) are to Hartmann's work.

Aside from their calling into question such speculative notions as the death instinct, the theorists of ego psychology countenanced no deviation from the axioms of individual depth psychology. A fault line thus opened in American psychoanalysis in 1942 when a group of early interpersonalists, who had begun to examine what hitherto had been regarded skeptically as the social epiphenomena of intrapsychic processes, left the New York Psychoanalytic Society in protest against Horney's removal from her faculty position. This group, which included Fromm and Thompson, formed the American Institute of Psychoanalysis, now known as the

American Institute of Psychoanalysis-Karen Horney Clinic. But as with the Lacanians in France, a series of further rifts occurred within the schismatic group. William Silverberg and other interpersonalists left the American Institute of Psychoanalysis to found a more medical, university-affiliated psychoanalytic group at New York Medical College. Fromm and Thompson left to establish the William Alanson White Institute, whose disciplinary orientation was a mixture of medical and psychological, and where Harry Stack Sullivan played a leading role. In the 1960s, Bernard Kalinkowitz, Erwin Singer, and Avrum Ben-Avi in turn moved from the White Institute, where they had trained, to found the New York University Postdoctoral Program in Psychotherapy and Psychoanalysis, which has since become an important center of relational thought. They did so in part because of their sense that psychologists were not accorded equal status at the White Institute and because they wanted to offer a less rigid training program.

Schisms are qualitatively different from ordinary disagreements because the parties break off contact and thereafter develop in isolation. Because they cease to know each other personally, the factions then construct fantasies of the rival group based on ignorance and fear. Horney's ouster set the stage for a half-century of struggle in American psychoanalysis in which issues of power and authority ran parallel with—and often took precedence over—theoretical debates. Although skirmishes continued to flare up periodically in the American Psychoanalytic Association, none led to a crisis on the order of the 1942 schism (Richards 1999). Even Sandor Rado's resignation from the New York Institute to found the Columbia Center, where his distinctive form of adapational psychoanalysis became ensconced, did not lead to an exodus of his group from the medically based umbrella organization of the American; not did the self psychology promulgated by Kohut and his colleagues result in a split at the Chicago Institute. Thus, in political terms, these two later controversies have more in common with the clashes between Anna Freud and Melanie Klein in British psychoanalysis than with the original Horney schism in America.

The series of rifts among Horney's adherents furnishes an important lesson for students of psychoanalytic history. For if divisions within the rebel camp replicate the one that generated the initial schism, this suggests that the two warring sides—the Greeks and the Trojans, as it were—are mirror images of one another, whatever substantive differences they may appear to have. In an interview with Peter Rudnytsky

(2000), Stephen Mitchell stated that "the internal politics and the generational battles" he witnessed at the White Institute and the NYU Postdoctoral Program "were just as pernicious and crushing" as any at Freudian institutes; "often," he added, "underneath an ideology of openness, there was an enormous concern with political correctness and control" (p. 115). Similarly, Rado asserted in an interview with Bluma Swerdloff (Roazen and Swerdloff 1995) that when a group leaves an institute it considers authoritarian, the new institute established by the group frequently turns out to be no less authoritarian than its predecessor. As Milton warned against the tendency of revolutionary Puritans to reimpose the oppressive institutions of the Anglican church, "New Presbyter is but Old Priest writ Large" (Hughes 1957, p. 145).

The persistence of exclusionary behavior in dissident analytic groups exposes the inadequacy of any simple opposition between Freudian authoritarianism and interpersonal egalitarianism. Until recently, the White Institute did not provide full training for social workers with a master's degree. As long ago as 1948, this marginalization of their discipline prompted a nucleus of social workers and their supporters to withdraw from the White and align themselves with Theodor Reik's grouping to found the National Psychological Association for Psychoanalysis. Freud, of course, had in 1926 written *The Question of Lay Analysis* to defend Reik in the Viennese context, but nonetheless, when Reik arrived in this country in 1938 as a refugee from the Nazis, he was denied full membership in the New York Psychoanalytic Institute because he had a Ph.D. in psychology rather than a medical degree. He was instead offered a research membership, which he refused.

If what I have recounted is in one respect a gloomy history, from another vantage point it gives us grounds for hope. Since there is enough blame to go around, there is no longer any good reason for one analytic tradition to feel superior to another. With a measure of humility on all sides, we might begin to lower the barriers between competing groups.

As I suggested at the outset, the world of psychoanalysis today is irrevocably pluralistic. In addition to the ubiquitous contemporary Freudians and relationalists, we have Kleinians, Bionians, Lacanians, self psychologists, intersubjectivists, and interpersonalists. And contemporary Freudians are themselves not all of a piece. Among them we can distinguish conflict theorists (Jacob Arlow, Charles Brenner, Dale Boesky, Leo Rangell), defense analysts (Paul Gray, Fred Busch), and developmentalists (Margaret Mahler, Fred Pine), to name only some of the more prominent subspecies. An organizational pluralism both reflects and informs this theoretical pluralism. At one time the American Psychoanalytic Association was virtually the only game in town. Now, however, a thousand flowers have bloomed: the Independent Psychoanalytic Societies, a federation of four groups that joined the International Psychoanalytical Association as a result of the lawsuit against the American and the IPA; Division 39, with its many affiliated but autonomous institutes; the Academy of Psychoanalysis, limited to medical psychoanalysts; the National Committee of Psychoanalytic Social Workers; and the International Federation for Psychoanalysis, an independent organization. Most recently, the International Society for Relational Psychoanalysis has come on the scene.

An accurate census of the psychoanalytic population even in the United States is difficult to come by. One estimate is that the members of the Academy, Division 39, and the Psychoanalytic Committee of Social Workers together number about 7,000. Section 1 of Division 39 has about 500 members, while Section 4 has thirty local chapters with over 3,000 members, of whom only 500 belong to Division 39. Of the psychoanalytic journals, about 1,500 people subscribe to *Contemporary Psychoanalysis,* the organ of the William Alanson White Society, while 2,400 are subscribers of *Psychoanalytic Dialogues,* the journal of relational perspectives. *Psychoanalytic Psychology,* the Division 39 journal, has 4,500 subscribers; *Psychoanalytic Review,* sponsored by NPAP, has 2,700. *The Journal of the American Psychoanalytic Association* has approximately 5,600 subscribers, and of that number approximately 3,000 belong to neither the American nor the IPA.

How are diverse groups to coexist in today's psychoanalytic world? The choice comes down to whether they choose to hunker down in entrenched positions or to embrace the challenges of pluralism. Obviously, I am in favor of reaching out; but in order to take that risk we must be prepared to listen to and learn from one another. There is, of course, a paradox in proposing oneself as a spokesperson for humility, since anyone claiming to be humble may well be perceived to be self-righteously claiming instead to be wiser than those whose pretensions are being deflated. It was for this reason that Socrates was put to death by the outraged citizens of Athens. But something of the same paradox inheres in the very practice of psychoanalysis, in which all of us—flawed though we are—take it upon ourselves to offer help and guidance to others. There is no escape from this dilemma except to recognize that we are imperfect messengers of the causes we espouse and to reconcile ourselves to accepting as gracefully as possible the criticism that comes with the territory.

There is, then, an interplay between the political history of psychoanalysis and the nature of psychoanalytic discourse. Because of the breakdown of the organizational structures that once ensured the hegemony of the American Psychoanalytic Association, we have an opportunity to discuss our differences in a genuinely scientific and open-minded spirit. As every psychoanalyst knows, the traumas of the past often continue to exert a hold on the present even when there seems no reason for them to do so; intellectual insight into the causes of a repetition compulsion may not suffice to free a patient from its grip. Like everyone else, psychoanalysts are not immune from the law that those who do not remember the past are condemned to repeat it; or rather, to put it analytically, that those who have not worked through the past are condemned to repeat it instead of remembering it.

In contrast to the groups led by Rado and Kohut, which never broke away from the American Psychoanalytic Association, (and were never in danger of being expelled), those who formed the White Institute had to seek recognition as a component society but were persistently rebuffed. The committee appointed to settle the matter included Merton Gill, who told the White delegation that the real reason for their exclusion was not the requirements imposed by the Board on Professional Standards but an entrenched hostility on the part of the powers-that-be. At one point, the American Psychoanalytic Association even sued the White Institute in an attempt to enjoin it from using the word psychoanalysis in its name. The White countersued, hiring the prestigious Washington antitrust firm of Fortas and Porter, and the American eventually dropped its suit. This skirmish foreshadowed the successful lawsuit brought by clinical psychologists against the American and the IPA in the late 1980s, which was financed in large measure by members of the White.

As a consequence of the politics of exclusion practiced by the American, those in the interpersonal tradition developed their form of psychoanalysis in isolation—on a kind of intellectual Galapagos island—and at times even seemed to cherish their outsider status. If the authoritarianism of the American bore the lineaments of Freud's personality, the truculence of the interpersonalists was consistent with the style of Sullivan, who cultivated a deliberate nonconformity. Although the interpersonalists' insularity led to some divergences in their theoretical evolution, there were also many striking parallels with contemporary Freudians, as both analytic species encountered similar clinical challenges. What was lost by this unfortunate severing of contact was the chance for a healthy cross-fertilization, a situation only now being redressed, with representatives of the groups meeting on a regular basis.

Although ignorance of the other's work has at times led both Freudians and interpersonalists to reinvent the wheel, such seemingly superfluous labors have at least the value of showing the extent of the convergence between erstwhile rival traditions. Charles Spezzano (1998), for instance, has pointed to the emphasis placed by both Paul Gray and Harry Stack Sullivan on anxiety in analytic work. In Freudian fashion, Gray argues that anxiety initiates maneuvers of "defense," maneuvers that Sullivan refers to as "security operations." The basic principle, however, is the same. There is likewise a meeting of minds between the Freudian Sheldon Bach and the interpersonalist Philip Bromberg in their conceptualization of narcissistic states of consciousness. Arlene Kramer Richards and I (Richards and Richards 2000) have also recently discussed an exchange between Irwin Hirsch and the late Benjamin Wolstein for a memorial tribute to the latter in Contemporary Psychoanalysis. Recognizing that Wolstein makes an unlikely ally for contemporary Freudians, we argue that Otto Fenichel's belief in the centrality of affect to the therapeutic process and Charles Brenner's approach to countertransference as the transference of the analyst are both consistent with Wolstein's point of view. On a broader level, both interpersonalists and Freudians have shown a heightened interest in the phenomenology of subjective experience and a corresponding decline in their concern with abstruse matters of metapsychology. Both groups have reopened fundamental questions about the ground rules of the analytic situation and how the dynamics of authority and power impinge on the analyst's functioning.

A turning point in recent psychoanalytic history came with the founding of the relational track at the NYU Postdoctoral Program in 1988. Having initially offered courses from Freudian, Sullivanian, and Frommian points of view, the NYU program had by the 1970s moved from theoretical eclecticism to a system of three specific tracks—the Freudian, the interpersonal/humanist, and the unaligned—an arrangement reminiscent of the "gentleman's agreement" reached by the British Society in the 1940s. But, as Lewis Aron (1996) has chronicled, the emergence of self psychology, together with the rapidly increasing popularity of the British object relations school, destabilized that arrangement by introducing new alternatives to both the Freudian and the interpersonal/humanist tracks.

The founders of the relational track—Emmanuel Ghent, Stephen Mitchell, James Fosshage, Bernard Friedland, and Philip Bromberg—took advantage of the publication of Greenberg and Mitchell's Object Relations in Psychoanalytic Theory (1983) five years earlier to make a definitive break with psychoanalytic orthodoxy. Relying on the "drive/relational dichotomy" postulated in that volume as a road map through the theoretical landscape, the NYU relationalists endeavored to unite under a single roof interpersonalism, object relations, Kleinian-ism, self psychology, and intersubjectivity. By connecting American interpersonalism with British object relations theory, this strategy effectively combatted the marginalization of the Sullivanian tradition and integrated it with a larger body of psychoanalytic thought.

But this positive achievement was not without its unintended consequences. First of all, the interpersonal/humanist track was effectively deprived of its reason for existence, though it managed to hobble on with a nominally separate identity. More profoundly, the struggle for power against what was deemed the common enemy—the Freudian establishment—was waged on two interconnected fronts: a theoretical and clinical one on behalf of the relational perspective, and a political one on behalf of antiauthoritarianism. As Aron observed, the political agenda to a large extent drove the intellectual debate. "One way of viewing Mitchell's achievement," he wrote "is to think of his having forged a multinational combination, consolidating diverse nations, some of which have conflicting interests in regard to other matters, but uniting them against a common adversary—classical theory. He has brought into one relational confederation a wide variety of alternative (non-classical) analytic schools, in the hope that even in their individual weaknesses, together they would be able to overcome the force of classical theory" (1996, p. 33).

This strategy was not only successful but also understandable in light of the injustices perpetrated as late as the 1980s by entrenched forces in the American Psychoanalytic Association. In the turmoil of the Vietnam War era, those with strongly left-wing leanings tended to see classical Freudian theory as an expression of the climate of social conformity of the preceding decades. The struggle for power in psychoanalytic organizational life had as its counterpart an attack on the alleged authoritarianism of classical analytic practice. Although the settlement of the lawsuit opened up the American and the IPA to several nonmedical groups (the Institute for Psychoanalytic Training and Research, the New York Freudian Society, and the Los Angeles Institute and Society for Psychoanalytic Studies), as well as to one predominantly Kleinian medical group (the Psychoanalytic Center of California), it ironically left both the White Institute of the interperson-alists and the Karen Horney Institute—the result of the original 1942 split—still on the outside.

Credit must be given to Greenberg and Mitchell for their articulation of the intellectual synthesis that lay the groundwork for a new political alliance, as well as to the founders of the relational track at NYU for using that synthesis to shape curriculum. A dozen years later, however, it is possible to see that their success came at a price. The energy of the dissidents was fueled at least in part by a sense of their status as victims, and the fundamental premise of a dichotomy between drive and relational theories fails to withstand scrutiny. Melanie Klein, for instance, was classified by Greenberg and Mitchell (1983) as an object relations theorist, though she endorsed the concept of the death instinct. Some in the relational camp, however, including Jessica Benjamin (1999), have questioned the binary opposition between drives, seen as nonrelational, and the need for relationships, seen as lacking instinctual urgency. In his later work, Greenberg (1991) made room for a concept of drives within a relational matrix when he proposed safety and effectance as primary motivations of human behavior.

In short, by elevating the antithesis between drives and relationships into a theoretical shibboleth, the relational turn made it difficult to engage in nuanced debate regarding their interaction. Relationalists hail what they consider their more empathic two-person psychology as the expression of an epistemologically sophisticated constructivism, while they fault the psychology of Freud and contemporary Freudians as noninteractive and as maintaining an allegiance to an outmoded sci-entistic objectivism. Stuart Pizer (1998), for example, asserts that all classical analysis is characterized by a "a nondisclosing analyst, who arrogates to himself the nonnegotiable position of arbiter of reality, who sits as a neutral observer outside the one-person dynamic situation, [which] is inherently humiliating to the patient, and may iatrogenically embed resistances to negotiation.... it may well be that the maximized power asymmetry of the classical (patriarchal, patronizing) analytic position in its very structure actually incites aggression by dichotomizing power in ways that inherently humiliate the patient with its a priori terms for negotiating the treatment" (p. 188).

Pizer's sketch of what he takes to be classical analysis is, however, a caricature of contemporary Freudian practice. Every analytic style has its dangers and excesses, just as every school has its share of bad analysts and doctrinaire thinkers. If, on the one hand, the Freudian ideals of neutrality and abstinence entail the risk of hardening into authoritarianism, so, on the other, do the relational ideals of empathy and participation risk yielding to inappropriate gratifications. Pizer makes no allowance for the fact that analysts of all persuasions proceed as they do because they believe they are acting in the best interest of their patients. For Pizer, it would seem, negotiation is possible with everyone except a contemporary Freudian analyst. This irony is reminiscent of the tendency of postmodernists to take for granted the truth of their own beliefs, while remaining condescendingly skeptical about the assertions of those with whom they disagree.

The fundamental problem with Pizer's claim that the classical analyst "arrogates to himself the nonnegotiable position of arbiter of reality" can be seen by contrasting his outlook with that of the late Merton Gill. Like Hans Loewald, Gill has the distinction of being revered by contemporary Freudians and relationalists alike, and he is acknowledged as a seminal influence on analysts in both traditions. Lacking political ambitions and belonging to no school, Gill was devoted to exploring psychoanalysis in theory and in practice. He also recognized the limitations of thinking in terms of mutually exclusive polarities. "To speak of internal and external factors as though they were a simple dichotomy," he wrote in his last book, "is false. In human psychological functioning the external world is significantly constructed by the internal world and the internal world is significantly constructed by the external world. In short, we deal with the mutually interactive constructivist circle" (1994, p. 16). As if anticipating Pizer's objection that the classical analyst "sits as a neutral observer outside the one-person dynamic situation," Gill recognized that "the analyst is always influencing the patient, and the patient is always influencing the analyst. This mutual influence cannot be avoided; it can only be interpreted. It is the analyst's awareness of the unremitting influence of patient and analyst on each other and his attempt to make that influence as explicit as possible that constitutes his 'neutrality'" (p. 50).

Gill's emphasis on the virtues of dialectical thinking in psychoanalysis has been carried forward by Irwin Hoffman (1998). Although

Hoffman shares the widespread belief that an irreversible paradigm shift has recently occurred in psychoanalysis, he holds that the decisive shift is not from a drive to a relational model, but rather from a posi-tivist to a constructivist one. This leads Hoffman to question the customary alignment of drive theory with positivism and relational theory with constructivism. As Hoffman notes, relational theories, including interpersonal psychoanalysis and self psychology, frequently retain an objectivist cast, whereas classical Freudian theory contains at least the seeds of a constructivist point of view. By clearing the ground for a meeting of opposing camps, Hoffman fosters intellectual exchange and helps heal old resentments. Once areas of agreement are established, any remaining differences can be addressed in a positive, even pleasurable, spirit.

Although, as I have argued, the success of the relational turn has been limited both by a penchant for dichotomies and by a lingering sense of resentment at having been oppressed, it was undoubtedly detrimental to American psychoanalysis to have had a single school hold the reins of power for so long. Historically, the responsibility for what I have termed the "politics of exclusion" in American psychoanalysis (Richards 1999) rests with the then dominant group. As the editors of the *Journal of Clinical Psychoanalysis* have admitted, theory in the late 1950s and early 1960s was stuck in a "blind alley" of remote abstraction and "seemed unable to progress" (Wyman and Rittenberg 1994, p. 315). What is more, in their zeal to defend classical theory, some distinguished analysts went too far, advancing an argument that echoed Ernest Jone's notorious claim that Ferenczi at the end of his life developed "psychotic manifestations that revealed themselves in, among other ways, a turning away from Freud and his doctrines" (1957, p. 45). By this logic, orthodoxy would be permanently immune to challenge and diagnosis substituted for reasoned discussion.

Thus, it must be recognized that relationalists and self psychologists have performed a valuable service in bringing to the fore issues that with few exceptions had been insufficiently addressed in the literature of ego psychology and structural conflict prior to the 1980s. That literature had focused on other aspects of mind, development, and technique and itself proved of lasting importance. My problem with some relational theorists is that they want not only to celebrate the relational school but also to dismiss the entire contemporary Freudian tradition as anachronistic, and to parlay the emphasis on interaction in the relational literature into a claim that even today no one else understands its importance as they do.

More than a decade has passed since the end of the lawsuit against the American Psychoanalytic Association (and the IPA) and the founding of the relational track at NYU. Taken together, these events mark the entry of American psychoanalysis into a new era. For better or worse—but mostly for the better—we are no longer faced with a cold war between monolithic powers, but with widening rifts on both sides of what once was an insurmountable barrier—a Berlin wall—between Freudians and interpersonalists. Differences within one's own group become muted and can be overlooked in the face of a common enemy, but they quickly reemerge once the external threat disappears.

But if the present situation might be viewed pessimistically as the balkanization of psychoanalysis, I prefer to think that it affords the prospect of creating a new intellectual and political order that allows all of us both to acknowledge our differences and to affirm our common psychoanalytic heritage. As Greenberg (2001) has written, "There are very few psychoanalysts around these days, only Freudians, or Kleinians, or Lacanians, or self psychologists" (p. 361). Because an analyst's subjectivity is his or her instrument, all of us are drawn to a school we find congenial to our temperament. But good analysts, I think, also try to cultivate a style antithetical to their innate disposition, in order to reach a golden mean between the conflicting tendencies of self-disclosure and self-restraint. In short, there is nothing wrong with being a Freudian, a relationalist, an interpersonalist, a self psychologist, or whatever, as long as the analyst does not succumb to the delusion that his or her school has a monopoly on the truth and that there is nothing to be learned from other approaches.

As we forge a new psychoanalytic identity, let us not renounce the discourse of dichotomy and polarization among ourselves only to allow it to creep into our dealings with other mental health professionals and the culture at large. Although we may be convinced that only those who have had personal experience of the unconscious, whether as patients in analysis or simply through reading and self-reflection, are likely to be persuaded of its existence, it does little good to accuse our detractors of resistance if they fail to see the light. For if we adopt this strategy, dialogue grinds to a halt. The only recourse is to speak with the quiet voice of reason, to try to learn as much from our critics as possible, to survive their destructive attacks if necessary, and to trust to time to sort out the merits of our competing claims.

It is the abiding lesson of psychoanalysis to be skeptical of utopian blueprints and protestations of a sudden conversion. The more exaggerated the promises of transformation, the more acute will be the disillusionment as reality sets in and life goes on much as it did before, though under altered circumstances. To a psychoanalyst, the dawn of a new millennium is simply another day, though one to which unusually intense fantasies may be attached. But this skepticism about revolutions does not mean that genuine change, usually as a result of long and painful struggle, is not possible. There are plastic moments in history—and in a person's life—in which, after a prolonged incubation, something new is hatched. For us in the American psychoanalytic community, this is such a moment, and it happily coincides with the turning of a page in the calendar.

Although I call myself a contemporary Freudian, my loyalty, as I said at the outset, is not to Freud as a human being, who for all his greatness had his share of frailties, but to psychoanalysis as a method of thinking, working, and living. This method, though it originated with Freud, has been enriched by Klein, Winnicott, Sullivan, Hartmann, Kohut, and all the other figures who form the tradition to which we are heir and to which we have the opportunity to contribute in our turn. In Winnicott's profound words (1971), "in any cultural field it is not possible to be original except on the basis of tradition" (p. 99). Psychoanalysis is a coat of many colors. Let us cease fighting over our inheritance and resolve instead to share it and to wear it with both humility and pride as we enter the twenty-first century.

REFERENCES

ARON, L. (1996). A Meeting of Minds: Mutuality in Psychoanalysis. Hillsdale, NJ: Analytic Press.

BENJAMIN, J. (1999). Review of I.Z. Hoffman, Ritual and Spontaneity in the Psychoanalytic Process. *J. Amer. Psychoanal. Assn.* 47: 883–891.

FREUD, S. (1909). An analysis of a phobia in a five-year-old boy. Standard Edition 10:5–149.

——— (1926). The question of lay analysis. Standard Edition 20:183–258.

GILL, M.M. (1994). Psychoanalysis in Transition: A Personal View. Hillsdale, NJ: Analytic Press.

——— (1991). Oedipus and Beyond: A Clinical Theory. Cambridge: Harvard University Press.

——— (2001). The analysts's participation: A new look. *Journal of the American Psychoanalytic Association* 49:359–381.

GREENBERG, J. & MITCHELL, S.A. (1983). *Object Relations in Psychoanalytic Theory.* Cambridge: Harvard University Press.

HARTMANN, H. (1959). Psychoanalysis as a scientific theory. In *Essays on Ego Psychology: Selected Problems in Psychoanalytic Theory.* New York: International Universities Press, 1964, pp. 318–350.

HOFFMAN, I.Z. (1998). *Ritual and Spontaneity in the Psychoanalytic Process.* Hillsdale, NJ: Analytic Press.

HUGHES, M.Y., ed. (1957). *John Milton: The Complete Poems and Major Prose.* Indianapolis: Odyssey Press.

JONES, E. (1957). *The Life and Work of Sigmund Freud.* Vol. 3. New York: Basic Books.

KING, P., & STEINER, R., Eds. (1990). The Freud-Klein Controversies 1941–1945. London: Routledge.

KOHUT, H. (1971). *The Analysis of the Self: A Systematic Approach to the Treatment of Narcissistic Personality Disorders.* New York: International Universities Press.

MITCHELL, S.A. (1993). *Hope and Dread in Psychoanalysis.* New York: Basic Books.

PIZER, S.A. (1998). *Building Bridges: Negotiation of Paradox in the Analytic Process.* Hillsdale, NJ: Analytic Press.

RICHARDS, A.D. (1999). A.A. Brill and the politics of exclusion. *Journal of the American Psychoanalytic Association* 47:9–28.

———— & Richards, A.K. (2000). Benjamin Wolstein and us: Many roads lead to Rome. *Contemporary Psychoanalysis* 36:255–266.

ROAZEN, P., & SWERDLOFF, B. (1995). *Heresy: Sandor Rado and the Psychoanalytic Movement.* Northvale, NJ: Aronson.

RUDNYTSKY, P.L. (2000). *Psychoanalytic Conversations: Interviews with Clinicians, Commentators, and Critics.* Hillsdale, NJ: Analytic Press.

SPEZZANO, C. (1998). The triangle of clinical judgment. *Journal of the American Psychoanalytic Association* 46:365–388.

WINNICOTT, D.W. (1971). Playing and Reality. London:Tavistock.

WYMAN, H., & RITTENBERG, S. (1994). The contributions of Charles Brenner, MD: Psychoanalysis rebooted. *Journal of Clinical Psychoanalysis* 3:315–316.

II. The Self-Psychologies with Emphasis on the Work of Heinz Kohut

This section presents three chapters that address the work of current theorists who organize their thinking around the concept of the "self". Beginning in Chapter 4, "Self Theory, Conflict Theory, and the Problem of Hypochondriasis," Richards looks at a complex case of an individual who suffers from hypochondriasis. He uses the findings of the case to discuss how contemporary conflict theory and self psychology might understand the problems provided by the case. In this chapter Richards ask:

- Can reliance on descriptive subjective states provide a sufficient understanding of the nature of the patient's problems?
- Can a theory or technical approach that relies on diagnostic categories capture the diversity of those who fall within the category? For that matter, can it capture the unevenness in mental functioning seen in the clinical presentation common to most patients?
- What happens to the narcissistic transferences (e.g., idealizing and mirror transferences) as the case progresses?
- Finally, are introspection and empathy the only necessary conditions for the analyst or can other important functions lead to change?

In chapter 5, "The Superordinate Self in Psychoanalytic Theory and in the Self Psychologies," Richards explores the role and function of the "self" in psychoanalytic theory. He asks:

- Do different self psychologies hold different definitions of the self for different self psychologists?
- Can any self-construct capture the variety of phenomena contained in a subjective-experience?
- Are George Klein's "self-schema" and subsequent clinical theory and John Gedo's "epigenetic model," comprehensive enough to replace metapsychology?

In chapter 6, "Extenders Modifiers and Heretics," Richards evaluates Martin Bergmann's taxonomy of psychoanalytic innovators. He establishes its core positions, and then tests its usefulness by questioning some of Kohut's basic assumptions.

• Does Kohut's rejection of unconscious mental functioning (via depreciation of the drives; diminished value of conflict, transference and resistance; and inflated use of introspection and empathy) constitute following a separate research tradition or is Kohut searching for a way to share in the growth of psychoanalysis with a new model?

CHAPTER 4

Self Theory, Conflict Theory, and the Problem of Hypochondriasis

[Richards, A.D. (1981). *Psychoanalytic Study of the Child* 36:319–337.]

The widening scope of psychoanalytic treatment has initiated a controversy in psychoanalytic theory and technique. Central to this controversy is the issue of the place of the self in psychoanalytic theory. Two broad and apparently antithetical positions have been taken. The first position is that radical revision of psychoanalytic theory is necessary to account for new data relating to the self and to explain specific forms of psychopathology, particularly narcissistic personality disorders. The second position, to which I subscribe, is that current psychoanalytic theory is adequate to account for the phenomenology and psychopathology of the self and that therefore an alternative model or an alternative theory is not necessary (Richards, 1979).

The first position is represented primarily by Kohut (1971, 1977) and his followers, whose theory appears to rest on four basic principles: (1) the concept of narcissism as a separate and independent line of development; (2) the centrality of a single metapsychological point of view—the economic—and the stress on contentless mental states; (3) the delineation of two specific self-object transferences, which I view as manifest-content, descriptive designations rather than as having inherent diagnostic, dynamic, and genetic significance; and (4) the overriding importance of empathic introspective modes of observation and the downgrading of the observational, cognitive, and synthetic aspects of the analyst's functioning in the analytic situation.

This theory, I believe, severely neglects the importance of the role of unconscious conflict in mental life and views unconscious conflict and developmental deficit as polar opposites rather than interactive variables. This exemplifies a general trend and an important weakness in Kohut's theorizing—theorizing in terms of forced dichotomies.

Kohut's metapsychology starts from the proposition of two kinds of libido: narcissistic and object; two kinds of patients: narcissistic and neurotic; two kinds of transferences: idealizing and mirror; two different conceptions of the mechanism of therapeutic action of psychoanalysis: transmuting internalization and change through insight; two kinds of anxiety: disintegration anxiety and anxiety stemming from drives; two kinds of aggression: nondestructive assertiveness and destructive aggression; two kinds of objects: self-objects and oedipal objects; two kinds of dreams: self-state dreams and wish-fulfilling dreams. The theory finally resulted in two broad classifications of the human situation: guilty man versus tragic man; guilty man suffering from conflicts and tragic man suffering from developmental defects caused by parental empathic failure. For Kohut, conflict theory is applicable only to guilty man, with self theory applicable to tragic man. It is therefore hardly surprising, since Kohut sees people today as essentially tragic rather than guilty, that he considers the conflict-drive model as less relevant and less applicable to psychopathology and the clinical situation than the self model. Nor should it come as a surprise that in his later writings, particularly in the Restoration of the Self, Kohut moves toward discarding the classical drive-conflict model and toward adapting a unitary position in which the psychology of the self is transcendent. This new psychology contains, according to Kohut, "a whole new concept of man," one quite distinct and different from the Freudian concept.

Since self-theory psychopathology results from developmental deficit, Kohut is in effect proposing a deficit model of psychopathology. This raises the question: should we limit ourselves to the consideration of two models—a conflict model versus a deficit or self model—or would we do better with three, as Arnold Cooper (1980) has proposed: the conflict model for neurosis, the self model for narcissistic patients, and an object relations model for borderline patients? Or why not the five models of the mind offered by Gedo and Goldberg (1973)?

In psychoanalysis, as perhaps in all sciences, questions are more easily asked than answered. But in psychoanalysis, unlike many other sciences, questions are particularly difficult to answer because of the special problems of access to its unique data and validation of its propositions. It is not an overstatement to assert that our methodological problems have no bounds. It is rarely possible to propose or execute the crucial experiment that will resolve a particular point of theoretical controversy. It seems to me that to make dialogue more fruitful we should focus on clinical as well as theoretical issues. In line with this idea, I shall attempt to move closer to the heart of the issues I have outlined by considering a single syndrome—hypochondriasis. I hope to be able through the clinical material to assess the relative explanatory power and therapeutic yield of the alternative psychoanalytic models: the conflict model of ego-id-superego psychology and the deficit model of self psychology. I believe that hypochondriasis is a particularly suitable focus because self psychologists view the syndrome as pathognomonic of the disorders of the self and indicative of a state of self-fragmentation and loss of self-cohesion rather than a compromise-impulsedefense constellation.

Although my focus will be on the clinical data, theoretical concerns are equally important. After all, the analyst's theoretical stance determines how he or she listens, what is heard, and how the analyst relates to the patient; all of these of course influence the data obtained.

CASE PRESENTATION

The patient was 27 years old, married, with one child, when he entered analysis because he was intensely anxious about his health. He presented bizarre somatic complaints and the conviction that he was sexually deteriorating. He was convinced that there was minimal but definite diminution in his public, axillary, and facial hair, that he was undergoing feminizing physiological alteration which was producing a feminine fat distribution, enlarged breasts, potbelly, and a change in the pitch of his voice. He experienced chest pains, which made him fear that he was going to have a heart attack, especially after intercourse. He was convinced that there was something wrong with the condition and configuration of his penis, a worry that could be resolved only by testing it through masturbation, often in front of a mirror. He worried that he was suffering from premature senility and that he was about to have a stroke. He linked these concerns to one another and explained them with the diagnosis that he had a generalized arteriosclerosis which was cutting off the blood supply to his heart and brain. He explained the fact that physicians had been unable to find any corroborating evidence of his diseases with the notion that the changes were subclinical: had the EEG or EKG been taken a day earlier or later, the results would have been different. He acknowledged that his thinking was illogical, and in spite of the strength of his hypochondriacal symptoms, he never ceased to function on an extraordinarily high level.

The onset of the symptoms had occurred about 4 years earlier, at a time when he was preparing to take a number of important independent steps, including going abroad (to study) and making plans to get married. During an examination occasioned by a minor illness, a physician commented that he might have a slight heart murmur; this touched off concerns about hypertension and heart disease. While he was abroad, he developed abdominal pains, which at first he attributed to bad food. A diagnostic GI series was negative for ulcer but made him worry that the X-ray had damaged his genitals. One psychiatrist he saw treated him with tranquilizers, and another saw him for psychotherapy twice a week for about a year. The latter referred him for analysis, which he agreed to start, not at all convinced that his problems were not physical, but willing to try anything to reestablish his health.

He described his childhood as "idyllic": his mother had doted on him, and his father, a passive, cautious, moderately successful businessman, had remained benignly enough in the background. It was only in the course of the analysis that more telling details emerged. The mother, whom the patient perceived as all-knowing and all-powerful, was ridden with fears and superstitions. She was afraid to handle her newborn son and worried about each new step in his development: that he would fall when he was learning to walk, would choke when learning to feed himself, would fall out of his crib during the night. Until he was an adult she advised him about his clothing, his diet, warned him about the dangers of sports, of other boys, and of encounters with girls, sexual or otherwise. And his childhood idyll was interrupted suddenly, when he was 5 years old, by the birth of a sister. So terrifying to him was his mother's pregnancy and the birth of his sister that he was totally amnestic for the year surrounding it. He was told, however, that he had responded to the loss of his mother's attention by completely refusing to eat until a doctor advised his parents to pay more attention to him. He also was told how pleased his father had been about having a daughter, and analysis revealed that the patient had felt particularly upset by his father's attention to the new baby.

The patient grew up in a one-bedroom apartment, sleeping in the same bedroom with his parents, who had twin deds. When his sister was born, she was given his crib, and he slept in one of the twin beds, his parents sharing the other. When he was 8 the family moved, and he and his sister shared a bedroom until he was 12. From then on, he slept in one bedroom with his father, his sister had a room for herself, and his mother slept in the living room. The patient described his father as quiet and passive, strong but not athletic, and not particularly bright. His mother encouraged him to think that he was intellectually superior to his father, an idea the patient absorbed as his own when he was still a boy. That he was exhibitionistic is attested to by one of his earliest memories, or it might have been a fantasy: when his grandmother was dying, he said, "Don't die, grandma, look at me in my new sailor suit." His parents, particularly his mother, severely discouraged expressions of his sexuality when he was a child. Although he did not remember her forbidding him to masturbate, a reconstruction of that possibility was made when he observed his mother's reactions to watching his own son play with his penis. He remembered how his mother made fun of any girls that he had an interest in. When the patient was in the latency period and as a young adolescent, his mother suffered several serious illnesses and operations, many details of which were replicated in his own physical symptoms.

He continued to live at home while going to college until his fourth year there, when he moved into the apartment of his girlfriendＣhis first girl and the one he married a few years later. I should add that this girl, the first with whom he had intercourse, found no fault with his sexual performance and had apparently had enough experience to have been able to judge. It was when he left her to go abroad that his symptoms appeared.

I turn to a brief account of the part of the analysis that is relevant to my thesis. Although the patient for many months insisted that there was nothing I could offer because his symptoms were physical and not psychological, a specific transference configuration soon emerged. He saw me as a dangerous, omnivorous person who was robbing him of his time, his money, and his independence, and who was placing him in great physical danger by treating his symptoms as though they were psychological rather than physical. A recurrent image that appeared in fantasies and dreams was that of a leech sucking his blood. He viewed me as strong and himself as weak, fragile, and needing to be taken care of. He spent many sessions ruminating about my penis, imagining himself sucking it as though it were a nipple. The accompanying fantasy was that he would thereby gain power from me which would make him more potent in relation to the woman, but would not incur the wrath of the male rival because he would be giving him pleasure as well. Other homosexual fantasies experienced in the analytic situation and about me, particularly fantasies of anal penetration, were elaborated with the idea that my penis would extend into his penis, making it harder and stronger and making him more potent.

He felt the more he told me about himself, the more he put himself in my power and control, and that only my death would liberate him. His dreams and fantasies of me as a devouring figure could be recognized as a replication of an unconscious childhood image of his mother, whom he had experienced as robbing him of his autonomy, his physical competence, and his independence by her overprotectiveness and anxious overconcern. He gradually came to see that successful independent action on his part resulted in an increase of suffering from his symptoms and was related to his symbolic movement away from his mother. His inability to tolerate autonomy and success stemmed from his identification with his weak, passive father, and even more from his need to feel inadequate and dependent in order to conform to his mother's idea of him. He feared that he would lose her as he became an adult; after all, she had told him that she was always afraid that she would lose him if he learned to do things on his own. He saw the delicate balance with which he had had to walk the line between ambition and illness, between autonomy and infantility.

When he had occasion to criticize a man considerably older than himself, he was immediately consumed with anxiety that the attack would cause him to lose the man's love and friendship. About his superiors in his firm, he brooded, "If they don't step down, how will I get ahead? But if they die, who will take care of me?" As the aggression implicit in these questions gradually became conscious, he was able to be more critical of his superiors.

The patient's conflicted feelings about surpassing his father were elucidated in the transference when he was aware of feeling anxious because he had the thought that he was intellectually superior to me. This was followed by ruminations that he had cerebral arteriosclerosis so that, on the one hand, he felt smarter than the analyst and, on the other, felt that his brain was deteriorating: the somatic concern disavowed his intense competitive wishes. He recalled how he had acquired considerable skill in playing ping-pong when he was an adolescent, but would deliberately lose when he played with his father because he did not want to embarrass him.

At the beginning of the analysis, he had no recollection of observing or hearing anything sexual going on between his parents. He could only imagine them lying motionless next to each other all night. He reported experiencing a profound sense of disbelief when he learned about the details of sexual intercourse. His denial of the relevance of primal scene experiences was countered by the following dream, which he reported: "I am in a large empty room sitting against the wall. A couple on the other side of the room are having intercourse. I can see the man's back and not his penis, and I feel relieved. He motions to me to have intercourse with my wife. I feel relieved because he will not be able to see me, just as I couldn't see him. I wake up and have a feeling that I am in a twin bed and my wife is in the bed next to me." The connection between the dream and the sleeping arrangement as a child was clear enough, given the fact that he and his wife slept in a double bed. Clarification of primal scene memories showed that he experienced intercourse as an attack by the woman on the man. His sickness had protected him from the dangers of a sexual relationship with a frightening woman. Success in the sexual area was just as frightening as it was at work: he consulted a physician for a recurring pain in the groin following intercourse, a time when he felt in greatest danger of suffering a heart attack. He could recognize the extent to which his sexuality had been discouraged by his mother, who viewed it as an area over which she had no control. For her, he realized, his sexual maturity meant that he would inevitably leave her to seek another woman. Fantasies of invagination or a vagina appearing on his abdomen suggested he would be willing to give up his penis altogether to please her. This fantasy had both positive and negative oedipal determinants, and could also be understood in context as a relinquishment of an organ which pushed him to be independent of his mother. He recalled that the development of his potbelly and the enlarging of her abdomen were parallel processes. I asked him what came to his mind about the thought that he was like a pregnant woman, and he replied, "A woman with a penis."

Turning into a woman, as in his almost delusional preoccupation with his feminizing changes, was both a regressive solution to his positive and negative oedipal conflicts and a means of avoiding separation from the preoedipal mother by identifying with her. Being sick fit nicely into this entire conflictual nexus because sick meant feminine, weak, and castrated, but also pregnant and powerful. The constant perusal of his body for suspected tumors as well as other features of his hypochondriacal concerns could be connected with pregnancy, specifically with his mother's pregnancy when he was 5. Repressed memories of that experience returned, directly represented in his symptomatology, and served to organize his illness. For example, he connected his concern about losing his hair with an image of the smooth, hairless skin of his baby sister. The disturbing nature of this experience for him had to do with his losing not only his mother's undivided attention but also the exclusive love of his father. Hence his refusal to eat until his mother's worry over his health restored her to him.

As these conflicts were worked through, the patient offered what seemed to me a telling insight: "I split myself into two persons when I am worried about my health. One is being taken care of and one is taking care of me. I have become in effect the child and the mother. I am my mother and my body is myself as a baby. I attend to every hair on my body. I attend to my own aches. There is no one to take care of me, to watch over me, so I do it myself. I am afraid to let go. I have a fear of something terrible happening if no one is watching me."

Although this insight was followed by marked improvement in his symptoms and a more positive feeling toward me and the analysis, this transference developed as a resistance to termination. He wished the analysis would go on forever, to achieve in this way the longed-for union with his mother. Contemplating termination, "a step toward independence," exacerbated symptoms that had abated considerably during the previous years. In fact, there was a recurrence of the very symptom that had plagued him during a previous period of decompensation. He developed abdominal pains and the conviction that he had an ulcer. This time, however, he was able to undergo a GI series without the dire psychological consequences that had occurred the first time. Central to this was his newly gained ability to see that his concerns were related to the impending termination and his fears of being independent. He was able to accept the negative findings of the internist, and the pains gradually subsided.

DISCUSSION

According to the psychology of the self, hypochondriacal preoccupations indicate the lack of a cohesive self, a lack consequent to the mother's failure to respond in a properly empathic fashion to the child's bodily and emotional needs. Hypochondriacal states are pathognomonic of self psychopathology and, along with feelings of fragmentation and depersonalization, can best be understood as indicating disturbance, or impending disturbance, of the self or self representation, rather than as a consequence of unconscious conflict. Kohut (1977) regards hypochondriasis as a displacement onto the body of what he calls disintegration anxiety—an unverbalizable dread of loss of the self, "the fragmentation of and the estrangement from his body and mind in space, the breakup of the sense of his continuity in time" (p. 105). The worries about physical defects are "replicas of the anxieties of childhood and [the] need for the attention of the missing self-objects" (p. 161). Kohut's concept seems to hark back to Freud's (1914) explanation of hypochondriasis as a withdrawing of libidinal cathexis from objects and a turning of it onto the self—of transforming object libido into narcissistic libido. Freud consistently placed hypochondriasis in the same category as actual neurosis. Both were "toxic" in nature and more medical than psychological (1916–1917, p. 389).

Freud's earliest reference to a case of hypochondriasis occurs in an 1893 letter to Fliess. There he writes of a man, age 42, who upon the death of his father developed hypochondriacal fears of cancer of the tongue. The man also reported that he had practiced coitus interruptus for the previous 11 years, a fact Freud considered of primary etiological significance. The death of the father, he felt, was only an immediate precipitating factor. In the discussion of masturbation, Freud (1912) said, "I see nothing that could oblige us to abandon the distinction between 'actual neuroses' and psychoneuroses, and I cannot regard the genesis of the symptoms in the case of the former as anything but toxic" (p. 248). Freud chided Stekel for "overstretching pathogenicity" and seemed concerned with maintaining his position that the symptoms of actual neurosis, whether neurasthenia or hypochondriasis, are essentially contentless and essentially unanalyzable. This is certainly evident in Beyond the Pleasure Principle (1920) where Freud refers to hypochondriasis as akin to traumatic neurosis, referring presumably to the view that it is caused by an unmanageable flood of sexual exertion which causes toxic changes in the hypochondriacal agents.

Although these references indicate that Freud included hypochondriasis in the category of the actual neurosis and stressed its traumatic and somatic origins, there is some evidence that at least prior to 1912 Freud struggled with choosing between a somatic and psychogenic etiology. Although his theoretical remarks clearly favor the somatic view, several clinical comments suggest the psychogenic view. In 1898, Freud was advancing the idea that hypochondriasis can be caused by self-reproach. He said, "Self-reproach (for having carried out the sexual act in childhood) can easily turn into shame (in case someone should find out about it), [or] into hypochondriacal anxiety (fear of the physical injuries resulting from the act involving the self-reproach)" (p. 171). Finally, Freud's uncertainty about the issue of a somatic versus psychogenic origin of hypochondriasis and his dissatisfaction with his classification of hypochondriasis as an actual neurosis may be indicated by the following comment in a letter to Ferenczi dated March 18, 1912. "I always felt that the obscurity in the question of hypochondria to be a disgraceful gap in our work" (see Jones, 1955, p. 453).

In the psychology of the self, the course of the analysis would focus on variations in the cohesiveness of the self, particularly as they can be related to empathic failures on the part of the analyst and manifested symptomatically in the patient by feelings of fragmentation, depersonalization, and hypochondriacal preoccupations. The analyst would help the patient see the connection between the empathic failures he experienced in the analysis and the empathic failures he had experienced as a child. This process would result in what Kohut calls transmuting internalizations, thus repairing the structural deficit in the patient.

A diagnosis would be based on the manifest content of the transference and of the patient's symptoms and pathology. Genetic explanation would be, on the one hand, very specific and, on the other hand, presented as universally operating; namely, of parental empathic failures in childhood. Issues related to drive derivatives and conflicts with regard to the patient's past or in the here and now of the analytic situation would not be stressed. I consider this view unidimensional, for it looks only at the self, a concrete and reified entity which is never really defined but whose state of being—cohesive, fragmented, overstimulated, understimulated, overburdened, or underburdened—is presented as of paramount importance. Clinical findings not relevant to this construct are discarded.

Certainly, the etiological significance of my patient's mother's intrusiveness is clear; but what has to be worked out in the analysis is the specific way in which conflicts produced by the unpleasure of this experience and others, the vicissitudes of both libidinal and aggressive drives, have influenced the patient's unconscious mental organization. Only by understanding how he defended himself against the anxiety evoked by conflict can the nature of the patient's symptoms and of his relations to his analyst and to others in his life be modified.

Before explaining my patient's symptom in terms of conflict theory, I had best define what I mean by conflict theory. I am in accord with Brenner (1976) who believes that intrapsychic conflict develops when a drive derivative or self-punitive trend is perceived as dangerous. The danger produces unpleasure—anxiety or depression—which evokes unconscious defenses against the unconscious wish. The resulting symptom is a compromise between the wish and the defense; anxiety is either diminished or abolished, depending on the success of the defense. The aim is to avoid unpleasure. The conflict may be between ego and id or between ego and superego. The four calamities producing unpleasure are object loss, loss of the object's love, castration anxiety, and superego condemnation. Conflict can thus be preoedipal as well as oedipal. I also agree that the origin of hypochondriasis is similar to that of conversion symptoms: the symptom expresses in body language a fantasy which is a compromise between wish and defense (Arlow and Brenner, 1964, p. 173). Clinical illustrations of this view in the literature include a paper by Macalpine and Hunter (1953) on the Schreber case which identifies an unconscious fantasy of intestinal pregnancy as underlying Schreber's hypochondriachal symptoms, and a paper by Broden and Myers (1980) who relate several hypochondriacal preoccupations in several of their patients to underlying unconscious beating fantasies.

Conflict theory is multidimensional: it stresses the principles of multiple function, multiple determination, the importance of the repetition compulsion, and of unconscious fantasies which are linked with childhood memories and perceptions, with all their distortions. Of course, this complicates both conceptualization and interpretation.

Returning to my patient, I contend that viewing his symptom in terms of cathexis, recathexis, and hypercathexis, or in terms of developmental deficit keeps us on a descriptive, manifest-content level which seriously impairs our ability to help the patient understand why he feels the way he does. I believe that this understanding is necessary for successful treatment. Equally inadequate are formulations that view the symptom simply as preoedipally rather than oedipally determined, or that rely on the positing of a prestructural, preconflictual realm, for they pose false dichotomies and result in excluding from consideration a large sector of the patient's experiences.

What were the childhood experiences that were crucial in this case? I would cite the following: (1) the patient's mother's oversolicitousness and overprotectiveness when he was an infant; (2) the child's exposure to great admiration for his intellectual achievements, simultaneously with strong physical discouragement of physical activities and equally strong discouragement of all sexual behavior; (3) his father's passivity, timidity, and remoteness, and the patient's sense that he was smarter than his father; (4) the sudden expulsion from his special position when his sister was born; (5) his observations of the bodily changes that occurred in his mother during her pregnancy, observations of her genital, and observation of the anatomy of his newborn baby sister; and (6) primal scene observations.

We can point out some of the multiple determinants of the patient's hypochondriacal symptoms with regard to both their form and content. In a general way the symptoms represent a continuation of his childhood relationship with his mother; he hovers over himself as she hovered over him. The symptoms enable him to maintain the illusion of the persistence of this special relationship between himself and his mother and to defend against the twin dangers of losing her and her love.

This state of affairs is very similar to the attitudes toward health of motherless, institutional children described by Anna Freud (1952). "The child actually deprived of a mother's care adopts the mother's role in health matters, thus playing 'mother and child' with his own body" (p. 79). Anna Freud asks whether this behavior does provide a clue to the understanding of adult hypochondriacal attitudes. She states, "With children analytic study seems to make clear that in the staging of the mother-child relationship, they themselves identify with the lost mother, while the body represents the child (more exactly: the infant in the mother's care)" (p. 80). The similarity between my patient's statement, already quoted, "I am my mother and my body is myself as a baby" and Anna Freud's formulation is striking indeed.

The danger of castration is warded off through identification with his mother in which the perception of her as being injured and castrated is countered by the unconscious fantasy of her having an internal penis (the illness growing inside), the model for which is pregnancy, in which baby equals penis. The danger of castration connected with his oedipal wishes is countered by his assertion that he is "old, ill, impotent, or female." Superego condemnation is also avoided by the formula: I am not bad, just sick. Castration anxiety is defended against by displacement—the body as phallus—and by turning passive into active: "You can't do it to me; I have already done it to myself."

The prospect of termination and the impending separation from the analyst were similar to the situation he experienced when he was abroad. In both instances he developed a hypochondriacal conviction that he had an ulcer. Both situations revived the childhood situation when he was 5. The danger then was loss of the object, his mother— and to some extent his father—as well as loss of their love. He also risked moral condemnation because of his aggressive wishes toward his father, his mother, and his sister. Being in the oedipal phase, his height- ened libidinal needs for his mother increased his competitive striving toward his father. His aggressive wishes as well as his libidinal needs toward his mother were exacerbated by her unavailability for him because of her attention to his sister. Finally, the aggression of sibling rivalry was ushered in for him by his sister's unwelcome appearance on the household scene. When he was 5, his compromise solution was not to eat, thereby at once infuriating his mother, forcing her attention from his sister to himself, and, as he himself put it, "punishing myself for my own greediness." Similarly, in the analysis, if his symptoms returned, I would continue to have to spoon-feed him and would not replace him with another patient.

During the termination phase of his analysis, as well as at the time of his mother's pregnancy, my patient was experiencing intense con- flicts. He wanted to depend on me and hated me for this dependency. He experienced both libidinal and aggressive feelings toward his moth- er, his father, and his sister. Yet, anger toward his parents made him feel diminished as an independent person and as a man. The patient's symp- tom of not eating during the crucial time when his mother gave birth was shortlived, and the basic conflictsCwhich were both oedipal and preoedipalCwere not resolved; a temporary peace was achieved at the expense of marked repression. He denied his angry feelings, remem- bered his childhood as idyllic, maintained the view that his parents never had intercourse with each other, became a model boy and student, looked after his sister and never teased her, and never masturbated. His envy of his sister was submerged; his envy of his father, the oedipal rival, was made nonoperative by the idea that his parents did not have a private sexual relationship which excluded him.

But the whole scenario became unstuck when he was confronted with the prospect of leaving home and getting married, and subsequently at times when independence, active mastery, sexual performance, and the surpassing of rivals were called for. The hypochondriacal symptom then appeared as a compromise formation. Why this particular choice of symptom rather than some other? This brings up the issue of choice of neurosis, which is one that Freud struggled with and one that has never been resolved. In this instance, however, the details of the hypochondriacal symptom, its specific content, can be related almost point for point to specific details of the traumatic childhood situation, his mother's pregnancy, and to a lesser extent her illnesses during his latency period and early adolescence. The symptom is meaningful in terms of conflict, content, and genesis, rather than merely indicative of a general failure to develop a cohesive or stable self representation in response to his mother's general failure of empathy.

I have reserved one question in order to raise it only after the patient had been described as fully as is possible in a brief presentationCthe question of diagnosis. Some analysts might ask whether the patient was suffering from a symptom neurosis or from a narcissistic personality disorder. I think he was suffering from both. Indeed, this brings me to my basic pointCthe unnecessary confusion caused by positing two separate lines of development. That my patient was narcissistic is indisputableChis intellectual grandiosity, his exhibitionistic traits, his preoccupation with his body, all attest to it. It did not occur to me at the time I treated him, nor would I find it particularly helpful today, to view these traits apart from his problems in separation from his mother, from his fiancée, or from me. The problem he had in separating from his mother profoundly affected his choice of a wife and his subsequent relationship to her, sexual and otherwise; his rivalry with his father affected his relations with other real or imagined rivals. At the same time, the difficulty he had in enjoying success when on his own made it harder for him to loosen the tie to an intrusive and engulfing mother.

The diagnostic question I asked myself was of a different order. It had to do with the severity of the illness. The high level of certain aspects of my patient's functioning and his capacity for meaningful object relations, many of the details of which I have not presented at length in this report, favor a "less sick" diagnosis. On the other hand, other features of the psychopathology, particularly the bizarre quality of some of the details of his preoccupation and the almost delusional way in which he clung to some of his beliefs suggest a "more sick" diagnosis. I would suggest that the unevenness manifest in the patient is not unusual in clinical work and points up the difficulty posed by setting up clear-cut diagnostic categories. It also calls into question theoretical approaches that rely upon clear-cut diagnostic categories to justify technical departures.

I return to the four basic principles of the psychology of the self which I enumerated at the beginning. I have already dealt with the issue of making a sharp distinction between narcissistic and object-libidinal developmental lines. It seems to me that for this patient these issues were interactive and intertwined. Secondly, the material points up the limitations of making a single metapsychological point of view, the economic, with its stress on contentless mental states the central issue. From time to time the patient said, during a session, that he felt as if his body was flying off in all different directions. Perhaps this is what is meant by disintegration anxiety. But this patient's mental states were never, as far as I could tell, devoid of specific mental content that could be expressed in everyday language—the language of current need and wish and fear, and the related language of childhood need, wish, and fear. With regard to the third principle, specificity of the two major self-object transferences, I found that I was able to understand the analysand-analyst interactions as they emerged without them. Idealizing and mirror transferences are broad, descriptive designations, useful in the early stages of treatment when we do not yet know too much about the patient. It seems to me that the self psychologists assign to these transferences more weight than they can bear and, even more to the point, thereby narrow the analyst's focus.

With regard to the final principle—the overriding importance of empathy and introspection—my position, in contradistinction to Kohut's, is that the psychoanalytic method of inquiry depends upon a wide range of affective, perceptual, and cognitive processes applied by the analyst to his own observations of, and reports from, the analysand. Empathy and introspection clearly are part of this method but are neither primary nor exclusive. In any case, it is my firm conviction that this patient's achievement of insight and the resulting change in his psychic structure and subsequent modes of adaptation would not have been possible without the calling into operation of the ego's cognitive and synthesizing functions on both my part and his.

I think there can be no question but that this patient was struggling with severe conflicts. He wanted to be rid of his sister, but he wanted to retain his parents' approval—and his own self-approval. He wanted to be close to his mother and win her approval by being like her; but if he did this, he would feel castrated because she did not have a penis. He wanted to replace his father in his mother's affections, but he also wanted to retain his father's love and approval. He wanted to be independent, but this would have meant losing his mother because to have her was to need her. And so he developed symptoms which expressed his need for his mother, his identification with her, his fear of castration, and punishment for his hostile wishes.

CONCLUSION

I do not argue against the usefulness of the concept of the self as it relates to the importance of certain broad identity themes which characterize each of us, themes by which we organize our experience. But I want to stress that these themes are inevitably the result of the outcome of the vicissitudes of the important childhood conflicts and are related to the expressions of these conflicts in adult life. And at the root of these conflicts are indeed the core calamities of childhood—loss of object, loss of love, castration anxiety, and guilt. Evidence of the importance of all four could be found in my patient.

If Freud's drive theory is not relevant to disorders of the self (see Kohut, 1977, p. 68), then perhaps we should add a fifth calamity—loss of the self—to the usual four. This, I would suggest, is the essential point raised by those advocating a psychology of the self. My own opinion is that, before we accept the fifth calamity, we should be certain that it is not reducible to the other four. I think the law of parsimony prevents us from doing otherwise. For the fifth calamity to be useful, it would have to be firmly rooted and situated in the conflict-compromise formation nexus that includes the other four dangers, the drive derivatives, and the concept of defense. This the psychology of the self has not achieved or even attempted. We must wonder why.

REFERENCES

ARLOW, J.A. & BRENNER, C. (1964). *Psychoanalytic Concepts and the Structural Theory.* New York: International Universities Press.
BRENNER, C. (1976). *Psychoanalytic Technique and Psychic Conflict.* New

York: International Universities Press.

BRODEN, A. & MYERS, W. (1980). Hypochondriacal symptoms as derivatives of unconscious fantasies of being beaten or tortured (unpublished).

COOPER, A. (1980). Some current issues in psychoanalytic technique (unpublished).

FREUD, A. (1952). The role of bodily illness in the mental life of children. *Psychoanalytic Study of the Child* 7:78–80

FREUD, S. (1893). Letter 14 [to W. Fliess]. *Standard Edition* 1:4–186

———— (1898). Further remarks on the neuro-psychoses of defence. *Standard Edition* 3:159–185.

———— (1912). Contributions to a discussion on masturbation. *Standard Edition* 12:239–254.

———— (1914). On narcissism. *Standard Edition* 14:67–102.

———— (1916–1917). Introductory lectures on psycho-analysis *Standard Edition* 9

———— (1920). Beyond the pleasure principle. *Standard Edition* 18:3–64.

GEDO, J. (1979). Beyond Interpretation New York: International Universities Press.

———— & GOLDBERG, A. (1973). *Models of the Mind.* Chicago: Chicago University Press.

JONES, E. (1955). *The Life and Work of Sigmund Freud.* vol. 2 New York: Basic Books.

KLEIN, G. (1976). *Psychoanalytic Theory.* New York: International Universities Press.

KOHUT, H. (1971). *The Analysis of the Self.* New York: International Universities Press.

———— (1977). The Restoration of the Self New York: International Universities Press.

MACALPINE, I. & HUNTER, R.A. 1953 The Schreber case. *Psychoanalytic Quarterly* 22:328–371

RICHARDS, A.D. (1979). The self in psychoanalytic theory, the self psychologies and the psychology of the self. *Issues in Ego Psychology* 2:20–29.

ROTHSTEIN, A. (1980). Toward a critique of the psychology of the self *Psychoanalytic Quarterly* 49:423–455.

The Superordinate Self in Psychoanalytic Theory and in the Self Psychologies

[Richards, A.D. (1982). *Journal of the American Psychoanalytic Association* 30:939–957.]

The last several years have seen the concept of the self replace the concept of identity as the focus of theoretical controversy in psychoanalysis. Even though many of the basic theoretical and clinical issues are the same as they were a decade ago when "identity" was the subject of intense debate, revisionary thrusts forming under the banner of the "self" seem to be stronger than those that adopted the banner of identity. A heightened trend toward polarization exists today; witness Ornstein (in Kohut, 1979), for example, who advocates placing self psychology in opposition to ego psychology. Rothstein (1980) attributes this trend to "narcissistic paradigm overevaluation," a perfectly valid descriptive phrase, but one that fails to explain the polarization that is now taking place.

In considering the controversy about the status of the self in psychoanalytic theory, two broad and antithetical positions can be discerned. The first maintains that contemporary psychoanalytic theory (the theory introduced by Freud and refined by Hartmann, Jacobson, and others) is by no means perfect, but remains the best theory available. Adherents of this position contend that no radical revision of theory is required either to account for new data that relate to the self or to account for specific forms of psychopathology (e.g., the narcissistic personality disorders). In disavowing the need for a new theory from which to survey the clinical terrain, they argue that terms and concepts which are part of the evolutionary growth of psychoanalysis since Freud's death—self-representation, ideal self, wishful self-image, self-feeling, and self-esteem—are entirely adequate to account for the relevant clinical phenomena.

Adherents to the second position, on the other hand, contend that a radical revision of psychoanalytic theory is necessary because traditional

Presented at the panel on "Psychoanalytic Theories of the Self" at the Fall Meeting of the American Psychoanalytic Association, New York, December, 1980.

theory is deficient, inaccurate, or in some way limited. Psychoanalytic theoreticians who have adopted this position include (1) the late George Klein and his collaborators, who maintain that metapsychology should be eliminated from psychoanalytic theory because it is primarily concerned with energic considerations and neurobiological concepts that are irrelevant and confusing; (2) John Gedo, who tends to agree with Klein about the inadequacy of traditional metapsychology, but who focuses on specific deficiencies in the psychoanalytic theory of therapy; and (3) Heinz Kohut and his collaborators who, unlike Klein and Gedo, do not quarrel with metapsychology and its energic metaphors, but embrace the need for a new theory of the mechanisms of therapeutic change in psychoanalysis along with a new conceptualization of psychopathology. The theoretical formulations of all these critics incorporate the use of a superordinate self-concept. Klein's system centers on his elaboration of a "self-schema," Gedo's work revolves around the centrality of his "self-organization," and Kohut's "self psychology" is anchored in the theoretical preeminence of the "nuclear" or "bipolar" self.

Unlike earlier differences in opinion about the concept of identity, indications now exist that the divergent perspectives of the self psychologists and their critics may eventuate in a rift in psychoanalysis rather than eventual integration. Ticho (1982), for example, has elaborated the parallels between Kohut's self psychology and the psychologies of Adler, Jung, Horney, and Sullivan, implying that self psychology is pursuing a direction similar to those taken by these alternative schools. Still more forcefully, Rangell (1982) argues that an oppositional stance toward self psychology is long overdue. Others, like Wallerstein (Panel, 1981), entertain a more optimistic view about the prospects for eventually integrating the two positions. This optimism stems partly from the fact that a dialogue between opposing theoreticians continues, thus providing some reason to hope for reconciliation.

Ticho's (1982) contribution is relevant to a pattern that reappears throughout the history of psychoanalysis, but which he does not spell out. I am referring to the fact that, despite important changes in the psychoanalytic theory of mental functioning over the past eighty years, such changes have resulted in little revision of the theory of therapy or of basic psychoanalytic technique. Indeed, psychoanalytic technique is noteworthy precisely because it has undergone so few changes during this period. This is not to say that major alterations in technique have not been advanced over the years, but only that proposed modifications have generally been rejected by the mainstream psychoanalytic community. Virtually without exception, the proponents of such modifications (Jung, Adler, Ferenczi, Alexander) have not remained within the mainstream, suggesting that psychoanalysts tolerate greater revision of psychoanalysis as a theory of mental functioning than as a theory of therapy incorporating specific technical procedures. Hartmann, for example, whose stature as the theorist of psychoanalytic ego psychology is uncontested, proposed fairly important changes in the theory of mental functioning without advocating significant alterations in technique. Eissler, on the other hand, did propose the use of parameters as a modification of technique as early as 1953, but he scrupulously insisted that such parameters be analyzed in the course of treatment; his suggestion came at a time when the scope of analysis was dramatically widening. Mahler has also presented significant new formulations while insisting that her findings should not alter psychoanalytic technique with adult patients. Kernberg likewise reserves his proposed technical changes for psychoanalytic therapy while retaining the conventional technique for psychoanalysis proper. Perhaps analysts find it easier to accept technical alterations when they apply to children or psychotics rather than the majority of adult patients who present themselves for psychoanalysis.

"Ich," Ego, and Self

Hartmann (1950) and Strachey (1923) underscored many years ago Freud's failure to distinguish clearly between the ego and the self. Freud's term Ich can refer either to the person as a whole or to a particular part of the person's mind, i.e., to a discrete mental system with particular functions. In Freud's writings, Ich most frequently has the latter systemic referent and can be profitably translated as ego. In certain cases, however, Ich is clearly equated with the subjective person, and it lends itself to translation as self in such circumstances. It should be noted that Freud did refer to early developmental states in which the demarcation of inner and outer, self and object, is not clear; consider his references to the "oceanic feeling" (1930), the "purified pleasure ego" (1915), and early experiential states that may be appropriately labeled "grandiose." Considerable evidence exists, then, that Freud did in fact deal with phenomena that we might presently consider aspects of the self; what is noteworthy is his persistent use of the ambiguous term Ich to encompass these dimensions of self-experience. Kernberg (1982) construes the dual referents of the Ich as parallel tributaries that jointly enrich Freud's conceptualization. Whereas Strachey felt Freud could have spoken more clearly by using different terms for the self and the ego, Kernberg commends Freud for using a single term to capture both the personal and systemic-organismic aspects of the ego-self. Correspondingly, he faults Strachey for translating Ich as ego, a term that sacrifices the personal connotations Freud had in mind. An alternative explanation of Freud's calculating ambiguity may pertain to his belief that, ultimately, the distinction between the person and the mental apparatus trenched on philosophy, i.e., that it implicated issues that exceeded the explanatory power of psychoanalytic theory (Freud, 1940).

It fell to Hartmann (1950) to propose a terminological clarification that would separate the subjective-personal from the objective-organismic realms. By redefining narcissism as the libidinal cathexis not of ego but of the self, Hartmann necessarily distinguished between an organismic ego and a subjective self. He was explicit about this:

> . . . in using the term narcissism, two different sets of opposites often seem to be fused into one. The one refers to the self (one's own person) in contradistinction to the object, the second to the ego (as a psychic system) in contradistinction to other substructures of personality [p. 127].

Of greater importance than this "energic" refinement was Hartmann's ensuing suggestion that a new expression, "self-representation," be invoked as the correct opposite of "object representation." In presenting this distinction, Hartmann provided analysis with a new handle with which to specify the contents of the inner experiential world—the "representational world" (Sandler and Rosenblatt, 1962) of wishes, fantasies, identifications, and attitudes. On the basis of these theoretical considerations, Hartmann advanced three separate meanings of Freud's Ich: (1) Ich as ego; (2) Ich as self in the sense of subject as opposed to object of experience (including awareness of one's own body); and (3) Ich as self in the sense of the whole personality, i.e., the individual or person.

The net import of Hartmann's distinctions was a new realization that the concepts of ego and self pertain to different domains. A recent discussion of the self by the philosopher William Alston (1977) is highly relevant to our understanding of the domain of the self. I quote Alston as length because his definition of the self enlarges on the very insight that led Hartmann to differentiate this self from the ego:

I would like to suggest that our commonsense conceptual scheme provides a sound, unconfused way of talking about the self. In our ordinary thought we make no distinction between the self, the person, the man/woman, the human being, etc. In fact, we have an indefinitely large repertoire of devices for referring to what we regard as one and the same entity—Wolfgang Amadeus Mozart, the composer of Don Giovanni, the son of Leopold Mozart of Salzburg, my favorite composer, and so on. Furthermore, each of these phrases picks out the man Mozart, the person Mozart, the human being Mozart. It would, of course, be unnatural to speak of the "self Mozart." . . . The term "self" (usually in compounds) is used for a person when that person is being spoken of as the object of a self-directed cognition, action, or attitude [pp. 67–68].

Rubinstein (1981) has distilled Alston's position into the following pithy formulation: "The self is the person a person is to himself." Arlow, on the other hand, has put his finger on the disjunction between this "self" and the psychoanalytic "ego" with beguiling simplicity: "The self has been described as residing within the body or, more likely, within the head. The ego, however, resides within textbooks and monographs on psychoanalytic theory" (1980, personal communication).

Hartmann's proposed distinction between the personal and organismic realms, as captured in these formulations, is a necessary one that does full justice to the dual nature of human psychological experience. The distinction remains as important to psychoanalytic work today as it was when Hartmann offered it. The remaining portion of this paper will examine the theories of George Klein, John Gedo, and Heinz Kohut by way of demonstrating how this distinction has become lost in the new psychologies of the self. Consideration of the "self-" conceptions of these theorists will highlight the fact that the introduction of a superordinate self-construct really offers no theoretical or clinical advantages over traditional psychoanalytic formulations; indeed, such consideration reveals that the new self psychologies are actually regressive in their tendency to gloss over Hartmann's meaningful distinction between the domains of ego and self.

George Klein and the Self-Schema

Klein's revision of psychoanalytic theory proceeds from his dissatisfaction with Freud's neurophysiological and energic assumptions. Arguing that concepts such as drive, energy, ego, id, and superego all reflect a "natural-science" view of the organism as subject to laws of physics, chemistry, and physiology, Klein proposed supplanting Freud's metapsychology with the construct of the "self-schema." His referent for this construct was the third of Hartmann's three meanings of Ich: the concept of self as person. Klein (1976) defined the self as

. . . a single apparatus of control which exhibits a variety of dynamic tendencies, the focus of which is either an integration experienced in terms of a sense of continuity, coherence, and integrity, or its impairment, as cleavages of dissonance [p. 8].

Klein's theoretical ambition was to postulate a concept or structure that had both systemic attributes and personal, "human" qualities. The self was presented as simultaneously more personal and less prone to reification or concretization than the ego. The self-schema thereby became Klein's proposed bridge over the divide separating "person" and "organism."

But Klein was far from successful in this respect. As soon as he incorporated into his definition of the self-schema the term "apparatus," he necessarily sacrificed the personal quality with which he sought to infuse his self-concept. When he referred to the developing self as a yardstick against which certain aspects of the personality could be measured, moreover, he came close to the very kind of reification (if not anthropomorphism) he sought to avoid. Klein's theoretical development, in this regard, approximates what Alston (1977) had in mind when he submitted that homunculus-fearing self-theorists who seek to rescue their psychologies from the homunculus fallacies ultimately evoke in their self-concepts the type of real and unitary agent they believe they are attacking.

So what does Klein's self-schema offer us that the ego of traditional theory does not? Was Klein proposing an actual conceptual change or a mere terminological shift? Is the self of the self-schema nothing but an ego in new clothing? Klein maintained that adopting the self-schema as the central theoretical construct would enable analysts to focus on two important aspects of "selfhood"—the need for personal autonomy and the need to be part of a larger social unit. He referred to these trends as "centrifugal" and "centripetal" and asserted that the source of conflict between them was a neglected area of psychoanalysis. In reply, however, one could ask whether a schema that elevates these aspects of personal development to a position of preeminence does not in fact move us away from the principal concerns of psychoanalysis. Analysts would certainly concur that personal autonomy is an important goal for most individuals. But is the aim of psychoanalysis to explore the relation between this goal and the need for social integration, or to help the patient understand the nature of unconscious conflicts that may prevent him from achieving both personal autonomy and social adaptation?

Although Klein did not recommend any significant shift in clinical approach, he did situate his self-schema in "a clinical theory of personal encounter" that is additionally problematic. Klein argued that his "clinical theory" had the self-schema as a central construct but included additional constructs deriving from developmental principles of differentiation, fractionation, and identification. Klein neglected, however, to define these terms in a clinically relevant way. The result, as Frank (1979) comments, is that Klein theorized at "increasingly abstract levels of conceptualization, using increasingly abstract principles of organization regarding the interaction of his primary entities and their derivatives" (p. 192). This propensity for abstractive conceptualization shorn of clinical referents underscores the paradoxical failure of Klein's self-schema to avoid the very pitfalls of metapsychological language that led to his new theory. Klein set out from the observation that psychoanalysis contains within itself two types of theories, a clinical theory and a metapsychological theory. He took as his task the execution of a "theorectomy" that would excise metapsychological theory from analysis and graft in its place an improved clinical theory based on the self-schema. Ultimately, however, Klein ended up with a clinical theory at least as abstract as the metapsychology he criticized and in certain respects just as biological. It is predictable, then, that the self-schema around which the theory revolved should offer very little clinical yield.

John Gedo and the Self-Organization

John Gedo, like George Klein, faults the metapsychological constructs of Freud and Hartmann for being too reductionistic, abstract, impersonal, and prone to reification. He agrees with Klein that traditional metapsychology slights the concept of person as agent, and he also follows Klein in offering the self as the antidote to the impersonal quality of ego-psychological constructs. Gedo's basic paradigm, however, concerns the "epigenesis" of a "self-organization" that he conceptualizes in terms of a hierarchy of values. In according the self a central organizing role in a psychology of personal aims, Gedo leans heavily on Lichtenstein (1977), who postulated "the acquisition of a primary identity that stamps all the individual's actions with their uniqueness, endures through all subsequential developmental vicissitudes and crucially limits his freedom of action" (p. 11). Gedo departs from both Klein and Lichtenstein, however, in his attempt to use the self-organization to bridge the gap between psychoanalytic explanations formulated in terms of hermeneutic-type "meanings" and in terms of natural-scientific-type "causes." Gedo undertakes this piece of mediation by giving biological motivations an important place in his scheme. Thus, the hierarchy of personal aims that are constitutive of the self-organization, for Gedo, includes a category of biological aims and patterns as well as a category of psychological goals and values. It remains unclear, however, what advantage this scheme offers over Hartmann's concept of an ego that includes both constitutional and experiential determinants. Furthermore, Gedo's focus on goals and values is frequently at the expense of a properly psychoanalytic concern with drives (libidinal and aggressive), wishes, and defense.

Gedo's conception of the self-organization posits personal autonomy as the highest aim of the organism. He believes that concepts such as basic core, basic identity, and self-cohesion all relate to a hierarchy of personal goals and values that culminates in autonomy, and he dissociates this conception from theories that dwell on the self as a mental content or a content of thought. Gedo submits that analysts who use the self in this way (e.g., Hartmann, Jacobson, Sandler, Rosenblatt, and others) "explicitly disavow" what he construes as the "cardinal importance" of the self-concept—"the epigenesis of human motivations, i.e., of mental structure itself" (1979, p. 177). But Gedo's apparent equation of the self with development or "epigenesis" makes for considerable confusion. Most notably, it obscures the fact that the epigenesis of personality is a given. It is self-evident, in other words, that both person and organism develop as a result of the complex interaction between developing biological givens and the environment. Surely, this process is not adequately explicated by affixing to it the noun "self." Arlow (1980, personal communication), commenting on the equation of self with a goal of personal autonomy taken to be the highest aim of the organism, asks how the aims of the organism are in fact established: "Is it a part of a divine scheme, the hand of the Lord moving in biology?" Gedo's scheme of the self-organization culminates in "a revised theory of psychoanalytic therapy." In brief, Gedo's theory of psychoanalytic therapy attempts to systematize the various interventions appropriate to early modes of psychic organization. Such interventions, which encompass noninterpretive strategies, the use of drugs, and other constraints, accomplish preinterpretive tasks that include "pacification," the fostering of a holding environment (which Gedo terms "the unification of self-organization"), and the "optimal disillusionment" of the patient. This systematization of therapeutic modalities generally coincides with the technical approach advocated by Kohut for the treatment of patients with narcissistic personality disorders. Unlike Kohut, however, Gedo rejects any one-to-one correspondence between nosology and therapeutic modality; he stresses instead that noninterpretive interventions are required in every analysis, inasmuch as patients rarely demonstrate a single mode of psychic organization throughout treatment. In every analysis, he insists, the analysand not only manifests a multiplicity of behaviors based on a variety of illusions, but experiences episodes of overstimulation accompanied by the temporary disruption of a cohesive self.

But Gedo's emphasis on interventions directed toward contentless tension states and functional deficits has the following negative consequence: it shifts analytic focus away from intrapsychic reality to the patient's environment. In fact, this shift in focus typifies all the self psychologies and makes for an interesting paradox. Intending to bring us closer to our patient's experience, the self psychologies really accomplish the very opposite. Thus, Dewald is right on target when he faults Gedo (1979) for:

> ascribing to the external objects primary responsibility for the construction and maintenance of the primitive, primary-process fantasy systems which are at the core of most neurotic phenomena. Clinical observation repeatedly documents the importance of unconscious core fantasy systems, the explanations for which are more appropriately ascribed to the child's immature, cognitive and reality-testing capacities, and to the child's tendency to interpret phenomena in accordance with his own intrapsychic organization and limited experiences [Dewald, 1981, p. 189].

Heinz Kohut and the Psychology of the Self

Of all the self psychologies, Kohut's is most clearly presented as a new theory and, due to the breadth of its concern, is the one most likely to threaten the cohesion of the psychoanalytic community. In contributions beginning with *The Restoration of the Self* (1977), Kohut accords the self a superordinate status only approached in the work of Klein and Gedo. In these writings, Kohut expounds a psychology of the self in the "broad" sense which, he believes, can explain human behavior and psychopathology more cogently than classical psychoanalytic theory. The latter, in its purported narrowness, is designated "drive theory" or "conflict theory."

This viewpoint represents a radical departure from the pre-Restoration writings in which Kohut resorted to the language of traditional metapsychology both in his differentiation of object libido from narcissistic libido and in his rediscovery of the importance of the "actual" neurosis (1971). Furthermore, Kohut originally introduced the self as a construct applicable to only one set of structures within the mental apparatus; this self-construct figures in the psychology of the self in the "narrow" sense. In accord with this early perspective, Kohut argued against the idea of making the self "the basic axiom of a psychoanalytic theory," claiming this strategy would lead to "an abrogation of the importance of the unconscious" (Kohut, 1979, p. 659). By viewing the self as a single content of the mind, Kohut felt we could "recognize the simultaneous existence of contradictory selves . . . of different selves of various degrees of stability and of various degrees of importance. There are conscious, preconscious, and unconscious selves, selves in the ego, the id, and the superego; and we may discover in our patients contradictory selves, side by side, in the same psychic agency (p. 660). It was in the context of this entirely operational viewpoint that Kohut first expressed a preference to designate one of these selves the "nuclear self."

Over the next five years, self psychology in the narrow sense was definitively transcended by self psychology in the broad sense. This development followed Kohut's extension of clinical concepts adumbrated in *The Analysis of the Self* (1971) beyond the specifically "narcissistic" psychopathology that had called the concepts into being. The psychology of the self became relevant not only to patients with narcissistic personality disorders, but to patients with perversions, depressive syndromes, and character disorders. As the obverse side of this expansion, the relevance of traditional theory to psychopathology became increasingly remote; by the time Kohut published *The Restoration of the Self* (1977), he believed the patient with neurotic conflicts centering on the oedipal phase of development was a rare bird—an endangered species, as it were. It was the new centrality of the self-concept in a variety of psychopathological conditions that induced Kohut to abandon his earlier positions and to espouse "two approaches: a psychology in which the self is seen as the center of the psychological universe, and a psychology in which the self is seen as a content of a mental apparatus" (1977, p. xv). The promulgation of the psychology of the self in the former "broader" sense embodied Kohut's recognition of "the limits of the applicability of some of the basic analytic formulations" (p. xviii).

The route Kohut has taken since 1972 has been punctuated by a series of sharply dichotomous positions with regard to important clinical and technical issues. Narcissism as a separate and independent line of development was initially part of a dichotomous formulation of narcissistic and object libido. This formulation, in turn, was predicated on the assumption that two kinds of patients present for analysis: patients with narcissistic personality disorders and patients with neurotic disturbances rooted in the Oedipus complex. These two categories of patients were further distinguished by two different types of transference—selfobject and object-libidinal—and the two types of transference yielded two different conceptualizations of the mechanism of therapeutic action in psychoanalysis—transmuting internalization and change through insight. Within this framework, Kohut went on to offer a number of further contrasts: between destructive aggression and nondestructive aggression experienced in response to an attack on the self, between self-objects and oedipal objects, and between nonconflictual, nonwish-fulfilling self-state dreams and conflictual, wish-fulfilling dreams. Kohut's various dichotomies culminated in a grand dichotomy encompassing the human situation writ large; the Guilty Man of traditional psychoanalytic theory was contrasted to the Tragic Man of self psychology. For Tragic Man, drive, conflict, and guilt are all but irrelevant. Unlike Guilty Man plagued by these dimensions of oedipal experience, Tragic Man suffers from developmental defects rooted in his preoedipal failure to receive adequately empathic parenting. From 1977, then, Kohut's belief in the paramount importance of Tragic Man and his self-psychological problems led him to all but discard a classical drive theory that could only address the problems of increasingly anachronistic Guilty Man.

The outcome of this judgment is the unitary position of the psychology of the self in the broad sense, a position tantamount to "a whole new concept of man." This new concept of man, in turn, is premised on a unidimensional view of human nature and psychopathology in which self-cohesion is the highest aim and loss of self the greatest danger. I am not prepared to argue that Kohut's position in this regard is inherently indefensible; I would argue, however, that it is sufficiently different from the viewpoint of traditional psychoanalytic theory, with its emphasis on infantile sexuality and oedipal conflict, to make the two perspectives irreconcilable.

This judgment can be highlighted by considering the discontinuity between Kohut's formulations and the more revisionist enterprises of Klein and Gedo. Kohut's theory derives from the clinical psychoanalytic situation, from what he terms "the experience-near realm." As a clinician, he observed a spontaneous unfolding of a specifically "selfobject" (initially designated "narcissistic") transference configuration. This discovery led, initially, to a new framework for approaching narcissistic personality disorders, but ultimately to a reconceptualization of both psychopathology per se and the mechanism of action in psychoanalysis. Klein, on the other hand, moved toward a theoretical revision because of his dissatisfaction with the epistemological status of classical psychoanalytic concepts: drive, energy, the structural model, physicalistic metaphors, etc. Gedo shared Klein's dissatisfaction, but was additionally motivated to provide a clinical theory that could do justice to a range of interventions that were implicated in many classically conducted analyses, but never accorded the systematic place within the traditional theory of therapy Gedo felt they deserved.

Kohut's major contribution has been clinical; he has sharpened our sensitivity to our patients' perceptions of what we say and how we say it, as well as our awareness of our patients' narcissistic vulnerabilities. Kohut does not follow the theoretical path of Klein and Gedo, who want to eliminate Freud's metapsychology and replace it with a language of motivations or personal aims. Instead, Kohut retains the metapsychological concept of the libido as a transitional phase in his theory building while effectively disowning the assumptions about psychic development that underlie the metapsychology. Thus, where Klein and Gedo would rid psychoanalysis of metapsychology while retaining what they consider Freud's fundamental principles, including the centrality of conflict and infantile sexuality, Kohut seems willing to retain for the time being the language of metapsychology while relegating conflict in general and infantile sexuality in particular to a position of relative unimportance. Kohut (1977) believes, in short, that the conceptual tools of conflict psychology can reveal but a partial view of man's inner life. But what are the analytic sacrifices that accompany Kohut's more encompassing view of the psychological field? For Kohut, as for Klein, the self is equivalent to everything that is psychologically meaningful about the person, and it becomes "superordinate" by subsuming everything within its fold that can be characterized as mental. For Kohut, as for Klein and Gedo, the self becomes both driving force and that which is driven. The problems embodied in this theoretical approach have been clearly stated by Palombo (1978). He refers to a

. . . kind of humanistic holism characterized by the effort to relate even the smallest units of psychic activity to the overall aims and interests of the "whole person." This achievement is of course the ultimate goal both of therapeutic practice and theoretical understanding. In pursuing this goal prematurely and indiscriminately at all levels of the hierarchic organization of the psychic apparatus, however, we are put in the false position of having to understand the whole person before being able to explain any of the details of his thought and behavior. The investigator who adopts this strategy tends to lose interest in the observation of lower level adaptive functions. He may even come to deny they exist on the ground that adaptation is a function of the whole organism and that "mechanisms" are by definition rigid and inflexible. To follow this course is to lose touch with the means by which adaptation is achieved. The organism, human or otherwise, survives through the incorporation of simple, mechanical performance into increasingly complex patterns of contingent organization [p. 9].

The problem with Kohut's continual stress on contentless mental states, on the self as over- or understimulated, fragmented or cohesive, is that the absence of content, conflict, and unconscious fantasy may be more apparent than real. Similarly, the designations "idealizing transference" and "mirror transference" may only embody manifest contents beneath which a multiplicity of latent meanings can be tapped. This possibility counters the tendency of self psychologists to give these

configurations considerable diagnostic weight, to view them as prefig-
ured structures with a predictable pattern of unfolding, and to attribute to
them a very specific genetic significance. The hypothesis that parental
empathic failure is the central cause of psychopathology is plausible for
some, even for many, patients. But validation in a particular case ultimately requires good analytic data. Good analytic data, in turn, derive
from a well-conducted analysis—an analysis in which the analyst's preconceived expectations are kept to a minimum and clinical phenomena
including the transference are explored in an open-minded way.

SUMMARY

The concept of the self has been used in several attempts to resolve the
epistemological problems of what is subjective and what is objective,
what is personal and what is organismic. In addition, it has been used
to mediate between the hermeneutic and natural-science approaches to
psychoanalytic explanation, between the motivational and causal dimensions of our theory and experience. In the case of Kohut, the self was
initially invoked to deal with clinical difficulties associated with the
analysis of patients with narcissistic personality disorders; more recently,
it has become the central article in a "self psychology" that addresses
presumed deficiencies in the traditional psychoanalytic picture of
psychopathology. But the concept of the self is not suited to be a
panacea for resolving theoretical or clinical difficulties. The self as person refers to an entity that is both enduring and changing; it describes
continuity in the face of change and change in the face of continuity.
Abend (1974) comes closest to capturing this attribute of the self in his
image of the tidal beach with a configuration that changes but an essence
that remains the same. Eisnitz (1980) evokes something similar in his
figure-ground conception of the self-representation. The crux of the
matter is that the notion of self-experience includes a variety of phenomena that cannot be contained within a single self-construct—be it normal
pathologic, grandiose, or otherwise.

As a result of these considerations, I have argued against the use of
the self as a superordinate concept in psychoanalytic theory and have
focused on the shortcomings of three self psychologies that use the self
in this way. I believe that Klein, Gedo, and Kohut all offer the self as a
kind of conceptual tranquilizer for the philosophical, theoretical, and
clinical dualities that are inherent in psychoanalytic work. Grossman

addressed himself to these dualities as far back as 1967 and elaborated on the problem with Simon (1969) in a pathbreaking paper on anthropomorphism in psychoanalysis. Grossman and Simon contended that the controversy about anthropomorphism in psychoanalytic theory pertains to the basic confusion in psychology between meaning and causality. They submitted that until this confusion was dispelled and until some superordinate concept was found that could "encompass both kinds of discourse," attempts to transform psychoanalysis into a general psychology would result in failure. In my view, the superordinate schema invoked by Grossman and Simon in 1969 remains to be formulated, the self psychologies of today notwithstanding.

REFERENCES

ABEND, S. (1974). Problems of identity: theoretical and clinical application. *Psychoanalytic Quarterly* 43:606–637.

ALSTON, W. (1977). Self intervention and the structure of motivation. In *The Self: Psychological and Philosophical Issues,* ed. T. Mischel. Oxford: Blackwell, pp. 64–102.

DEWALD, P. (1981). Commentaries on John Gedo's Beyond Interpretation. *Psychoanalytic Inquiry* 1:187–204.

EISNITZ, A. (1980). The organization of the self representation and its influence on pathology. *Psychoanalytic Quarterly* 49:361–392.

FRANK, A. (1979). Two theories or one? Or more. *Journal of the American Psychoanalytic Association* 27:169–207.

FREUD, S. (1915). Instincts and their vicissitudes. *Standard Edition* 14.

———— (1930). Civilization and its discontents. *Standard Edition* 21.

———— (1940). An outline of psycho-analysis. *Standard Edition* 23.

GEDO, J. (1979). *Beyond Interpretation.* New York: International Universities Press.

GROSSMAN, W. (1967). Reflections on the relationships of introspection and psychoanalysis. *International Journal Psychoanalysis* 48:16–31.

GROSSMAN, W. & SIMON, B. (1969). Anthropomorphism: motive, meaning and causality in psychoanalytic thinking *Psychoanalytic Study of the Child* 24:79–114.

HARTMANN, H. (1950). Comments on the psychoanalytic theory of the ego *Psychoanalytic Study of the Child* 5:74–96

KERNBERG, O. (1982). Self, ego, affects, and drives *Journal of the American Psychoanalytic Association* 30:893–917.

KLEIN, G. (1976). *Psychoanalytic Theory* New York: International Universities Press.

KOHUT, H. (1971). *The Analysis of the Self.* New York: International Universities Press.

————— (1977). *The Restoration of the Self.* New York: International Universities Press.

————— (1979). *The Search for the Self.* New York: International Universities Press.

LICHTENSTEIN, H. (1977). *The Dilemma of Human Identity.* New York: Aronson.

PALOMBO, S.R. (1978). *Dreaming and Memory: A New Information Processing Model.* New York: Basic Books.

PANEL (1981). The bipolar self, S.J. Meyers, reporter. *Journal of the American Psychoanalytic Association* 29:143–159.

RANGELL, L. (1982). The self in psychoanalytic theory. *Journal of the American Psychoanalytic Association* 30:863–891.

ROTHSTEIN, A. (1980). Toward a critique of the psychology of the self *Psychoanalytic Quarterly.* 49:423–455.

RUBINSTEIN, B.B. (1981). Person, organism, and self. Presented to New York Psychoanalytic Society, Jan. 27.

SANDLER, J. & Rosenblatt, B. (1962). The representational world *Psychoanalytic Study of the Child* 17:128–145.

STRACHEY, J. (1923) Editor's introduction The ego and the id. *Standard Edition* 19.

TICHO, E. (1982) The alternate schools and the self. *Journal of the American Psychoanalytic Association* 30:849–862.

CHAPTER 6

Extenders, Modifiers, Heretics

[Richards, A.D. (1994). In *The Spectrum of Psychoanalysis, Essays in Honor of Martin S. Bergmann*, eds. A.K. Richards, M.S. Bergmann, & A.D. Richards. Madison, CT: International Universities Press.]

In his 1991 plenary address to the American Psychoanalytic Association, Martin Bergmann (Bergmann, 1993) put forward a classification of psychoanalytic innovators as modifiers, extenders, or heretics.

The heretics, rare in recent years but prevalent in Freud's lifetime, were typically close to Freud for some time, made important contributions and then bolted to start their own schools. They include Adler, Steckel, Jung, Rank, and Wilhelm Reich. During Freud's lifetime there were only heretics and extenders; modifiers appeared after Freud's death. . . .

Modifiers recast psychoanalytic theory or modified psychoanalytic practice but did not leave the psychoanalytic field. A typical strategy for a modifier is to claim that his or her modification is implicit in Freud's writing or flows directly out of Freud's idea. While modifiers create controversy in psychoanalysis, they also keep it alive and protect it from stagnation. Earlier modifiers were Ferenczi and Federn. Later ones were Hartmann, Melanie Klein, Winnicott, Lacan, and Kohut. . . .

Extenders, the third group, usually extend psychoanalysis into areas as yet unexplored but their findings do not demand modification. Unlike modifiers, they evoke no enmity and their contributions are appreciated. Some of the important extenders are Karl Abraham, Hermann Nunberg, Waelder, and Fenichel [p. 930].

In what follows we will attempt to probe this taxonomy for its adequacy in characterizing psychoanalytic history and the current situation of theoretical diversity.

At the outset we might note a certain asymmetry in the terms. Whereas *extender* and *modifier* present themselves as descriptive judgments, *heretic* injects into the discussion a note of the normative. Clearly, heresy requires an orthodoxy agamst which it may be defined. This realization, however, should occasion our looking beyond the secular appearance of the other two terms, as on closer inspection they reveal a conceptual dependence on the very orthodoxy whose rejection, in whole or in part, would bring down the judgment of heresy. The question then becomes, is this orthodoxy in fact the one true faith? Or, in terms perhaps less loaded, are we dealing here with a scientific consensus? The problem is that orthodoxy, religious or scientific, varies over time (as it is extended and modified), and it is often difficult to identify a core set. of beliefs that remain constant.

The situation is complicated further by the fact that each of the terms in question may he used in reference either to another or to oneself. Heresy, when self-ascribed, is more properly referred to as apostasy. The apostate makes a formal renunciation of the faith and becomes a defector; in contrast, those who might be branded heretics often consider themselves within the fold. Heretics may believe that they are struggling there for hegemony, the power tb define the tradition along lines they consider orthodox, or they may in all innocence believe that they accept the reigning version of orthodoxy, only to be branded by some inquisitor as heretical and subversive. Often heresy is diagnosed when some peripheral belief that once admitted variation becomes a central article of faith and so is shored up against equivocation. When charged, heretics may either submit to authority (either sincerely or with mental reservations and subversive intent) or declare their apostasy openly. If in the latter instance they escape unburned, they may either drift off as individuals or make over what was once a mere school or sect into a new religion.

In any case, these judgments, whether of self or others, are not incorrigible; we may be mistaken in the application of these terms, a difficulty compounded by the historical variability of orthodoxy (and of its tolerances: these may he quite generous when hegemony is firmly established or, conversely, when it is extremely attenuated). And, finally, these judgments may be altered retrospectively, as in scientific textbooks. Thomas Kuhn (1962) has shown how the synchronic presentation of a field, using seamlessly contemporary terminology, obliterates past and future while demarcating for would-be extenders the range of normal (or orthodox) science. In subsequent revised editions the historian of science can often detect the unremarked rehabilitation of a figure once anathematized or the retrocondemnation (by simple omission) of an erstwhile scientific saint.

With these refinements in mind, let us now apply Bergmann's categories to the theoretical diversity of contemporary psychoanalysis. Bergmann argues that extenders and modifiers exhaust the field here, as heretics are no longer (or are only rarely) to be found. "It is likely," he observes, "that the concept of modifier became a reality in organized psychoanalysis after the controversies between Kleinians and ego psychologists did not result in a split. The outcome demonstrated that after Freud's death, no one, not even his daughter, could claim to be his only legitimate heir" (1993, p. 950).

Is it then that while Freud was alive heresy was simply whatever he determined it to be, and that this was a judgment that depended solely on his personal authority, however well earned? And might this not be explained in part by the fact that psychoanalysis was still quite young then, its tensions, ambiguities, and potential directions brought together nowhere more comprehensively than in the head of its founder? If so, Freud's death might be seen as having plunged the field into a situation in which, in order to avoid a series of schisms that would undermine its efforts to institutionalize itself, a pact of toleration had to be made. To that end, a dilute creed that almost anyone could agree with was tacitly accepted. (Perhaps it is no mere coincidence that this was played out largely in Anglican Britain, where, as Bergmann notes, Kleinians, ego psychologists, and a middle school settled their differences without a formal split.)

Organizational integrity thus overrode theoretical consensus, which in any case could not be arrived at in the former's absence. This situation allowed views that might previously have been branded heretical to exist within the pale of psychoanalysis. Early on, this stance may have paid dividends, as these views, given enough time to develop, could often be woven into the theoretical fabric accepted by most analysts. It is open to question, however, whether this toleration may not also have spawned systems of ideas (and clinical practice) that on closer scrutiny prove incompatible with psychoanalysis. One result of this situation is that theoretical divisions could no longer be neatly charted along organizational lines.

As a salient instance of theoretical diversity, then, let us consider the work of Heinz Kohut. Bergmann, though he considers Kohut a modifier, notes "a great dividing line in psychoanalysis" between Freudian analysts, who "believe that cure depends on reliving the traumatic past in the transference," and self psychologists, who "see the analysand as a new selfobject and through empathy can avoid or at least postpone the appearance of the traumatic repetition compulsion in the analysis" (p. 28). Some psychoanalysts, rather less charitable than Bergmann, come very close to considering Kohut a heretic. Others, including a number of self psychologists, consider his contribution an extension of fundamental Freudian ideas. Other self psychologists, however, including at times Kohut himself, present his contributions as disjunctive with classical psychoanalysis. We will, incidentally, see how much turns in these disputes on the adjective *classical,* which, depending on its utterer's point of view, can be either (1) an epithet, in two of its dictionary senses (i.e., a pejorative and a taxonomic term denoting a species within a genus [classical psychoanalysis from this perspective is but one species of psychoanalysis, and not a particularly esteemed one at that]; or (2) an honorific, serving to distinguish its bearer from false claimants (in this view, classical psychoanalysis is the only valid form of psychoanalysis).

In the posthumously published *How Does Analysis Cure?,* Kohut (1984) differentiated the self psychologically informed psychoanalyst from the classical analyst by remarking that the former will:

> [O]nly very rarely look at his patient in terms of his drive, wishes and defenses; if he does, moreover, he will do so in the framework of his overall understanding of the needs of the patient's self. Defense motivation in analysis will be understood in terms of activities undertaken in the service of psychological survival, that is, as the patient's attempt to save at least that factor of his nuclear self, however small and precariously established it may be, that he has been able to construct and maintain despite serious inefficiencies in the development-enhancing matrix of the selfobjects of childhood [1984, p. 115].

Kohut distinguished between a mechanistic classical psychoanalysis and a humanistic self psychology. Although he acknowledged that the original model of analytic technique, close as it was to the model of hypnosis, was changed by ego psychology, the latter in his opinion occasioned more a refinement of psychoanalytic theory than of the theory of technique and the conduct of clinical analysis. The distinction was ultimately between the Freudian analyst as surgeon and the Kohutian analyst attuned to the "needs of the patient's self." For the self psychologist, classical psychoanalysis rests on "a penetration to the unconscious via the overcoming of resistance model, a model that looks for slips of the tongue, dreams, and the vicissitudes of the transference neurosis but does not explain personality disturbances, . . . especially disturbances within the essential psychopathology that results from the thwarted development of the self" (1984, p. 113). Kohut argued the desirability of the self psychological theory of pathogenesis on the basis of value considerations. The analysis of drives, wishes, defenses, and resistances was for him "a moralistic framework provided by the pleasure principle and promoted by traditional psychoanalysts" (p. 114).

Although Kohut argued strongly against the idea that when drives, wishes, defenses, and resistances are thoroughly analyzed and worked through, "everything else will follow," he insisted that his approach retained a place for the concept of resistance, and defense analysis (p. 114). Despite these assurances, however, Kohut asserted the opposition between an approach that focuses on psychic mechanisms and one that attempts to grasp the position of the self over time. In a clinical example intended to illustrate the difference between the traditional approach and that of self psychology, he formulated the underlying dynamic of the patient's resistive struggle as a need for self-enhancing reflection rather than a struggle for objective love. He faulted classical analysts for not recognizing that the patient's need for self affirmation is neither defensive nor resistant, but rather is a move taken in the service of psychic survival.

In response, the classical analyst might point out that Kohut disregards the adaptive dimension of compromise formation; at any given moment, that is, patients are doing the best they can to mediate among various pushes, pulls, needs, desires, conflicts, wishes, and superego attitudes. The advantage of the drive-compromise formation model is that it accommodates a richer array of forces, requirements, and contingency demands than does the concept of a self struggling against under- or overstimulation.

In his last book Kohut linked the notion of the therapeutic centrality of truth-facing with the scientific model whereby the unconscious is made conscious. According to him, classical analysts are preoccupied with progress or its lack, with success or failure, and function within a cognitive orientation. By contrast, self psychologists work within a self-state orientation. Knowing or not knowing is not for them the most salient issue; rather, it is being or not being.

Technically, the self psychological approach develops out of the conviction that at bottom there are two distinct ways of working in the analytic situation. One finds the analyst interpreting active mechanisms; the other, favored by self psychologists, has the analyst offering broad, genetically based reconstructions of chronic attitudes. Trop and Stolorow (1992), commenting on similar issues in regard to defense analysis, view traditional analysts as engaged in a continual battle with their patients, thereby ignoring Kohut's dictum that "the analyst's aim should not be to break through or overcome resistance, but rather to accept, understand, and explain its necessity in terms of the psychological dangers being mobilized by the analytic process" (p. 427).

How Does Analysis Cure? was published thirteen years after Kohut's first book, *The Analysis of the Self* (1971) in which he first presented ideas arguably disjunctive with classical Freudian analysis. Since then, reviews, critiques, and commentaries have flowed endlessly, it seems. One of the most cogent of these critiques is that of Friedman. By the end of *The Analysis of the Self,* Friedman argues, Kohut was at a crossroads:

> On the one hand he could describe structure-building. That is, he could extend the classical account of the birth of the ego, generalize the process to include the superego, coordinate specific feeling states with it, and advance the process forward from infancy into adult life. Alternatively he could announce a newly-discovered drive [1980, pp. 404–405].

Friedman's conclusion is that Kohut, though "he never wanted to do either, . . . wanted the advantages of both approaches" (p. 405).

Wallerstein (1983) has gone even further and argued that:

> [S]elf psychology denies that the drives in interaction with the environment and with experience (and since Hartmann with the maturational unfolding of inborn ego apparatuses) are the primary developers of the maturing coherent ego and/or self. Instead, self psychology hypothesizes . . . the primacy of the organizing, cohering self organization with drive manifestations considered the "breakdown products of the vulnerable self under fragmenting pressures" [p. 562].

This, Treurniet (1983), would seem to consider an instance of self psychology "in its broader superordinate sense attack[ing] and tr[ying] to destroy the central explanatory concepts of psychoanalysis" (p. 59). The self, he explains, invoking Rangell (1963), "is not an explanatory concept; [it] pertains to the outcome of conflict rather than [to] its cause" (pp. 98–99). He concludes that self psychology diminishes greatly the central explanatory role of conflict, transference, and resistance, a point on which Curtis (1985) would seem to concur:

> Efforts to extend the application of self psychology to include the psychoneuroses lead to an interactional reparative therapy that compromises interpretations of transference and resistance. Therapeutic change resulting from this approach is seen as essentially different from the processes and transformations set in motion by classical analysis [p. 339].

Modell (1986), an object relational theorist at odds with classical analysis on several points, nevertheless focuses on the disjunction between Kohut and Freud. "Although Kohut gives lip service to innate biological predisposition and acknowledges Freud's complemental series, he believes in essence that neurosis is the consequence of a defective or faulty sense of self" (p. 368); in his conclusion that Kohut rejected Freud's instinct theory, Modell is joined by Friedman (1986), who holds that: "in the end, Kohut believed more strongly than ever that Freudian drive theory by its nature fosters the unattractive qualities of the analyses he had seen" (p. 339).

This Kohutian belief is turned on its head by Reed (1987). Arguing that "self psychology adheres to a system of interpretation that is contrary, not complementary, to that of psychoanalysis," she finds "the two systems are incompatible" (p.422). Moreover, she maintains that Kohut's characterization of classical analysis as an "understanding by imposing an objective theory on the patient's material is more the basis for his restriction of its applicability" (p. 423). Quite the reverse, Reed argues, self psychology treats the product to be interpreted didactically. The product to be interpreted reveals the theory of the self. She suggests that Kohut "wove the same rules of understanding into the fabric of self psychology as he applied when using the classical paradigm; that is, he attempted to reveal classical theory truth to the patient in order to restore meaning (p. 432). Regarding Kohut's first analysis of Mr. Z (1979), which occurred at a time when the extent of his divergence from Freud was evident neither to himself nor to others, she comments that:

> [W]hat is most striking is the impression one receives of the analyst's insistence that he is in possession of the truth to be imparted to the patient no matter what. That the truth the analyst attempts to reveal resembles formulations familiar to classical psychoanalytic theory does not make this procedure a classical psychoanalysis. Indoctrination remains indoctrination regardless of the discipline [Reed, 1987, p. 433].

An article on empathy by Spencer and Balter (1990) throws into sharp relief another essential difference between self psychology and classical analysis. Discussing Kohut's 1959 claim that "introspection and empathy are the essential constituents of psychoanalytic fact-finding" (pp. 464-465), the authors point out a different analytic tradition, one exemplified by Arlow and Brenner who "adopt a more positive, natural scientific or mechanistic view of psychoanalytic observation. While recognizing the importance of empathy and introspection . . . they do not consider them central or even essential to psychoanalytic method" (p. 395). Noting that introspection is "preeminently a psychology of consciousness," Spencer and Balter remark on the incompleteness (not to say the absurdity) of analyzing only manifest content (p. 398).

Examining Kohut's formulation of empathy as "vicarious introspection" (the analyst puts himself in the position of the analysand while listening to the analysand's introspective observations), they find an inverse correlation between empathy and free association. The latter they connect with nonempathic behavioral observation in which the subject's behavior "is not seen from the empathic vantage point but rather from the point or view of a spectator without regard to the subject's own thoughts or feelings" (p. 402). Although allowing that Kohut "apparently did not at first mean to discard free association" (Kohut, 1959, p. 464), they maintain that by 1984 the concept had essentially disappeared from his discussions of psychoanalytic method. The index of *How Does Analysis Cure?* lists but three instances of the term's use, in each of which it refers rather generally to the patient's production of material. As Freud's fundamental rule requires that patient and analyst treat associations as verbal behavior, affording access to the unconscious, Spencer and Balter view Kohut's de-emphasis of the method as evidence of a disinclination to acknowledge the unconscious in the classical Freudian sense. They write:

> There is no discussion of unconscious mental functioning as an aspect of the theory and method of self psychology. The index references to the term unconscious are either to clinical discussions of its use by Freud or casual references to its use by classical analysts [p. 419].

If Spencer and Balter are right, then Kohut has jettisoned what for many is Freud's single most important contribution. The authors cited here focus, at their most charitable, on Kohut's inconsistencies. All note, however, what they consider subversions and misunderstandings of Freud's fundamental ideas. Under what dispensation then can Kohut, certainly no extender, be considered a modifier? With respect to the term *heretic*, Bergmann is surely correct with regard to the political fate of psychoanalytic innovators: no longer are they read out of the movement. But if it is true that Kohut has abandoned the concept of the unconscious, does not the organizational fact of self psychology's inclusion within the analytic pale present a problem? Must we conclude that there is no core set of beliefs and practices to which analysts owe their allegiance? And if there is not, then it would seem that the name of psychoanalysis must be granted to any group that might choose to so label itself.

A possible stratagem for removing ourselves from this dilemma is suggested by Larry Laudan's concept (1977) of the scientific research tradition, a notion applied by Stepansky (1983) to the subject of analytic dissent. Stepansky reminds us again that the very notion of what counts as dissent is a historical issue. "Certain formal comparabilities between Adler's self psychology of 1911 and Kohut's self psychology," he notes, "may belie a striking incommensurability between the dissident status of their respective theories" (p. 52). This is because the research tradition within which psychoanalytic theories are situated has evolved over the seven decades separating Adler's work from that of Kohut.

Stepansky's elaboration of the affinity of certain Adlerian concepts to Kohut's ideas is compelling. In the winter of 1911, at the point of breaking with Freud, Adler rejected "the analytic concept of ego instincts" as "redundant and empty," arguing that "these instincts should not be viewed as rigidified and discrete but as part of an expansive outlook . . . directed toward the environment" (p. 53). He went on to reject "the idea of primary instinctual aggression" and developed the notion of the masculine protest. At this point, Adler's language strikingly anticipated the terminology later adopted by Kohut. "Precociously stimulated sexuality entered into neurosis because it represented a type of safeguard or security device . . .through which the neurotically predisposed child could mitigate its feelings of inferiority and achieve adequate self-esteem or self feeling . . ." Stepansky, 1983, p. 54–5). Within the Adlerian schema, Freud's drives became "derivative phenomena that functioned as compensatory attempts to ward off the inferiority (i.e, the lack of self feeling) occasioned by deficient early parenting" (p. 55), and the "Oedipus complex was derivative to the masculine protest, Adler's 'overpowering neurotic dynamic' " (Adler, 1911, p. 114, quoted in Stepansky, 1983, p. 55).

According to Stepansky, Kohut's "Thoughts on Narcissism and Narcissistic Rage" (1972) "undertook to resuscitate Adler's notion of 'organ inferiority' by refracting this concept from the standpoint of narcissistic energetics. For Kohut, the 'inferior organ' regained its status as a valid object of analytic focus when reconceptualized as a reservoir of archaic, narcissistic cathexis of the child's body/self " (pp. 56, 67). Stepansky argues that these claims "pave the way for the more radical reassessment of aggression and of classical drive theory" to be found in *The Restoration of the Self* (1977). From developmental assumptions regarding the "assertive quality of healthy self-development," Kohut, paralleling Adler in certain respects, posits that the child's destructive aggressiveness is not an expression of primary instinctuality but rather as a product of regression, a "fragment of the healthy, assertive potentiality of the nuclear self" (p. 57).

Now Stepansky, as we have seen, does not claim that Kohut must be judged a heretic simply because Adler, who espoused similar ideas, was found to one in 1911. At the time Freud expelled Adler from the psychoanalytic movement, after all, psychoanalysis "did not entail methodological commitments that transcended the basic content of Freud's early clinical discoveries. . . . In 1911, Freud clearly believed that acceptance of the clinical theories encompassing his early discoveries was always at issue in the attribution of a specifically 'psychoanalytic' identity" (p. 60). By the time Kohut formulated his ideas, however, psychoanalysis had become a research tradition transcending Freud's theories. Now psychoanalysis openly aspired to the status of a "general psychology," an aspiration, that could no longer be summarily equated with "resistance" to the theory of infantile sexuality. Correspondingly, after the work of Anna Freud, and Hartmann, Kris, and Loewenstein, it no longer seems reasonable to reject as nonanalytic an "ego psychology deepened by the knowledge of the psychology of the unconscious—the very formulation Freud invoked to underscore the incompatibility of Adler's viewpoint with analysis" (p. 65). Stepansky adds that Kohut's indebtedness to the work of Hartmann, acknowledged in one of his final essays (Kohut, 1984), "should not be taken lightly by analysts, because it points to the historicity of self psychology within a psychoanalytic research tradition" (p. 65).

Nevertheless, Stepansky, in a Kuhnian appreciation of the relation between scientific community and scientific progress, believes that the psychoanalytic community, with its collective understanding of the research tradition it has evolved, "must ultimately appraise the psychoanalytic admissibility of Kohut's formulations" (p. 66). His analysis is helpful in reminding us that terms like *extender, modifier,* and *heretic* are historically variable; a "heretic of 1911 may today be regarded as a modifier. Nonetheless, an ostensible modifier moves into the realm of outright dissidence once he abandons certain elements of the psychoanalytic research tradition that are sacrosanct and cannot be rejected without repudiating the tradition itself " (p. 64).

So in the end these categories of psychoanalytic difference and dissidence may ultimately rest more on issues of methodology than of content. If Reed and Spencer and Balter are right, Kohut is promoting a different kind of observation, one in which empathy and vicarious introspection purportedly replace free association and behavioral observation. It would follow that Kohut's self psychology qualifies as a separate research tradition. Other theoretical schools now current might also be viewed as reflecting fundamental methodological differences rather than conceptual differences involving only content. Not only do they listen for different things in their patients' productions—issues of security, validation, developmental arrest—but they claim to listen with a different ear and seem to use different criteria for the validation of hypotheses and interpretations in the analytic situation.

We are left with the question whether the practitioners of these schools in fact participate in the research tradition of psychoanalysis. At a minimum, they do not really conduct analyses using a different instrument of observation; they *cannot,* as none exists. It is arguable that they have available to them in the consulting room the same mix of perceptions any of us have, but their participation in the common ground of psychoanalysis (in Wallerstein's sense) may be precluded by their flawed understanding of what it is they do. To the extent that they cannot put aside a theory that would direct their attention exclusively to a particular type of phenomenon, which seems always to be found, they are neither observing nor analyzing; to pick up on Reed's discussions of indoctrination, they are "schooling" their patients. If, however, they can avoid such closure, they may operate as analysts but at the disadvantage, it would seem, of having only the vaguest understanding of psychoanalytic principles to guide them in their work. But then, of course, we would have a case of mistaken identification. A group considered, by both themselves and others, to be either modifiers, or heretics would in practice turn out to be quite orthodox, not even extenders, though perhaps only minimally competent.

A recent exercise in psychoanalytic dialogue will perhaps show how treacherous these waters are. In a discussion (Richards, 1992) of a case presentation by Trop and Stolorow (1992), the point was made that the nature of the report made it impossible to decide the relative truth value of their formulation of the patient's pathology and course of treatment and an alternative formulation in terms of drive, conflict, and compromise formation. Mitchell (1992) offering yet a third formulation and advancing the belief that there is no such thing as truth in a positivistic sense, argued that the reader could not choose, using any objective criterion, between Stolorow and Trop's interpretation and his alternative reading. And yet, paradoxically, he asserted that within his relativistic framework he was nonetheless certain that the classical analytic formulation was in error. For Mitchell, it is classical psychoanalysis that is now deemed heretical, and the new orthodoxy comprises a number of relational schools whose differences can be characterized using the modifier/extender distinction alone. Mitchell remarked:

> Taken together, these various relational theories have provided a compelling and comprehensive alternative to the classical model of orthodox psychoanalysis. In my view, the battle against orthodoxy has been largely won; the real vitality and creativity in the field has shifted to efforts . . . to develop postclassical, broadly relational approaches to mind, development, and the analytic situation. Because the battle has been won, it is now less interesting to recount the deficiencies of the classical model than to

explore the subtle but quite important differences among post-classical perspectives . . . [p. 443].

It may well be, then, that Bergmann's taxonomy is not fully adequate to the description of the relationships currently obtaining among theoretical trends in psychoanalysis. The concept of scientific research traditions may well represent the foundation for a new and more fruitful approach to the problem, and yet Bergmann's distinction, perhaps as refined here, will no doubt continue to figure in our exercises in comparative psychoanalysis, and these are important both historically and pragmatically. They provide an opportunity to delineate specific differences with regard to theories of pathogenesis, the treatment process, and cure, and are modifications, extensions, or heresies (or, alternatively, as embodying different scientific research traditions) relevant to the extent to which discussion shifts from considerations of conformity and orthodoxy to important features of human experience that are neglected by one or another approach. Different scientific research traditions, provided they are that, can certainly learn from one another and increasing our awareness of overlooked scripts or themes can only be helpful, to patients and analysts alike.

REFERENCES

ADLER, A. (1911). Zur kritik der Freud schen Sexual theorie der Nervositzet: 11 "Verdaengurg" und "Maennlicher Protest": Ihre Rolle urd Bedeutung fuer die neurotische Dynamik. In: Heuten on Bilden: Aerztich-paedagogische Arbeiten des Vereins fur Individual Psychologie, ed., A. Adler & C. Furtmueller. Munich: Ekst Reinhardt, 1914.

BERGMANN, M.S. (1993). Reflections on the history of psychoanalysis. *Journal of the American Psychoanalytic Association* 41:929–955.

CURTIS, H.C. (1985). Clinical perspectives on self psychology. *Psychoanalytic Quarterly* 54:339–377.

FRIEDMAN, L. (1980). Kohut: A book review essay. *Psychoanalytic Quarterly* 49:393–423.

——— (1986). Kohut's testament. *Psychoanalytic Inquiry* 6:321–347.

KOHUT, H. (1959). Introspection, empathy and psychoanalysis: An examination of the relationship between mode of observation and theory. *Journal of the American Psychoanalytic Association* 7:459–483.

——— (1971). *The Analysis of the Self.* New York: International Universities Press.

——— (1972). Thoughts on narcissism and narcissistic rage. *The Psychoanalytic Study of the Child* 27:360–400.

————— (1977). *The Restoration of the Self.* New York: International Universities Press.

————— (1979). The two analyses of Mr. Z. *International Journal of Psycho-Analysis.* 60:3–18.

————— (1984). *How Does Analysis Cure?*, ed. A. Goldberg & P. Stepansky. Chicago: University of Chicago Press.

KUHN, T. (1962). *The Structure of Scientific Revolutions.* Chicago: University of Chicago Press.

LAUDAN, L. (1977). *Progress and its Problems: Towards a Theory of Scientific Growth.* Berkeley: University of California Press.

MITCHELL, S.A. (1992). Commentary on Trop and Stolorow's "Defense Analysis in Self Psychology." *Psychoanalytic Dialogues* 2:443–453.

MODELL, A. (1986). The missing element in Kohut's Cure. *Psychoanalytic Inquiry* 6:367–385.

RANGELL, L. (1963). The scope of intrapsychic conflict. *Psychoanalytic Study of the Child* 18:75–102.

REED, G. (1987). Rules of clinical understanding in classical psychoanalysis and in self psychology: A comparison. *Journal of the American Psychoanalytic Association* 35:421–455.

RICHARDS, A.D. (1992). Commentary on Trop and Stolorow's "Defense Analysis in Self Psychology." *Psychoanalytic Dialogues* 2:455–465.

SPENCER, J.H., & BALTER, L. (1990). Psychoanalytic observation. *Journal of the American Psychoanalytic Association* 38:393–420.

STEPANSKY, P. (1983). Perspectives on dissent: Adler, Kohut, and the idea of a psychoanalytic research tradition. *Annual of Psychoanalysis* 11:51–74. New York: International Universities Press.

TREURNIET, N. (1983). Psychoanalysis and self psychology: A metapsychological essay with a clinical illustration. *Journal of the American Psychoanalytic Association* 31:59–98.

TROP, J.L., & STOLOROW, R.D. (1992). Defense analysis in self psychology: A developmental view. *Psychoanalytic Dialogues* 2:427–453.

WALLERSTEIN, R.S. (1983). Self psychology and "classical" psychoanalytic psychology: The nature of their relationship. *Psychoanalysis & Contemporary Thought* 6:553–593.

————— (1985). How does self psychology differ in practice? *International Journal of Psycho-Analysis* 66:391–403.

III. The Hermeneutic Science of Merton M. Gill and Z. Hoffman

Section 3 contains four chapters that review of the works of Merton Gill from his early works through his innovative work on transference and his collaborative efforts with Irwin Z. Hoffman, to his final contributions on hermeneutic science. This review is complemented by an assessment of some of Hoffman's efforts to integrate social constructivism into psychoanalytic thinking.

In chapter 7, "Transference Analysis: Means or End?", Richards (1984) explores:

- Should any single aspect of technique achieve centrality over other aspects?
- Further, is "resistance to the awareness of the transference" really ubiquitous?
- Finally, can and should pathology always be translated into the transference?

Richards next turns to Gill and Hoffman's (vol. 2, 1982) attempt to empirically test their hypotheses. After a critique of their research methodology Richard wonders:

- Does Gill's recommendations technically skew the interpretive process and threaten reliance on a restrictive formulaic approach?

In chapter 8, "Merton Gill: A View of His Place in the Freudian Firmament," Richards (with Lynch) reviews the many and varied contributions of Merton Gill spanning his 50-year career. They ask:

- Where did Gill fit theoretically at the end of his long and productive career?

In Chapter 9 and 10 Richards turns his attention to Hoffman's social constructivist view. In this perspective, the analysand's psychic reality is not discovered but constructed by both the analyst and the analysand. In chapter 9, "Irwin Hoffman: Ritual and Spontaneity in the Psychoanalytic Process," Richards examines Hoffamn's use of: (1) the position of the dialectic in psychoanalytic practice, (2) the nature of therapeutic change, and (3) the question of a new paradigm in psychoanalysis.

Regarding the analyst's persistent influence on the patient, Richards wonders:

- Does the analyst persistent influence mandate a shift in clinical focus that elevates 'intersubjective subjectivity' or is this an additional perspective from which to listen to the unconscious?
- Does psychoanalysis really need to wholeheartedly adopt a social constructivist's perspective to find the true nature of the patient's struggles or is this perspective another contribution that enhances psychoanalytic theory?
- Does the analyst's main function, as Hoffman proposes, only lead to a process of re-socialization connected to affirmation?

In chapter 10, "How New is the "New American Psychoanalysis?", Richards critiques Hoffman (1998) efforts to establish a paradigmatic shift. Richards wonders:

- Is this an attempt to render the old theories obsolete, to dismiss all that preceded the shift? Or, is this simply an attempt at self-promotion by inflating the uniqueness of one's views?

Richards uses Hoffman's evaluation of the concept of a "blank screen" and neutrality to illustrate how Hoffman's technical conclusions are limiting his intervention strategies. In contrast to Hoffman, Richards wonders:

- Whether the creation of a "predictable atmosphere," that allows for openness and compassion, is not only possible but essential?

Richards takes another tack and suggests a redefinition of the concept of neutrality. Using Freud's term of "Indifferenz," he asks:

- Doesn't "disinterestedness" whose essence is in the response of the analyst as detached contemplation better define the idea of neutrality?

CHAPTER 7

Transference Analysis: Means or End?

[Original version: Richards, A.D. (1984). Psychoanalytic Inquiry 4:355–366.]

I would like to begin with the definition of transference.

The patient is not satisfied with regarding the analyst in the light of reality as a helper and adviser who, moreover, is remunerated for the trouble he takes and who would himself be content with some such role as that of a guide on a difficult mountain climb. On the contrary, the patient sees in him the return, the reincarnation, of some important figure out of his childhood or past, and consequently transfers on to him feelings and reactions which undoubtedly applied to this prototype. This fact of transference soon proves to be a factor of undreamt-of importance, on the one hand an instrument of irreplaceable value and on the other hand a source of serious dangers. This transference is ambivalent: it comprises positive (affectionate) as well as negative (hostile) attitudes towards the analyst, who as a rule is put in the place of one or other of the patient's parents, his father or mother [Freud, 1940].

The Universality of Transference

An analysis without transference is an impossibility. It must not be supposed, however, that transference is created by analysis and does not occur apart from it. Transference is merely uncovered and isolated by analysis. It is a universal phenomenon of the human mind, it decides the success of all medical influence, and in fact dominates the whole of each person's relations to his human environment. We can easily recognize it as the same dynamic factor which the hypnotists have named 'suggestibility', which is the agent of hypnotic rapport and whose incalculable behaviour led to difficulties with the cathartic method as well. [Freud, 1925].

Over the years psychoanalysts have invoked different organizing frameworks as vehicles for theoretical and clinical discourse. The concept of "identity" was a prominent theme in the 1960s, to be supplanted by a focus on the "self" in the 1970s. Now, in the 1980s, preoccupation with the self and its vicissitudes is giving way to a revived interest in the psychoanalytic process per se. In part the result of a growing disillusionment with proliferating alternative theories, this renewed interest may have been kindled as well by the debate over Kohut's "self psychology" and its attentiveness to the role of empathy in the analytic transaction. Schafer's The Analytic Attitude (1983) and Anton Kris's Free Association: Method and Process (1983) exemplify this new focus on the psychoanalytic process. It is in this emerging tradition that Merton Gill's two-volume study, The Analysis of the Transference (Gill, 1982; Gill & Hoffman, 1982) must be situated as well. Like Schafer and Kris, Gill seeks to explicate the methods and goals of psychoanalysis by concentrating on a particular dimension of the analytic process. What narrative content is to Shafer and free association is to Kris, the analysis of transference is to Gill.

Gill's position is informed by the conviction that the analysis of the transference, which he considers "the heart of psychoanalytic technique," has not been consistently pursued in practice. By and large, he believes, analysts have concerned themselves with "classical genetic interpretation" at the expense of "the largely implicit manifestations of the transference in the current analytic situation" (p. 1). His conviction regarding the preeminent role of transference analysis proceeds from a definition of transference that encompasses virtually all aspects of the analytic interaction. He distinguishes, for example, between "conscious appropriate elements of the person's way of relating as manifestations of transference" and "inappropriate unconscious elements" (p. 10), adding that the so-called "unobjectionable" roots of transference cannot be excluded from clinical scrutiny. Here he takes issue with analysts like Zetzel (1956) and Greenson (1965) who believe that the "therapeutic" or "working" alliance is exempt from analytic scrutiny. He similarly disputes Leo Stone's notion of the "mature transference" (1961) as something to be partially gratified rather than analyzed.

Gill's perspective on transference interpretation is comparably broad, encompassing interpretations of resistance to the awareness of transference and interpretations of resistance to its resolution. It is mainly with respect to the first category that Gill propounds his main thesis regarding the technical centrality of transference analysis. In pointing to the analysand's "resistance to the awareness of transference," Gill is referring to associations containing implicit allusions to the transference—allusions the analysand cannot or will not recognize. Holding latent transference associations of this sort to be ubiquitous in analysis, he enjoins analysts to decipher their hidden transference meanings. This recommendation follows from his belief that analysts have to date stressed the analysis of resistance to transference resolution while paying insufficient attention to the more pervasive resistance to transference awareness. The latter resistance encompasses what analysts have traditionally characterized, somewhat confusedly, as defense transference, transference of defense, and defense against the transference. Gill's terminological proposal that we henceforth conceptualize transference phenomena in terms of "resistance to the awareness of transference," "resistance to the resolution of transference," and "resistance to involvement in transference" is a welcome advance over the prevailing nomenclature; his categories are experience-near, readily verifiable, and integral to the conduct of analyses.

But if Gill's attempt at terminological revision would seem unexceptionable and indeed useful, the same cannot be said of his claim that resistance is always expressed via transference. Gill correctly reminds us that resistance (unlike defense) is an interpersonal phenomenon manifesting itself only in the transference. His estimation of the compulsion to repeat as it operates in therapy is integral to his argument here. Citing Freud, he argues that resistance manifests itself primarily by repetition "both inside and outside the analytic situation." Without the compulsion to repeat, there would be no replication of the past and nothing for the analyst to analyze. Gill realizes, of course, that resistance may be rooted in id, ego, or superego; his point is that, whatever its source, resistance becomes evident and analyzable only in the analytic situation and with respect to the analyst. In adopting this position, Gill apparently wishes to impress upon us that when the analysand offers resistance to the discussion of a particular issue, thought, or fantasy, this resistance necessarily takes the form of a reluctance to relate the relevant information to the analyst. But Gill does not allow for the possibility that the analysand may be reluctant to acknowledge something to himself, with the reluctance to relay the relevant material to the analyst having a secondary, derivative quality. Certain patients, for example, may experience certain alterations in their ability to recall dreams, not simply because such recollections would involve reporting these dreams to their analysts, but also because the act of recollection involves painful (i.e., conflictual) self-awareness. Surely the term "resistance" may properly be applied to clinical situations of this sort as well as to those cited by Gill.

A similarly perceptive but overgeneralized insight is to be found in his core argument regarding the centrality of transference analysis. Pointing to the contributions of Bergmann and Hartman (1976), Gill contrasts the analytic stance of the "observer and purveyor of interpretation" with that of the participant observer who learns from the analytic interaction itself. In opting for the latter, Gill adopts a model of analysis based on the primacy of translating the patient's presenting neurosis into a transference neurosis. A consequence of this position (which, according to Gill and the sources he relies on, conforms to Freud's theory of technique though not to his technical practices) is a seeming depreciation of the analytic need to recover memories systematically. Gill believes that if resistance to awareness of the transference is overcome and the ensuing resistance to its resolution is worked through, then relevant childhood memories will automatically achieve consciousness.

In subordinating the recovery of early memories to transference analysis and thereby identifying the therapeutic action of analysis with the latter, Gill allies himself with Strachey's (1934) position. Like Strachey, Gill believes that only transference interpretations can be truly mutative. But Gill departs from Strachey, and from Leo Stone (1961) as well, in contesting the importance of additional, "extratransference" interpretations to the analytic process. Unlike Stone and Strachey, he rejects the theoretical possibility that in certain analyses the presenting neurosis might prove intractable to wholesale translation into the transference neurosis. He believes such translation can always be effected, without residue, provided the analyst does what is clinically necessary to facilitate expansion of the transference in the analytic situation. Just how this expansion is to occur—through what particular analytic activities and through what degree of analytic activity—is the crucial issue here. In general, he would seem to view this expansion as directly proportional to the degree of activity. He argues against an inactive stance that assumes the transference will emerge and clarify itself spontaneously; "on the contrary," he quotes Glover (1955, p. 130), "the transference-neurosis in the first instance feeds on transference-interpretation" (p. 62). Gill disclaims, to be sure, any reading that would take his stress on transference interpretation as a calculating disregard of other elements of the patient's life; he forcefully insists, however, that it is necessary to work on the premise that of the many things the patient could associate to, his choice is often dictated by a topic which can serve as resistance to the transference. It is therefore the transference implication that matters for the process. Thus Gill does not view early interpretive activity as simply mobilizing a transference readiness (Nunberg, 1951), but rather as exposing and overcoming transference "resistances" intrinsic to the analytic transaction from the very outset. In his insistence that the analyst continually exert himself to enlighten the patient as to the transferential "hidden meaning" of everything being said, Gill ultimately equates the analytic process itself with educating the patient to accept transference interpretation as the royal road to understanding psychopathology—and hence to cure.

In the second volume of The Analysis of Transference Gill and his collaborator Hoffman attempt to verify their claim that "transference is organized around significant contributions from the analyst in the here and now." To this end, they present, and offer commentary on, the transcripts of nine therapeutic sessions. It should be noted at the outset that only six of these sessions come from analyses, and one of these was with a patient seen sitting up. The remaining three patients were seen in therapy once a week. Of five sessions conducted by therapists attempting to apply Gill's point of view, three involved the once-a-week-therapy patients and one involved the analytic patient who did not use the couch. In sum, then, Gill and Hoffman present us with four "bad" analytic sessions, one "good" analytic session, one "good" analytic session in which the patient was seen sitting up, and three "good" psychotherapy sessions. They do not tell us how they arrived at this selection of sessions, or why they elected to analyze the sessions in vacuo—i.e., without the benefit of any historical background material or clinical data from earlier or later sessions. It is particularly regrettable that we have but one "good" analytic case conducted on the couch. A rigorous test of their proposals would require more adequate clinical data, perhaps a combination of longitudinal case studies with verbatim transcripts of pivotal sessions.

As a result of these methodological problems, Gill and Hoffman are more persuasive in criticizing sessions evincing faulty technique than in demonstrating the unquestioned primacy of here-and-now transference interpretation in those they deem successful. In their discussion of Patient B, for example, they have little difficulty demonstrating the inappropriateness of a penis meaning arbitrarily imputed to the patient's dream associations by the analyst. More perceptively, they point to the analyst's failure to appreciate the import of a significant interaction at the analyst's door as the session began: the patient expressed her perception of the analyst as impatient and critical on opening the door. Rather than probing the meaning of this perception in terms of issues, say, of initiative and self-assertion, the analyst permitted the session to begin with a four-minute silence.

In the case of Patient C, Gill and Hoffman criticize the similarly forced imputation of castration meaning on the productions of a woman patient. When this patient responded angrily to the interpretation, adding that she wished to knock all the analyst's books off the wall, the analyst responded in turn that this latter wish was really a wish to knock his penis off. Gill and Hoffman deem this remark "an almost unbelievably pat interpretation that exemplifies our point: Instead of finding out what she means by wanting to knock down his books, the analyst uses what she has said to reiterate his fixed conviction—which she has just characterized as unhelpful" (p. 58). Interestingly enough, however, this patient proceeded to relate books and reading to compensatory feelings for not having a penis; thus, as Gill and Hoffman subsequently acknowledge, the session may actually provide an example of a correct interpretation proceeding from faulty technique. Gill's point is that the analyst had in any event missed the fact that the patient experienced him as an unreasonable dictator and that this perception was based on the patient's actual experience of the analyst: he indeed seemed to foist interpretations on the patient without due concern for either the evidence or her feelings.

In the case of Patient D, Gill and Hoffman discuss a session in which the patient responded to the analyst's interpretation with the remark, "That's obvious now." They point to the analyst's failure to analyze their comment as a "significant and common flaw." Their insistence that analysts attend to the pseudocompliant aspects of such seemingly facile acceptance of interpretations is certainly a useful technical proviso, but there is no way of determining whether their inference about Patient D is correct on the basis of the transcript of this single session. Had the patient's "That's obvious now" generated relevant memories or associations, or a modulation of the character trait being explored, it might well have betokened a deepening of the analytic process and a working through of the patient's comprehension of the issues.

It is with respect to Patient A that Gill and Hoffman provide examples of what they mean by inferring latent transference meaning from the overt products of the patient. To give but one example: the patient tells an involved story about her cat and the ASPCA. This agency delayed in treating the cat for an illness, and the animal subsequently died. The authors comment that "the cat died because they fooled around instead of operating. The latent meaning may be that the analyst's silence is doing nothing and the analysis may die. She may be growing increasingly angry at his inactivity" (p. 19). Now this interpretation is surely one possibility, but it is the only one? How can the analyst know this to be the case? The only technical dictum that follows from clinical data of this sort is that the analyst must "listen" to the patient's productions and attempt to "read" unconscious meanings and themes in them. These meanings and themes invariably pertain to wishes and fantasies, which, to be sure, may include transference wishes and fantasies. But the analyst can hardly assume that such wishes and fantasies are necessarily limited to the patient's reactions to the analyst in the here-and-now. In many cases, the discernment of unconscious meanings will proceed from the analyst's sense of what has transpired in recent sessions, from his understanding of the latent content of a series of dreams—indeed, from his cumulative knowledge of the entire analysis to that point. The analyst's imputation of unconscious meaning proceeds from a complex process of "knowing," which must take into account the patient's achieved level of cognitive, intuitive, and empathic functioning. This presupposes an ongoing attentiveness to a whole host of nonverbal cues, bodily movements, and additional data processed by what is sometimes called the "analytic instrument." When the analyst, on the basis of this material, undertakes to communicate his inference of unconscious meaning to the patient via an interpretation, he must synthesize knowledge from a variety of sources, judge the adequacy and persuasive force of the evidence for a connection between current productions and latent meaning, and make a further judgment as to the patient's readiness to assimilate the interpretation.

The problem with Gill and Hoffman's clinical strategies, as with Gill's theoretical exposition, is that they seem to skew the interpretive process along a single dimension. The patient speaks, and the analyst thinks, "What is the patient trying to say about me and the analytic situation?" It seems to me that the aggressive pursuit of transference meaning may actually impair the analyst's "hovering" attention, his ability to attend to the range of unconscious meanings intrinsic to the productions of the analysand. The result may well be a tendency to respond to the patient's productions in a stereotypical, automatic way. Transference fantasies and attitudes in the here-and-now are indeed important and may even warrant a certain priority in our interpretive strategies. An entire analysis, however, cannot be spent analyzing the patient's feelings about the analyst's silences, missed sessions, vacations, aspects of the analyst's office, and the like. Ultimately, transference analysis must be absorbed in the broader attempt to uncover and understand significant unconscious wishes and fantasies which emerge in childhood and, via the compulsion to repeat, continue to affect the patient's current life adjustment.

It is with this caveat in mind that we must assess Gill's closely reasoned principles of psychoanalytic interpretation. The issue of the relative importance of transference analysis with respect to, say, genetic interpretation and noninterpretive activities pursuant to the establishment of a holding environment cannot be addressed in topical isolation; it is an issue secondary to the more encompassing question of the nature of therapeutic change. Gill's presentation, cogent though it is in certain respects, does not systematically address the precise relationship of transference analysis to the principal constituents of cure—i.e., structural changes in the personality. These include the realignment and alteration of defenses, the removal of inhibitions, and the lifting of repressions.

The criticism to which Gill's prescriptions are subject are those invited by any conceptual tour de force intent on establishing the preeminence of a perspective which, its proponents argue, has not received its just due. Despite his illuminating terminological suggestions and his persuasive case for the importance of transference analysis, Gill fails to prove the ubiquity of transference meanings or to demonstrate that analysis in fact amounts to transference interpretation. All analysts have worked with analysands for whom "transference" indeed seemed to lurk everywhere, but this clinical impression can hardly be taken as evidence that everything such patients are concerned with relates to the transference. Moreover, we often deal with patients who simply do not develop transference neuroses; our understanding of them and the implications of this understanding for our theoretical conceptualizations continue to be hotly debated. Even Gill seems to retreat from the extreme one-sidedness of his views in his chapter on "Transference and the Actual Analytic Situation." Here he attempts to differentiate between the "positive transference" rooted in the past and those "realistic" cognitive attitudes which, he admits, are appropriate to the actual analytic situation. We now learn that such attitudes, "which do not have the same interpersonally determined roots in the past," must also be taken into account in matters of technique. Similarly, he points out that the distinction between the analyst's "technical" and "personal" roles should not be collapsed, reasoning that the analyst's "real behavior" and the patient's realistic attitude toward this behavior are also part of the psychoanalytic process. These admissions, inconsistent with his basic views, stand out as a brief but telling exception to his otherwise continuing insistence that the analysand's "realistic" attitudes invariably mask transference meanings that the analyst is duty bound to uncover.

The strengths and limitations of Gill's position can be highlighted by positing three extreme approaches to the analytic situation: (1) an approach emphasizing the analyst's passivity, inaction, and silence; (2) an approach involving the aggressive pursuit and uncovering of repressed childhood memories; and (3) an approach involving the aggressive pursuit and interpretative uncovering of latent transference meanings in everything the patient says or does. I am to a certain extent sympathetic to Gill's argument, for I believe the pursuit of transference meaning to be the least dangerous of the three to therapy. Gill is correct in maintaining that it is ultimately the transference that is the most difficult dimension of analysis for the patient to discuss and for the analyst to conceptualize. To this degree, Gill's work provides a valuable corrective; he alerts us to the fact that analysts probably err more often by being too inactive or too intent on interpreting "deep" meanings than from an overzealous pursuit of transference meanings. Nonetheless, exclusive commitment to any one of these approaches will interfere with the unfolding analytic process. The three orientations are not mutually exclusive, a point that is particularly clear with respect to the integral relationship between the recovery of childhood memories and the development of the transference and the analytic process. Analysts are surely familiar with the ways in which the recovery of early memories facilitates both the unfolding of the transference and the patient's understanding of its nature. But it is equally true that the experience of the here-and-now transference leads to the recovery of memories centrally implicated in the analysand's psychopathology. The analyst, we might say, functions from both inside and outside, simultaneously participating in the here-and-now interaction and providing interpretations from his "observer" vantage point; he is both observer and observer participant, or, to put it somewhat differently, he is not merely an observer participant but simultaneously a participant and an observer. In Gill's presentation, it is the complex, interdependent nature of the analyst's multiple orientations toward the analysand that is occasionally obscured.

The same criticism may be leveled at Gill's repeated insistence that translation of the presenting neurosis into a transference neurosis is the "aim" of analysis and is, as such, central to its therapeutic efficacy. As an abstract commentary on the analytic process, this formulation is theoretically unassailable. But Gill's extreme position overlooks the fact that, as therapists, we are continually dealing with a means-end problem that calls for flexible clinical judgment. The goal of psychoanalytic treatment is to provide the analysand with insight that will enable him to achieve significant personality change on behalf of enhanced creativity and productivity in his work life, along with more satisfactory adaptation in his human relationships. Analysis of the transference is a central means to this end, certainly, but is not tantamount to it: the goal of analysis is not merely to leave the patient with a "resolved" relationship with his analyst. In view of the differing needs of different analysands, it is not self-evidently true that resistance to the awareness of transference must be relentlessly pursued by the analyst, as if every stone must be turned to see if some hidden transference meaning might be found lurking beneath it. Does translation of the presenting neurosis into a transference neurosis really require this dogged pursuit of transference meanings in virtually everything the analysand says or does in a given session? In arguing that this is the case, Gill unwarrantedly assumes that throughout the course of treatment analysis is the preeminent activity—and the analyst the preeminent object—for every analysand. Although this situation may frequently obtain when a patient first enters analysis, even here we overlook the significant others in the new analysand's childhood and current life only at great clinical peril. To be sure, attitudes toward childhood figures are inevitably transferred onto the analyst along with the strong affects associated with such attitudes, but the power underlying these affects originates from, and continues to be connected to, the important primary objects in the life of the analysand.

In short, the here-and-now transference may be pursued so vigorously and exclusively that the genetic roots of transference conflicts in infantile sexuality and aggression may ultimately be lost in the transferential shuffle. It is always a test of clinical judgment to work out, in the context of the psychopathology and therapeutic requirements of a given analysand, an appropriate balance between analytic interventions focusing on primary objects and those focusing on relationships to these objects as mediated by the unfolding transference. This basic fact of clinical psychoanalytic life belies Gill's formulaic zeal regarding the preeminence of transference interpretations; it further belies the associated belief that patients can be "taught" that analysis of the transference is central to their psychopathology and ultimate cure. Such "learning" can occur only when a specific series of associations and interpretations makes it self-evident to the analysand that the transference and its analysis have indeed become crucial to therapeutic progress. The analysand's appreciation of the transference can only be the dynamic by-product of a successful analytic process. If it were constitutive of that process, its necessary precondition, analysis could never begin nor, on Gill's assumptions, would it have to.

As I began with Freud, I would like to end with Freud's (1925) words on the role of transference in the psychoanalytic technique:

> It is perfectly true that psychoanalysis, like other psychotherapeutic methods, employs the instrument of suggestion (or transference). But the difference is this: that in analysis it is not allowed to play the decisive part in determining the therapeutic results. It is used instead to induce the patient to perform a piece of psychical work—the overcoming of his transference resistances—which involves a permanent alteration in his mental economy. The transference is made conscious to the patient by the analyst, and it is resolved by convincing him that in his transference-attitude he is re-experiencing emotional relations which had their origin in his earliest object-attachments during the repressed period of his childhood. In this way the transference is changed from the strongest weapon of the resistance into the best instrument of the analytic treatment. Nevertheless its handling remains the most difficult as well as the most important part of the technique of analysis (Freud, 1925).

REFERENCES

BERGMANN, M.S. & HARTMAN, F.C. (1976). The Evolution of Psychoanalytic Technique. New York: Basic Books.

FREUD, S. (1925). An autobiographical study. *Standard Edition* 20:1–74.

——— (1940). An outline of psycho-analysis. *International Journal of Psycho-analysis* 21:27–84.

GILL, M. (1982). Analysis of Transference, vol. I: Theory and Technique: *Psychological Issues, Monograph 53.* New York: International Universities Press.

——— & HOFFMAN, I.Z. (1982). Analysis of Transference, vol. II: Studies of Nine Audio-Recorded Sessions. *Psychological Issues, Monograph 54.* New York: International Universities Press.

GLOVER, E. (1955). *The Technique of Psycho-Analysis.* New York: International Universities Press.

GREENSON, R. (1965). The working alliance and the transference neurosis. *Psychoanalytic Quarterly* 34:155–181.

KRIS, A. (1983). *Free Association: Method and Process.* New Haven: Yale University Press.

NUNBERG, H. (1951). Transference and reality. *International Journal of Psycho-analysis* 32:1–9.

SCHAFER, R. (1983). *The Analytic Attitude.* New York: Basic Books.

STONE, L. (1961). *The Psychoanalytic Situation.* New York: International Universities Press.

STRACHEY, J. (1934). The nature of the therapeutic action of psychoanalysis. *International Journal of Psycho-analysis* 15:127–159.

ZETZEL, E. (1956). *The concept of transference. In The Capacity for Emotional Growth.* New York: International Universities Press, 1970, pp. 168–181.

CHAPTER 8

Merton Gill: A View of His Place in the "Freudian" Firmament

[Richards, A.D. & Lynch, A.A. (1996). *The Annual of Psychoanalysis*, 24:49–61.]

Merton Gill's psychoanalytic career spanned the 50 years from the early 1940s to 1994, what some might consider the American era of psychoanalysis. The early part of that period had the major figures of continental psychoanalysis (primarily from Central Europe, Austria, and Germany) torn from their roots and dispersed mostly to New York City but also to Chicago, Los Angeles, Philadelphia, San Francisco, and Boston. The development of psychoanalysis was affected, to varying degrees, by where emigrés settled and by their interaction with their American colleagues.

Those rescued by the New York Psychoanalytic Committee, most of them Viennese, accepted the invitation to become a part of that society and, in effect, took over. Hartmann, Kris, Loewenstein, Nunberg, Robert Bak, Edith Jacobson, and the Eisslers established themselves as the dominant theoretical and political force in New York, and their influence carried over to other institutes as well. Sandor Lorand, for example, founded the Downstate (now NYU) Institute. Influential Europeans on the West Coast included the Bernfelds, the Simmels, the Fenichels, and Susan Deri. Although the psychoanalytic community in Topeka, Kansas, where Gill trained, was primarily American, David Rapaport, a Hungarian whom Karl Menninger had found working in a state hospital, transmitted the echt Freudian vision, corpus, and doctrine to his coworkers and students there (and later in Stockbridge, Massachusetts).

Merton Gill's career in psychoanalysis can be viewed as part of a turn that American psychoanalysis took in its increasing disenchantment with Freud's Central European metapsychology. It is no accident that two of the foremost psychoanalytic theoreticians who maintain aspects of the form, if not the content, of metapsychology are European born. Both Otto Kernberg's theories and Heinz Kohut's psychology of the self include a set of reified concepts that have the same Central

European flavor as Freud's. The repudiation of metapsychology by Rapaport's students—Gill, Roy Schafer, George Klein, Robert Holt—is well known and has been underscored by Irwin Hoffman's (1996) recent contribution, "Merton Gill: A Study in Theory Development in Psychoanalysis." What Hoffman does not mention is yet another American psychoanalytic theoretical line that has moved to question the place of reified structures and agencies in psychoanalytic theory. That line is represented by Charles Brenner, Leo Rangell, Jacob Arlow, Sandor Abend, David Beres, Dale Boesky and their collegues and associates.

Like Gill, they have moved in the direction of questioning the drive and energetic aspects of Freud's metapsychology. Arlow and Brenner, in their 1964 monograph, valorize the structural model over the economic model, championing it as the proper framework for psychoanalytic theory and explanation. Most recently, Brenner, in his paper "Mind as conflict and compromise formation" (1994) has come down full force against the notion of psychic agency. Brenner here is espousing a position very similar to that taken first by Schafer (1976) and by Gill (1976). It is striking to us that Gill and Schafer, on the one side, and Brenner and his colleagues, on the other, fail to recognize the convergence of their approaches to psychoanalytic theory. In our view, Gill and Arlow and Brenner take a similar route. Hoffman (1996) cites Apfelbaum as describing Gill's monograph *Topography and Systems in Psychoanalytic Theory* (1963) as "giving the coup de grace to the topographic model" (p. 12). The Arlow and Brenner work published in 1964 is similarly critical of the topographic model.

Gill (1963) precedes Arlow and Brenner, however, in raising questions about "the validity of the structural model in so far as it connotes a set of internally consistent, relatively well demarcated systems of the mind" (Hoffman, 1996, p. 14). Gill is anticipating by almost 30 years a position arrived at by Brenner. Hoffman (1996) refers to Gill as moving toward a "holistic approach, which places the whole person at the center of the theory" (p. 14). The parallel here is Brenner's replacement of the concept of the ego with his reference to the person. Hoffman (1996) observes that Gill's proposals are actually quite radical since, in challenging the structural model they argue instead for an emphasis on continuity. Again, Arlow and Brenner, too, are all more comfortable with a continuum point of view. Their discussion of psychoanalytic theories of psychosis, where they stress the continuance between neurosis and psychosis, is a clear case in point. And finally, Gill's moving from what Hoffman refers to as "an energy discharge point of view," as distinct from a "person point of view," in psychoanalysis is paralleled by Brenner's shift from instinctual drives to personally unique wishes.

There are, of course, fundamental differences in outlook between Merton Gill and the other Americans. In his wide-ranging essay on Gill's work, Hoffman (1996) points out the centrality of Gill's perspectivism and its social basis and the centrality of "interpersonal human relatedness and human interactions" (p. 25). Moreover, Gill's emphasis on "the psychoanalytic situation as one in which two people interact and continually try to establish the meaning of that interaction as one of them experiences it" (p. 25) is a far cry from Arlow and Brenner's conception of psychoanalytic technique, which privileges a neutral analyst and a more positivist epistemology. But here again, one can make the case that there is some movement on the part of Arlow and Brenner towards Gill's position. Arlow (1995), for example, refers to psychoanalysis and the analytic process as conversations. Hoffman (1996) refers to Gill's stressing "the irrelevance of the arrangement—either the frequency of visits or the use of the couch—to a definition of technique" (p. 36). Likewise, Brenner (1995) does not view the use of the couch as essential for the conduct of a psychoanalysis.

Although Gill has been adopted by the relationalists and interpersonalists as someone who is firmly in their camp, a careful reading of his last work, *Psychoanalysis in Transition,* raises some questions about locating him in this way. Charles Spezzano (1995), reviewing the book in the Psychologist Psychoanalyst, represents the American Psychoanalytic Association and Merton Gill as having a less-than-positive relationship. In fact, however, when Gill was being considered for the Sigourney Award, eighty members of the American Psychoanalytic Association signed a letter on his behalf, and that number could have been increased severalfold without much difficulty.

The question of whether, in the end, Gill was a Freudian or a relational/interpersonal analyst is not a simple one. In his last book, he writes that "it remains true that the great discovery peculiar to psychoanalysis, the internal factor in the sense of unconscious fantasy, is the one that psychoanalysis must zealously protect" (1994, p. 28). This view of the fundamental core of psychoanalysis is profoundly Freudian but more in keeping, we think, with the position of writers such as Arlow, Brenner, and Boesky than it is with the theoretical stance of Mitchell, Greenberg,

Aron, and others. What separates Gill's thinking from that of the developing relationalist tradition is Gill's discomfort with dichotomies of any stripe. He (1994) writes,

> It is equally important to make clear that to speak of internal and external factors as though they were a simple dichotomy is false. In human psychological functioning the external world is significantly constructed by the internal world and the internal world is significantly constructed by the external world. In short, we deal with the mutually interactive constructivist circle. I am taking the position that their dichotomy, in the sense of simple independent entities, is epistemologically untenable [p. 16].

If one views the drive/relational dichotomy as indeed a variant or subset of the internal/external dichotomy, one sees Gill as firmly positioning himself against Mitchell's approach, for example. But Gill argues against the dichotomist position for classical analysis as well as for relational psychoanalysis. He writes (1994) that, in classical analysis,

> Subject and object remain dichotomous. The subject construes the object, but if the analyst differs with the analysand about how an object is to be construed, the analysand's construal tends to be regarded as a distortion. It is recognized that sometimes it is the analyst who is mistaken if he differs with the analysand, but the analyst's misconstrual then tends to be regarded as an unfortunate countertransference departure from objectivity [p. 17].

We would argue that Gill is overstating the case here and that there is nothing inherent in classical psychoanalytic theory that necessitates viewing the analysand's misconstruals as distortions or the analyst's misconstruals as countertransferential. Rather, the differences are probably a matter more of personality than of theoretical persuasion. There are certainly analysts, of all persuasions, who are convinced that they are always right and who tend toward that position with the analysand. Gill's conviction that the dichotomy of object and subject exists in classical analysis goes along with his conviction that it is overcome by the constructivist position, which recognizes "the constraints, or, more generally the influences, that each exerts on the other" (1994, p. 17). Nevertheless, we ourselves have relied on a reasoned approach very similar to Gill's (Bachant, Lynch, and Richards, 1992; 1995a).

Gill extends this constructivist point of view, applying it to transference; the result is a redefinition of "transference and countertransference as being contributed to by both participants and being shaped by one another" (1994, p. 17). The central proposition of classical analysis, at least as defined by writers such as Brenner, is that transference is ubiquitous in human nature, and if that is the case, it makes sense to believe that there are distortions in perceptions on both sides such that the perceptions are determined by the contributions of each participant. Arlow's (1969) image of two projectors showing on the same screen is an especially vivid metaphor for the relationship between subject and object, and it may not be pushing things too far to offer it as a model of co-constructive perceptions, with contributions by subject and object.

Following from this conception, Gill considers the self-psychological view of the relationship between self and object denoted by the term selfobject. Here Gill contrasts a classical view of narcissistic transference, which implies a developmental push toward autonomy and mutuality, with selfobject transferences, where the selfobject tie is part of normal development and "remains a life-long necessity," with autonomy given somewhat short shrift.

Gill sees the relational school, exemplified by the work of Mitchell, as constructivist and thus regards the subject and object as shaping each other. It is hard to find disagreement on this score, but less clear is the claim that classical analysis leaves out the mutual influences of subject and object. Anna Freud and other ego psychologists, for example, who stress the influences of id, ego, and superego on reality, recognize the mutual influences of reality externals and intrapsychic internals. It may be that Kleinian theory, which "sees the infant's construal of the parental object as determined solely by the infant's fantasies and unrelated to the qualities of the object" (Gill, 1994, p. 18), involves the kind of selfobject dichotomization that Gill attributes to the more mainstream contemporary Freudian point of view. Gill brilliantly demonstrates the complexity of Freud's own approach to the relationship between internal and external. After reviewing several texts of Freud's, he notes, "So here we find Freud, the champion of the innate, insisting that the innate should be considered seriously only after an exhaustive effort to account for a phenomenon by experience. In Haeckel's terms, this would translate as ontogeny taking precedence over phylogeny, in matters of technique at least" (1994, p. 22).

In short, Gill was able to maintain this reasoned point of view because he was not engaged in political efforts to establish the hegemony of one "new" point of view against an allegedly "old" point of view—to establish a school, to attract candidates, to become a leader. Gill was committed to exploring psychoanalysis as a scientific and intellectual discipline and as a clinical practice, rather than to promoting internecine warfare that divided the psychoanalytic landscape into rival camps. He very nicely lines out the internal and external distinctions in psychoanalysis—constitution versus experience, innate versus experiential, drive versus object relational, intrapsychic versus interpersonal, fantasies versus perceptions, psychic reality versus material reality, inner world versus outer world, and asocial versus social—and cogently remarks that, although the pairs are presented dichotomously, "the controversy is actually a matter of emphasis or hierarchy" (p. 24).

Gill quotes a passage from Freud's introduction to *Group Psychology and the Analysis of the Ego* (1921) that lays the basic theme for the entire work: "In the individual's mental life someone else is invariably involved, as a model, as an object, as a helper, as an opponent; and so from the very first, individual psychology, in this extended but entirely justifiable sense of the words, is at the same time social psychology as well" (Freud, 1921, p. 69). Gill notes how the concepts of intrapsychic and interpersonal are understood for their connotative, rather than their denotative, value. This follows as well for the equation of innate drives with the intrapsychic and of experience with the interpersonal. Gill rejects these paired antitheses as a misleading caricature, since the intrapsychic and the interpersonal are, in fact, both recognized in the other. He emphasizes, as do current classical theorists, that "of singular importance is to avoid adopting a general position on the relative importance of the two factors [internal and external]. Each case . . . must be decided on its own merits. . . . Deciding where the emphasis should lie in a particular instance remains the art of psychoanalysis" (p. 27). This fundamental clinical principle holds true for all theoretical concepts applied to the psychoanalytic situation.

Starting in the section "One-Person and Two-Person Psychology" and extending through the piece on "Theory and Technique," Gill focuses on the technical concepts that affect the psychoanalytic situation and the psychoanalytic process. "One-Person and Two-Person

Psychology," which reviews transference, alliance, and silence as an interaction, opens with the observation that the intrapsychic structure can be considered from a one-person psychology when seen as a closed system and from a two-person psychology when interaction between the internal and the external is stressed. Noting that Freud's theory always comprised both viewpoints, Gill adds that the focus on drives led to the depiction of Freudian thinking as a one-person psychology. Here again we would argue that it is a matter of emphasis as well as a matter of denying drive. The difference in emphasis in contemporary classical perspectives can be seen in the works of Schwaber and Sandler. Schwaber (1983, 1986) stresses the intrapsychic dimension of the analysand's subjectivity. She appraises her own feeling states as a measure for understanding the analytic interactions from the analysand's experience. Sandler (1976a) suggests that only through compromise can the analyst come to appreciate the value of the reciprocal interactions between intrapsychic self and object representation, as well as with the external world. Within the representational field, Sandler emphasizes the affective nature of the relatedness. This is strikingly similar to Brenner's concept of drive derivative and its accompanying affect state. These two approaches also highlight different features of the analyst. Schwaber holds for an intrapsychic focus in which the analyst puts aside his or her subjectivity and engages the analysand's experience. For Sandler, on the other hand, the analyst's personality is continually and inescapably communicated to the analysand and therefore always greatly influences the impact of the analytic interventions. Schwaber's and Sandler's views of the analyst are not mutually exclusive; they are a matter of emphasis that requires a broad and adaptable framework. Gill (1994) notes that analysts have always worked in both one-person and two-person contexts (p. 40), a point we have supported elsewhere (Bachant, Lynch, and Richards, 1995b). Current concepts of drives and their derivatives are also highly interactional, as we will discuss.

Turning to the transference, Gill states that the analyst always participates in its construction. The analyst must acknowledge having "contributed to what he is now passing judgment on" (p. 36). This contribution may be experienced with a sense of uncertainty and vagueness; in fact, the basis of the analyst's contribution may not be known. Gill next examines the concept of alliance, which he sees as an attempt "to correct what had come to be considered the overly rigid, withdrawn, silent stance of the analyst" (p. 41). In following Freud's evolution of the concept from the unobjectionable positive transference to the analytic alliance, Gill points out how this alliance reflects a true transference as well as being an outgrowth of the analytic process. He supports his position by citing Stein (1981), who argues that the unobjectionable positive transference can itself function as a critical resistance. Gill also cites Stone's (1961) attempt to change the view of the analyst as "the uninvolved bystander" (p. 43). Interestingly enough, Gill criticizes Brenner's (1979) view of the working alliance as tending to encourage deviation from analysis when invoked as grounds for reassuring the patient. Our reading of Brenner on this issue is similar to Gill's. Brenner does not see the working alliance as extending beyond the transference and as uninterpretable. He also doubts whether it can be facilitated by anything other than precise and well-timed interpretations and so, like Gill, believes it is "an outgrowth of the work if it goes well" (Gill, 1994, p. 43).

Throughout his career, Gill focused a great deal of attention on the topic of transference, and in his final work, he emphasizes the analyst's co-construction of the transference and its essential position in the analysis. He charts the underexplored dimension of constructivism in the transference, while maintaining the need for both a one- and two-person context. Elsewhere, we (Bachant, Lynch, and Richards, 1995a) have reviewed the relational theorists' concept of transference. Here we will simply focus on the evolution of the classical theory of transference to which Gill and others have contributed. In *Psychoanalysis in Transition,* Gill touches, but does not elaborate, on the spectrum of interactions involving the concept of transference, including acting out, transference actualization, countertransference, and enactment. Like Gill, we have noted (Bachant, Lynch, and Richards, 1995a) that, conceptually, interaction lies at the center of the transference. Freud (1905b, 1912, 1915b), Loewenstein (1969), Bird (1972), and Brenner (1982) have all pointed out how these dynamics are found in all adult relationships. By the early 1940s, Fenichel (1941) had reemphasized the role of reality by noting that all relationships are a mixture of realistic and transference reactions (p. 72). Although relying on the mirror metaphor, he redefined its use of the metaphor: "The statement that the analyst is only a mirror has been misunderstood. It has been correctly emphasized (by Bibring-Lehner [1936]) that the personality of the analyst influences the transference. Different analysts act differently and these differences influence the behavior of patients" (p. 72). This early insight has led to our current focus on the spectrum of interactions. The classical analyst's commitment continues to be analysis of the conflicts that persist in shaping the analysand's perception of the analyst and the world. In the classical approach, transference is distinguished from other perspectives by the analyst's ability to understand and use the transference in analyzing psychic conflict.

Current theorists have focused on transference actualization as an evolving construct (Sandler, 1976a, b; Sandler and Sandler, 1978; McLaughlin 1981, 1991; Boesky, 1982; Chused, 1991; Panel, 1992). Dynamically, the analysand, cued from many potential sources, seeks to shape the analyst's actions and attitudes with the aim of fulfilling wishes or expectations. Most signifiers come from the analytic interaction. In highly complex forms of communication, the analysand depicts what is left out and what is followed, from the conspicuous to the elusive shifts in expression, for example, in form and content.

Unfortunately, Gill does not dedicate a section of *Psychoanalysis in Transition* to countertransference. He does, however, redefine the concept as "being contributed to by both participants and shaped by one another" (1994, p. 17). McLaughlin (1981), approaching this position, believes that counter-transference is the transference of the analyst in an analytic situation and does not require a separate term. Brenner (1976, 1985) attempts a fresh approach by asserting that "counter-transference is ubiquitous and inescapable, just as is transference" (1985, p. 156). Both Brenner and McLaughlin view this phenomenon as multiply determined by the analyst's personal life, as well as by the manifold impingements of the private worlds of his patients. So far as we can see, these insights parallel Gill's contributions.

When we include the concept of enactments, we see the similarity even more clearly. McLaughlin (1991) offers a broad and a narrow definition of enactment. The broad definition encompasses all behaviors of the analytic participants. The narrow definition denotes "those regressive (defensive) interactions between the pair experienced by either as a consequence of the behavior of the other" (p. 595). The narrow definition provides a better perspective for attending to the intrapsychic dynamics of both participants that contribute to the interaction. Unlike others, McLaughlin (1991) does not assert that enactments must re-enact the dynamic under consideration. In a panel on interaction (Panel, 1992), he further specifies that enactments are "events within the analytic relationship experienced as interpersonal happenings co-constituted by both parties in consequence of shared regression" (p. 828).

Clinically and conceptually, enactments and actualizations are attempts to describe a more sophisticated and elaborate understanding of interactions in the analytic process. Enactments "serve as indispensable guides in our efforts to explore the subtle and pervasive interactions between patient and analyst that form the core of the analytic process" (Jacobs, 1986, p. 836). Like Gill, these theorists have worked within the one-person/two-person and the constructivist/positivist dialectics. Gill equates the latter dialectical tension with constructivism. "A construction," writes Gill (1994), "is subject to the constraints of reality even if we cannot say what reality really is" (p. 2).

In the section on "Neutrality," Gill addresses the clinical construct of neutrality and redefines it: "The analyst is always influencing the patient, and the patient is always influencing the analyst. This mutual influence cannot be avoided; it can only be interpreted. It is the analyst's awareness of this unremitting influence of patient and analyst on each other and his attempt to make that influence as explicit as possible that constitute his 'neutrality'" (Gill, 1994, p. 50). Gill begins with Anna Freud's (1936) definition of neutrality, in which the analyst keeps an equidistance from id, ego, and superego, not siding with any agency's strivings. He also cites Levy and Inderbitzin's (1992) suggestion that neutrality extends to external reality. But his discussion proceeds to show how misdirected treatment becomes when neutrality is taken to mean noninvolvement. He comes away from this discussion defining one of the goals of analytic treatment: "to understand that everything we say and don't say, do and don't do, in interpersonal relations has interactive implications" (p. 54). And further: "Once an analytic situation is established so that the two participants are agreed on the centrality of the analysis of interaction, it may be helpful to relax the strictures against interaction for a more effective therapy" (p. 57).

But has classical psychoanalysis been so far off the mark as to prescribe noninvolvement with analysands? Does neutrality equal noninvolvement? Freud didn't see it that way. Rather he thought that the analytic situation served to facilitate the transference (Freud, 1905b, 1912). The analyst's work was to elucidate the transference through interpretation and reconstruction and not to try and create them. The analyst attempted to maintain a position of neutrality to facilitate the analysand's contact with inner experience so that fantasies about the analyst could be more clearly observed. Freud (1913) showed that neutrality did not mean cold detachment or loss of spontaneity and recommended an attitude of "sympathetic understanding" (p. 140). Earlier, Freud alluded to the analyst's need for neutrality in his observation that "no psychoanalyst goes further than his own complexes and internal resistances permit" (1910a, p. 145). Later he added that "we ought not to give up the neutrality towards the patient, which we have acquired through keeping the countertransference in check" (1915b, p. 164).

Neutrality is critical to the interpretive process. And Gill is correct when he indicates that noninvolvement is destructive to this process. But neutrality involves more than a technique of listening with impartiality and an approach that favors interpretation over influence in the resolution of conflict (A. Freud, 1936); it implies as well a *state of receptivity* in the analyst, an inner neutrality in which the analyst is able to listen to, understand, and meet the diverse demands and conflicts of the analysand with interest and without conviction. That is to say, the analyst must not be unduly impeded by the unconscious conflicts of the analysand. Jacobs (1991) has pointed out that the tensions and disharmonies between these two aspects of the analyst's neutrality frequently underlie its countertransference distortions.

In the section entitled "Free Association and the Analytic Process," Gill questions whether free association should be defined as the patient's response to the analyst's instruction to free associate or as a manifestation of primary process. He opts for the former. Gill explores how the instruction to free associate can variously become an authoritarian stance, an expanded communication, an altered state of consciousness, a resistance, a primary-process production, or a one- or two-person situation or a combination of both. Maintaining his emphasis on interaction, Gill concludes that "analysis is a two-person situation" (p. 92). Later, he elaborates this definition: "A truly interactive concept is one in which both parties are contributing to an interaction, not one in which one party is merely responding to the other" (p. 103). Free associations for Gill are necessarily coherent communications, and over the course of an analysis, the forms become more coherent still. Arlow (1975) also agrees that the process of analysis is progressive. Like Freud (1926), Arlow refers to the analytic process as conversations. In a similar vein, Brenner (1995) stresses the communicative nature of analytic interaction and notes that "the best technique is the best way for an analyst to learn what a patient's conflicts are and to communicate what has been learned about those conflicts to the patient" (p. 415). Gill concludes that free association is necessary, regardless of how one understands it. "The point," he says, "is to enable the patient to speak as freely as possible" (p. 99).

In the section entitled "Theory and Technique," Gill (1994) addresses the theory of motivation, beginning with the biology of Freud. He asks, "Is it possible for psychoanalysis to be solely a psychological discipline even though humans are not only persons but also biological organisms?" (p. 127). This is a crucial question given today's theoretical diversity. People are the products of their biological, psychological, and social interactions, and while psychology as a science and a discipline addresses a great deal that goes on in the mind, it also excludes a great deal; a broader perspective is clearly needed. Turning to the subject of "Drive," Gill provides a wonderful historical overview of theories of motivation, from Freud to Lichtenberg (1989). In his attempt to force Freud (1915a) into a biological box, however, Gill loses sight of Freud's greater complexity. When, for example, Freud remarks "All his drives [*Triebe*], those of tenderness, gratitude, lustfulness, defiance, and independence, find satisfaction in the single wish to be his own father" (1910b, p. 173), Gill sees "an illustration of the way Freud (1910b) himself could play fast and loose with the word drive" (p. 135). It is curious that, having laid down such a carefully thought-out overview of the drive concepts, Gill should come this conclusion. Whatever Freud's struggle to develop his drive theory, the "aims" of drives were about the wishes and fears associated with people and complex states of living. Like Gill, Brenner (1982) attempts to simplify the clutter in this theory and arrive at a cleaner and more experiential version of drives. We have elaborated on this view of drives elsewhere (Bachant, Lynch, and Richards, 1995b).

Gill sees the theories of motivation as the main distinction among the different schools of psychoanalysis. Such theories do indeed seem to be distinctive hallmarks of these schools, as they are played out in theories of pathology, technique, development, and mental functioning. Sometimes the differences are small and sometimes quite significant. In "The Body in Psychoanalysis," Gill argues that it is essential that psychoanalysis focus on the psychological meaningfulness of the biological and the sociocultural. Gill does not, however, limit himself to the psychological realm. He links the bio-psycho-social contributions to the dialectic of the actual material reference and the metaphor created to capture a meaning. Gill's contributions confer on him the status of a theoretical extender (Bergman, 1993). His efforts in *Psychoanalysis in Transition* highlight for a final time the idea that differences in theory are best understood as an emphasis of issues within a dialectic. Like Freud (Holt, 1973), Gill chooses not to come down too heavily on any single point. Instead, he looks for emphasis, appreciates dialectical interplay, and seeks the value of the specific contribution. In doing so, he definitively rejects as simplistic any attempts at dichotomization. His focus can be thought of as truly Freudian in this regard. We see him as going beyond Freud in an authentic Freudian spirit, challenging to psychoanalytic theory in a way that has helped us all. He consistently went to the edge of theory, beating new paths into the future. We are grateful to have known him and to be the beneficiaries of the outstanding body of work that he leaves behind.

REFERENCES

ARLOW, J.A. (1969). Unconscious Fantasy and Disturbances of Conscious Experience. *Psychoanalytic Quarterly* 38:1–27.
————— (1975). Discussion of paper by M. Kanzer. The therapeutic and working alliances *International Journal of Psycho-Analysis* 4:69–73.
————— (1985). Some Technical Problems of Countertransference. *Psychoanalytic Quarterly* 54:164–174.
————— (1995). Stilted listening: Psychoanalysis as discourse *Psychoanalytic Quarterly* 54:215–233.
————— & Brenner, C. (1964). *Psychoanalytic Concepts and the Structural Theory.* New York: International Universities Press.
BACHANT, J.L., LYNCH, A.A. & RICHARDS, A.D. (1992). Commentary on Reisner's "Reclaiming the Metapsychology" *Psychoanalytic Psychology* 9:563–569.
————— ————— ————— (1995). Relational Models in Psychoanalytic Theory. *Psychoanalytic Psychology* 12:71–87.
————— ————— ————— (1995). The Evolution Drive in Contemporary Psychoanalysis *Psychoanalytic Psychology* 12:565–573.
BERGMANN, M.S. (1993). Reflections on the History of Psychoanalysis. *Journal of the American Psychoanalytic Association* 41:929–955.
BIBRING-LEHNER, G. (1936). A Contribution to the Subject of Transference-Resistance. *International Journal of Psycho-Analysis* 17:181–189.
BIRD, B. (1972). Notes on Transference: Universal Phenomenon and Hardest Part of Analysis. *Journal of the American Psychoanalytic Association* 20:267–301.

BOESKY, D. (1976). *Psychoanalytic Technique and Psychic Conflict.* New York: International Universities Press.
——— (1979). Working alliance, therapeutic alliance, and transference *Journal of the American Psychoanalytic Association* 27:137–158.
——— (1982). Acting Out: A Reconsideration of the Concept. *International Journal of Psycho-Analysis* 63:39–55.
——— (1982b). *The Mind in Conflict.* New York: International Universities Press.
——— (1994). Mind as conflict and compromise formation. *Journal of Clinical Psychoanalysis* 3:473–488.
——— (1995). Some remarks on psychoanalytic technique. *Journal of* 4:413–428.
BRENNER, C. (1985). Countertransference as Compromise Formation. *Psychoanalytic Quarterly* 54:155–163.
CHUSED, J.F. (1991). The Evocative Power of Enactments. *Journal of the American Psychoanalytic Association* 39:615–639.
FENICHEL, O. (1941). Problems of Psychoanalytic Technique. New York: The Psychoanalytic Quarterly, Inc.
FREUD, A. (1936). *The Ego and the Mechanisms of Defense. The Writings of Anna Freud, 2.* New York: International Universities Press, 1966.
FREUD, S. (1905b). Three essays on the theory of sexuality. *Standard Edition* 7:130–243.
——— (1910a). The future prospects of psycho-analytic therapy. *Standard Edition* 11:139–151.
——— (1910b). A special type of choice of object made by men. *Standard Edition* 11:163–177.
——— (1912). The dynamics of transference. Standard Edition, 12:97–108. London: Hogarth Press, 1958.
——— (1913). On beginning the treatment: Further recommendations on the technique of psycho-analysis: I. *Standard Edition,* 12:121–144.
——— (1915a). Instincts and their vicissitudes. Standard Edition, 14:117–140. London: Hogarth Press, 1957.
——— (1915b). Observations on transference-love: Further recommendations on the technique of psycho-analysis III. *Standard Edition* 12:157–171.
——— (1921). Group psychology and the analysis of the ego. *Standard Edition* 18:69–143. London: Hogarth Press, 1955.
——— (1926). Inhibitions, symptoms and anxiety. *Standard Edition* 20:87–175.
GILL, M. (1963). *Topography and Systems in Psychoanalytic Theory.* New York: International Universities Press.
——— (1976). Metapsychology is not psychology. In: *Psychology Versus Metapsychology,* ed. M. Gill & P. Holzman. New York: International Universities Press, pp. 71–105.
——— (1994). *Psychoanalysis in Transition: A Personal View.* Hillsdale,

NJ: The Analytic Press.

HOFFMAN, I. (1996). Merton M. Gill: A Study in Theory Development in Psychoanalysis.

HOLT, R. (1973). On reading Freud. In: *Abstracts of the Standard Edition of the Complete Psychological Works of Sigmund Freud,* ed. C.L. Rothgeb. New York: Aronson, pp. 5–82.

JACOBS, T.J. (1986). On Countertransference Enactments. *Journal of the American Psychoanalytic Association* 34:289–307.

JACOBS, T. (1991). The Use of the Self: Countertransference and Communication in the Analytic Situation. Madison, CT: International Universities Press.

LEVY, S.T. & Inderbitzin, L.B. (1992). Neutrality, Interpretation, and Therapeutic Intent. *Journal of the American Psychoanalytic Association* 40:989–1011.

LICHTENBERG, J. (1989). *Psychoanalysis and Motivation.* Hillsdale, NJ: The Analytic Press.

LOEWENSTEIN, R.M. (1969). Developments in the Theory of Transference in the Last Fifty Years. *International Journal of Psycho-Analysis* 50:583–588.

MCLAUGHLIN, J.T. (1981). Transference, Psychic Reality, and Countertransference. *Psychoanalytic Quarterly* 50:639–664.

——— (1991). Clinical and Theoretical Aspects of Enactment. *Journal of the American Psychoanalytic Association* 39:595–614.

——— & Johan, M. (1992). Enactments in Psychoanalysis. *Journal of the American Psychoanalytic Association* 40:827–841.

SANDLER, J. (1976a). Actualization and object relationships. *Journal of the Philadelphia Association of Psychoanalysis* 3:59–70.

——— (1976). Countertransference and Role-Responsiveness. *International Review Psycho-Analysis* 3:43–47.

——— & Sandler, A. (1978). On the Development of Object Relationships and Affects. *International Journal of Psycho-Analysis* 59:285–296.

SCHAFER, R. (1976). A New Language for Psychoanalysis. New Haven, CT: Yale University Press.

SCHWABER, E. (1983). Psychoanalytic Listening and Psychic Reality. *International Review Psycho-Analysis* 10:379–392.

——— (1986). Reconstruction and Perceptual Experience: Further Thoughts on Psychoanalytic Listening. *Journal of the American Psychoanalytic Association* 34:911–932.

SPEZZANO, C. (1995). *Psychoanalysis in Transition* by Merton M. Gill *Psychoanalytic Psychology* 15:25–26.

STEIN, M. H. (1981). The Unobjectionable Part of the Transference. *Journal of the American Psychoanalytic Association* 29:869–892.

STONE, L. (1961). *The Psychoanalytic Situation.* New York: International Universities Press.

A Book Review   CHAPTER 9

(1998). New York: Routledge, 344 pp.

Ritual and Spontaneity in the Psychoanalytic Process: A Dialectical-Constructivist View   By Irwin Z. Hoffman

[Richards, A.D. (1999). *Psychoanalytic Psychology* 16:288–302.]

Irwin Hoffman is a well-known exponent of the social constructivist view of the analytic process; that is, according to Hoffman, one in which the analyst is involved in the construction, rather than merely the discovery, of the patient's psychic reality. In his book, *Ritual and Spontaneity in the Psychoanalytic Process: A Dialectical-Constructivist View,* he explores from this perspective many (currently) widely debated aspects of the psychoanalytic treatment situation, and contrasts his findings with those of classical psychoanalysis as he understands it. This latter point of view, which he calls objectivist or positivist, he characterizes as a rationalist stance, an intellectual belief that the psychoanalytic therapies are based on "very specific, rather narrowly defined approaches or treatments to the amelioration or cure of symptoms or to further psychological development" (p. viii). By comparison, the constructivist point of view does not understand the analyst as the uninvolved applier of defined methods to a defined reality. It sees the analyst as profoundly involved subjectively in a reality that he helps to create, and rather than turning to objective methods for "cure," keeps a sharp eye out instead for "partially blinding emotional entanglement, for the uniqueness of each interaction, for uncertainty and ambiguity, for cultural bias, for chance, for the analyst's creativity, for the moral dimensions of choice, and for existential anxiety in the face of freedom and morality" (p. xii). The constructivist analyst understand the psychoanalysis not as working upon by the analyst of the patient's "fantasies," "perceptions," and "realities," but rather "a world of mutual influence and constructed meaning" (p. xii).

Nonclassical perspective on psychoanalysis are many and complex now and require careful sorting to avoid obscuring differences and stepping on toes. Hoffman shares in some measure the views of his colleagues in the relational and intersubjective camps, but he feels himself as very distinct from them in important ways. He agrees with Greenberg's (1991) assertion that both positivism and an asocial view of transference are very much alive and well in contemporary psychoanalytic practice. Hoffman is a very tough vetter indeed of constructivist credentials. He dismisses interpersonalists Sullivan and Levinson ("the actuality of events," p. 79) as positivists in one way or another, as well as Weiss and Sampson who "go about identifying pathogenic beliefs" (p. 139). In self-psychology he maintains that the emphasis on introspection and empathy precludes the involvement of the analyst as a true participant—constructivist. (He cites Eagle, 1984, and Mitchell, 1988, who have pointed out that the self-psychologist is just as invested in the possibility of an objective or accurate reading of the patient's experience as is the classical analyst.) Even the intersubjectivist Stolorow does not escape being placed squarely within a positivist tradition. As Hoffman writes, "For the theory of intersubjectivity to be consistent with the social constructive paradigm, it must encompass interaction on multiple levels of psychological organization and consciousness. Any divorcing of the interpsychic and the interpersonal is unacceptable in this model" (pp. 141–142). He does apparently feel some kinship with the early theorist, Racker (1968), who seems to Hoffman to have been "ahead of his time and perhaps our own" (p. 142), with a view of countertransference which is not simply reactive, and the idea that analysts cannot keep their subjective experience from contaminating their patient's transferences. But ultimately he believes that pure constructivism stands alone: "In the end I'm not sure that the gulf that separates Kohut, Winnicott and Sullivan from the social constructivist point of view is less wide than the gulf that separates Freud from that perspective" (p. 143).

Even within that camp Hoffman has taken pains to separate himself from what he calls "radical constructivism," and this singles him out even further from his colleagues. He quotes von Glasserfeld, who typifies this approach:

> Knowledge does not reflect an "objective" ontological reality but exclusively an order and organization of a world constituted by our experience and a critical constructivism in which the individual is not a self-sufficient producer of his or her own experience . . . rather, the individual is conceived as a co-creator or co-constructor of personal realities with the prefix "co"

emphasizing an interactive interdependence with their social and physical environments [p. 21].

Aron (1996) has maintained that such varied epistemological approaches are all part of what has come to be called postmodern thought, and as such are central to the development of a new sensibility in psychoanalysis. But Hoffman points out, correctly I think, that postmodernism is too broad a concept to accept without qualifications, that it includes approaches that Hoffman, to say nothing of more traditional analysts like myself, would not sign on to, and therefore cannot be accepted wholesale. Hoffman comments pointedly, "I would locate myself much more with the critical constructivists. Indeed I have no more in common with the radical group than I do with the objectivist camp" (p. 22).

So much for what Hoffman rejects. What he is interested in, or at least what concerns him in this work, is what he calls the dialectic between interpersonal influence and critical interpretive exploration. He does not distinguish in this book between psychoanalysis proper and psychoanalytic psychotherapy. Rather he considers there to be a "single psychoanalytic modality in which there is a dialectic between non-interpretive and interpretive interactions" (p. xiii). Much of the interest in this study lies in his vision of this dialectic.

Hoffman does not deny that there may be bedrock "givens" of the conscious and unconscious aspects of human action, but apart from these givens he insists that mental life and action are constructed. He sees the analyst as always caught up in interactions with his patients at the very same time that he is reflecting on the meaning of this involvement as it occurs. This is such a fundamental aspect of the analytic situation, in his view, that he asserts "To some extent, free association as the central focus of analytic attention is replaced in this model with the free emergence of multiple transference/countertransference scenarios" (p. 78). For Hoffman, in other words, the method of psychoanalysis is centered primarily not on the patient's words or associations, but on the interactions between patient and analyst (transference/countertransference). In this book he examines how these beliefs fit into psychoanalysis as a whole, from the small details of analytic practice and discourse, to the nature of therapeutic change, and finally to the huge and abstract body of psychoanalytic theory. I want to discuss three aspects of his exploration: the position of dialectic in analytic practice and inquiry, the nature of therapeutic change, and the question of whether there is a new paradigm of psychoanalysis.

The first of these, the use of dichotomy and dialectic as investigative tools in psychoanalytic inquiry, is a matter of great interest to Hoffman, and to me as well. It is compelling in itself, and it also contains the peculiar paradox that haunts the dialogue between positivist and (supposedly) nonpositivist psychoanalysts, to the endless confounding of both. Hoffman is a unusual writer in that he is very attuned to the vicissitudes of dichotomy and dialectic in psychoanalytic thought, and I am very much in synch with some of his conclusions. He says, for instance, that he used to think that the great divide in psychoanalysis was between objectivist and constructivist thinking, but that he now thinks it is between dichotomous and dialectical thinking. Here, here say I. I think that the single most commendable aspect of Hoffman's work in general, and of this book in particular, is his close attention to dialectic in psychoanalytic theory and technique, and the consistency with which he avoids the temptation of seductive but untenable dichotomies. (This is another way in which Hoffman has pursued a very different path from Mitchell, Aron, and others, who base their thinking on what they view as a fundamental dichotomy—the division between drive theory and relational theory—which they use as the foundation upon which to build a case for the superiority of relational psychoanalysis over the classical point of view.) Hoffman eschews such dualities. He accepts readily, for example, that paying more attention to the subjectivity of the analyst does not negate the tension between his visibility and invisibility in the analytic situation, nor does it diminish its value. And as I mentioned above, he understands the interpretive and the noninterpretive aspects of psychoanalysis as a dialectic, rather than a struggle for supremacy in which only on can triumph, or worse, an illusion in which only one exists.

When he does tackle an apparent dichotomy, he does so in a thoughtful and discriminating manner that also sets him apart. He maintains, for instance, that it is false to equate the drive-relational axis with the objectivist—constructivist one, on the grounds that relational (including interpersonal and self-psychological) theory as yet retains a significant objectivist cast, whereas, conversely, drive theory has always contained within it "the seeds of a constructivist point of view" (p. xiv). (I've mentioned his reasons for the former assertion above; he gives as an example of the latter the tension in Freudian theory between "the environmentalism of the trauma theory and the endogenous excesses of the drive theory, a tension that virtually begs for a dialectical constructivist resolution" [p. xv]).

Yet, as much as I admire Hoffman's slowness to partisanship and his reluctance to polarize, he does still sometimes "dichotomize" in his discussions of dichotomy. The paradox of constructivist thinkers embracing a positivistic position about the importance of constructivism can make dialogue confusing. As a specific example, for instance, I do not concur with his belief that dichotomous thinking in integral to objectivism and dialectical thinking to constructivism. (This assertion seems to stem from what he sees in objectivism as a dichotomy between the things believed to come from the analyst and those believed to come from the patient, and the belief that these can be definitively distinguished—as opposed to the constructivist belief that transference and countertransference exist in a dialectical relationship that creats "a zone of irreducible ambiguity and indeterminacy as to the nature of their interaction and reciprocal influence, a zone that is open to multiple possible interpretive constructions" [p. 26.]) And I do not at all believe that a nonconstructivist view of psychoanalysis must preclude awareness of some of the interpersonal aspects of the treatment situation that Hoffman presents as integral to his constructivism. In a more general way, I think that any search for singular answers to the question of how psychoanalysis works and what psychoanalysis is is too simple an approach to such an immensely complex and multifaceted undertaking as psychoanalysis.

I would hope that Hoffman would apply his own dialectical thinking to his view of the analytic situation. Surely we can have some ambiguity and some certainty, or some indeterminacy and some sense of the determinate at the same time. Indeed, surely, there are tensions operating between these two poles, and other, all the time. There are no absolutes in psychoanalysis and in that sense everything is ambiguous and indeterminate. However, that does not prevent our making intelligent guesses at any given time about what may be going on between analyst and patient and what is influencing what. (The capacity to do that is a good piece of what makes the difference between analyst and someone who is not.) Nor does it preclude the possibility (the likelihood, in fact) that at different times the nature of the "what is going on" may be quite different—at times focused and intellectual, and at other occult and interpersonal.

There is no doubt that different schools of psychoanalysis vary in the extent to which they see the influence of the analyst's subjectivity, personality, and values as being central to therapeutic action. We may say that there is a spectrum of opinion about these matters. One point of view considers only interpretive interchange as therapeutic, and minimizes, if it doesn't exactly deny, more personal effects. A middle position sees noninterpretive interventions as important to the relationship but not necessarily to therapeutic change. The third position is that noninterpretive therapeutic interactions are indeed where the money is—that this is the locus of change. But along that spectrum there is plenty of room for overlapping models.

For instance, I consider myself a classical analyst, yet I agree comfortably with Hoffman's assertion that there are many questions in the analytic situation that cannot be avoided and probably can't be finally "answered." I agree that the analyst will always be influencing the patient in some way. I agree that the analyst's presence is never strictly neutral. Yet I do think that an analyst may function from a "neutral-enough" stance (which is not the same as a moralistic, coercive, or suggestive one) to provide an occasional useful interpretation.

For example, questions about the patient's experience of the analyst come up again and again as a central divide between classical and relational analysts. Relational analysts fault classical analysts for not acknowledging that patients' transference-based speculations are not necessarily untenable and that therefore the tern distortion is not apt.

Classical analysts, however, do not necessarily deny that their patients' speculations may be tenable. They do, however, prefer to keep their attention on the patient's experience of the analyst as the patient displays it (rather than as it "really" is or isn't), their belief being that the patient's choice is transferentially determined and that therapeutic gain derives from looking at transference-based phenomena, whereas little therapeutic benefit derives from emphasizing the correctness or not of the patient's speculations about the analyst.

The way models overlap and separate is illustrated in an interesting discussion in chapter 4, the Hoffman points out that critiques of the blank screen model can be found as early as 1950s, although current relational authors challenging the centrality of neutrality, anonymity, and abstinence tend to write as if the blank screen concept has been a sacred cow until very recently. Hoffman himself, however, believes that the blank screen view in psychoanalysis is part of a larger phenomenon, what he refers to as asocial conceptions of the patient's experience in psychotherapy.

Hoffman is therefore too careful a thinker to be allowed to make "unconstructivist" demands for a constructivist understanding of the analytic situation, at least without some ironic acknowledgment on his part of the paradox. This paradox has shadowed the debate between relationalists and other for years, and as we move from the at least slightly concrete microcosm of analytic practice to the progressively larger and more abstract issues of therapeutic change and theoretical "paradigms" and models, it becomes less benign.

Therapeutic Change

Hoffman discusses carefully and at length the importance of the tension between the patient's subjectivity and that of the analyst in the treatment situation. I know no one at this moment who would argue against the existence of this dialectic. Hoffman, however, leaps from recognition of its existence to the assertion that it is the primary vehicle of psychoanalytic change. Not one factor in an interacting dialectic of factors, but the one that supersedes all others. Here again, the constructivist edifice seems to be built on a positivistic substratum. Where else does the conviction come from that one type of interaction rather than another is singularly responsible for the changes that take place in such an immensely detailed and complicated thing as a psychoanalysis? Why do we not hear of interpretive and intersubjective experiences influencing each other and constructing together what eventually becomes recognizable as psychotherapeutic change? Why, if we agree that the analyst's subjectivity is a significant factor in the establishment of the analytic milieu, are we expected to support as well such a positivist position as Mitchell's, say, that a new relational theory of therapeutic action has emerged that is radically disjunct from the classical one? To agree that constructivist tendencies may be at work in a given situation does not demand agreement as well that their operation is the only, or even the central, factor in therapeutic change.

For example, Hoffman reviews articles by Aron (1991), Greenberg (1991), and Modell (1991) in *Psychoanalytic Dialogues.* He notes their emphasis on the importance of the personal presence and participation of the analyst in the analytic process. About the therapeutic action issues Hoffman says first that "exploring the patient's perceptions of the analyst's immediate experience in the analytic situation as well as perceptions of the analyst's general attributes is at least in keeping with the value of bringing resisted aspects of the patient's experience to consciousness" (pp. 133–134). I understand this to mean that "bringing to consciousness" retains in Hoffman's system at least some of the value it has in mine as a therapeutic experience. Here would seem to be another example of overlapping models where a constructivist analyst can concur with the values of a classicist without completely converting to the fundamentalist Freudianism. Hoffman appears to back off from classically tainted position, though, eventually restating it: "Such exploration creates the opportunity for a special kind of affective contact with the analyst that is thought to have therapeutic potential" (p. 150) What does this statement mean? How does it coexist with the earlier one? How do we know if this is a central therapeutic potential, or a peripheral one? How, if we want to test it, can we set up the analytic situation to maximize this kind of contact, as opposed to setups that maximize the "bringing to consciousness" kinds?

Another example: Aron (1991) and Greenberg (1991) have asserted that their patients are actively interested in exploring their personal qualities, that this is part of a basic tendency with roots in the infant's interests in the subjectivity of the mother, and that this interest needs to be encouraged and to some extent gratified because it is presumably therapeutic. Even if this basic tendency exists in fact, though, I question how universal the interest is among analysands. In my observation it is quite variable, and determined by inner wishes, desires, and defenses as intersubjective curiosity. It is certainly possible that in this kind of interaction the analyst may discover something new about himself as Aron (1991) maintained, but I think it remains to be demonstrated that this new knowledge in the analyst leads to therapeutic effect for the patient, although Aron's (1991) belief and Greenberg's (1991) as well is that it does make a positive difference and that it is separate from the possibility that the analyst's attitude, and his openness to the patient's exploration of his life, create a certain kind of atmosphere that the patient can use.

In addition to the theoretical question of how unilateral a phenomenon intrapsychic change is (or isn't), these endless assertions about the therapeutic action of psychoanalysis raise more concrete problems of proof, or at least clinical demonstration, because psychoanalysis is not so far susceptible to the kinds of objective proof in which the hard sciences delight. So far the best we can do is to test the explanatory power and predictive adequacy of our theories in the clinical situation, and compare them against the explanatory power and adequacy of alternative theories. And so I wish Hoffman had done more than to propose abstract theories of therapeutic change. We need opportunities to examine these assertions in practice.

Hoffman does provide us with clinical vignettes, good examples of the importance of timing, tact, and "menschliness" in clinical work. But they do not address or answer the question about how, or even whether, differences in perspective may or may not relate to the actuality of what happens in a psychotherapeutic treatment. Or, to put it differently, of the nature of the relationship between psychoanalytic theory and practice; the relationship between the theory and the facts of therapeutic change. How we think about these matters is one thing; how we demonstrate their truth is something else. Central to Hoffman's discussion is the assumption that our theoretical models inevitably influence and reflect practice. This may be true, but how they influence and reflect is not so clear.

One may or may not agree with Hoffman that Gill underrates the power of noninterpretive interventions—I do agree, as it happens. Still, when one is thinking about different theories of the mode of action of psychoanalysis and of the nature of therapeutic change, the issue becomes not so much the relative importance-rankings of different interventions as a rather pragmatic examination of which kind of actual encounters enhance psychoanalytic processes when they happen, which don't seem to have much of an effect, and which may in fact derail our efforts.

I think that in this time of rapidly proliferating theories we must requires of those who propose the superiority of one therapeutic point of view over another evocative, compelling, and—let it be said until psychoanalysis becomes capable of more objective proof—convincing clinical examples. We need to see how the principles of theoreticians are or aren't reflected in their practice.

What does it mean to say that we participate as "intimate partners with our patients?" How in actual behavior is the intimate participation of the classical analyst different from the intimate participation of the relational analyst? How can that be illustrated? And how can we gain sufficient intimacy with each other's work to form an informed opinion that the patient's therapeutic purposes and goals are better served from one stance than from another? Does attention to one theory as opposed to another really lead to a different kind of practice, or a different pathway to analytic goals? Are these ideas that exist only in principle, or practical guidelines that can be demonstrated in process? We need abundant illustration of their clinical behavior, abundant demonstration of their results, and abundant opportunity to compare and test their practices against the clinical practices of others. Does the understanding of therapeutic change specific to relational psychoanalysis offer the analyst a new set of tools for bringing about a positive therapeutic outcome? What are they? Can we have them defined, see them at work in the hands of an experienced relational analyst, and observe their action in clinical examples? If we are to make countertransference disclosure a central part of technique, as relational theory seems to suggest, how do we handle it? The lack of this kind of material for scrutiny is a flaw in this book, but Hoffman is not alone in this.

When Hoffman proposes that the central task of the analyst is "to find forms of engagement through which the patient's own capacity for love and for courageous, honest and creative living despite and because of full awareness of mortality can be newly discovered and inspired" (p. 30), one can at the same time applaud the goal, ponder the question of engagement versus insight, and recognize that either way one is still no closer to knowing how to go about accomplishing it.

A final example: Hoffman considers the analyst as moral authority. He examines the hierarchical qualities intrinsic to the analytic relationship (as opposed to the ones resulting from a specifically authoritarian stance of the analyst) and raises the possibility that psychoanalysis may be in some way a process resocialization. This can come about, he suggests, because the analyst's "culturally sanctioned power [is] sustained and cultivated in an ongoing way by the ritual features of the psychoanalytic process itself" (p. 82).

Connected with this phenomenon, and central to the process of analysis and presumably to the nature of its therapeutic action, is what Hoffman calls the factor of affirmation. He considers that this process occurs authentically when

> regard for the analyst is fostered by the fact that the patient knows so much less about him or her than the analyst knows about the patient. The analyst is in a position that is likely to promote the most tolerant understanding and generous aspects of his or her personality. On the other side, the analyst's regard for the patient is fostered by the fact that he or she knows so much about the patient [p. 83].

This conjunction of more and less knowledge, according to Hoffman, promotes the idealization of the analyst that, in turn, enables the analyst to play this affirming role.

Acknowledging that there is always a tension between a patient's perception of his analyst as a person like himself and his perception of him as a person of superior knowledge, wisdom, judgment, and power and that the balance of these two factors emerges "from an authentic kind of participation by the analyst rather than from adherence to some technical formula" (p. 84), Hoffman feels that there is a special affirming power associated with an analyst's willingness to engage a patient in a way that is personally expressive and spontaneous. In fact, he thinks, because the analyst is functioning in a ritualized asymmetrical system, the analyst's emotional and personal availability, his love, when it is made evident, takes on an even more powerful valence than it might in relationship that is more symmetrical and discourse more "ordinary." He puts it this way:

> I am arguing . . . that the analyst's personal involvement in the analytic situation has potentially a particular kind of concentrative power because it is embedded in a ritual in which the analyst is set up to be a special kind of authority. (p. 84)

By this and other arguments Hoffman makes the point that the analyst's effect as influential moral authority is inevitable, and he reminds us that even if we follow Kohut and Winnicott and function to the best of our ability as empathic self-objects or as responders to our patient's true selves, we are still responding on the basis of our own dispositions and values. He states, "Effective attunement and empathic responsiveness no less than traditional interpretation are colored by each therapist's cultural, theoretical and personal bias" (p. 85).

The bottom line for Hoffman is that in no treatment does the analyst's own personality ever disappear from the field, and he asks us to acknowledge the inevitable impact of the analyst's subjectivity on the patient. I think that all of us are prepared to do that.

Yet having made this acknowledgment does not mean we must proceed any further down the constructivist road. We can acknowledge this impact as an important part of the analytic process without specifically considering it curative. If it is curative, that does not necessarily mean that nothing else is. There is little evidence so far that these are all-or-nothing phenomena, or that to admit the existence of constructivist aspects of treatment requires the dismissal of insight and interpretation as irrelevant. A perspective like Hoffman's can enlarge our own without engulfing our own. In fact, there can be a dialectical tension between two perspectives, or within one person aware of them both, at least as commonly as two perspectives dichotomously exist in two people. There is also, of course, always the possibility that neither perspective is the absolutely last word, and that both will some day be transcended by another more inclusive one.

New Paradigm

Discussions of therapeutic action and the so-called new paradigm are both fundamentally evaluations of theories—our relationships with them, and ultimately their relationships to the things they are intended to explain. There will always be more than one way to think about anything, and we can make theories endlessly, to enlighten or confuse us, but they are still only theories, and not to be confused with fact. The development of a good theory leads eventually to more accurate predictions of events and more detailed understanding of observed phenomena, but until it does it is still a speculative endeavor, and not a model of real explanatory power. A theory without a real world to explain is incomplete, and so is a world without theories to explain it. They make each other. This would seem to me to be a very comfortable view of things for constructivists.

Therefore, I don't quite understand the intensity of the search for a monolithic primary cause of psychoanalytic cure, or for a "new paradigm" of psychoanalysis that by definition replaces the old one. And I feel keenly, as I said above, the need for enough clinical material to bring all this theorizing back to its roots in the real world, which is the only place where we have any chance of evaluating it.

Hoffman does not satisfy my wish for empirical demonstration of his theories of psychoanalytic action, but he does display a satisfying skepticism and independence of thought in the matter of the much-touted, much-to-be-desired (in some neighborhoods) and much-to-be-deplored (in others) "new paradigm of psychoanalysis."

He devotes a fair amount of discussion to his colleagues Modell (1991), Aron (1991), and Greenberg (1991), and to the question of whether their approach "amounts to a new paradigm" (p. 134). He presents as his own personal view the conviction "that there is a new paradigm struggling to emerge in the field, but it has not yet fully arrived, much less been firmly established" (p. 135). Hoffman is reluctant to announce that the new paradigm infant has been successfully "delivered," but the implication of his position clearly is that its birth is not only expected but very much to be desired. He implies that psychoanalysis as praxis very much needs a new social constructivist paradigm to replace what he sees no longer accurately as the pregnant positivist—objectivist nonconstructivist approach.

But at the same time that Hoffman acknowledges his wish for a paradigm shift, he makes very clear that what he has in mind is not the shift from the drive model to the relational model. In this he definitively parts company with Greenberg (1991), Mitchell (1988), and Eagle (1984), who all have argued that the fundamental revolution in psychoanalysis has been the shift from the drive model to the relational model, and the long battle against classical Freudian orthodoxy (drive theory) has now been won. My understanding of "paradigm shift" is that it does not refer primarily to an alternative theory or a new way of understanding something, but rather to the shift that occurs when an explanation of lesser explanatory power is replaced by one of much greater. We have alternative theories in plenty at the moment, but the greater explanatory power of any one of them has so far escaped me.

For Hoffman, though, the essential shift is from a positivist to a constructivist model for understanding the psychoanalytic situation. He does not see the struggle as aimed at classical Freudianism.

In fact, interestingly enough, Hoffman observes that "there are aspects of classical theory that are . . . conducive to a shift to a constructivist point of view" (p. 135). This is a position that I have not read before in contributions from relational and interpersonal authors; however, it is accurate. Freud's constructivism can be found, for example, in his essay "The Unconscious" (Freud, 1914), where he referred favorably to the idea that there is no immaculate perception. Hoffman's important point (his talent for fine distinction shows again here) is that the social constructivist paradigm is not the same as the relational model.

Hoffman feels that in order for a theory to be truly constructivist, it has to do more than emphasize the importance of the patient's awareness of the analyst as a person, more than move from the view of the transference as illusory to a view of the transference as real, more than move from exploration of endogenously based fantasy to exploration also of realistic perceptions of the analyst. What Hoffman thinks is essential for this social constructivist paradigm is the idea that "the personal participation of the analyst in the process is considered to have a continuous effect on what he or she understands about himself and about the patient in the interaction" (p. 136).

SUMMARY

As I have pointed out repeatedly, relationalists exalt their subjective perspectival point of view, yet they still seem to be quite positive about the singular superiority of their approach. I would not say that classical analysts aren't similarly positive about the therapeutic advantage of their approach; however, they do not claim not to be positivists. It would seem to me that a little more humility from both sides would be a good thing, along with the recognition that in the end the question of what works best for one patient or another may be an empirical one. Empirical questions are hard and important in such an abstract enterprise as psychoanalysis; it is not weaseling to recognize them where they exist, nor is it likely that they will be easy to answer. Hoffman is an interesting writer. Let me conclude by offering a few more selections of his own words:

> We can trace a movement, . . . decidedly nonlinear, from Freud's solitary reflection on his own dreams which sets up self-analysis as the ideal, to the detached presence of the analyst as a scientific observer and facilitator of the transference and its interpretation, to a view of the analyst as responsive in a therapeutically corrective way to the patient's needs and deficits, to an appreciation of the usefulness of countertransference in the process, to an understanding that the analyst's interpretations do not simply map on to a prestructured reality but rather contribute something to the construction of that reality, to a recognition of the culture's relative and ironic aspects of the analyst—authority, to an appreciation of the full extent and implications of our personal involvement with out patients as they struggle to make sense of and modify their ways of experiencing and constructing their worlds. . ... Stated succinctly, . . . we have traversed a distance from analysis as solitary reflection to analysis as relational struggle. In the latter, against a backdrop of the ritualized asymmetry of the psychoanalytic situation from which we draw special moral power, we participate as intimate powers with our patients as they wrestle with conflict and they choose from among and struggle to realize, their multiple potentials for intimacy and autonomy, for identification and individuality, for work and play, and for continuity and change [p. 94].

Hoffman presents eloquently here the goals of analysis for the patient. Clearly these goals are not inconsistent with the classical goal of psychoanalysis, the achievement of maximum insight, because obviously the achievement of insight is a means to the ends, the ability to work and play and change that Hoffman proposes. He is a lover of paradox and figure—ground reversals:

> the analyst within the patient and the patient within one's self, . . . the resonance of the past in the present, and the impact of the present upon one's reading of the past,. . . the analytic arrangement as emotionally deadening and the analytic arrangement as a framework for liberating understanding and affirmation [p. 30].

His contributions to psychoanalysis are interesting and provocative. I think he could improve them even further by listening to his own words of wisdom, which I quoted above, but will remind us all of here:

> What the analyst seems to understand about his or her own experience and behavior, as well as the patient, is always suspect, always susceptible to the vicissitudes of the analyst's own resistance and always prone to be superseded by the point of view that may emerge [p. 136].

Surely if this is true in the analytic consulting room, it is true outside of it as well.

REFERENCES

ARON, L. (1991). The Patient's Experience of the Analyst's Subjectivity *Psychoanalytic Dialogues* 1:29–51.

ARON, L. (1996). A meeting of minds: Mutuality in psychoanalysis. Hillsdale, NJ: Analytic Press.

EAGLE, M. (1984). Recent developments in psychoanalysis. New York: McGraw-Hill.

FREUD, S. (1914). The unconscious. *Standard Edition* 14:166–204.

Greenberg, J.R. (1991). Countertransference and Reality *Psychoanalytic Dialogues* 1:52–73.

HOFFMAN, I.Z. (1998). *Ritual and Spontaneity in the Psychoanalytic Process: A Dialectical-Constructivist View*. New York: Routledge.

MITCHELL, S. (1988). *Relational Concepts in Psychoanalysis*. Cambridge, MA: Harvard University Press.

MODELL, A.H. (1991). The Therapeutic Relationship as a Paradoxical Experience *Psychoanalytic Dialogues* 1:13–28.

RACKER, H. (1968). Transference and Countertransference. New York: International Universities Press.

CHAPTER 10

How New is the "New American Psychoanalysis"? The Example of Irwin Z. Hoffman

[Richards, A.D. (2002). *Journal of Clinical Psychoanalysis* 11:379–401.]

In reflecting on the state of American psychoanalysis today, I am inspired by the memory of Lester Schwartz. When I returned to New York in 1964 from a two-year tour of duty as the chief medical officer and psychiatrist at the Federal Reformatory in Petersburg, Virginia, I accepted a position at Montefiore Hospital as assistant director of the Outpatient Department, of which Lester Schwartz was then acting chairman. He became a mentor, a colleague, and a dear friend, and these bonds continued until his death. Lester was for me the model of a contemporary Freudian psychoanalyst. He remained open to new ideas if they were supported by clinical data, just as he was receptive to technical innovations if they were shown to be effective. But he was not for change for its own sake. He was not for short cuts, quick fixes, or expediency. He was not for going with the latest Zeitgeist, whether it happened to be postmodernism, constructivism, narratology, or neurobiology.

But if, as Lewis Aron has observed, "psychoanalysis as an intellectual endeavor is part of an ongoing conversation between people" (1996, p. 29). I think Lester Schwartz would have joined me in celebrating the fact that most of us who work in the field today are speaking a common language. With the possible exception of the Lacanian school, which seems to show little interest in integrating its ideas with those of other traditions, the world of contemporary analysis has, after a long and often painful process, come together in a way that could not have been foreseen twenty or even ten years ago. The chasm that once divided the tradition of ego psychology taught at institutes affiliated with the American Psychoanalytic Association from the interpersonal tradition associated with the William Alanson White Institute in New York has, in response to a combination of political and theoretical pressures, given way to a productive dialogue in print and on public platforms. Drawing a parallel to the history of British psychoanalysis, in which the split between Anna Freudians and Kleinians during World War II led to the emergence of a Middle Group (or Independents). Charles Spezzano has referred to this new conglomeration as "the American Middle School" (1995, cited by Aron, 1996, p. 15).[1] No less distinguished a representative of the mainstream than Robert Wallerstein has noted that "we collectively agree . . . that indeed, at least in America, we have been engaged, over the past fifteen years or so, in a major shift—call it a paradigm shift or not-in our conceptualization of the nature of the psychoanalytic enterprise, both in theory and in practice" (1998, p. 1021). Like Spezzano, Wallerstein compares this "new conceptualization, or reconceptualization," to that which had occurred decades ago in "the British object relations school," and he likewise notes its indigenous antecedents in "Harry Stack Sullivan's interpersonal perspective."

Just as it has become commonplace to assert that a "paradigm shift" has taken place in American psychoanalysis, there is also agreement as to its nature. Some characterize the shift as a parallel movement from drive to relational theory and from an objectivist (or positivist) to a constructivist epistemology (Aron, 1996, p. 256). The former reconceptualization has been advocated above all in a series of books by the late Stephen A. Mitchell (Greenberg and Mitchell, 1983; Mitchell, 1988, 1993,1997, 2000). while the latter has found its foremost champion in Irwin Z. Hoffman (1998). Indeed, Aron (1996, p. 27) employs the terms *relational-perspectivism* or *relational-constructivism* interchangeably to show the links between the epistemological and metapsychological aspects of this shift. In Wallerstein's summary, the trend in contemporary American psychoanalysis can be defined as being:

> [A]way from a natural science, positivistic model anchored in a one-person psychology based on intrapsychic vicissitudes of the patient's instinctual strivings and the defenses ranged against them, all of this authoritatively surveyed by an objective, neutral analyst, the privileged arbiter of the patient's reality, and on the patient's neurosis as projected onto the analytic blank screen—away from all that to the ramifications of a two-person psychol-

---

[1]For a valuable account of how this orientation came into being in the context of the New York University Postdoctoral Program in *Psychoanalysis and Intensive Psychotherapy,* see Aron (1996, chapter 1).

ogy focused on the always subjective interactions of the transferential internalized object relationships of the patient with the countertransferential (or equally transferential) internalized object relationships of the analyst [1998, p. 1022].

Not only on an intellectual but also on a political level, the winds of change that have swept through American psychoanalysis in recent decades have had some beneficial effects. Although I remain skeptical whether the present upheavals amount to a paradigm shift, I share Wallerstein's conviction that contemporary Freudians should reject nostalgia and stagnation in favor of adaptation and growth. There can be no turning back. The question is, where do we go from here?

In trying to sift the wheat from the chaff in the so-called relational-constructivist turn, I find an unexpected dialectical counterpart in Jay Greenberg, who in a paper in the *Journal of the American Psychoanalytic Association*, has sought to address some of the excesses in the relational approach from the perspective of someone who has participated in its development and embraced its fundamental principles. In other words, whereas I, as an outsider to the relational approach, am prepared to concede its merits, Greenberg, a relational insider, has become increasingly troubled by its "excesses." This reversal is, I think, a positive development since it means that we are no longer polarized into warring camps of "Us against Them," but are once again (as in the halcyon days before the first schisms) all simply psychoanalysts, each of whom is free to think critically about his or her own tradition while drawing creatively on those of others.

Underlying the specific debates over the two main pillars of relational-constructivism is a broader question about the concept of a paradigm shift itself. Although I agree that the impact of the relational orientation on contemporary psychoanalytic thought has been positive in some respects, I have in a series of previous papers—including an exchange with Mitchell (1999) in the *Round Robin*—argued that relational theorists, out of an understandable desire to magnify their claims to originality, often define the contrast between their point of view and that of contemporary Freudians in unnecessarily polarized terms. The same point is made by Greenberg at the outset of his paper when he remarks that psychoanalysis as a discipline has grown through "one inspired theoretical excess after another" (p. 359). and that relationality "is in danger of becoming the latest wonderful idea to coalesce into a movement" (2001, p. 361).

In large part, the debate over whether something constitutes a paradigm shift comes down to a matter of historical perspective. Often enough, a startling new idea that seems at first to represent a fork in the road for psychoanalytic theory—the example of self psychology comes to mind—is in surprisingly short order absorbed by the community at large and thereby transformed into a bend in the river. Of course, almost everyone in our profession would agree that Freud's original discovery of psychoanalysis represents an intellectual breakthrough of such proportions that it rises to the level of a paradigm shift. Even this claim, however, might be challenged by medical model critics who see psychoanalysis and its offshoots as simply a temporary aberration in the great tradition of descriptive psychiatry that extends from Kraepelin to the *DSM-IV*.

Everything is relative, therefore, and the friction between those who, caught up by the latest "inspired theoretical excess," press the case for its novelty and those who, like myself, take a longer view and stress the degree to which, in Greenberg's words, "the new idea could then be seen as supplementing, or not productively competing with rendering obsolete everything that had come before" (2001, pp. 360–361). is an inevitable byproduct of the process by which psychoanalysis as a whole has always evolved. If, as Aron (1996, p. 255) has proposed, contemporary relational psychoanalysis should take as its "anthem" Racker's proclamation that "the first distortion of truth in 'the myth of the analytic situation' is that analysis is an interaction between a sick person and a healthy one" (1968, p. 132). I would antiphonally nominate as the "anthem" of contemporary Freudianism Winnicott's reminder that "in any cultural field *it is not possible to be original except on a basis of tradition*" (1971, p. 99).[2] Winnicott goes on to say that "the interplay between originality and the acceptance of tradition as the basis for inventiveness" is "just one more example . . . of the interplay between separateness and union." Read as a metaphor for the history of psychoanalysis, Winnicott's comparison

---

[2]The latest revelations (Godley, 2001) of the scandalous conduct of Winnicott's protégé, Masud Khan, certainly cast not only Khan but also Winnicott himself in an unfavorable light. But as the example of the Frink affair shows, Freud too was capable of actions that we would regret today; and Winnicott's positive contributions should not be allowed to become tarnished by his laxity with Khan.

implies that contemporary Freudians, as representatives of tradition, are equivalent to the mother, while relationalists and other proponents of originality are in the position of the child. In this perpetual tug-of-war between the pulls to separation and union—what Ferenczi (1928) would call "elasticity"—lies the ever renewable resource of true intellectual creativity.

Although I have previously addressed the issue of polarization in my colloguy with Mitchell and elsewhere, it bears reexamination as it pertains to the work of Hoffman. According to Hoffman, as I have indicated, the change that is believed to be "fundamental and still germinal in psychoanalytic theory and practice" is "not the shift from the drive model to the relational model" but that "from a positivist model for understanding the psychoanalytic situation to a constructivist model" (1998, p. 135).[3] Nonetheless, the key point is that Hoffman, no less than Mitchell, is heavily invested in the notion of a paradigm shift and consequently tends both to exaggerate the novelty of his own views and to present those with which he disagrees in a reductive and even trivializing fashion.[4]

A prime example of this tendency is Hoffman's treatment of the concept of a blank screen. Hoffman's opening move is to divide the critiques of this concept into two types: conservative and radical. Needless to say, he then endorses the radical critique because it "amounts to a different paradigm, not simply an elaboration of the standard paradigm, which is what the conservative critics propose" (1998, p. 103). At the core of the radical critique is the premise that "free association, as the central focus of analytic attention, is replaced in this model with the free emergence of multiple transference-countertransference scenarios, a sample of which

---

[2]The latest revelations (Godley, 2001) of the scandalous conduct of Winnicott's protégé, Masud Khan, certainly cast not only Khan but also Winnicott himself in an unfavorable light. But as the example of the Frink affair shows, Freud too was capable of actions that we would regret today; and Winnicott's positive contributions should not be allowed to become tarnished by his laxity with Khan.

[3]Hoffman's book includes papers published between 1979 and 1994, as well as several new chapters. There is thus some inconsistency between his earlier and more recent views, which he addresses from time to time in footnotes. But since the book as a whole appeared in 1998, I shall use this date for all citations of Hoffman's work.

[4]In his blurb for Hoffman's book Mitchell lauds him for being "a central figure in the broadscale paradigmatic shift from classical psychoanalysis to a psychoanalysis congruent with our own time."

is more or less reflected upon and interpreted over time" (p. 117). It is noteworthy that Hoffman does not say that the contemporary emphasis on enactments should *supplement* the traditional focus on the patient's free associations; rather, it must *replace* it. This style of dichotomous thinking, to which Greenberg also objects, is part and parcel of Hoffman's automatic assumption that what is new must be better than what is old.

Hoffman proceeds to take to task several leading proponents of the conservative critique. He rejects categorically the idea that the analyst may be able to distinguish between transferential and nontransferential components of the patient's communications. For instance, Kohut is rebuked for his assertion that transference "is defined by pre-analytically established internal factors in the analysand's personality structure" (1977, p. 217; cited in Hoffman, 1998, p. 110). Hoffman's position implies that, since everything that occurs in analysis is jointly created by the two participants, the causes of the patient's problems should not be sought in his or her past life or inner world. Robert Langs, likewise, though he is lauded for his "interactional emphasis," nonetheless fails to pass muster because "the main thrust of all Langs's writings is that a certain environment can be established that will be relatively free of countertransference and in which the patient will therefore feel safe to engage in a very special kind of communication, one that can take place in this environment and nowhere else" (Hoffman, 1998, p. 112). Indeed, Hoffman concludes that Langs "actually takes a step back from his own sources of inspiration rather than a step forward" (p. 114).

I agree with Hoffman that there are genuine differences between conservative and radical critiques of the blank screen concept. But just as his highlighting of interaction becomes one-sided when it leads Hoffman to dispute the legitimacy of Kohut's concern with "pre-analytically existing internal factors in the analysand's personality structure," so too it is Langs and not Hoffman whose conception of countertransference is on the mark. Langs does not claim that it is possible for the analyst to create an environment that is *entirely* "free of countertransference," but only one that is *"relatively" free*. As Langs (1978) notes, only by doing so can one provide the atmosphere of safety that is a precondition in order for analysis to take place. The problem is that Hoffman casts the issue in all-or-nothing terms. Although the analyst can never be perfectly neutral or a completely blank screen, it makes a crucial difference whether or not the analyst is able to remain "blank enough" or "neutral enough." To put it metaphorically as articulated by Sheldon Bach, we know that the water of a lake is always moving; but only if the surface is sufficiently still can one detect the ripples of a stone that has been thrown in from the shore (personal communication).

In addition to resorting to polarized formulations, as I have suggested, a further consequence of Hoffman's desire to proclaim a paradigm shift is that he exaggerates the novelty of his views. In order to drive home the point that "the paradigm changes . . . only when the idea of the analyst's personal involvement is wedded to a constructivist or perspectivist epistemological position," Hoffman elaborates: "By this I mean, very specifically, that the personal participation of the analyst in the process is considered to have a continuous effect on what he or she understands about himself or herself and about the patient in the interaction" (p. 136). But what contemporary analyst of any school would disagree with this statement? I do not dispute that the relational orientation has made a contribution in enlarging the horizons and redirecting the aims of psychoanalytic inquiry. But when Hoffman's zeal leads him to proffer commonplace ideas as though they were breakthroughs I am reminded of Daniel Webster's caustic observation about the platform of the Democratic Party in the 1848 election (quoting an earlier remark by Lord Brougham): "I see nothing in it both new and valuable: 'What is valuable is not new, and what is new is not valuable.'"

In order to gain some historical and theoretical perspective on the issues raised by Hoffman's work, it is helpful to turn to Searles's paper, "The Patient as Therapist to His Analyst" (1972). Like Racker, Searles is one of the leading recent precursors of the current relational orientation, and, again like Racker, he is known especially for his writings on countertransference. Homage to this paper in particular is paid by both Hoffman when he titles one of his chapters, "The Patient as Interpreter of the Analyst's Experience," as well as by Aron in his chapter title, "The Patient's Experience of the Analyst's Subjectivity." Hoffman singles out Searles, along with Gill, Racker, and Levenson, as one of the radical critics of the blank screen concept whose main difference "from conservative critics like Strachey and Langs is in their acceptance of a certain thread of transference-countertransference enactment throughout the analysis, which stands in a kind of dialectical relationship with the process by which this enactment, as experienced by the patient, is analyzed" (1998, p. 128).

But just as it is a misconception to suppose that contemporary Freudians are oblivious to enactments, so Hoffman misrepresents the views of Searles, who in fact belongs to the camp of "conservative" rather than "radical" critics of the blank screen concept. In his indictment of Langs, Hoffman cites Langs's statement that "within the bipersonal field the patient's relationship with the analyst has both transference and non-transference components" (1978, p. 506, cited in Hoffman, 1998, p. 112). But Searles himself draws a clear distinction between "reality relatedness" and "transference relatedness," noting that "the evolving reality relatedness . . . pursues its own course, related to and paralleling, but not fully embraced by, the evolving transference relatedness over the years of the two persons' work together" (Searles, 1972, quoting from Searles, 1961, p. 383). As we shall see, the price paid by Hoffman for his one-sided preoccupation with enactments is precisely that he loses sight of transference as the necessary illusion by which psychoanalytic treatment produces its real effects; and Searles, unlike Hoffman, remains on guard against this fundamental error.

Indeed, Searles's paper now reads as an uncannily prescient caveat against the excesses of Hoffman's technique. He notes the "extremely frequent instances" of "regression in the therapist" in which, "under the stress of his efforts to cope with his patient's intense ambivalence, and his own responsive ambivalence," the therapist "has lost touch with the transference context of what is happening" (1972, p. 435). The therapist's vision, he continues, then becomes "so narrowed by the anxiety and guilt aroused in him by his awareness that he indeed possesses, as parts of his real self, increments which give immediate reality to the patient's transference to him, that he cannot achieve sufficient emotional distance from the immediate interaction to see what is happening as being a part of the patient's overall life history." The analyst, in other words, becomes so caught up in viewing the interaction as a real experience, for which he himself bears responsibility, that he fails to see it as the manifest content of a transference on the patient's part that it is the analyst's duty to analyze. In such cases, Searles cautions, the overwhelmed analyst resembles "the typical therapeutically striving patient in childhood who, in his or her efforts to bring therapeutic help to another family member has, of course, no awareness of the dimension of transference—a dimension which Freud, among his other fundamental contributions to mankind, recognized and enabled us, in turn, to recognize" (p. 435).

It is impossible for me to read Searles's commentary without thinking of the already famous—or notorious—clinical examples in which Hoffman describes "throwing away the book" in his work with patients.

Greenberg draws out the implications of Searles's line of argument by directing our attention to Hoffman's work with his patient, Diane, a single woman in her late twenties, which he rightly sees as characteristic of the clinical examples throughout the relational literature. As part of his trenchant autocritique, Greenberg notes that although "the very idea of the possibility of a standard or uniform technique has been debunked" by relational theorists, this seeming flexibility is paradoxically undercut by the fact that "the examples in so many of the important relational texts sound so much the same," to the point where the reader begins to feel that he or she is being indoctrinated by "a morality play, a series of stories that are highly prescriptive of a way that we should all be working" (2001, p. 365).

Hoffman's case of Diane has become known primarily because of his capitulation to her demand, on a day when he had been unable to grant Diane's plea for a session earlier than her usual time, that he aid her in obtaining Valium by calling an internist who could prescribe the medication. Greenberg, however, astutely highlights an earlier episode, in the second year of the analysis, in which the two of them had struggled over Diane's reluctance to continue lying on the couch. When the patient pressed Hoffman as to whether it was really necessary to the treatment for her to use the couch, saying that preserving eye contact was more important to her than lying down, Hoffman (who was a candidate in training at that time) replied, "Well, I don't know about the process, but it might be necessary for me to graduate" (1998, p. 205).

Although Hoffman objected verbally to Diane's violation of the classical rules, he colluded with her nonverbally when he met her "mischievous smile" with "a slight smile in return" (p. 205). But despite Hoffman's undeniable wit, I find his riposte troubling. It is not that I think it is always better for the patient to lie on the couch than to sit up. If Diane preferred to sit up, that may well have been what she needed to do, though of course this issue could have been explored in analysis. Rather, as Greenberg puts it, the problem with Hoffman's remark is the message it conveys to the patient that "this analysis is about both of us. . . . We each have our own motivations for being here, and in understanding what happens it is necessary to take account of my desires and my needs as much as of your own. In short, we cannot get to the bottom of your experience unless we understand it as significantly reactive to my own" (2001, p. 373).

One of the crucial components of the relational orientation, as Greenberg has pointed out, is the premise that "the analyst influences the analysand's experience in a myriad of ways. . . . Suggestion and personal influence, once the base metal of the despised and disdained psychotherapies, have become the coin of the realm" (2001, p.362). Hoffman, too, as we have seen, emphasizes that a paradigm shift in analytic thinking occurs only when the "analyst's personal involvement is wedded to a constructivist or perspectivist epistemological position" (p. 136). Theodore Jacobs, who, coming out of the mainstream tradition, has brought into prominence the term *enactment*, and likewise underscores that countertransference reactions are conveyed not simply through the analyst's obvious lapses, but also in "ways that are even more covert, as aspects of well-accepted methods and procedures" (p. 435). When countertransference takes this form, Jacobs elaborates, it is "intricately intertwined with and embedded within customary, and even unexamined, analytic techniques and the attitudes and values that inform them" (1986, p. 64; see also Ellman and Moskowitz, 1998, for papers on enactment by Boesky, McLaughlin, Chused, Renik, and others).

I am prepared to agree that the emphasis of Jacobs, Hoffman, and Greenberg on the covert aspects of the analyst's influence is an important contribution. Indeed, by inviting analysts to pay greater heed to the impact of "methods and procedures" that we might otherwise take for granted, Jacobs and the others provide a critique that, in Greenberg's words, "does what psychoanalysis at its best has always done, reminding us to attend to the inattended and forcing us to acknowledge that it is always what we don't know that affects us most deeply" (2001, p. 363).

But though I accept the initial premise of the relationalists' argument, I would draw from it the opposite conclusion. For if the analyst's influence is as great as they say it is, this should lead the analyst to exercise greater restraint and caution, not less. If we take Hoffman's conduct with Diane as an example, he seems to assume that because some degree of "personal involvement" on his part is inevitable, this gives him a license to make the analysis as much about himself and his needs as it is about the patient and her needs. Far from being an aberration, such an usurpation of the patient's rightful place as the center of attention in the analytic process follows directly from Hoffman's radical critique of the blank screen concept. In contrast to Langs's recognition of the importance of creating an environment that is "relatively free of countertransference" so that the patient will "feel safe to engage in a very special kind of communication," Hoffman seems to set out to infuse the analytic atmosphere with countertransference in order to ensure that it will approximate an ordinary relationship as closely as possible.

The fallacy in Hoffman's procedure is clearly articulated in a passage from Strachey's classic paper on therapeutic action that Hoffman himself quotes in order to criticize Strachey's distinction between the analyst as a real and a transference object. Strachey writes:

> The analytic situation is all the time threatening to degenerate into a "real" situation. But that actually means the opposite of what it appears to. It means that the patient is all the time on the brink of turning the real external object (the analyst) into the archaic one; that is to say, he is on the brink of projecting his primitive introjected imagos on to him. . . . It is important, therefore, not to submit [the patient's sense of reality] to any unnecessary strain; and that is the fundamental reason why the analyst must avoid any real behavior that is likely to confirm the patient's view of him as a "bad" or a "good" phantasy object [Strachey, 1934, p. 146, cited in Hoffman, 1998, pp. 107–108].

Strachey's reasoning is subtle and paradoxical. He shows that when the analytic situation is allowed to become "real," this means that the influence of unconscious fantasy has been intensified, not diminished. And the way that this unfortunate result comes about is that the analyst, instead of simply interpreting the patient's verbal and nonverbal communications, engages in some form of "real behavior" that serves to "confirm the patient's view of him as a 'bad' or 'good' phantasy object." In Winnicott's (1971, p. 91) terms, by magically fulfilling the patient's fantasies in reality, the analyst remains a "subjective object," instead of creating the conditions in which it is possible for him to become an object that is "objectively perceived." The analyst's real behavior colludes with the patient's unconscious belief in the omnipotence of his or her fantasies, and thereby defeats the aims of analysis.

Thus, the very passage that Hoffman quotes from Strachey to illustrate the inadequacy of a "conservative critique" of the blank screen concept offers, on closer inspection, an incisive refutation of both the theory and practice of his own "radical critique." As Hoffman himself explains the reasons for his "nonverbal acceptance of Diane's sitting up," he was "consciously disidentifying with her father," an "extraordinarily self-centered and stingy" businessman in whom she became "bitterly disappointed and disillusioned" (1998, p. 206). The crucial phrase here is "consciously disidentifying." For what it means, of course, is that Hoffman perceives his job to be one of making up in reality for the failures of Diane's father, instead of being the analyst who weathers the storms that are bound to be unleashed when she experiences him as a reincarnation of her father in the transference. Such a misconception of the analytic process, however well-intentioned, underlies Alexander and French's (1946) concept of the "corrective emotional experience." Even more to the point, it likewise underlies Ferenczi's early experiments in mutual analysis, which have been so important for the relational orientation.[5] As Aron has judiciously remarked—in words that are no less applicable to Hoffman than to Ferenczi: "It was in getting caught up in the compulsion to be the 'good' object that Ferenczi lost the ability to see the ways in which he, in fact, was failing his patients" (1996, p. 175).

The consequences of Hoffman's initial missstep with respect to Diane's conflicts over using the couch come home to roost in the later episode involving her demands first to change the time of her session, and then for a prescription for Valium. As Greenberg sums it up, because Hoffman on the earlier occasion had "taught her that what she feels is manufactured within the dyad," rather than being a manifestation of her inner world, when she subsequently becomes angry at him for refusing to change the time of her session, "she does not think about her feelings, or about her transference, or about her history, or about herself and her own private experience very much at all. Instead, she focuses her gaze on the analyst's behavior" (2001, p. 374). One could not ask for a more articulate formulation of the contemporary Freudian position on technique than this statement by Greenberg. To put the matter aphoristically, now that psychoanalysts have absorbed what the relational orientation has to teach us about the "dyadic unconscious," it is time for a return to Freud's founding insights into the *dynamic unconscious*, and a concomitant rediscovery of his lessons about transference.

---

[5]As Gedo (1996, pp. 78–79) has noted, although Alexander was Hungarian, he was analyzed by Abraham and does not appear to have had any significant contact with Ferenczi before moving to Berlin in the 1920s. Thus, the similarity between Alexander's views and Ferenczi's should be ascribed to a shared cultural heritage rather to any direct influence.

Greenberg spells out the steps of the slippery slope down which Hoffman's technique leads him and Diane. From the initial premise that everything is "manufactured within the dyad," it is "a small step for the patient to make the analyst responsible for her experience" (2001, p. 374). And then, when Diane feels pressure that she believes to be unbearable, "it is a small further step to demanding that the analyst must change his behavior in a way that will relieve some of her pain." Finally, because Hoffman "agrees with her that he is significantly responsible for her emotional experience," it is virtually impossible for him "simply to observe and to explore that experience; his anxiety and guilt about his role in causing her despair must lead him to want to act in ways that will help the patient to feel better."

As I remarked earlier, notwithstanding Hoffman's attempt to claim Searles as a sponsor of his own views, Searles's most seminal paper is in fact a prescient critique of Hoffman's excesses. Just how uncannily Searles hits the nail on the head can be seen from a comparison between Greenberg's reference to Hoffman's "anxiety and guilt" at causing Diane's distress that unseats him from his role as an analyst and the warning issued by Searles in 1972 against allowing "anxiety and guilt" aroused in the therapist by his belief that he "indeed possesses, as parts of his real self, increments which give immediate reality to the patient's transference to him." Once this occurs, as Searles understood, the therapist has "lost touch with the transference context of what is happening" and, blinded by his own regression, he "cannot achieve sufficient emotional distance from the immediate interaction to see what is happening as being a part of the patient's overall life history" (p. 435).

The problems I have pinpointed in Hoffman's analysis of Diane surface also in a second well-known specimen of his clinical work—that with a male patient, Ken, who suffered from a severe fear of heights. Due to changes in both Hoffman's schedule and Ken's, it became more convenient to hold some sessions in Hoffman's downtown office, on the twenty-first floor, rather than in his university office, where Ken rarely felt anxious. The key moment came at the end of their first downtown session when Ken asked Hoffman to walk with him to the elevator. Hoffman complied, with what appears to have been beneficial results.

My objection is not to Hoffman's spontaneous decision, which exemplifies that intangible quality of *menschlich* that should be possessed by any good analyst. It is rather to what Hoffman says about his motivations. For just as he reports responding in kind to Diane's "mischievous smile," so Hoffman writes that his decision to bend the analytic frame with Ken was "a kind of transgression that I am joining the patient in, a bit of mischief in relation to the psychoanalytic 'authorities' . . . as they are internalized as part of my own (and may be the patient's) psychoanalytic conscience" (1998, p. 234). And just as he describes his technique with Diane as one of "consciously disidentifying" with her father, so too, Hoffman explains that he went along with Ken's request because he "certainly didn't want to be like [Ken's] father blocking his shots in basketball" (p. 242). In both instances, Hoffman attempts to provide his patients with a corrective emotional experience, the impetus for which has much to do with his own desire to perpetrate "mischief" with the "psychoanalytic 'authorities.'" By throwing away the book, in short, Hoffman substitutes a countertransference enactment for an analysis of the patient's transference neurosis.

My interrogation of Hoffman's technique as he represents it in these two cases brings me to the topic of analytic neutrality. The concept of neutrality is, of course, closely allied to that of the blank screen; and it too has been subjected to a stern critique by proponents of the relational orientation. In Greenberg's summary of the current consensus, "there is no posture that the analyst can adopt that will guarantee the creation of a predictable atmosphere in the analysis. Neutrality and abstinence, keystones of classical technique, are mythic and therefore empty concepts" (2001, p. 362). "Detached objectivity," he reiterates, "is a myth" (p. 5). Greenberg sets forth this view with admirable clarity, though he himself does not embrace it wholeheartedly. Indeed, in his discussion of the issue a decade ago in *Oedipus and Beyond*, he concluded that "the neutral posture" was the one that "best serves the goals of psychoanalytic treatment" (1991, p. 224).

Clearly, I cannot agree that it is impossible for the analyst to create a "predictable atmosphere," though this does not mean one that precludes spontaneity or compassion. This was the point of the metaphor of the stone thrown into the water. Nor can I endorse the notion that neutrality and abstinence are "empty concepts." If, as Greenberg writes in his recent paper, "countertransference is the air that our patients breathe" (2001, p. 363). it surely makes a real difference whether that air is pure or polluted. Just because the ideal of neutrality can be realized only imperfectly, that does not mean that it is not worth pursuing, just as the possibility that it can be abused by being followed too rigidly is no argument against its proper use.

What is needed is a way out of the all-or-nothing absolutism of Greenberg's formulations, which accurately reflect the quality of much relational thinking, if not of his own more nuanced views. Such an alternative is proffered in the work of Loewald, which has the distinction of being held in high esteem by relationalists and contemporary Freudians alike. As Loewald describes the aim of his influential paper on therapeutic action, "what I am attempting to do is to disentangle the justified and necessary requirement of objectivity and neutrality from a model of neutrality which has its origins in propositions which I believe to be untenable" (1960, p. 227). This is precisely my aim as well. The flaw in Hoffman's extreme constructivist position is the assumption that because he has successfully attacked a simplistic version of "objectivity and neutrality," he has therefore demolished these concepts altogether. He does not consider the possibility that they may be redefined in a way that meets his objections while continuing to be a "justified and necessary requirement" of contemporary analytic practice.

It must be said that Loewald's exposition does not always make it clear to the reader where he stands in relation to the ideas he is presenting. When he states that "theneutrality of the analyst appears to be required to guarantee a *tabula rasa* for the patient's transferences" (1960, p. 223). for example, he neither accepts nor rejects this formulation unequivocally.[6] He then he goes on to say that "a specific aspect of this neutrality is that the analyst must avoid falling into the role of the environmental figure (or of his opposite) the relationship to whom the patient is transferring to the analyst" (p. 223). This is, of course, the main problem to which I have drawn attention in Hoffman's work with Diane and Ken. In his discussion of Loewald, Hoffman recognizes that, like Langs, Searles, and the other "conservative" critics of the blank screen concept, Loewald upholds the distinction between transference and countertransference experience, which Hoffman himself wishes to reject. He quotes the following passage, which certainly reflects Loewald's own ideas: "In his interpretations [the analyst] implies aspects of undistorted reality which the patient begins to grasp step by step as transferences are interpreted. This undistorted reality is mediated to the patient by the analyst, mostly by the process of chiseling away the transference distortions" (1960, p. 225, cited in Hoffman, 1998, p. 107).

---

[6]Lear (1998, p. 141) assumes that Loewald is endorsing the view of the analytic field as a *"tabula rasa."*

As we have seen, contemporary relational theory takes as its "anthem" Racker's (1968) proclamation that "the first distortion of truth in 'the myth of the analytic situation' is that analysis is an interaction between a sick person and a healthy one" (p. 132). But before we join the chorus, I think we should pause to consider whether it might be possible to "disentangle" more and less credible versions of this "myth." Loewald himself points the way when he observes that "the analyst functions as a representative of a higher stage of organization and mediates this to the patient, insofar as the analyst's understanding is attuned to what is, and the way in which it is, in need of organization" (1960, p. 239).

In other words, although it may be invidious to define the analytic relationship in terms of a distinction between "sick" and "healthy" individuals, it is entirely appropriate to conceive of it in terms of individuals who, at least by virtue of the roles they occupy, embody a lower and a higher degree of psychic organization. For Loewald, the prototype for analytic interaction at different levels of integration is "the early understanding between mother and child" (1960, p. 239). Strikingly, Hoffman employs the same parental model, which is commonplace in the analytic literature. Noting that "people usually come to therapy with problems they would like to handle better, with symptoms they want to be rid of, or with ways of being that they would like to change," Hoffman elaborates: "In many respects, the functions of the analyst are analogous to those of a parent, promoting development and change through a close relationship that is valued by both participants for its own sake, but is also always in the process of being outgrown" (1998, p. 257).

That Hoffman's views coincide in this respect with Loewald's, and are indeed compatible with those of contemporary Freudians, is all to the good so far as I am concerned. But what then becomes of Hoffman's vaunted radicalism? What is valuable here is certainly not new. According to Aron, "what may be the critical difference between most Freudian analysts and most relational analysts is that Freudian analysts assume a relatively well-analyzed, relatively healthy analyst who can monitor intermittent countertransference disruptions through continual self-analysis" (1996, p. 127). But what is the alternative? It is, to quote Aron again, an analyst who "is inevitably drawn into ongoing enactments with patients" and who "will not be detached enough (if working properly) to observe and work through these unconscious participations on [his or her] own" (pp. 127–128). This strikes me as an excellent description of Hoffman's technique. But, looking at it from the patient's point of view, to which of these analysts would one turn for help with a problem, a symptom one wanted to be rid of, or a way of being one wanted to change?

In the debates over neutrality, it generally passes unnoticed that Freud nowhere uses this term (*Neutralität*) in his technical or theoretical papers (see Hoffer, 1996). It is, rather, Strachey's translation of the German word *Indifferenz*, though Joan Riviere preferred the literal "indifference." Thus, when Freud warns, "We ought not to give up the neutrality towards the patient, which we have acquired through keeping the countertransference in check" (1915, p. 164). a silent emendation is required in order to interpret the passage correctly. Perhaps the best definition of "indifference" is the beautiful old word *disinterestedness*, employed by Matthew Arnold to describe the proper attitude to adopt toward works of art, though (in the form "disinterest") it is almost always misused today to mean "boredom" or "lack of interest."

The essence of the idea of disinterestedness, which is rooted in the Kantian tradition, is that the response of a spectator to a work of art is fundamentally different from that to other phenomena that serve a utilitarian purpose or meet a need. The disinterested spectator is not objective, but he or she is in a state of detached contemplation and does not seek to use the aesthetic experience for any ends beyond itself. Exactly the same is—or should be—true of the analyst.

As Greenberg has remarked with reference to Hoffman's clinical examples, "the issue of the analyst's desire . . . is far too rarely discussed" (2001, p. 375). Even when gross abuses such as financial or sexual exploitation are not involved, the problem of the analyst's desire surfaces whenever his or her "indifference" gives way to any other ulterior motive—to be the patient's friend, to make up for the failures of the patient's parents, etc.—however altruistic these ambitions may seem at first glance.

One of the leitmotifs of relational-constructivism has been its indictment of Freud because, in Greenberg's words, his "vision of the analyst's stance is based on the position of the observing scientist as it was understood in the nineteenth century" (1991, p. 210). Variations on this theme occur in virtually all the leading representatives of the relational orientation. For Aron, "Freud's insistence on the neutrality, abstinence, and anonymity of the analyst is a reflection of the principle of scientific detachment that insists on the rigid demarcation between the observer and the observed" (1996, p. 24). And Aron again: "Positivist principles of absolute objectivity exclude subjectivity, as Freud did, leading to an a perspectival objectivity or a 'view from nowhere,' a 'God's eye view'" (p. 261). Hoffman concurs: "the positivist or objectivist paradigm," implicitly attributed to Freud, assumes that analysts are "capable of standing outside the interaction with the patient, so that they can generate rather confident hypotheses and judgments about the patient's history, dynamics, and transference" (1998, p. 164).

It is striking that such statements about what is wrong with Freud are very rarely buttressed with quotations from passages in which Freud says what his detractors claim that he does. Rather, it seems to be taken for granted that Freud can be equated with a certain nineteenth-century "objectivism" or "positivism," which has also self-evidently been superseded by the more epistemologically sophisticated constructivism of the twentieth—now, twenty-first—century. In order for there to have been a paradigm shift, it is necessary for an old way of thinking to be supplemented by a new way of thinking. There is, accordingly, a polemical logic that drives these characterizations of Freud's thought, which are so reductive as to border on caricatures.

Ironically, in stigmatizing Freud for his alleged espousal of "aperspectival objectivity," these relationalists find themselves in the company of Adolf Grünbaum (1984). whose berating of psychoanalysis for failing to be a natural science is increasingly recognized to be based on a false dichotomy between science and hermeneutics as well as on willful misreadings of Freud's texts. In his effort to deny any hermeneutic dimension to Freud's work, Grünbaum begins *The Foundations of Psychoanalysis* with the following declaration:

> Throughout his long career, Freud insisted that the psychoanalytic enterprise has the status of a natural science. As he told us at the very end of his life, the explanatory gains from positing unconscious mental processes "enabled psychology to take its place as a natural science like any other." Then he went on to declare: "Psychology, too, is a natural science. What else can it be?" [1984, p. 2].

Grünbaum weaves two quotations from Freud into his argument. Their meaning seems to be clear-cut: Freud himself consistently regarded psychoanalysis as a natural science, and anyone who contests this fact—by proposing that it might, for example, be an interpretative discipline—is disregarding Freud's own unmistakable pronouncements on this crucial point.

How drastically Grünbaum has misread Freud becomes evident as soon as the quoted passages are restored to their contexts.[7] The second of the two, from *An Outline of Psychoanalysis* (1940a). deserves to be quoted in its entirety:

> Psychoanalysis is part of the mental science of psychology. . . . Psychology, too, is a natural science. What else can it be? But its case is different. Not everyone is bold enough to make judgements about questions of physics; but everyone—the philosopher and the man in the street alike—has his opinion on psychological questions and behaves as if he were an amateur psychologist [1940a, p. 158].

The first passage, from the posthumously published "Some Elementary Lessons in Psycho-Analysis" (1940b). where Freud seems to assert without equivocation that psychology is "a natural science like any other," continues in the following paragraph: "Every science is based on observation and experiences arrived at through the medium of our psychical apparatus. But since *our* science has as its subject that apparatus itself, the analogy ends here" (1940b, p. 282).

In both instances, therefore, Grünbaum fails to quote Freud's immediately ensuing sentences that radically qualify any attempt to equate psychoanalysis with the natural sciences. What Freud gives to natural science with one hand, he takes away with the other. The question, "What else can it be?" is not simply rhetorical. Psychoanalysis is both like and unlike other sciences; and what makes it unique is precisely its fusion of the subjective with the objective dimensions in a way that engages people in a visceral way about the obstacles that confront them in everyday life. Whether Grünbaum's omissions are due to deliberate bad faith or simply to inadvertent carelessness, they deal a death blow to his project of trying to turn Freud's own definitions of psychoanalysis against him by showing that psychoanalysis fails to live up to the scientific claims that he allegedly made for it.

Grünbaum's sins should not, of course, be visited on the heads of the

---

[7]Grünbaum's taking of Freud's passages out of context is noted by Forrester (1997, p. 241).

relationalists; but I think it remains telling how closely their unflattering picture of Freud as a thinker who would "exclude subjectivity" in favor of an "aperspectival objectivity" resembles Grünbaum's tendentious distortions. Let us, by all means, take Freud to task whenever it is warranted; but let us at least do so on the basis of a scrupulous and fair-minded scrutiny of what he actually wrote.

How new, then, is the new American psychoanalysis? Is it a fork in the road, or simply one more bend in the river? Time will tell, and there are no views from nowhere. If I have engaged Irwin Hoffman in a psychoanalytic dialogue, it is meant to pay tribute to the stimulus that his work, like that of his colleagues, has given to my own thinking. As Aron has truly written, analysts "should do nothing with patients that they would not in principle be willing to discuss with colleagues, with the professional community, and with the public" (1996, p. 264). Hoffman has enriched us all by making public his often risky but always honest and compassionate labors as a clinician. Like Freud in his case histories, he gives us the evidence we need to form our own conclusions and to hold him accountable where we think he may have been mistaken. If Hoffman can thus be compared to Freud, so too, as I have suggested, my own effort in this paper to reach out from the contemporary Freudian to the relational tradition finds its counterpart in Greenberg's self-critical examination of the relational orientation that he himself has helped to call into being. That such dialectical crossings are possible—and increasingly common—seems to me the best possible omen for the future of American psychoanalysis.

REFERENCES

ALEXANDER, F., & FRENCH, T.M. (1946). *Psychoanalytic Theory: Principles and Applications.* New York: Ronald Press.

ARON, L. (1996). *A Meeting of Minds: Mutuality in Psychoanalysis.* Hillsdale, NJ: Analytic Press.

ELLMAN, S.J., & MOSKOWITZ, M., Eds. (1998). *Enactment: Toward a New Approach to the Therapeutic Relationship.* Northvale, NJ: Aronson.

FERENCZI, S. (1928). The elasticity of psychoanalytic technique. In: *Final Contributions to the Problems and Methods of Psycho-Analysis,* ed. M. Balint; tr. E. Mosbacher. London: Karnac Books, 1980, pp. 108–125.

FORRESTER, J. (1997). *Dispatches from the Freud Wars.* Cambridge, MA: Harvard University Press.

FREUD, S. (1915). Observations on transference-love (Further recommendations on the technique of psycho-analysis III). *Standard Edition*

12:157–171. London: Hogarth Press, 1958.

——— (1940a). An Outline of Psycho-Analysis. *Standard Edition* 23:139–207. London: Hogarth Press, 1964.

——— (11940b). Some elementary lessons in psycho-analysis. *Standard Edition* 23:279–286.

GEDO, J. (1996). O, patria mia. In: *Ferenczi's Turn in Psychoanalysis,* ed. P.L. Rudnytsky, A. Bókay, & P. Giampieri-Deutsch. New York: New York University Press pp. 77–88.

GODLEY, W. (2001). Saving Masud Khan. *London Review of Books,* February 22:3–7.

GREENBERG, J. (1991). *Oedipus and Beyond: A Clinical Theory.* Cambridge, MA: Harvard University Press.

——— (2001). The analyst's participation: A new look. *Journal of the American Psychoanalytic Association* 49:359–380.

——— & MITCHELL, S. (1983). *Object Relations in Psychoanalytic Theory.* Cambridge, MA: Harvard University Press.

GRÜNBAUM, A. (1984). *The Foundations of Psychoanalysis: A Philosophical Critique.* Berkeley: University of California Press.

HOFFER, A. (1996). Introduction. In: *The Correspondence of Sigmund Freud and Sándor Ferenczi, 1914–1919,* Vol. 2. Cambridge, MA: Harvard University Press, pp. xvii–xlvi.

HOFFMAN, I.Z. (1998). *Ritual and Spontaneity in the Psychoanalytic Process.* Hillsdale, NJ: Analytic Press.

JACOBS, T.J. (1986). *Enactments: Toward a New Approach to the Therapeutic Relationship,* ed. S.J. Ellman & M. Moskowitz. Northvale, NJ: Jason Aronson, 1998, pp. 63–74.

KOHUT, H. (1977). *The Restoration of the Self.* New York: International Universities Press.

LANGS, R. (1978). *Technique in Transition.* New York: Jason Aronson.

LEAR, J. (1998). *Open Minded: Working Out the Logic of the Soul.* Cambridge, MA: Harvard University Press.

LOEWALD, H. (1960). On the therapeutic action of psychoanalysis. In: *Papers on Psychoanalysis.* New Haven, CT: Yale University Press, 1980, pp. 221–256.

MITCHELL, S.A. (1988). *Relational Concepts in Psychoanalysis: An Integration.* Cambridge, MA: Harvard University Press.

——— (1993). *Hope and Dread in Psychoanalysis.* New York: Basic Books.

——— (1997). *Influence and Autonomy in Psychoanalysis.* Hillsdale, NJ: Analytic Press.

———— (2000). Relationality: *From Attachment to Intersubjectivity.* Hillsdale, NJ: Analytic Press.

RACKER, H. (1968). *Transference and Countertransference.* New York: International Universities Press.

RICHARDS, A.D. (1999). Squeaky chairs and straw persons: An intervention in the contemporary psychoanalytic debate. *The Round Robin,* 14:6–9.

SEARLES, H.F. (1961). The evolution of the mother transference in psychotherapy with the schizophrenic patient. In: *Collected Papers on Schizophrenia and Related Subjects.* International Universities Press: Madison, CT, 1996, pp. 349–380.

———— (1972). *The patient as therapist to his analyst. In: Countertransference and Related Subjects: Selected Papers.* New York: International Universities Press, 1979 pp. 380–459.

SPEZZANO, C. (1995). "Classical" vs. "contemporary" theory. *Contemporary Psychoanalysis* 31:20–46.

STRACHEY, J. (1934). The nature of the therapeutic action of psychoanalysis. *International Journal of Psycho-Analysis* 15:127–159.

WALLERSTEIN, R.S. (1998). The new American psychoanalysis: A commentary. *Journal of the American Psychoanalytic Association* 46:1021–1043.

WINNICOTT, D.W. (1971). *Playing and Reality.* London: Tavistock.

IV. Interpersonal and Relational Theory

Relational theorists began their re-examination of psychoanalytic concepts in the late 1970s and early 1980s. In Section 3, we find Richards engaged in a spirited dialogue and debate with these theorists. The atmosphere was charged as the Relational theorists, of the day, rejected all things Freudian, including contemporary classical theory, yet claimed any critique of their work as "trenchant" (Meissner, 2000) or "mean spirited" (Bromberg, 2002). Since this time, new and seasoned voices have been added to the relational roster (e.g., Aron, Renik, Hirsch, Benjamin, Altman) and older voices, from many camps, have engaged the dialogue with greater tolerance and reflection (e.g., Abend, Gill, Greenberg, Ogden, Rangell, Rothstein, Stolorow). The current section has three chapters. The first two (1993, 1995) are early critiques of relational theory.

In Chapter 11 - Review Essay: Relational Concepts in Psycho-analysis: An Integration by Stephen A. Mitchell, (with Bachant) reviews Mitchell's 1988 work. Their basic question was:

- How does centralizing the "relational matrix" benefit or detract from the clinical situation?

Chapter 12, "Relational Models In Psychoanalytic Theory" (with Bachant and Lynch) provides a broader critique of the growth of this perspective with a particular focus on psychoanalytic technique. This task was complicated, at the time, because "relational theory" was made up of a variety of contributions and points of view, which made any generalization difficult. The authors chose five exponents of relational theory for discussion—Mitchell, Greenberg, Ogden, Aron, and Slavin and Kriegman) the overriding question for the reader is:

- How do Relational tenets affect the structuring of the psychoanalytic situation?

In Chapter 13, "Benjamin Wolstein and Us: Many Roads Lead to Rome," Richards (with A.K. Richards) assess the work of Benjamin Wolstein. Wolstein is considered by many as a forefather of relational theory. The Richardses comment on this work with special interest in the psychoanalytic situation and the therapeutic action of psychoanalysis. Three main goals of the paper are addressed in the following questions:

- What was lost to the broader psychoanalytic community during the period where Wolstein's contributions were isolated?
- What were the areas of convergence in clinical findings between Wolstein and his contemporaries?
- What are the possible solutions to address an end to theoretical estrangements?

Book Review Essay   CHAPTER 11

(1988). Cambridge, MA: Harvard University Press, ix + 306 pp.

Relational Concepts in Psychoanalysis: An Integration By Stephen A. Mitchell

[Bachant, J.L. & Richards, A.D. (1993). *Psychoanalytic Dialogues* 3:431–460.]

In *Relational Concepts in Psychoanalysis: an Integration,* Stephen A. Mitchell presents a challenging, creative articulation of the ways in which relations with others shape and color psychic life. Bringing prodigious talent and breadth of knowledge to his task, Mitchell portrays contemporary psychoanalysis as dominated by two competing perspectives: Freud's drive theory and a cluster of theories that he depicts as relationally based. Mitchell sets as his goal the unification of an array of relational perspectives (primarily British object relations theory, interpersonal psychoanalysis, and self psychology) into a comprehensive theoretical framework. This perspective, which describes relations with others as the building blocks of psychic structure, is contrasted with aspects of Freudian drive theory throughout the book and occasionally with contemporary classical thought.

Within Mitchell's framework, "mind is composed of relational configurations" (p. 3). Mind becomes dyadic in nature and is defined as "transactional patterns and internal structures derived from an interactive, interpersonal field" (p. 17). His system rests on the premise that repetitive patterns within human experience are derived from a tendency to preserve the continuity, connections, and familiarity of one's personal, interactional world. Mitchell describes the "relational matrix" as an organizing principle, a counterpart to drive (the generalization drawn from internally motivated, unconscious wishes), and contends that the fundamental question is whether drive and relational thinking can "work together in a smooth, consistent manner that is mutually enhancing" (pp. 52–53).

His answer to this question is a resounding no. Describing attempts at integrating drive and relational constructs as ultimately not very useful because they characteristically lack clearly defined terms, Mitchell opts instead for a system unmixed with drive-model premises, in which "all meaning is generated in the context of the relational matrix" (p. 61). He asserts that what matters in theory construction is the operational metaphor of mind and offers us a choice between two dichotomous positions: "psychological meaning is either regarded as inherent and brought to the relational field, or as negotiated through interaction" (pp. 4–5). Freud would disagree. But by counterposing one aspect of Freud's theory (what Mitchell has decided is his drive model) with his own relational perspective, Mitchell continually asks the reader to choose between the purely relational mode perspective and his version of the Freudian drive model. The message is clear—you cannot have both. Thus Mitchell frames an inherent opposition between drive and relational premises into the structure of his argument. What are the grounds for the establishment of this opposition, for deciding that relational considerations should be primary? Are they clinical? Philosophical? Logical?

The Freudian perspective has sustained the continuity of a theory that has proven useful over time not only because of the strength of its fundamental points but also because of the ability of those positions to be modified within a continuous framework. The assertion that an integration of drive and relational concepts is unworkable dismisses the extensive clinical descriptions found in Freud's case histories, 50 years of psychoanalytic development, and a host of theoreticians (Freud, Klein, Loewald, Modell, Brenner, Kernberg, and Pine among many others) who have insisted on the fundamental complementarity between drive and relational contributions to psychic functioning. Mitchell appears to want to nail Freud to the mast of a nonsocial, noninteractive, nonrelational drive theory—to see Freud as oblivious to, or uninterested in, object relations.

In fact, all Freud's ideas about human development and about infantile sexuality include a theory of object relations. They make no sense unless one sees them as part of a theory of object relations. Friedman (1988) warns of the ease with which the comparative theoretician can lose sight of the interdependence of Freud's *multiple perspectives,* which contain drive-discharge features, transformational features, hermeneutic features, structural features, and object relations features. Referring to the earlier book written with Greenberg (Greenberg and Mitchell, 1983), Friedman (1988) comments:

> These authors do recognize that Freud's theory is an amalgam of considerations. But in order to set up a basis for comparison,

they assume that Freud was essentially trying to construct what they call a drive-structure theory, and that other aspects of his system were attempts to accommodate drive-structure theory to object relations considerations. That is an interesting way to organize an exegesis, but it may confuse the reader, who is likely to forget that extracting the essence of a drive-structure model from Freud's theory (Greenberg and Mitchell, 1983, p. 24) is not the same thing as extracting the essence of Freud's theory. We would need quite an elaborate argument to establish any one aspect of Freud's system as its essence rather than just a facet that interests the investigator [p. 668].

Unfortunately, *Relational Concepts in Psychoanalysis* continues in the earlier tradition. Moreover, the propensity to organize the field into dichotomies is curiously *misattributed* to Freud. For example, Mitchell (p. 44) quotes Freud (1916–1917) speaking of the calamities of childhood:

These events of childhood are somehow demanded as a necessity . . . they are among the essential elements of a neurosis. If they have occurred in reality, so much to the good; but if they have been withheld by reality, they are put together from hints and supplemented by phantasy. The outcome is the same, and up to the present we have not succeeded in pointing to any difference in the consequences whether phantasy or reality has had the greater share in these events of childhood. . . . Whence comes the need for these phantasies and the material for them? There can be no doubt that their sources lie in the instincts [p. 370].

Mitchell continues with the following thesis:

In this crucial shift Freud replaced one set of ideas, emphases and foci with another, establishing two clusters of dichotomous concepts which later became associated with the terms "intrapsychic" and "interpersonal": fantasy vs. perception, psychic reality vs. a theory of environmental influences. One might argue that Freud's shift in theory in 1897 split the different sides of these dialectics unnaturally from each other, and that we have been trying to heal that split ever since [p. 44].

In his zeal to support the contention that Freud created an unnatural split and thereby established two clusters of dichotomous concepts, Mitchell omits a key sentence. In the original, Freud's (1916–1917) statement "up to the present we have not succeeded in pointing to any difference in the consequences, whether phantasy or reality has had the greater share in these events of childhood" is followed by: "Here we simply have once again one of the complemental relations that I have so often mentioned; moreover it is the strangest of all we have met with" (p. 370).

That sentence substantially changes the reader's perception of Freud's view of the relation between fantasy and reality. In particular, it renders Mitchell's contention that Freud "replaced one set of ideas, emphases, and foci with another" a distortion of Freud's position. Freud argues in this passage, as he does in many other passages throughout his clinical (see especially the Wolf Man case) and theoretical work that reality and fantasy stand in a "complemental relation" to each other, not that they are dichotomously split. The complementary nature of internal and external processes can hardly be more clearly stated. Far from a conceptual split, Freud proposes here what he articulates even more clearly in his "History of the Psycho-Analytic Movement" (Freud, 1914), that disposition and experience are "linked up in an indissoluble aetiological unity" (pp. 17–18). To ignore this assertion leaves the less than diligent reader with a completely erroneous understanding of Freud's position. Even a cursory look at the development of psychoanalysis, from the evolution of the method of free association, to the discovery of the value of the transference, to Freud's (1900) demonstration in *The Interpretation of Dreams* that "pathological" processes are operant in normal mental functioning, establishes that Freud thought in continuums and dualities, not dichotomies.

It is instructive and, perhaps, essential, in grappling with the question of whether we must choose between a drive and a relational perspective, to examine further the thinking of *contemporary* classical analysts on the nature of drive. Loewald's (1972) understanding of the relationship between drive and relational determinants of psychic structure is in marked contrast to Mitchell's position. In a paper that emphasizes the importance of preoedipal early disturbances in the negative therapeutic reaction, Loewald (1972) states:

> Instincts, in other words, are to be seen as relational phenomena from the beginning and not as autochthonous forces seeking dis-

charge, which discharge is understood as some kind of emptying of energy potential, in a closed system or out of it. Instinctual drives, their qualities and intensities, their fusions and defusions, and their proportional strength are codetermined by the "environmental factors" that enter into their very organization as motivational forces [p. 322].

Brenner (1982) speaks directly to the issue of the nature of drive in contemporary classical psychoanalytic thought. In questioning Freud's conception of drive as a phenomenon on the frontier between mind and body, Brenner redefines drive as a purely psychological phenomenon. He contends that the idea that there is a frontier between the mind and the body is a "relic of the time when the separateness of mind and body was arguable" (p. 20), a disguised version of the belief in an incorporeal soul.

Since all mental functioning is somatic, it is unnecessary and, in some respects, even misleading to separate one group of psychological phenomena from others by labeling them as somatic in nature. . . . All psychological phenomena are somatically dependent. All are an aspect of brain functioning. . . . Everything psychic is somatic as well. One need not hesitate, therefore, to base a theory of drives on psychoanalytic data, despite Freud's reluctance to do so himself. . . . The evidential basis for psychoanalytic drive theory is the conscious and unconscious wishes of patients as disclosed by the psychoanalytic method of observation. It should be noted that each observation is personal and unique. It is the wish of a particular patient for a particular kind of gratification from or at the hands of a particular person under particular circumstances. . . . It is a wish that has a uniquely personal history, a uniquely personal form and a uniquely personal content. Nor is a wish ever just "an aggressive wish." It is always a wish to do something to somebody, again with a special history, a special content and a special form [pp. 19–22].

An emphasis on the interrelation between drive and object is an integral part of this formulation. Drive is here clearly and explicitly redefined, articulated in a way that is intricately tied to the "relational matrix." It is represented in the mind as a conscious or unconscious "wish to do something to somebody, again with a special history, a special content and a special form."

Brenner clearly differentiates between the *concept* of drive, which is a theoretical construct (as is relational matrix), and the *manifestation* of drive, that is, specific conscious and unconscious wishes. Mitchell confuses these levels of discourse throughout *Relational Concepts in Psychoanalysis*. He refers to the concept of drive as a generalization when he should be speaking of the clinical manifestations, the drive derivatives. For example, when describing the differences between the interpretive strategies of the drive and relational models, Mitchell says that in the drive model (is this Freud's drive model or the contemporary drive model?), "elements of the patient's life and free associations are broken down and grouped according to the categories provided by the drives. In essence, the variety of life is seen as an array of metaphors for sexual and aggressive wishes" (p. 91).

Interest in the particularities of the clinical situation, the "who is doing what to whom," is replaced by the contention that what is important in drive theory is a classification of experience into "preformed categories." Nothing could be farther from the truth. The essence of the contemporary classical position is rooted in *examining the individual patient's unique* fantasies, fears, and wishes that emerge through the method of free association. Mitchell is here demonstrating a misunderstanding both of drive theory and of the distinction between drive as a theoretical generalization and the clinical manifestation of drive, the *specific* wishes (conscious and unconscious) we observe or infer from the analysand's associations.

It is exceedingly unclear throughout the book where Mitchell is speaking of Freudian drive theory as it existed half a century ago and where he is contrasting a purely relational perspective with that of current classical psychoanalysis. For example, although Mitchell says on page three that his book is based on the belief that there is a fundamental distinction between Freud's drive theory and the major trends within *contemporary* psychoanalytic thinking, on the next page he uses Freud's (1924, p. 178) statement that "anatomy is destiny" as illustrative of the way in which the integration between considerations of biology and culture is handled by the drive model. We are led to believe that when Mitchell speaks of the drive model, he is talking only about Freud's drive model and not about how contemporary classical analysis is practiced or thought about today. And yet in the preface to his book, Mitchell identifies Freud's drive theory as one of the two broad, competing perspectives in contemporary psychoanalysis (p. viii). Which is it? Is there a distinction between contemporary psychoanalytic thinking and what he describes as Freud's drive theory, or is Freud's drive theory one of the two "competing perspectives" in psychoanalysis today? This confusion permeates the book and once again leaves the reader with some serious misunderstandings of both Freud's drive theory and how contemporary psychoanalysis is practiced today.

This is not the place to undertake an exhaustive compendium of the ways in which contemporary classical psychoanalysis has integrated drive and relational constructs into a theoretical system. (In this regard see Rangell, 1985; Spruiell, 1988; Knapp, 1991.) Rather, we shall examine the ways in which Mitchell describes the purely relational perspective as differing from the classical psychoanalytic perspective. Specifically, how does application of the "relational matrix" point of view change our apprehension of the clinical situation? What is the added value? What is the cost? This particular comparison addresses differences between the relational and the contemporary classical positions; although other comparisons would, no doubt, have much to contribute, it is beyond the scope of the present paper to consider them here. Among the issues delineated by Mitchell, we focus here on sexuality and the importance of early experience in the development of psychic structure, because the differences between the perspectives in these areas are particularly significant.

In addition, although it is not given the status of a focused presentation by Mitchell, we examine his use of transference and attempt to conceptualize the differences between the classical and relational perspectives on this issue. Finally, we have a word to say about the politics of model making.

Sexuality

Mitchell poses for himself the task of retaining the phenomenological accuracy and clinical utility of Freud's theory of sexuality without yoking it to outmoded notions of drives. Arguing that sexuality is not driven from within but is evoked from without, by others, he cites George Klein (1976), Holt (1976), and Schafer (1976) as making rich contributions to this debate. He suggests that sensual pleasure is not sought after simply for its own sake and that the view of sex as an internally arising drive or tension that causes the organism to seek out the object is unsupported by animal research. Sexuality becomes a response or an action rather than an internal pressure.

Mitchell proposes a theory of sexuality within an explicitly relational perspective in which sexuality is not "mandated by a pressured expression of inner necessity" (p. 94), that is, not structured by drive derivatives (specific, unconscious infantile wishes). He describes two areas of contribution to the development of a relational view of sexuality, one stressing "the tie to the other, how it is established and how it is preserved," the other area emphasizing "self continuity and the preservation of identity" (p. 94).

Paradoxically, Mitchell appeals to the work of Melanie Klein (1945, 1957) and Kernberg (1988)—both include in their theories the concept of drive—to elaborate a vision of sexual functioning as "a response or action within an interactive context" (p. 89). Mitchell is willing to borrow one aspect of a conceptualization (the object-relational aspect of Klein and Kernberg's formulations) but sees no problem with simply discarding the drive component of these concepts. Mitchell here confounds drive and relational premises. He borrows concepts from Freud and those who extended his theories that assume the existence of the drives, represented in the mind as *internally motivated, unconscious wishes,* yet he does not see the contradictions involved in attempting to combine his relational understanding with the Freudian conceptual base. For example, the concepts of transference and such other mental mechanisms as defense contain, as part of their conceptualization, assumptions of unconscious, infantile wishes that push for expression in the current reality. Mitchell uses one aspect of these concepts but simply discards the full conceptual foundation and thus leaves the reader with concepts whose meanings have been excised from their foundations.

A second aspect of the relational understanding of sexuality described by Mitchell, centers on the role of sexual experience in shaping and maintaining a sense of self or identity. This perspective proposes that the most pressing human concern is to maintain a sense of identity; sexual experiences are understood as deriving their meaning and intensity through their connection to this vital need. Here Mitchell, referring to the work of Person (1980) and Simon and Gagnon (1973), suggests that male sexuality only appears to be more driven and compulsive because male gender identity is more fragile than is female gender identity and is more easily threatened.

What are we given in exchange for discarding the body's role in sexuality? Mitchell's own contribution to the relational understanding of sexuality resides in his suggestion that the predominant meanings of sexuality often derive from the basic patterns of search, surrender, and escape. He writes: "Here the establishment of strong connections to others, in reality or in fantasy, is presumed to be primary. Forms of relationship are seen as fundamental, and life is understood largely as an array of metaphors for expressing and playing out relational patterns" (p. 91).

He further maintains that if "sexuality is not a powerful, dangerous, preconstituted push from within but a response or action within an interactive context, *sexuality becomes a function, an expression of the relational matrix*" (p. 89; italics added). Thus, according to Mitchell, the relational matrix is the primary organizer, and sexuality is a function of it, not an organizer of experience in its own right.

This description of sexuality raises several important questions. If sexuality is a result of particular patterns of connectedness to others, if everything hinges on the unique specificities of interactions with others, how do we account for the demonstrable commonalities of human nature? Mitchell is asking us to eliminate sexuality as an organizing force in its *own right,* but what does he add? How does categorizing the metaphors for expressing and playing out our relational patterns into "search, surrender and escape" take us beyond a descriptive level of discourse? What does it add to our theoretical understanding, our clinical apprehension of the individual case? What is lost?

Consider Mitchell's example of the analysand who

> had a passing acquaintance with psychoanalytic theory and considered himself to be wholly understandable in terms of Freud's theory of instinctual drive and the structural model. He was filled with bad, bestial drives and therefore had to keep himself always on a short leash. It was crucial to be solicitous always of other people, providing what they seemed to expect, as a way to keep his badness concealed. He felt he had a harsh superego, a projective extension of the primitivity of his own bestial impulses [pp. 120–121].

Mitchell's application of relational model thinking generates the following:

> Involvement with his parents, particularly his scapegoating and abusive mother, necessitated the internalization of her image of

him as bad and animalistic, and the fashioning of a false-self personality, extremely attentive to the expectations of the other, hiding any spontaneous needs or wishes. This compulsive compliance with others regularly generated considerable rage and a longing to escape this interpersonal pressure, to be free of the need to be good—to be, in fact, the bestial bad boy his parents had felt him to be. Thus, the superego introjects came first, and the bestial wishes and impulses were a defiant reaction to them, a protest in which he asserted his right to his own existence and pleasure in the only form available to him, the image of himself as greedy and animalistic. These experiences redoubled his need for the harsh parental introjects, prodding him with critical judgments he felt necessary to keep himself under control and out of trouble.

The phenomenology of bestiality thus is often part of a neurotic loop (see Wachtel, 1982), within the relational matrix. It is generated as a defiant reaction to compliance and a compulsion to elevate [pp. 120–121].

Mitchell provides in this report a compelling analysis of one dimension of this case that contributes a valuable understanding of the patient's relationships. But does it provide the reader with the most comprehensive understanding of this patient's functioning? Mitchell presents us with a one-sided analysis that would blind the clinician to other crucial dynamics. Because the clinical material is insufficient, additional commentary can be only speculative, but a contemporary Freudian would certainly be alert to other complexities. For example, this analysand's noisy emphasis on his "bestiality" may serve a defensive purpose. Beyond protecting the patient from recognizing the badness of the object, the emphasis on bestiality may ward off the possibility of becoming aware of his own sexual impulses. Both defenses are important and involved, simultaneously. Perhaps this analysand prefers to see himself as a beast rather than as the passive object of his mother's desire. He may be dealing with a primitive sexual identification with the man as the passive recipient of the sadistic, phallic woman (the father is nonexistent in this example; we know him only from his absence). Typically, such an intrusive mother will invoke and even force the child's sexuality into a passive reciprocal mode, with little room to express his own phallic assertive strivings.

Demonstrating that sexuality is going to be influenced by the relational context is nothing new. It is part of Freudian theory and always has been. The free and uninhibited expression of this patient's "bestiality," his greedy and animalistic aspect, may have been the assertion of his autonomy, but it might also have served, simultaneously, as a defense against the passive side of his sexuality, which might have been more deeply frightening. Mitchell's analysis is fine as far as it goes, but it does not relate to the underlying need for the patient to put himself in a passive position that he then has to defend against. The classical position, by granting sexuality an organizing capacity in its own right, enable the clinician to grasp additional levels of meaning in the clinical material.

Mitchell's example illustrates another significant difference between relational and classical approaches to sexuality: it ignores the role of oedipal dynamics as a topic worthy of discussion. Despite the fact that the passions involved in this dynamic are exemplars of the power of experience-in-relation to interact with the unconscious fantasies typically generated during this period, there is in Relational Concepts not one reference to the oedipal complex that reveals Mitchell's understanding of oedipal dynamics from a relational point of view. Even more to the point, Mitchell's clinical examples yield nothing of the passions of oedipal desires being played out, even in the "relational configurations" of the analysand, intrapsychically or interpersonally. Stripped of its genitality, the oedipus complex becomes for Mitchell more of a struggle for self-definition while the incest taboo is likened to "a bulwark against dedifferentiating regression" (p. 87). Elimination of the Oedipus is necessary for Mitchell to sustain his contention that relational configurations alone are capable of organizing experience. To acknowledge that there is a readiness to organize experience in particular ways at particular times is to undermine this premise, and so one of the most powerful relational configurations in human development must be tossed aside.

The Freudian concept of the oedipal dynamic as an intrinsic, "organized body of loving and hostile wishes which the child inevitably experiences toward its parents" (La Planche and Pontalis, 1973) structures an integration of drive and relational issues at the very heart of psychoanalytic thinking. The individual is seen as inevitably experiencing drives and adaptations in the context of relationships with others. The other (from the perspective of the subject) can be understood in part *as a symbolic representation of endogenous processes.* Not only are we affected by our significant others, but we, in turn, affect those others and use them to carry and represent certain aspects of ourselves, just as during the preverbal era, we use our own bodies to carry inner urges and meanings *in addition to relational ones.* Although there is considerable difference among current Freudian thinkers about the *centrality* of the Oedipus (some analysts place great weight on preoedipal issues), the power with which the oedipal complex integrates passionate unconscious wishes with powerful relational considerations is appreciated by all as contributing an invaluable dimension to our understanding of development and the treatment situation.

Continuing to frame the issue of sexuality dichotomously, Mitchell asks a key question: "Is the child driven toward certain predetermined experiences and fantasies or do the exquisite sensations provided through bodily experiences with others take on passionate significance and meaning from the relational context in which they occur?" (p. 92). To maintain theoretical consistency, Mitchell needs not only to avoid any mention of oedipal dynamics but also to pit himself against the entire idea of the existence of a readiness to organize experience in a particular way. If experience is determined by relational configurations and relational configurations alone, then similarities in experience are simply coincidental or the result of similar interactions.

A second aspect of Mitchell's question concerns the nature of the driven quality of sexuality. This is, in fact, a central issue and one that decisively differentiates between relational and contemporary classical perspectives. *Is* there a driven quality to sexuality and those experiences that symbolize it, or is passion something that resides in the "significance" (however it may be internalized) of the relational context in which the child finds himself? Does it have to be either/or?

Mitchell does not seem to recognize that Freud's ideas about infantile sexuality are deeply embedded in ideas about the child's place in the nuclear family, with all the passions and conflicts that the relational environment creates. What Mitchell misses is that it is not just any others who are important to the child; it is certain, very specific people: mother, father, sister, brother. These individuals loom large because of who they are and how they are represented in the child's mind. The nature of this representation is determined by contributions from both drive derivatives (specific wishes in specific contexts) and the unique manner in which they hook up with relational considerations. To purge the unique manifestations of libidinal and aggressive drive derivatives from the arena of discourse leaves us with a cleaner theory but one whose explanatory power is compromised. It does not address the relation between temperament and instinct, and it does not account for transference, defense, and other drive-based phenomena. Sexuality, for Mitchell, becomes a response, a function of the relational matrix, rather than an organizer of experience in its own right. The driven quality of sexuality in the Freudian corpus is transformed into a passive kind of arousal, an arousal that is caused by relationships rather than generated from within. Turning Freud's argument on its head, Mitchell portrays a world in which "sex does not bring us to relationships, relationships bring us to sex" (Hatcher, 1990, p. 130). The contemporary classical position, contained within a framework that incorporates multiple perspectives, including drive and relational factors, understands human beings both as passionately driven and as deriving meaning from the relational context. There is, to use Freud's term, a "complemental" relationship. Bodily experiences and events are understood not only as "evoked potentials which derive meaning from the way they become patterned in interaction with others," but as *actively* "pushing and shaping experience" in addition. Mitchell proposes an essentially passive understanding of sexuality, one in which sexuality is used in the service of other functions (i.e., ties to others, maintenance of identity, and so on), one in which potentials are evoked, and one that derives meaning primarily from relational considerations but one that serves no function of its own.

The Role of Early Experience in the Development of Psychic Structure

The Oedipus complex is not the only casualty of Mitchell's revision of psychoanalytic theory. His effort to derive all experience from relational considerations alone, to purge every aspect of drive from his conceptualization results in the necessary abandonment of powerful technical and theoretical principles. The consequences of this abandonment are profound and create decisive differences between his relational model and that of contemporary classical psychoanalysis.

According to Mitchell, what appears to be the influence of early experience structuring psychic life is, instead, the manifestation of patterns of relating that have been repeated in different forms throughout development. Thus, Mitchell contends that the importance generally ascribed to early experience in the development of psychic structure is illusory and would be better understood as an expression of needs that are active throughout life.

Mitchell cites Stern (1985) and Rutter (1979) to bolster his claim that there is little evidence to support the notion that early trauma causes later emotional damage. He goes even further, suggesting that although children from deprived and disturbed backgrounds suffer all sorts of difficulties, even this does not necessarily implicate the earliest years as developmentally crucial. Mitchell is stretching some very recent, incomplete research data to support a sweeping dismissal of clinical theory that has considerable data to back it up. In its place, he proposes that

> developmental continuity is a reflection of similarities in the kinds of problems human beings struggle with at all points in the life cycle. . . . In this view the interpersonal environment plays a continuous, crucial role in the creation of experience. The earliest experiences are meaningful not because they lay down structural residues which remain fixed, but because they are the earliest representation of patterns of family structure and interactions which will be repeated over and over in different forms at different developmental stages [p. 149].

Mitchell's rejection of early experience as exercising a critical role in the formation of psychic structure substantially changes psychoanalytic theory, particularly in relation to the pleasure principle, the theory of the dynamic unconscious, and technique. Gratification, in the contemporary classical perspective, is a central experience, especially for the young child who experiences so much mediated through the body. Gratification or the lack of it is understood by classical analysts as playing a decisive role in developing psychic structure and motivating behavior. The pleasure principle proposes that unsatisfied wishes of drive origin persistently seek gratification. Childhood wishes that remain ungratified because they arouse unpleasure and conflict are understood to remain active and to drive the person continually in the direction of gratification. This is what Freud speaks of as the dynamic unconscious, a concept that Hatcher (1990), in a recent review of *Relational Concepts in Psychoanalysis,* claims that Mitchell has omitted in a "strategy of simplification" (p. 134). It does make a difference whether we think that infantile fears and fantasies play a central role in the creation of adult anxiety and the repetitive reenactments that symbolize them or whether we imagine that the persistence of patterns of relating are wholly accounted for by relational configurations. Technically, the contemporary Freudian looks for the way in which primitive wishes and fears, manifest in unconscious fantasy, exert a powerful and structuring influence on adult experience. Working through these primitive wishes and fears is seen as a necessary component of change. We can see the application of this thinking in the understanding of the dream as an attempt to fulfill an *infantile* wish, as well as in the exploration of enactments that carry and symbolize conflicted wishes and fears that have been cut off from conscious awareness. The ability to structure hypotheses that speak to the *intrapsychic* conflicts of the analysand adds a powerful and profound dimension to the treatment that is not addressed in Mitchell's formulations. Mitchell is a master at fleshing out the variety and complexity of the ways in which we seek to maintain connectedness with patterns of relating that have come to feel like home to us, but he neglects to consider intrapsychic dynamics except insofar as they are represented in relational configurations.

Contemporary classical psychoanalysts, on the other hand, believe that in addition to providing "strong connections to others," relational configurations become infused, intertwined, and symbolized with sexual and aggressive drive derivatives—*specific, unique wishes* with "a special history, a special content and a special form" (Brenner, 1982, p. 22). To remove gratification from our understanding of development and to ignore the dynamic unconscious in our understanding of mental functioning is to disconnect a major dimension of human motivation from psychoanalytic explanation. We are left, in Mitchell's system, with the fully explanatory weight falling on relational patterns and no significance attributed to the fact that gratification itself and the dynamic unconscious wishes generated in early development add a deeply felt, powerful motivator to experience.

Can we not appreciate the impact that the interpersonal environment plays in the creation of experience and, at the same time, believe that early experience has a powerful and pervasive role in shaping psychic structure? The classical analyst is, indeed, impressed with the way in which the vast panoply of encounters with a limitless reality is telescoped into a rigidly controlled myopia. The contemporary Freudian *does* see evidence, clinical evidence, for the belief that there are experiences that are formative in nature, that not only influence the development of psychic structure but contribute significantly to pathological reenactments. But maintaining this belief does not mean that early experience is the sole contributor to the development of psychic structure or that it is not influenced by interpersonal experience.

It is a mistake to assume that because the profound impact of early experience on development is appreciated, reality factors are devalued in the classical approach. We need not be misled by Mitchell's belief in a dichotomized reality. McDougall (1970) has this to say about the interaction between internal states and external reality:

> We cannot advance too far on the basis of fantasy alone. Certain reality experiences leave their imprint. Children caught in the nets of their parents' unconscious desires weave their fantasies out of an amalgam of primitive instinctual drives organized around what they have decoded of their parents' wishes and around what they believe they represent to their parents. Of such stuff is ego identity made [p. 173].

Transference

Surprisingly little is written on transference in *Relational Concepts in Psychoanalysis*. Mitchell's most explicit discussion of the concept resides in the book's final chapter, where he likens the relational matrix to a tapestry woven on Penelope's loom and pathology to Penelope's nighttime sabotage of her work, reflecting deep and often unconscious loyalty to the familiar. Specifically, he describes the process of understanding and engaging the transference as involving a fluctuation between old and new relational configurations, an aspect of the transference that is reminiscent of Freud's (1905) postscript to the Dora case, where he speaks of transference as "new editions or facsimiles of the impulses and phantasies which are aroused and made conscious during the progress of an analysis" (p. 116). It calls forth, too, Loewald's (1960) description of the treatment relationship. In that therapeutic action paper, structural change is attributed to a resumption of ego development in the therapeutic process, a resumption that is contingent on the relation with a new object, the analyst.

In one of his most explicit descriptions of transference, Mitchell characterizes the process as follows:

> In the relational-conflict model, there is a continual oscillation between old and new relational configurations, between the articulation of the passions and organizational structures of the analysand's phenomenology and the introduction of the analyst's perspective (as neither more "real" nor more "mature," but as

different and possibly useful). The analyst is constantly in the midst of the transference-countertransference integrations, shaped by the analysand's relational configurations and struggling to understand and thereby reshape them from within [pp. 299–300].

What is Mitchell saying about transference? To grasp his position fully, it is necessary to tease out some of the assumptions inherent in how he conceptualizes the process. These assumptions revolve around three notions: *first,* that transference in the relational model involves an interplay of old and new relational configurations; *second,* that the analyst introduces his own perspective into the transference in order to move the treatment in the direction of greater intimacy and increased possibility for varied experience; *third,* that the analyst is an active participant in a process that is dyadic in nature, interactive in style, and egalitarian by design.

The notion of transference as an oscillation between old and new relational configurations is implicit throughout Relational Concepts but is especially highlighted in Mitchell's description of the relational perspective on interpretive strategies:

> Here [in the relational model] the establishment of strong connections to others, in reality or in fantasy, is presumed to be primary. Forms of relationship are seen as fundamental, and life is understood largely as an array of metaphors for expressing and playing out relational patterns" [p. 91].

Exemplifying this aspect of transference is the example of Sam, whose depression was eventually understood

> as a vehicle for the perpetuation of old object ties and his characteristic mode of integrating relationships with others, as well as a means for controlling anxiety. . . . To relate in other ways and to assume full ownership of his resources and successes was to be pervaded by intense anxiety, the anxiety of the unfamiliar and of options incompatible with the familial mode of contact [p. 304].

The understanding of transference offered by Mitchell here is reminiscent of the position Zetzel (1956) outlined in her delineation of the theoretical premises underlying the Kleinian and ego psychological conceptualizations of transference. Here, transference for those emphasizing the importance of early object relations is described primarily as a revival or repetition of early struggles in respect to others, whereas, for those who emphasize the analysis of defense, transference is viewed as a compromise formation that serves the purposes of resistance.

Mitchell's conceptualization of transference as a *relational configuration* differs in important respects from the contemporary classical perspective of transference as a *compromise formation* that is multiply determined and that serves multiple functions. The contemporary classical analyst is cognizant of the layers of understanding that every transference dynamic embodies. In addition to viewing transference as an oscillation between old and new relational configurations, structural theory adds an approach to understanding the mechanics of object relations. Most basically, the structural theory is a way of organizing mental processes "according to aims and functions" (Anna Freud, 1955, letter to Lawrence Kubie, quoted in Young-Bruehl, 1988, p. 162). Transference, then, can be understood as an expression of, and an attempt to gratify, powerful instinctual wishes (specific wishes for a particular form of gratification), as well as serving ego and superego functions. Moreover, each of these functions will be represented by, and manifest in, particular patterns of relating, what Mitchell describes as relational configurations.

It may bear emphasizing that we are not describing here a need to review the structural theory for every transference interpretation that comes to the analyst's mind. Rather, we are describing a way of *organizing* the analyst's thinking in terms of the multiple *functions* that a transference dynamic may be serving. At one moment, for example, transference may be dominated by powerful wishes to get the analyst to feed the analysand an unending supply of good interpretations, symbolically capturing the imperatives of early oral wishes in the transference reenactment; at another moment, the interpretations may become the vehicle for gratifying powerful primitive needs to punish either self or object; at still another moment, defending oneself against anxiety or depression by distancing oneself from the analyst may be most salient. In the contemporary classical model, listening for other ways in which the transference is used is as important as recognizing that all mental functions will be expressed in relation and may serve as a "tie to old objects" (p. 304). The contemporary classical position can thus be understood as occupying a middle position relative to organizing one's thinking about the transference: not as radical as Levenson's (1983) deconstructionism, which admonishes the analyst to listen without any metapsychology, nor as conservative as Mitchell's *specific* focus on relational configurations alone. Let us turn now to the idea of transference involving the development of a broadened ability to function. In addition to the passage quoted above, where the relational analyst is described as introducing his perspective "as neither more 'real' nor more 'mature' but as different and possibly useful" (p. 300). Mitchell writes:

> The analyst becomes the various figures in the analysand's relational matrix, taking on their attributes and assuming their voices; the analyst and the analysand generally rewrite the narrative, transforming those characters in a direction which will allow greater intimacy and more possibilities for varied experience and relatedness [p. 296].

Those passages generate a great many questions about how these processes actually work. How does "rewriting the narrative" transform character? How does broadening the analytic relationship differ from the development of an ordinarily good therapeutic relationship? How does delineating a difference enable analysands to break through their investments in remaining as they are? If it were possible for the analysand to learn to change simply by being confronted with a difference, would not change be much more easily accomplished than it is? Is it even *possible* for the analyst to point out a difference to an analysand and have it perceived "neither as more real nor more mature"? How does this differ from attempts to educate the analysand according to the analyst's sense of appropriateness? To think that analysis heals because we are more honest, more authentic, or more intimate is both naive and grandiose. Until we are able to begin to address these issues, Mitchell's ideas about transference as involving a broadening of the relationship raise more questions than they answer.

Finally, let us examine the third premise about transference embedded in Mitchell's writing: in transference the analyst is an active participant in a process that is dyadic in nature, interactive in style, and egalitarian by design.

> If one views the analysand's experience of the analysis and the analyst as fundamentally interactive, as an encounter between

two persons, the analysand is struggling to reach this analyst. Familiar timeworn strategies are employed, to be sure, but as pathways to connect with what the analysand has experienced about this particular analyst as a person. The problem is no longer past significant others, but how to connect with, surrender to, dominate, fuse with, control, love, be loved by, use, be used by, this person [p. 300].

This comment, also found in the section on understanding and engaging the transference, posits the analytic situation as "fundamentally interactive, as an encounter between two *persons*. . . .The problem is no longer past significant others." Mitchell here virtually *abandons* the notion of transference, thereby losing the uniqueness of the analytic relationship. The essence of transference is that there is a transfer *from an earlier* object or pattern of relating *to a contemporary situation.* To describe, as *transference,* the struggle "to find an authentic voice in which to speak to the analysand, a voice more fully one's own, less shaped by the configurations and limited options of the analysand's relational matrix, and, in so doing, [to offer] the analysand a chance to broaden and expand that matrix" (p. 295) is to fail to understand the impact of the past on the present and the role that significant others and patterns of functioning play in the analytic situation.

Understanding that history has a role to play in the analytic encounter is not to focus the entire treatment on the past. In a similar vein, attending to that aspect of transference that does involve distortion and misperceiving does not imply that this is the totality of the classical understanding of transference or that the analyst contributes nothing to the transference. By framing another question in terms of a dichotomy— "Does the analysand experience the analyst in terms of the past (what Freud called earlier editions), or is the transference at least partially a response to input from the analyst?" (p. 297)—Mitchell *himself* distorts the classical position. He suggests that only in the relational position is transference "at least partially a response to input from the analyst." Yet in the very paper by Arlow (1985) from which he obtained the passage on transference as distortion, Arlow maintains the following: "The patient's unconscious fantasy of the past, *during transference,* intrudes on the reality of the present, and *conscious experience comes to represent an amalgam of current events and unconscious fantasy* (p. 526; italics added). This dichotomizing type of thinking leads to serious oversimplifications of the analytic process, a process that deserves to be presented in all its rich complexity. Instead, the reader is offered Mitchell's revisionist statement: "for the analyst to view the analytic situation as monadic and the analysand's experience of him as by definition distorted—this is a powerful and destructive form of interaction indeed" (p. 300). How does seeing transference as containing the patient's distortions make it a "destructive form of interaction?" Further, Mitchell offers no hint in his version of the classical point of view that the importance of the object in the development of psychic structure and of the relationship in the analytic situation is represented by a fertile and varied tradition within the classical perspective.

Knapp (1991) describes the understanding of individual personality that Freudians have gained by treating their patients as persons who experience drives and adaptations in the context of relationships with significant others. Among these analysts are Loewald (1960, 1972), Kernberg (1988), Modell (1990), Kohut (1971, 1977), Gedo (1979) and Gill (1982). These analysts are noteworthy in that each espouses a system that "recognizes the power of the relationship but seeks to maintain the focus on the individual" (Knapp, 1991, p. 6). Knapp credits Gill (1982) with reframing the essence of transference in a way that makes room for the interpersonalists and with tying together several key points regarding the transference:

> Gill deftly addresses the problem raised by interpersonalists, i.e., their criticism of the notion of the blank screen, neutrality and the transference as distortion by using the term "plausibility." With the notion of plausibility Gill demonstrates that he accepts the potential accuracy of the patient's perception. His concern, however, is with what sense the patient has made of this perception. By doing so Gill acknowledges what is, and thereby clears the way for a focus on the patient. It is a resolution of the one person/two person dilemma by acknowledging the two but focusing on the one [Knapp, 1991, p. 6].

A consequence of framing the analytic situation in the dyadic, interactive mode described by Mitchell is that it positions the analyst squarely on the participatory side of the observer/participant dimension of analytic functioning. Aron (1990) discusses the limitations of a theoretical commitment to the priority of interactional material and to the newly exclusive focus on transference as the therapeutic factor in psycho-analysis. Commenting on the interpersonal-interactional tradition as explicated by Levenson (1983) and Gill (1982), he warns that an exclu-sively interpersonal focus may interfere with the curative aspects of regression and puts the analyst at risk of meticulously engaging and analyzing the false self. A related issue is raised by Rangell (1988), who maintains that castration anxiety is not easily or typically revealed in the transference but often needs to be uncovered through extra-analytic sources. The technical implications of these points are profound and direct us toward maintaining a balance in our stance, both theoretically and transferentially. Mitchell's primary focus on the interactive contri-bution to the transference ("There is no examination of intrapsychic processes except as they are transformed and in a sense uniquely created in the encounter with the analyst," pp. 297–298) by definition interferes with following the chain of associations by shifting the focus of the work from the discovery of unconscious conflict and fantasy to the current interaction between the participants. One cannot *simultaneously* follow the *analysand's* associations *and* offer him an association that is not his. The contemporary Freudian does value the unique specificity and access to the unconscious that are generated by use of the method of free asso-ciation. This is not to say that one method is right and the other wrong. Nor is it to assert either that those who use an interactive method never follow the associative flow or that those who use the method of free asso-ciation do not acknowledge that transference is responsive to the current stimulus of the individual analyst. There is, however, a real difference in emphasis, which leads to substantive differences in technique and in the data available for analytic investigation.

Finally, a comment is necessary about the assumption, implicit throughout much of *Relational Concepts,* that the analytic situation in the relational model is basically egalitarian. A typical comment is that "analytic change entails a struggle by both participants to overcome precisely these kinds of imbalances which characterize pathological patterns of interpretation and in which differences in experience threaten the interpersonal connection rather than enrich it" (p. 296).

Imbalances (and here Mitchell is referring to what he describes as the *imbalance inherent in the structure of the analytic situation in other mod-els*: those brought about by "exploring and mirroring or 'holding' the analysand's subjective experience" and those brought about by "entreat-ing the analysand to realign his hopes and wishes according to the analyst's sense of appropriateness" (p. 296) are characterized as "pathological" and as differences in experience that "threaten the interpersonal connection rather than enrich it." Mitchell raises a critical issue here. Is an imbalance between the analytic participants in the structure of the analytic situation properly conceived as something to "overcome"? A classical analyst, acknowledging the analysand's freedom to choose to engage the analyst in a myriad of ways, would be interested in how an imbalance is experienced and would see it as something to be analyzed and understood rather than corrected.

Attempting to make the analytic situation egalitarian is appealing. It appeals to the democratic ideal internalized in many of us. But it also appeals to those aspects of ourselves that are conflicted and threatened by authority. Can we ever escape the fact that the analytic situation is not an equal one? Just as no matter what parents do, they cannot escape the fact of parenthood, similarly, analysts always retain the authority of their position, at least in the unconscious of their analysands. To attempt to structure a model of psychoanalysis that denies the inescapable authority of the analyst places crucial experiential data out of reach of the analytic process. A refusal to acknowledge this aspect of the analytic situation inevitably undermines the analytic process by implicitly telling the analysand that a relation of authority does not exist, indeed, that it will not be tolerated. It also puts out of reach what could be an opportunity to work through in the analytic setting a relationship with an authority. To acknowledge the analyst as an authority (Why else does the patient come? He does not turn to an encounter with a friend) does not imply that the analytic situation is bent on demanding a "surrender to the analyst's illusory wisdom and control" (p. 301). To allow the experience of authority to exist in the structure of the analytic situation does not preclude the development of a relationship with the analysand that is collaborative in nature, nor does it deny that the analyst can learn from the analysand. That analyst and analysand are characterized by different levels of authority is a reality of the analytic situation. The situation is not inherently a "threatening" one but can be perceived as bad and dangerous when it carries unconscious, malevolent fantasies. It is the analyst's responsibility to explore and analyze those fantasies, not to pretend that they do not exist.

On Model Making

The drive theory Mitchell contrasts with his relational model is a fascinating creature: "bestial" in nature; monadic in premise ("the analyst is outside the [analysand's experience of the analysis] and should stay that way," p. 300); "destructive" in interaction, demanding the patient's "surrender to the analyst's illusory wisdom and control" (p. 301). It bears little resemblance, however, to the contemporary classical perspective as it is practiced today. We ask, therefore, where Mitchell's relational paradigm is positioned vis-à-vis current psychoanalytic thought.

The contemporary psychoanalytic landscape has been determined, in part, by certain historical sequences in the development of psychoanalysis. Freud came first. He offered a model of the mind, of symptom formation, transference, and other key concepts as early as 1894. He expanded and modified his theory over the course of the next 50 years. In a series of papers he struggled to define the relationship between the individual and society, and he seemed to realize the difficulty involved in the task; he never concluded that he was either all right or all wrong. Comfortable with the psychological-biological duality of mental functioning, he framed some of his concepts with certain linguistic emphases to acknowledge these two dimensions of human experience. His metapsychology includes the personal and the organismic dimensions of human experience. Built into Freud's reasoning are both hermeneutic and natural science principles that help us retain a place in our theory for causes and reasons. It is not surprising, therefore, that current perspectives stress very different aspects of Freudian thought.

Psychoanalytic metatheory now has constituents in five major parties. First is the group led by Robert Wallerstein and including Joseph Sandler, who espouse a position of common ground for almost all psychoanalytic theoretical approaches. Second are those who advocate a multimodel approach. This group is best exemplified by Fred Pine, who believes that common ground can be achieved only by an approach that includes and integrates the "four psychologies" of drive, ego, object, and self. Third are those who reject the drive-object relations polarity—a position most articulately elucidated by Leo Rangell in his concept of "total composite theory." This group believes that psychoanalysis has from its inception closely tied together drive, defense, and object-relational concepts. Fourth are the antimetapsychologists, those who strive to minimize theory about theory in psychoanalysis. They are represented by the interpersonalists Levenson and Zucker and by Schafer, Klein, and Holt. The fifth group is the "dichotomizers," those who separate all theory into two mutually exclusive positions. This group is typified by self psychology with its bipolar self and its division into tragic versus guilty man. Also among the dichotomizers is Mitchell, who divides the field into two competing perspectives of drive theory and object relations theory. According to the dichotomizers, Freud and the Freudians are conflict/defense drive theorists and therefore fundamentally distinct from the earliest and still most important proponents of object relations theory, namely, the British object relations school.

The "common-grounders," in contrast, find common theoretical ground in positions as different as those held by the British object relations school, the self psychologists, the ego psychologists, Sullivan, and possibly Lacan. Essentially, the "common ground" position is that psychoanalytic theoretical differences at the present time are not consequential clinically. Vastly different and sometimes mutually exclusive theories are referred to as metaphors, as comforting mental models, as opportunities for forming political allegiances, organizations, friendships, and languages; but the different approaches are not seen as having theoretical or technical consequences. Sandler (1992), for instance, has stressed the idea that people say one thing and do another. He concludes that psychoanalysts who claim to be following entirely different models all do or say the same thing in the consulting room.

The third group, the "composites," stress that at no point did Freud and his successors declare independence of the mind from its social and relational surround. Although at times drive theory has been given greater emphasis, and object-relations, at other times, Freud never intended to divorce either theory from the other. They were always interdependent.

What the "composites" and the "common-ground" proponents have is a belief in the fundamental principles of the Freudian corpus. Thus, there is actually more commonality in their approach than either group would care to admit. A difference between them lies in their threshold of tolerance for deviation: for the composites the threshold is low, for the common-grounders it is relatively high. The common-grounders might be seen as permissive, and the composites, as more orthodox in their allegiance to Freud. For Pine, in the multimodel group, common ground is a virtue; for Wallerstein, common ground is pursued as an expedient. Wallerstein holds forth the idea of someday possessing sufficient data to accept one theory or reject another. Pine, in contrast, feels such theory choice is impossible both now and in the future.

Mitchell's perspective, most boldly stated, proposes that there has been a paradigm shift—in Kuhn's sense of the term—in psychoanalytic theory. The shift is from a model in which drive/intrapsychic conflicts are central to one that is characterized by a relational/interpersonal focus. Although Mitchell would characterize his emphasis as both intrapsychic and relational/interpersonal, his intrapsychic focus is narrowly conceived. Its clinical applications are limited. For modern Freudians, a concept of the unconscious includes the repressed, or the childhood repressed, and in particular, the love/hate conflicts of early psychological eras. Mitchell's stress on patterns of relationships and their variants throughout the life cycle focuses attention on the interpersonal at the expense of the intrapsychic.

Mitchell's thesis actually incorporates two subtheses. The first is that traditional, classical, orthodox Freudian psychoanalysis and its various schools, including ego psychology, have not recognized this paradigm shift—they have remained tied to outmoded 19th-century neurological and mechanistic concepts. Perhaps only a return to the actual clinical data will clarify this issue. We are not advocating (as Mitchell does in Relational Concepts) the presentation of clinical examples that are composites of work with "different analysands having similar psychodynamic configurations and posing similar theoretical questions and technical problems" (p. 12). Rather, as Klumpner and Frank (1991) contend in a paper that bewails the paucity of clinical data in the most frequently cited psychoanalytic articles, there is a need to balance the requirements of confidentiality against the dangers of misleading the reader. It is essential that we keep as close as we can to the immediacy of the unique, clinical encounter if we are to be able to judge the extent to which psychoanalysts suffer from theoretical deficiencies that are technically consequential. The development of comparative psychoanalysis would be promoted if Mitchell were to present examples of his own clinical work that illustrate his point of view, as well as samples of the clinical work of contemporary "traditional" analysts in which he spelled out in vivid, dramatic detail how relational considerations have been underemphasized or omitted.

Mitchell's second subthesis is that it is both useful and possible to group together various psychoanalytic theories under a relational umbrella. As Mitchell would have it, British object relations, interpersonal theory, and self psychology all acknowledge relations with others as the "very stuff of experience" (p. 20). Mitchell holds that these traditions "generate what is essentially the same story line, but in different voices" (p. 35). Not everyone agrees, however, that British object relations, interpersonal theory, and self psychology share a common set of assumptions. (For example, see Zucker, 1989, for an account of the premises of interpersonal theory and the way in which they *differ* from those of object relations theories and self psychology; Levenson, 1991, for a discussion of how the interpersonal point of view, by emphasizing distortion as a collusive agreement, is essentially incompatible with both object relations and drive theory; Goldberg, 1986, for an articulation of the differences between self psychology and interpersonal theory, especially in regard to the input of the analyst; and Spruiell, 1988, for an overview of the ways in which object relations theories often contradict one another.)

Zucker's (1989) discussion of interpersonal theory is important because it elucidates the ways that the basic premises of both classical psychoanalysis and object relations theory are very different from the premises of interpersonal theory. These include the role of social influence in general, the degree of plasticity in aspects of human biology, and the significance of fantasy in personality formation and functioning. Mitchell, who claims Sullivan as one of his intellectual ancestors, is critical of contemporary classical thinkers who integrate theories that are not characterized by a conceptual base of shared premises and assumptions. His goal, however, of the unification of these different theoretical perspectives into a "coherent, comprehensive theoretical framework" (p. viii) requires him to meet this standard as well, rather than to gloss over fundamental differences or extract from theories those concepts with which he feels most sympathetic.

Finally, from a metatheoretical point of view, that is, from the point of view of theory about theories, Mitchell's perspective is at odds with three of the metatheoretical approaches that we have described: common ground, composite theory, and the multimodal theory set forth by Pine. Although we could elaborate many differences, the most fundamental difference is that these perspectives do not share Mitchell's conviction about a paradigm shift. All three approaches see the development of theory as evolutionary rather than revolutionary. Basically, they are integrationist positions, offering different perspectives on theoretical pluralism.

A close reading of Freud, especially the case studies (written at the height of his drive/id psychology phase), persuades that there has been no such shift. From the perspective of current clinical practice, it appears that the fundamental concepts of psychoanalysis, including an integration of drive and relational considerations, are supported by generations of clinical experience. This is not to say that there have been no changes, but there has not been the radical shift that Mitchell suggests. Mitchell appears not to be joined in his view by most contemporary theoreticians; there are exceptions, notably Gill and the antimetapsychologists. Those thinkers argue against the use of metapsychology on the grounds that its concepts are easily reified and reifiable but do not realize that the real problem lies not with the concepts but *with their use.* They do not accept the idea that an experience-near, experience-distant problem cannot be resolved by purging a theory of its metapsychological language. The majority of contemporary psychoanalysts, however, remain evolutionary, rather than revolutionary, in their approach.

With his concept of the radical shift in paradigms, Mitchell has gone out on a theoretical limb, and it remains to be seen whether history will judge him a prophet or the vanguard of a new movement. His theory is daring—daring enough to challenge in a very specific way the long-standing Freudian model and well worth grappling with.

REFERENCES

ARLOW, J. (1985). The concept of psychic reality and related problems. *Journal of the American Psychoanalytic Association* 33:521–535.

ARON, L. (1990). One-person and two-person psychologies and the method of psychoanalysis. *Psychoanalytic Psychology* 7:475–486.

BRENNER, C. (1982). *The Mind in Conflict.* New York: International Universities Press.

FREUD, S. (1900). The interpretation of dreams. *Standard Edition* 4–5. London: Hogarth Press, 1953.

———— (1905). Postscript to fragment of an analysis of a case of hysteria. *Standard Edition* 7:112–122.

———— (1914). On the history of the psycho-analytic movement. *Standard Edition* 14:1–66.

———— (1916–1917). Introductory lectures on psycho-analysis. *Standard Edition* 15:16.

———— (1918). From the history of an infantile neurosis. *Standard Edition* 17:3–122.

———— (1924). The dissolution of the Oedipus complex. *Standard Edition* 19:171–179.

FRIEDMAN, L. (1988). The clinical popularity of object relations concepts. *Psychoanalytic Quarterly* 57:667–691.

GEDO, J. (1979). *Beyond Interpretation.* New York: International Universities Press.

GILL, M. (1982). *Analysis of Transference,* Vol. 1. New York: International

Universities Press.

GOLDBERG, A. (1986). Reply to P. Bromberg's discussion of "The wishy-washy personality." *Contemporary Psychoanalysis* 22:387–388.

GREENBERG, J. & MITCHELL, S. (1983). *Object Relations in Psychoanalytic Theory.* Cambridge, MA: Harvard University Press.

HATCHER, R. (1990). Review of *Relational Concepts in Psychoanalysis. Psychoanalytic Books* 1:127–136.

HOLT, R. (1976). Drive or wish? A reconsideration of the psychoanalytic theory of motivation. In: *Psychology Versus Metapsychology: Psychoanalytic Essays in Memory of George Klein,* ed. M. Gill & P. Holzman. *Psychological Issues,* Monograph 36. New York: International Universities Press.

KERNBERG, O. (1988). Object relations theory in clinical practice. *Psychoanalytic Quarterly* 57:481–504.

KLEIN, G. (1976). Freud's two theories of sexuality. In: *Psychology Versus Metapsychology: Psychoanalytic Essays in Memory of George Klein,* ed. M. Gill & P. Holzman. Psychological Issues, Monograph 36. New York: International Universities Press.

KLEIN, M. (1945). The Oedipus complex in light of early anxieties. In: *Contributions to Psychoanalysis, 1921–1945.* New York: McGraw Hill, 1964.

——— (1957). Envy and gratitude. In: *Envy and Gratitude and Other Works, 1946–1963.* New York: Delacorte Press, 1975.

KLUMPNER, G. & Frank, A. (1991). On methods of reporting clinical material. *Journal of the American Psychoanalytic Association* 39:537–551.

KNAPP, S. (1991). American object relations. *Parameters* 2:3–7.

KOHUT, H. (1971). *The Analysis of the Self.* New York: International Universities Press.

——— (1977). *The Restoration of the Self.* New York: International Universities Press.

LA PLANCHE, J. & PONTALIS, J.-B. (1973). *The Language of Psychoanalysis.* New York: Norton.

LEVENSON, E. (1983). The Ambiguity of Change. New York: Basic Books.

——— (1991). *The Purloined Self.* New York: Contemporary Psychoanalysis Books.

LOEWALD, H. (1960). On the therapeutic action of psychoanalysis. *International Journal of Psycho-Aanalysis* 58:463–472.

——— (1972). Freud's conception of the negative therapeutic reaction, with comments on instinct theory. In: Papers on Psychoanalysis. New Haven, CT: Yale University Press, 1980.

McDOUGALL, J. (1970). Homosexuality in women. In: *Female Sexuality,* ed. J. Chasseguet-Smirgel. London: Maresfield Library, pp. 171–212.

MITCHELL, S.A. (1988). *Relational Concepts in Psychoanalysis: An*

Integration. Cambridge, MA: Harvard University Press.

MODELL, A. (1990). Some notes on object relations, "classical" theory and the problems of instincts (drives). *Psychoanalytic Inquiry* 10:182–196.

PERSON, E. (1980). Sexuality as the mainstay of identity: *Psychoanalytic perspectives. Sigma,* 5:605–630.

RANGELL, L. (1985). On the theory of theory in psychoanalysis and the relation of theory of psychoanalytic therapy. *Journal of the American Psychoanalytic Association* 33:59–92.

——— (1988). The future of psychoanalysis: The scientific crossroads. *Psychoanalytic Quarterly* 57:313–340.

RUTTER, M. (1979). Maternal deprivation, 1972–1978: New findings, new concepts, new approaches. *Child Development* 50:283–305.

SANDLER, J. (1992). Reflections on developments in the theory of psychoanalytic technique. *International Journal of Psycho-Aanalysis* 73:189–198.

SCHAFER, R. (1976). *A New Language for Psychoanalysis.* New Haven, CT: Yale University Press.

SIMON, J. & GAGNON, W. (1973). *Sexual Conduct.* Chicago: Aldine.

SPRUIELL, V. (1988). The indivisibility of Freudian object relations and drive theories. *Psychoanalytic Quarterly* 57:597–625.

STERN, D. (1985). *The Interpersonal World of the Infant.* New York: Basic Books.

WACHTEL, P. (1982). Vicious circles: The self and the rhetoric of emerging and unfolding. *Contemporary Psychoanalysis* 13:259–273.

YOUNG-BRUEHL, E. (1988). *Anna Freud: A Biography.* New York: Summit.

ZETZEL, E. (1956). Current concepts of transference. *International Journal of Psycho-Aanalysis* 37:369–375.

ZUCKER, H. (1989). Premises of interpersonal theory. *Psychoanalytic Psychology* 6:401–420.

CHAPTER 12

Relational Models in Psychoanalytic Theory

[Bachant, J.L., Lynch, A.A., & Richards, A.D. (1995).
Psychoanalytic Psychology 12:71–87.]

There are tides in the theoretical affairs of psychoanalysts—tides that originate in the struggle to understand the complexities of mental functioning, the problem of motivation, the impact of family and culture on personality, and the nature of transference. The current state of theoretical pluralism and multiple perspective is part of the continual ebb and flow of theoretical development that has characterized psychoanalysis during the past 50 years.

Psychoanalysis as a science encompasses a therapeutic technique, an observational method, and a theory derived from a method of inquiry. It is not a single theory, but a series of theories nested within each other: a theory of development; pathogenesis; how the mind is structured and functions; and technique, therapeutic action, and cure. A particular psychoanalytic perspective has con-sequences for the way in which the psychoanalytic situation is structured. These con-sequences, although essential to the clinical practitioner, are not often made explicit.

The relational perspective has positioned itself as offering a "revolutionary" view of how psychoanalysis has evolved (Mitchell, 1993, p. 466), declaring that its development represents a radical departure from the classical tradition. Given that the discontinuities with the Freudian tradition are described as more important than the continuities, a careful look at how its tenets affect the structuring of the psychoanalytic situation is in order. The task, however, is complicated because relational theory represents an array of diverse contributions and points of view, some of which are more radical than others. It is difficult, therefore, to make generalizations, and the major contributors of this perspective need to be considered separately. In this article, we outline some of the theoretical assumptions of the relational model and the implications for technique as presented by five exponents—Mitchell, Greenberg, Ogden, Aron, and Slavin and

Kriegman—focusing on the way relational theory organizes the psycho-analytic situation.

The Evolution of Psychoanalytic Theory

A proper understanding of contemporary psychoanalytic theory requires an appreciation of both an experiential–historical and a metapsychological understanding of the psyche. Historically, these dimensions have given rise, from Freud's continuous reformulations, to two streams of investigation and to schools of thought known as object relations and ego psychology. These currents, though separate in some respects, are related. We contend that the opposition set up between relational theory and drive theory is a false dichotomy (see Bachant, Lynch, & Richards, 1992). It emerged in the 1930s as Klein, Fairbairn, Sullivan, and others incorporated the burgeoning ideas of general systems theory and sought to elaborate aspects of psychoanalytic theory that had not been adequately developed. This group of contributors proposed that we are motivated as much by our emotional investments and forms of relatedness to others as by primitive wishes and fears. As the discourse developed and refinements were offered, these perspectives became integrated into the evolving psychoanalytic theory.

Some relational theorists have resurrected the drive–object dichot-omy, misinterpreting the present structure of psychoanalytic theory and turning a blind eye to the contributions from the 1930s on. It is necessary to differentiate between relational psychoanalysis as a school of thought and the body of relational considerations that have been a part of the psychoanalytic tradition since Freud looked at the relationship between Breuer and Anna O and asked himself what was going on. Greenberg and Mitchell (1983) agreed that "the clinical centrality of object relations is accepted by virtually all current psychoanalytic schools" (p. 3). Nonetheless, there are significant differences in how this centrality is understood. It is important to distinguish between theories that include relational aspects in their approach and those in which the relational perspective becomes dominant, even exclusive. Accordingly, we reserve the term *relational—perspective* model, theory, or school for those theories that would account for the individual's subjectivity, as well as its development, from relational considerations alone—that is, for those which eschew any drive component in their formulations. It is important to note that this is the primary distinction made by the relational school itself. In their now classic text, *Object*

Relations in Psychoanalytic Theory, Greenberg and Mitchell (1983) described the fundamental problem of object relations thinkers as

> the transformation of psychoanalytic metapsychology from a theoretical framework based on drives to a framework which makes relations with others, real and imagined, the conceptual and interpretive hub. While physiological needs, bodily events, temperament, and other biological factors significantly affect human experience and behavior, they operate within the context of an interactive matrix and are subsumed by the preeminent motivational thrust toward the establishment and maintenance of relations with others [p. 220].

Relational Theory

Greenberg and Mitchell (1983) were concerned that the proliferation of different theoretical approaches threatens to dissolve the field. They attributed this development to various efforts to achieve an adequate conceptualization of the role of object relations. They concluded that psychoanalytic theories are inherently dichotomous and asserted that drive and relational views are fundamentally incompatible in "the content each attributes to the operative dynamic forces, especially to those which are most commonly a part of the repressed unconscious" (p. 382). Model mixing is to no avail; the theorist must choose between accommodation (the drive model) and the radical alternative posed by the relational model. Greenberg and Mitchell (1983) opted for the latter, as they believed a change in the unit of study from the individual to the relational matrix[1] is essential. In addition, they pushed for a shift in our understanding of human development. But they misrepresented drive theory when they maintained that in classical theory, the individual's personality is formed primarily in response to the pressures of drive. They proposed that both normal and pathological dynamics emerge from the interpersonal field. This is not quite as reasonable as it might first appear. Conceptualizing development as primarily derived from the interpersonal field mitigates the role

---

[1]The relational matrix is "constituted by the individual in interaction with significant others" (Greenberg & Mitchell, 1983, p. 220). In this regard, according to Gill (personal communication, November 18, 1992) it is "the name used by Mitchell for the offshoot of interpersonal theory." See Zucker (1989) and Levenson (1991) for an opposing point of view.

in psychic development of the intrapsychic dimension; restricts our understanding of conflict; and substantially redefines the concepts of resistance, transference, and the method of free association. This has far-reaching implications for theory and technique. The role of the unconscious is particularly affected.

The relation between endogenous factors and relational experiences in development is a question that now divides even relational thinkers. Greenberg (1991), Ogden (1992a, 1992b), and Slavin and Kriegman (1992), for example, have all argued that some form of drive theory is essential in explaining the individual's development and differentiation. This has kept theorists like Ogden, Slavin, and Kriegman outside of the relational theory camp proper and has moved Greenberg from its center to a broader, more integrated perspective that he characterized as representational.

The Dynamic Unconscious

In *Relational Concepts in Psychoanalysis: An Integration,* Mitchell (1988) advocated abandonment of the drive framework entirely and proposed that the "establishment and maintenance of relational patterns [is] the deep structure of experience" (p. 90). For him, meaning is generated in interaction, and conflict is derived totally from relationships with others. Mitchell attempted to develop his purely relational model by combining British object relations theories with interpersonal and self psychological theories—a combination that he clearly believed is possible.

The problem with Mitchell's approach is that many of his ideas rest on an oversimplified view of key aspects of Freud's theoretical system. Most glaring is Mitchell's insistence on offering Freud's tension reduction, drive discharge model as Freudian theory. But this model bears little relation to the contemporary view of drive as a part of unconscious fantasies that organize childhood memory and experience. In contemporary classical theory, the drive component is part of a broader theory of the dynamic unconscious. The crucial dimension of the interface between theory and practice is the clinician's understanding and use of the dynamic unconscious, as this understanding organizes the structure of the analytic situation. Indispensable to this concept is the idea that certain drive derivatives, specific wishes and fears denied access to consciousness by various defensive actions, have a profound impact on the development of psychic structure and a continuing influence on psychic life. This is exemplified by the endless transformations of fantasies that emanate from core unconscious issues which we see played out in the patient's life. The dynamic unconscious is at the heart of transference, reflecting the individual's specific motivational imperatives and the way these are played out in the analytic situation.

According to classical theory, the development of the mind occurs as a dynamic, unfolding process determined by complex interactions between the child's innate, biologically determined characteristics and influences from the environment. Inappropriate care (cruelty, neglect, abandonment) or other stresses, traumas, or accidents of fate may adversely affect developmental progress, creating pathological development or a predisposition for later psychological difficulties.

While growing up, children face the fundamental existential questions of life, death, truth, and justice with immature cognitive functions. For the child, psychological urges are imperious, self-centered, and sincere. Throughout early development, however optimal, children are confronted with inevitable frustrations because of the limitations imposed by development. The child's solutions are a mixture of experience and fantasy that expresses the powerful wishes, fears, and self-punitive ideas characteristic of each developmental phase. In the course of development, the wishes and fears of earlier phases have been repressed and take on dangerous and primitive attributes. The unacceptable wishes of childhood are part of the persistent unconscious fantasies that seek resolution in the present through compromise formation. As we develop, these fantasies mature and shape our special interests and character traits, determine our behavior, and produce our neurotic symptoms. The essential plot or narrative of unconscious wishes and fears endures even as their manifestations are transformed. The consolidation of moral values, the advance in reality testing, and the developing cognitive capacities all contribute to the child's maturing solutions. Unconscious fantasies are unique and individual. They are part of the patterning and integration that emerge out of the important experiences, relationships, traumas, and conflicts of childhood. Unconscious fantasies provide a mental set that affects how we interpret the sensory data we perceive and how we respond.

Although many relational thinkers pay lip service to the concept of the dynamic unconscious and try to address some aspects of it, the concept, which is pivotal in the contemporary classical tradition, becomes a mere whisper in relational theory. One can discern in the relational perspective a definite, although often implicit, shift away from the centrality and importance of the concept of the dynamic unconscious—

a shift that has to affect the interpretive process. The relational perspective's focus on the interaction between patient and analyst and on the "new relationship" with the analyst as the major determinant of change, and its emphasis on the power and importance of present experience, diminish the clinician's attention to this critical factor (see Bachant & Richards, 1993).

Mitchell (1988, 1990) offered the unconscious as a static concept—like a file cabinet or archive for old records. Greenberg's (1991) unconscious is more dynamic, but it is viewed as ideas that are walled off from the corrective potential of interpersonal exchange. Lost in this perspective is an understanding that patients must work through the gratifications afforded by a mode of relating that satisfies primitive desires and fears and overcome their resistances to the threat of moving on before they are able to see a broader picture.

For Mitchell (1988, 1990), infantile wishes and fears are important no in and of themselves, but because they are embedded in relational patterns to which the patient is deeply committed.

> It is true that I don't think of infantile wishes as drive derivatives which are structurally preserved in time through repression, as did Freud. I believe that infantile wishes and the fears associated with them are powerful dynamic factors in the present because they are embedded in relational patterns which the analysand believes in and is deeply committed to in the present [1990, p. 138].

For Mitchell, infantile wishes and fears are important because they "ag along" with relational patterns which the patient is reluctant to give up, not because they represent passionate desires for particular forms of gratification that will be played out in the relational field. Implicit here is a substitution of the concept of will for that of the dynamic unconscious (Hatcher, 1990). As Mitchell (1988) described it, the unconscious is composed not of conflictual, repressed forces but "of all the characteristics of conscious mentation, including strong commitment and effort" (p. 264). "At any particular moment, the will is free—but free amid the clutter of the derivatives of past choices" (p. 263). Mitchell wrote, "What keeps the repressed unknown is the combination of the obstacles produced by the residues of past choices and the will that does not want to begin the search" (p. 265). The concept of a dynamic unconscious as enduring fantasies that continue to structure he experience of the adult is impoverished if not lost entirely. Presumably, if he patient decides to want to search for unconscious meaning, if he or she is inspired to give up cherished relational patterns, the wishes and fears themselves would be of little consequence.

Hatcher (1990) noted, in addition, that Mitchell's espousal of the dyadic position renders any consideration of the dynamic unconscious untenable:

> Mitchell requires that his theory be dyadic rather than monadic, that it describe the mind at all times in interaction with others— this *is* the mind. . . . Mitchell realizes that relational theories, criticized for lacking [an account of conflicting motives and how patterns are stored], are poorer without it. There is strong pressure to see conflict as internal, that is, as intrapsychic. But this view yields a theory no longer dyadic; it is a monadic theory operating on dyadic concerns [p. 133].

In summary, this reframing of the psychoanalytic situation within a dyadic theory, focused on interaction and organized along social constructivist lines, greatly vitiates this most important concept in contemporary psychoanalysis.

The Psychoanalytic Situation

The profound alteration of the conception of the dynamic unconscious in Mitchell's work affects his view of the psychoanalytic situation. Significant is Mitchell's (1988) statement that the analytic situation is "fundamentally interactive, and an encounter between two *persons*. . . . The problem is no longer past significant others, but how to connect with, surrender to, dominate, fuse with, control, love, be loved by, use, be used by, this person" (p. 300). On this view, "the past does not underlie the present, but rather provides clues for understanding the way in which meanings in the present are generated" (Mitchell, 1993, p. 465). But because central to the concept of transference is the "transfer" of an earlier object or pattern of relating to a contemporary situation, something essential about transference has been lost in Mitchell's notion. Further, the unrelenting focus on interaction—"there is no examination of intrapsychic processes except as they are transformed and in a sense uniquely created in the encounter with the analyst" (Mitchell, 1988, pp. 297–298) may *iatrogenically* direct the patient's attention away from inner process to an excessive focus on the analyst as person. With this approach, unconscious conflict in general and issues such as castration anxiety in particular (Rangell, 1985) may be obscured. Paradoxically, the recognition that transference may also serve important defensive functions (Arlow, in press) may be lost as well.

In addition, there is a subtle but significant shift in the way conflict is conceptualized within the relational perspective. Conflict in some relational models is limited to conflict between relational configurations—between conflictual passions within relationships as well as between different relationships and identifications (Mitchell, 1988). But how does the individual arrive at which aspect of experience with others is identified with and which is rejected? Appreciably diminished in Mitchell's perspective is an understanding of the intrapsychic dimension of conflict, of those factors *in the person,* engendered by unconscious wishes and fears from the earliest phases of life, that interact with how the environment is experienced.

Aron (1990b) acknowledged the limitations of any theory committed to the priority of interaction. Nevertheless, he still got caught in a dichotomous presentation of issues in his recent articles (Aron, 1990a, 1990b, 1991a, 1991b). From the beginning, he argued, "psychoanalytic clinical concepts and procedures were formulated . . . as one-person phenomena . . . [based in] quasibiological drive theory" (1990b, p. 475). To illustrate his belief that a shift to the two-person "relational" perspective is in order, he took up the ideas of transference and the free-associative method. Transference, he suggested, is viewed by classical theorists as a process occurring in the patient's mind and is determined by the patient's past as it unfolds, as a result of specific technical procedures in the psychoanalytic situation. The person of the analyst is "irrelevant" (1991b, p. 47). By contrast, a two-person or relational perspective is presented as viewing infantile wishes as "reflections of the actual interactions and encounters with the unique, individual analyst with all of his or her idiosyncratic, particularistic features" (1990b, p. 479).

Aron's understanding of the classical position implies that classical analysts lack any awareness that transference is an interpersonal process occurring between analyst and analysand. This does not accurately reflect the contemporary classical position on transference. Brenner (1976), for example, noted:

The "real personality" of an analyst is important only as a patient perceives it and reacts to it. It is a stimulus to a patient's mental activity like any other. The patient's reaction to it must be analyzed before one can tell what is real to him. This is not to say that an analyst's appearance, manner, way of speaking, and surroundings are unimportant. They are very important, but their effect will never be the same on any two patients and is often very different on the same patient at different times in his analysis. It is reasonable to expect, to be sure, if an analyst is very unconventional in one way or another, and still more if he is unusually inconsiderate, roughly disapproving, or ingratiatingly seductive, that any or all of those characteristics of behavior and attitude will interfere more or less seriously with the analytic progress of many of his patients. Nevertheless, even in such an extreme and obviously undesirable case the nature of the interference will be different for every patient and only if it can be analyzed can one hope to know what it actually is [pp. 126–127].

The patient's encounter with the unique, individual analyst who plays a pivotal role in the analytic situation is very much a part of this tradition (Greenson, 1967; Loewald, 1960, 1971; Stone, 1967; Zetzel, 1956). What is distinguishing, however, is the classical analyst's commitment to the importance of analyzing the unconscious, which shapes the patient's perception of the analyst. Arlow added that this "unconscious dimension can give an exactly opposite tone to the nature of the overt phenomena as they appear in the patient–analyst interaction" (cited in Valenstein, 1974, p. 315). Central is the need for the analyst to attend to the complex phenomenological data in an evenly hovering manner.

Freud (1915), Loewenstein (1969), Brenner (1982), and Bird (1972), in the classical tradition, pointed out that transference is found in every adult relationship. What is transferred in our relationships with others are unconscious wishes and fears, woven through a variety of themes in unconscious fantasy. This dynamic is not specific to the analytic relationship. Brenner noted that what distinguishes that relationship is not the presence of transference, but the use the analyst makes of it in analyzing psychic conflict. As is apparent from what we just discussed, this account certainly includes the variable of "who the analyst is" that Aron finds only in the two-person model.

The structure of the analytic situation, and of analytic neutrality in particular, serves a function: that of facilitating exploration of the wishes and fears fueled by the patient's dynamic unconscious. Neutrality and the other conditions structuring the analytic situation developed not to hide the person of the analyst from the analysand (an impossible goal), but rather to facilitate the analysand's contact with inner experience so that fantasies about the analyst can be more clearly observed.

The use of the concept of transference, then, distinguishes the classical and relational perspectives. For the relational thinker, interaction precipitates transference, and transference involves adaptation to an interpersonal reality. Both analyst–patient interaction and the transference itself are mutually constituted. Change comes about through the impact of the relationship. Adaptation in the present, in particular to the presence of the analyst in the transference, becomes the focus of the psychoanalytic situation, and the importance of the unconscious recedes into the background.

In classical thinking, the patient brings to the interaction the systemic reflection of the unconscious demands posed by wishes and fears, moral dictums, anxiety, misery, and defense. All meet in reality to create the nature of the transference. Transference is part of all adult relationships and is not unique to analysis. Unconscious wishes and fears, woven through a variety of themes in unconscious fantasy, are transferred to all our relationships with others. Change comes about through the analysis of these unconscious manifestations in the context of the relationship with the analyst.

Aron approached the method of free association in a similarly dichotomizing manner. He suggested that classical analysts believe that free association will lead, barring resistance or analyst interference, to the presentation of conflict from the dynamic unconscious, ignoring present day or interpersonal factors. Quoting Arlow (1987) as evidence, "the stream of the patient's free associations is the record of the vicissitudes of the analysand's intrapsychic conflicts" (p. 70). Aron (1990b) concluded that the classical model of the mind is that of a closed system "impervious to outside influence" (p. 480), with the analyst's interventions focused simply on keeping the process going. In the relational or two-person perspective, by contrast, all associations are determined by the ongoing interaction. In every aspect of the analyst's activity—remaining silent, formulating conjectures, timing interpretations—the analyst's personality influences the patient's associations. As is discussed later, the analyst's activities are, in fact, understood in this way in classical theory; the difference, however, lies in the emphasis on analytic focus.

Aron believed that the classical perspective has developed a set of conditions that the analyst must adhere to as part of the psychoanalytic situation and that classical analysts use this to disguise their own interactive influence on the analysand's associations. Although it may be acknowledged that some analysts may do this, it is by now commonplace that virtually anything, including humanity, warmth, and interpersonal relatedness, can be used defensively (Brenner, 1982). The notion that the analytic situation has been structured precisely to obscure interactive effects is a profound misunderstanding.

In broadening his concept of relational perspectivism (which is equated with Hoffman's (1991) notion of "social-constructivism"), Aron (1991a, 1992) suggested major technical revisions which flow from the patient's encounter with the analyst's subjectivity.[2] Adopting the two-person model, he (1991a) accepted Wolstein's (1983) redefinition of resistance as a relational phenomenon—the defensive efforts used by the patient to "accommodate to some aspect of the analyst's unconscious psychology" (p. 35). Fantasies about the analyst are seen not as complex compromise formations but

> as patients' attempts to grapple with and grasp, in their own unique and idiosyncratic way, the complex and ambiguous reality of their individual analyst. Ultimately, an analysis of these fantasies must contribute to a clearer understanding of both the patient's and analyst's psychologies [p. 35].

Thus, resistance reflects the patient's attempts to cope with the analyst's unconscious rather than the patient's effort to deal with an inner conflict in a particular interpersonal situation. For Aron, this occurs as a result of the patient's attempts to connect with others in an emotionally authentic manner. In an interesting attempt to wed interpersonal theory with his perception of drive theory, Aron (1991a) noted that "the analytic stance being described considers fantasies and memories not just as carriers of infantile wishes and defenses against these wishes, but as plausible interpretations and representations of the patient's

---

[2] Hoffman's (1991) concept of social constructivism will be addressed later in this article.

experiences with significant others" (p. 37). Aron (1991a) suggested technical considerations that would emphasize this down-played dimension (the analyst's subjectivity) as a central aspect of the analysis of transference: "The analyst needs to listen to all of the patient's associations for clues as to the patient's experience" of the analyst (p. 39). This directive shifts the analyst's clinical stance substantially. Instead of listening with evenly hovering attention to the patient's multiple demands and conflicts, the task of the analyst is now to focus his or her attention on the patient's experience of the analyst's subjectivity. Pursuing this line of exploration, Aron (1991a) noted, leads inescapably to self-disclosure; "Self-revelation is not an option; it is an inevitability" (p. 40). This is a shift echoed most dramatically in a recent work by Mitchell and cited in Aron (1991a):

> If the analytic situation is not regarded as one subjectivity and one objectivity, or one subjectivity and one facilitating environment, but two subjectivities—the participation in the inquiry into this interpersonal dialectic becomes a central focus of the work [p. 44].

This stance is problematic. It requires a fundamental change in the analytic attitude. It involves substituting a directed attention, a focus on listening for specific referential material containing clues to the analyst's subjectivity for an equidistant stance among the demands of the ego, superego, id, and external reality (A. Freud, 1936). In Aron's restructuring of the psychoanalytic situation, intimacy—represented by the need of children to find their parents' subjectivity (Aron, 1991a)—bears the weight of being the predominant human motivation. The need for intimacy is undoubtedly a powerful force. But it is only one of many driving forces infused with unconscious wishes and fears. As a need, it can be satisfied only when the strictures of morality, the limitations of reality, and the affects that accompany intimacy are taken into account. The contemporary classical framework asks the analyst to be aware of the complex nature of human motivation and to avoid premature closure, because the possible meanings of the patient's communications are manifold. One of those meanings will inevitably concern the patient's perception of the analyst's subjectivity. An interest in this dimension is not new to psychoanalysis. It was raised in Freud's (1905) postscript to the Dora case and developed in Greenson's (1967) book on technique in a section called "Pursuit of the Transference Trigger" (pp. 305-308). But it is only one of many factors. Listening to the patient with evenly hovering attention allows the analyst to attend to the complexity of the patient's experience within a broad framework, including but not limited to a focus on the interpersonal dialectic.

Contributions from a Broader Relational Perspective

Mitchell and Aron's relational perspective tends to "take a revolutionary view" (Mitchell, 1993, p. 466) and put forward a systematically elaborated alternative to the analytic mainstream. In the next set of relational thinkers we look at, dichotomization gives way to a more dialectical approach. Greenberg (1991) departed from the stance he took with Mitchell in the 1983 collaboration. He distanced himself from the "narrow" relational point of view and shifted to a position closer to traditional classical thinkers who see the relational and drive perspectives as mutually enriching.

Most relational model theorists, impressed by the theoretical, empirical, and clinical shortcomings of the particular drive theory that Freud built, believed that they could eliminate the drives entirely and put nothing explicit in their place. I don't think that's possible. Somewhere in everybody's theory—or in their implicit vision of human nature—there is something that does conceptually what the drives did for Freud. Sidestepping the issue . . . doesn't make for good theory. This accounts for my reservations about the relational model and why I haven't relied heavily on its framework in developing my own point of view [Greenberg, 1992, p. 191].

In his recent work, *Oedipus and Beyond: A Clinical Theory,* Greenberg (1991) affirmed the importance of the oedipal complex and preserved a central place for triangular relationships in psychoanalytic thought. He questioned the assumption that the analytic dyad creates a new experience that broadens the patient's experience by introducing alternative perspectives. This notion is at the heart of change, not only for relational and interpersonal theorists, but for social constructivists as well (Gill, 1992; Hoffman, 1991). Greenberg (1991) shifted his clinical focus to the internalized object, which is often a representation of the patient's observed self—an earlier version of the self in interaction with another. This representation, strongly influenced by fantasy, endows the patient's self-experience with a "momentum that resists rectification by subsequent experience" (Greenberg, 1991, p. 204).

A major change for Greenberg involves the question of motivation. Greenberg's designation of safety and effectance as the primary drives in motivating behavior and experience[3] is a shift from his earlier view that the individual is motivated by relational configurations. Greenberg did not make explicit what differentiates safety from a need to avoid displeasure. The contemporary approach to conflict and compromise formation understands the person as seeking to minimize misery and anxiety. What is the difference between this conception and Greenberg's motivational emphasis?

Greenberg's conceptualization of transference relates to the place of the dynamic unconscious in his theory (Bachant, 1994). He differentiated transference of impulse, in which unconscious wishes determine the characteristics of the object relation, from transference of conviction, in which ideas about the analyst depend on the experiential context. In Greenberg's model, conviction is the bedrock out of which wishes arise; the wish is determined by the idea, the representation, the experiential context. It is the idea that is clinically consequential here, whereas in the contemporary classical perspective, it is unconscious wishes and fears that determine our experience of the world. Greenberg's (1991) reversing "the direction of analytic inquiry" (p. 229), from the wish to the idea, risks depriving the analytic process of its richness and complexity. Applied, however, within a dialectical framework, Greenberg's formulation becomes a significant contribution. In the clinical process, the wish to capture a certain kind of gratification in a very particular kind of situation with a specific type of object—the pulsating, passionate, infantile, "gotta have it" experience—is always framed within a dialectical tension dependent on experiential context. This context varies with the types and levels of pathology and holds for the fear as well as the wish.

Slavin and Kriegman (1992) captured this notion quite well.

> Transference occurs as the means by which the psyche is designed to experience new situations as opportunities for the revival and reorganization of intrapsychic structure. This reorganization

---

[3]Greenberg's (1991) safety drive aims at producing a particular feeling state: "The sense of physical and emotional well-being—freedom from the pressure of any urgent need and the absence of unpleasant affects of which anxiety is the prototype" (p. 129).

is part of a continuing process of redefinition and revision of the complex set of proximal mechanisms (i.e., the structure of the self) that psychologically mediates inclusive fitness [p. 61].

In this broader conceptual frame, there is a place for Hoffman's (1991) contribution of a social-constructivist view of transference; the "creative repetition" defined by Loewald (1971); and the dimensions of intersubjectivity developed by Stolorow, Brandchaft, and Atwood (1987). Many of the points addressed by Hoffman's social-constructivist position, including the observation that the analyst is revealing himself or herself all the time and that the analytic situation is constructed by two people, are recognized in the classical tradition.[4] Hoffman's (1991) push, however, to eradicate positivist thinking in the psychoanalytic arena and replace it with an absolutistic social constructivism (a variant of relativism) is problematic. In particular, Leary (1994) warned that this perspective "purges the analytic situation of the need to grapple with history, with things that once were and had an effect . . . and diverts attention from that which endures in persons, in social transaction, and in the world" (p. 457). In addition, the distinction between the interpersonal and the intrapsychic falls away, key distinctions between fantasy and reality are obscured or disavowed, the enduring aspects of self are lost in a cacophony of multiple selves, and the importance of the role of the body in development is profoundly limited. Although Gill saw positivism and constructivism as a dichotomy that cannot be resolved "because the two are truly opposites" (personal communication, November 18, 1992), we feel that these constructs are dimensions that must not be understood dichotomously. There are reasons why "positivistic" language is often part of descriptions of even committed constructivists. As Damasio (1994) pointed out, there is a remarkable consistency in the constructions different people make of the essential aspects of the environment, although it is improbable that we will ever know what "absolute" reality

---

[4]For a commentary on this issue, see Erdelyi's (1992) discussion of Freud as "one of the great exponents . . . [of] . . . the mainstream Continental tradition of constructivism" (p. 784). Erdelyi speaks in this paper of the way in which Freud's constructivism was different from the traditional Continental approach. Freud extended the constructivist tradition to include emotionally motivated reconstructions (including defensive ones) as well as those based on intellectual considerations (the need for intelligibility, coherence, and consistency with cultural expectations). This is not simply an additive understanding, and specifically carries the idea of internal and external shaping each other.

is like. The patient's unique history has specific consequences that transcend different relationships. Multiple meanings between the analyst and analysand are part of understanding the impact of the analytic relationship. These multiple meanings are interpreted by the analyst as an approximation of the actual experience that occurs in the context of their relationship. Ogden (1991) made the point that the

> best we can hope for is an uneasy coexistence of a multiplicity of epistemologies. . . . Each epistemology is separate unto itself and at the same time stands in dialectical tension with the others. Each is slowly and sometimes painfully being transformed by the others, and, as a result, one is not dealing with linearly expanding body of knowledge [p. 368].

We contend that there is a place for both constructivistic and positivistic epistemological perspectives in psychoanalysis. They exist in a dialectical tension with each other. Rather than asking the analyst to choose between these two dimensions, this understanding requires that the analyst develop a sense of what emphasis will be most helpful at a given time. Maintenance of evenly hovering attention to this aspect of the psychoanalytic situation guards the analyst against immersion in one while neglecting the other.

The work of Slavin and Kriegman (1992) and Ogden (1992a, 1992b) does not fit a narrow definition of relational psychoanalysis. Slavin and Kriegman tried to provide a contemporary evolutionary dimension for psychoanalytic theory that recognizes that the mind is an adaptive organ whose structure and function evolves. They trace the development of this idea in Freud's work and in the more contemporary psychoanalytic theories of Bowloy, Hartmann, and Erikson. Today's "paradigmatic clash" is the result of polarizing tendencies characteristic of much current analytic thought. Many recent theoretical developments avoid the understanding that the human condition is part of a broad naturalistic context. The time is ripe, however, for a synthesis within a new paradigm.

Slavin and Kriegman (1992) highlighted Greenberg and Mitchell's (1983) two dichotomies. The first dichotomy contains the two paradigms that determine the basic unit of analysis: the individual mind and the interpersonal field. The second is the endogenous–relational dichotomy in the understanding of psychic structure and human experience. There are also two further dimensions: (a) inherent conflict versus inherent mutuality, and (b) subjective experience as deceptive distortion versus valid communication.

Slavin and Kriegman (1992) were on point with contemporary thinking when they described the classical agenda as

> a set of metaphors about the innate, evolved structure of driveness and the repression of versions of the self—metaphors that create a "narrative of conflict"—the classical agenda captures certain major, significant features of the relational world and the inherently "divided" way human beings are adapted to it. In the vast range of both analytic perspectives and nonanalytic psychologies, only the classical psychoanalytic perspective (and its derivatives), with its metaphors of inner conflict, fully depicts the deep divisions and tensions within the self that are indispensable concomitants of an adaptation to the conflictual relational world [p. 70].

All psychoanalytic models must include some biological assumptions. Slavin and Kriegman's evolutionary biological perspective embraces both classical and relational constructs. In doing so, they attempted to demonstrate the dialectic nature of these constructs.

Ogden (1992a, 1992b) offered a conceptualization that bridges many of the issues current in psychoanalytic theory and provides us with a lens through which we could view its evolution. Like mind, Ogden views psychoanalytic theory as evolving through a series of overlapping dialectics whose terms are reciprocals. This continuous communication and tension creates both the illusion of unified experience and a permanent state of conflict.

Ogden developed some intriguing ideas pertaining to basic concepts within the overall corpus of object relations theory (e.g., on projective identification, the nature of analytic knowledge, the structure of experience, psychological deep structure, and the oedipus complex). Ogden (1988, 1992a, 1992b) also emphasized the need for a synthesis of psychoanalytic theory based on an acceptance of the dialectical tensions that have evolved during the theory's development. In two recent articles, he (1992a, 1992b) returned to traditional theorists in his effort to rework the psychoanalytic concept of the nature of subjectivity in the works of Freud, Melanie Klein, and Winnicott.

These relational theorists have generated some interesting questions about the nature of subjectivity and the influence of the external world. Their approach to contemporary theoretical and clinical problems is shaped by psychoanalytic tradition and more recent scientific and intellectual trends.

Conclusions

Psychoanalysis is advanced by focused attention on specific conceptual issues. However, each new approach must address the contradictions that may follow from the effort to recast major aspects of the theory as it works to develop a codified and consistent set of hypotheses.

The relational perspective's contribution to psychoanalysis is the elaboration of the psychic dynamics generated in the interpersonal field. The systematic study of the way in which interpersonal influence shapes development and experience focuses our attention on important issues: the impact on the analytic process of the person of the analyst, the role relational configurations play in the development of psychic structure, the nature of interaction, and the structure of the unconscious. This focus has enriched psychoanalytic dialogue but has also generated questions concerning the theoretical foundations of the relational model. In this article, we tried to make explicit some of the assumptions of the relational perspective—assumptions that may alter the psychoanalytic situation significantly—with the concepts of transference, the dynamic unconscious, resistance, the method of free association, and the nature of conflict being especially affected. In addition, when relational thinking rests on a dichotomy of endogenous and exogenous factors, it limits the integrative possibilities of psychoanalytic theory and diminishes a rich view of personality.

The present state of theoretical pluralism requires that we continue our efforts to define the dialectic processes that contain the complexity of biopsychosocial determinants found in human experience within an integrative perspective. This task is currently being confronted by a multitude of psychoanalytic thinkers: those who opt for total integration, like Rangell; those who prefer model parity, like Pine; those who seek common clinical ground, like Wallerstein; and those who, like the relational thinkers we examined, struggle with a multiplicity of epistemologies, each of which is an essential aspect of the psychoanalytic corpus. Any attempt at providing comparative coherence to this diversity is a Herculean effort.

REFERENCES

ARLOW, J.A. (1987). The dynamics of interpretation. *Psychoanalytic Quarterly* 56:68–87.

ARON, L. (1990a). Free association and changing models of mind. *Journal of the American Academy of Psychoanalysis and Dynamic Psychiatry* 18:439–459.

———— (1990). One person and two person psychologies and the method of psychoanalysis. *Psychoanalytic Psychology* 7:475–485.

———— (1991). The patient's experience of the analyst's subjectivity *Psychoanalytic Dialogues* 1:29–51.

———— (1991). Working through the past—working toward the future. *Contemporary Psychoanalysis* 27:81–108.

———— (1992). Interpretation as expression of the analyst's subjectivity. *Psychoanalytic Dialogues* 2:475–507.

———— (1994). Review of Oedipus and beyond: A clinical theory by J. Greenberg. *Bulletin of the Psychological Association of New York* 31(1):12–14.

BACHANT, J.L., LYNCH, A.A., & RICHARDS, A.D. (1992). Commentary on Reisner's "reclaiming the metapsychology" *Psychoanalytic Psychology* 9:563–569.

———— & RICHARDS, A.D. (1993). [Review of] *Relational Concepts in Psycho-analysis: An Integration* by Stephen A. Mitchell *Psychoanalytic Dialogues* 3:431–460.

BIRD, B. (1972). Notes on transference: universal phenomenon and hardest part of analysis. *Journal of the American Psychoanalytic Association* 20:267–301.

BRENNER, C. (1976). *Psychoanalytic Technique And Psychic Conflict.* New York: International Universities Press.

———— (1982). *The Mind In Conflict.* New York: International Universities Press.

DAMASIO, A.R. (1994). *Descartes' Error: Emotrion, Reason, And The Human Brain.* New York: Putnam.

ERDELYI, M.H. (1992). Psychodynamics and the unconscious. *American Psychologist* 47:784–787.

FREUD, S. (1905). Fragment of an analysis of a case of hysteria. *Standard Edition* 7:112–122.

———— (1915). Observations on transference love. *Standard Edition* 12:157–171.

GILL, M.M. (1992). Paper delivered at New York Psychoanalytic Institute for the Heinz Hartmann award, November 12.

GREENBERG, J. (1991). *Oedipus And Beyond: A Clinical Theory.* Cambridge, MA: Harvard University Press.

────── (1992). Reply to Hirsch. *Psychoanalytic Books* 3:190–193.

────── & Mitchell, S. (1983). Object relations in psychoanalytic theory. Cambridge, MA: Harvard University Press.

GREENSON, R. (1967). *The Technique And Practice Of Psychoanalysis.* New York: International Universities Press.

HATCHER, R.L. (1990). [Review of the book] *Relational Concepts In Psychoanalysis: An Integration. Psychoanalytic Books* 1:127–136.

HOFFMAN, I.Z. (1991). Discussion: toward a social-constructivist view of the psychoanalytic situation. *Psychoanalytic Dialogues* 1:74–105.

LEARY, K. (1994). Psychoanalytic "problems" and postmodern "solutions." *Psychoanalytic Quarterly* 63:433–465.

LEVENSON, E.A. (1991). *The Purloined Self: Interpersonal Perspectives In Psychoanalysis.* New York: Contemporary Psychoanalysis Books, William Alanson White Institute.

LOEWALD, H.W. (1960). On the therapeutic action of psycho-analysis. *International Journal of Psycho-Analysis* 43:16–33.

────── (1971). Some Considerations on Repetition and Repetition Compulsion. *International Journal of Psycho-Analysis* 52:59–66.

LOEWENSTEIN, R. M. (1969). Developments in the theory of transference in the last fifty years. *International Journal of Psycho-Analysis* 50:583–588.

MITCHELL, S. (1988). Relational concepts in psychoanalysis: An integration. Cambridge, MA: Harvard University Press.

────── (1990). A reply. *Psychoanalytic Books* 1:136–140.

────── (1993). Reply to Bachant and Richards *Psychoanalytic Dialogues* 3:461–480.

OGDEN, T.H. (1988). On the dialectical structure of experience—some clinical and theoretical implications. *Contemporary Psychoanalysis* 24:17–45.

────── (1991). An interview with Thomas Ogden. *Psychoanalytic Dialogues* 1:361–376.

────── (1992). The dialectically constituted/decentred subject of psychoanalysis. I. the freudian subject. *International Journal of Psycho-Analysis* 73:517–526.

────── (1992). The Dialectically Constituted/decentred subject of psychoanalysis. II. the contributions of Klein and Winnicott. *International Journal of Psycho-Analysis* 73:613–626.

RANGELL, L. (1985). On the theory of theory in psychoanalysis and the relation of theory to psychoanalytic therapy. *Journal of the American Psychoanalytic Association* 33:59–92.

SLAVIN, M. O., & KRIEGMAN, D. (1992). Psychoanalysis as a Darwinian depth psychology: evolutionary biology and the classical–relational dialectic in psychoanalytic theory. In *Interface of Psychoanalysis and*

Psychology, Eds., J.W. Barron, M.N. Eagle, & D. L. Wolitzky, pp. 37–76. Washington, DC: American Psychological Association.

STOLOROW, R.D., BRANDCHAFT, B., & ATWOOD, G.E. (1987). *Psychoanalytic Treatment: An Intersubjective Approach.* Hillsdale, NJ: The Analytic Press.

STONE, L. (1967). The psychoanalytic situation and transference—postscript to an earlier communication. *Journal of the American Psychoanalytic Association* 15:3–58.

VALENSTEIN, A.F. (1974). Panel on 'Transference'. *International Journal of Psycho-Analysis* 55:311–321.

ZETZEL, E.R. (1956). Current concepts of transference. *International Journal of Psycho-Analysis* 37:369–375.

ZUCKER, H. (1989). Premises of interpersonal theory. *Psychoanalytic Psychology* 6:401–419.

CHAPTER 13

Benjamin Wolstein and Us:
Many Roads Lead to Rome

[Richards,A.K. & Richards,A.D.(2000).Contemporary Psychoanalysis36:255–265.]

We are delighted to have this opportunity to comment on the work of Benjamin Wolstein and on his very interesting understanding of the psychoanalytic situation and the therapeutic action of psychoanalysis. We also want to express our appreciation and admiration for Irwin Hirsch's masterful interview of Wolstein, who many consider to have been one of the true masters of interpersonal psychoanalysis.

As contemporary Freudian analysts, we have to acknowledge that it took us aback at first to realize that until now we have had almost no exposure to Wolstein's work. One of us had read Fiscalini's chapter on Wolstein in *Pioneers of Interpersonal Analysis* (Stern, Mann, Kantor & Schlesinger, 1995), but that was all. This lack of familiarity is worthy of note, and so is the fact that when we searched the PEP CD-ROM, which includes the publications through 1994 of five psychoanalytic journals, we found that Wolstein had published forty papers and commentaries in *Contemporary Psychoanalysis* and none in any of the other four journals (*Journal of the American Psychoanalytic Association, Psychoanalytic Quarterly, International Journal of Psycho-Analysis*, and *Psychoanalytic Study of the Child*). Furthermore, there are sixty-one references to Wolstein in *Contemporary Psychoanalysis*, but only two in *JAPA*, one in *PQ*, three in *IJP*, and none in PSC. The two *JAPA* citations are by Irwin Hirsch himself. This left us wondering: Did Wolstein ever submit a paper to any of the other four journals? If he did, were they rejected? If he didn't, was it because he thought they would be? Whatever the truth is, the bibliographic facts attest to the great divide that has existed since the 1940s between interpersonal psychoanalysis and the rest of the psychoanalytic world.

We speculate sometimes about how interpersonal psychoanalysis—and therefore, psychoanalysis at large—might have developed if William Silverberg had been elected president of the American Psychoanalytic Association in 1942 instead of Karl Menninger, to whom he lost by one vote. What if the members of the William Alanson White Institute who were also members of the American Psychoanalytic Association had succeeded in getting the White Institute approved as a training institute in the American? Wolstein's analyst, Clara Thompson, undoubtedly would have been accorded the status of training analyst by the APsaA's Board of Professional Standards. What impact would that have had, for better or worse, on the creativity of Thompson and her analysands? What would any of this have meant in the development of Wolstein's own work? Of course, we will never know. But at least now we *do* have the opportunity to observe, and to participate in, exchanges that can promote a cross-fertilization of ideas among formerly estranged schools of psychoanalysis. The PEP CD-ROM, which was developed and financed by the APA and the British Society, has changed the nature of psychoanalytic scholarship. The works of the interpersonal analysts, including Wolstein, are now accessible to all the psychoanalytic schools and traditions in all parts of the world.

In our hopes for the success of this new ecumenicism we would like to expand on a point that Hirsch made in his interview about the names of psychoanalytic schools. He gives a very cogent argument that interpersonal analysis came of age when, through the work of Wolstein, Clara Thompson, and Edgar Levenson, transference-countertransference dynamics took center stage. For that reason he designates a "post-Sullivanian" *contemporary* interpersonal analysis. Hirsch points out that Sullivan did not seem to have much use for the concepts of transference and countertransference in his understanding of the therapeutic interaction. Hirsch's differentiation of contemporary interpersonal psychoanalysis from what we are inclined to call *historical interpersonal psychoanalysis* is a helpful one, and we think that the historical-contemporary distinction can be helpful in understanding other schools as well. We also think that it could reduce the obfuscation and confusion that often mar comparative psychoanalytic discourse. It is clarifying, for example, to distinguish between the historical Kleinian psychoanalysis that developed in the 1930s and a contemporary Kleinian psychoanalysis advanced by Betty Joseph, Elizabeth Spielius, and their colleagues. Similarly, we can contrast the historical self psychology developed by Heinz Kohut and his original close associates and a contemporary self psychology espoused by Goldberg (1999) and the Shades; the historical object relations theory developed by Fairbairn and Guntrip and a contemporary one expounded by Kernberg, Ogden,

Newman, and Bacal; and finally, and most significantly for the two of us, a historical Freudian analysis developed by Freud and his circle and a contemporary one whose proponents include Arlow, Brenner, Rangell, Boesky, Poland, and many others. We strongly believe that the terms "orthodox" and "classical" are no longer useful categories in scholarly psychoanalytic discourse.

Now, to Wolstein himself. We discuss the interview itself, without reference to Wolstein's published work, and offer some thoughts about the ideas he expresses there. We then look outside the "interview situation" and offer some further thoughts based on our recent wider reading of Wolstein's work.

As we approach this, we want to anticipate a response that often greets our efforts at comparative study of the psychoanalytic schools: that we are trying to claim that "Freud said everything first." This is not what we think at all. In pointing out the parallels between Wolstein's work and that of some contemporary Freudian theorists we are in no way contesting Wolstein's mastery, creativity, or originality, nor are we challenging the importance of his contributions. On the contrary, we are trying to convey a sense of what has been *lost* to the psychoanalytic community as a whole by these decades of estrangement. The same problems and questions vex all psychoanalytic theorists, and all the schools have brought their most creative minds to bear on them. It is startling to realize how differently people can grapple with the same problems and come to similar conclusions, although from profoundly diverse starting points. These areas of convergence, precisely because they have been arrived at independently by thinkers of such dissimilar styles, seem to us to be potentially our areas of greatest strength, and to demonstrate why we so badly need to end the estrangement and allow the various traditions to come to know each other. Many roads lead to Rome, and because we are all trying to reach that elusive metaphorical city, we need the most complete map we can make.

For Wolstein, individuation is a central idea of psychoanalysis. The fact that each individual and each dyad in the analytic situation is unique is presented in the interview as "Wolstein's Law." For Wolstein (and for us, and probably for every other analyst), the uniqueness of each treatment and each participant is what makes the analytic situation both fascinating and tolerable. The work of an analyst would be unbearably boring if there were one framework into which all psychic difficulties could be fitted neatly and which dictated a single course of action from which all else followed. We believe that if such a principle existed, it wouldn't matter whether it were based on interpretation, relation, or any other single first principle. Analysis would be an endless reenactment of the same drama, a sort of psychoanalytic *No Exit*: the same routines of greeting, the same lines, the prescribed listening and reactions, and the resulting same emotions. Wolstein here makes a case against not only the idea, but also the ideal of the generic analyst and the generic analysis. This is a position we strongly endorse, and so, we believe, do most contemporary Freudian practitioners. Without such a framework and the certainty that it would create, the analyst is continually entering into unknown territory. So courage is a requirement of those who would conduct analytic treatment. Wolstein describes the courage that he saw in Clara Thompson: the courage to allow the analysand the freedom to change the analyst, the courage to do without a script, the courage to improvise. To accept the uniqueness of the dyad means to accept the need for courage. Yet courage is only definable in terms of fear. If there is nothing to be afraid of, there can be no courage. What are analysts so afraid of that they long for theories to make individual situations less than unique? What did Clara Thompson's therapeutic courage stand up to? A fear of not being liked? Of not being thought helpful? Was it fear that the analysand would show her that she was causing pain? That she was unlovable? That she longed for his love? Was it fear of the loss of herself—that she might be changed into another sort of person than she thought herself to be? Of not living up to her own values? Of having her theories belittled? And aren't these sorts of fears the ones Wolstein (or anyone else) faces with each new analysand?

In the broad sense, Wolstein is talking about the same things Freud (1926) talked about when he enumerated the fears that plague young people in the course of their psychic development, and then haunt them as adults for the rest of their lives: fear of loss of the loved one, fear of loss of love from that person, fear of loss of bodily parts, pleasures, or functions, and fear of guilt and loss of self-esteem. By this we are not implying that Wolstein's contribution is negligible or not original. We want to indicate that in spite of past divisions, and in spite of accusations to the contrary, interpersonal analysis is *not* beyond the pale. To face these fears requires great courage from any young child, and from any person, child or adult, who has actually experienced enough of these calamities to know the intensity of the pain they cause. In the course of development, everyone has experienced at least *some* of each of these calamities, and "everyone" includes all analysts. Perhaps it is even true that those who become analysts have known such pains in sufficient quantity or intensity to make the fear of repetition the central feature of psychic life. Perhaps we are, to extend Wolstein's analogy, the body-surfing instructors, the ones who cannot get enough of the danger, who have to fill our working lives with overcoming it and teaching others how to do the same.

Wolstein's views on countertransference are his central contribution to the theory and practice of psychoanalysis. It was a groundbreaking theory. It was paralleled by contributions from Heinz Racker (1953), a Kleinian, and Virginia Tower (1956), a contemporary Freudian who explored the same cutting edge. There was also convergence between Wolstein's ideas and those of another contemporary Freudian, Charles Brenner, whose ideas many interpersonalists view as alien to their way of thinking. Brenner's (1983) position was that both countertransference and transference are compromise formations. The analyst is a human being, therefore necessarily has transferences. Brenner asserts that the countertransference is the transference of the analyst toward the analysand. The analysand seems to the analyst to have some of the power of the original loved ones: the power to leave, to withhold love, to cause bodily harm or deprivation, and, perhaps worst of all, because most likely of all, to withhold approbation. The analyst is vulnerable to the analysand in exactly the way that the analysand is vulnerable to the analyst. Their positions in the room are parallel. Wolstein comments concisely: "Any basic observation of psychoanalysis is as true of the therapist as it is of the patient. To run through them: transference, resistance, anxiety, unconscious experience." It is possible to reach similar conclusions from very different vantage points.

Another parallel—a technical one this time—exists between Wolstein and another contemporary Freudian, Jacob Arlow. The analyst empathically experiences the fear and pain of the analysand. The analyst is required to serve the analysand by withdrawing the empathic connection long enough to put into words the affect that the analysand may be either feeling or anticipating (Arlow & Beres, 1991). It is important to the analysand that his unexpressed affect be attended to. This is the central part of the analytic work. It is the uniqueness of the affect that makes defining it work. Wolstein also believed that attending to affect is crucial.

Again, lest in our appreciation we give the impression that we are trying to co-opt Wolstein and claim him as a contemporary Freudian like ourselves, we want to repeat that our interest is in demonstrating how independent thinkers may arrive at related conclusions. And in that context we want to illustrate a difference between his ideas and ours; it seems to us to be a difference more in practice than in theory, but it may be worth clarifying the theoretical reasons behind it. As we understand it, Wolstein believes that it is inevitable that the analyst's thoughts and feelings will come into the room and that a choice must be made about how and whether to recognize them. In his experiential therapy field, they must be voiced. For Wolstein, not voicing the thoughts and feelings would be a failure of nerve, while for us it would be a proper focusing of attention on the analysand.

This is because the contemporary Freudian gives primary analytic attention to affect (Fenichel, 1941) in the belief that that is the opening through which analyst and analysand touch each other's minds. Because affect is ultimately private and unknowable except by description, the analyst puts the analysand's feeling into words, thus making the affect known. Affect may be inferred from nonverbal communications, repetitions, omissions, distortions, or any other evidence of psychic work. But it must also be named, because the naming evokes fantasies, memories, and desires *specific to the analysand*. The analyst's ideas, memories, fantasies, and current experiences may provide information for the analyst about the analysand, but sharing them with the analysand may diminish the intensity and therefore the clarity of the affect, and in this way obscure the analytic work. Aron put it well with this question: "Whose analysis is this anyway?"

This brings up one of our favorite questions: how different ways of working in the clinical situation reflect, or don't reflect, differences in theory. Whether or not Wolstein's practice is more effective than ours is an empirical question, and a very difficult one to answer. One possible answer, though, is that in some cases it might be, and in some it might not. It could also be that Wolstein's approach in our hands would be a disaster, or ours in his. We offer a hypothesis about the purpose of clinical theory: An analyst creates a theory of clinical practice that corrects for those aspects of her or his character that would thwart the analytic enterprise. In this view, adopting a theory means adapting it to fit one's own proclivities. We all know from experience that imitating someone else's way doesn't work; we all have to find our own. So how do we make theoretical sense out of a situation in which analysts select the technique that fits them best and patients choose the analyst whose technique they believe creates the right setting for them? Our plea in these matters is for a measure of dispassion, a willingness not to take our theoretical preferences personally, and to consider them in the context of the broader analytic community whose achievements as a whole are only just becoming available.

Wolstein quite sensibly points out that some of the concepts of interpersonal psychoanalysis were new names proposed by Sullivan for similar ideas already in use in ego psychology. It seems to us that Wolstein rejects the ego-psychological concept of "frame" at the same time as he sets up certain rules of his own that correspond to the idea of a "frame." For instance, and notably, he makes clear that the analysand may not sit on his lap, that telephone sessions and contacts during vacations are out, and that kissing is not a possibility. These limits are part of a frame established by the analyst. Other analysts might set other limits, but the idea that there *are* limits is the operative imperative. Because the frame involves limits, the limits will be tested and negotiated (Peyser, 1998), especially when the limits are the choice of the analyst and not the analysand. There are limits to what any analyst will tolerate, and to choices that all analysands make about whether to accept or contest those limits. The analysand may leave, withdraw love, withdraw approval, or act in ways that imply harm to the analyst; telling the world how bad the analyst is is a salient example.

There are other convergences between Wolstein's concepts and those of contemporary Freudians. What Wolstein calls "direct experience" seems to us comparable to what Fonagy (1999), and Daniel Stern (1998) have called "moments." These are experiences that are curative, even if they are not articulated interpretations. They feel crucial to analyst and analysand alike, even though neither of them may be able to put into words why they felt so. But certainly, Wolstein does not downplay the role of verbal communication in enlarging self-knowledge: "The therapeutic focus is consistently the expansion of awareness, searching for what is beyond conscious awareness. What are you keeping out of your shared communication? Out of your thoughts? Your feelings? And why not seek these things? It is a steady self-inquiry pointed toward modifying and enlarging self knowledge. . . . It's a questioning, it's exploration." Wolstein thus apparently considers "bringing into consciousness," which is a linguistic experience and not a direct one, to be therapeutic. We agree with this position, and we appreciate the dialectic that results between direct experience and linguistic experience. Hirsch gets to the heart of the matter when he asks: "So here's, I think, a good question. Does your increased freedom lead to, or [is it] likely to lead to, the patient's increased freedom? Is that how patients become freer, because you become freer?" Wolstein's response is "No, of course not. I think patients become freer because they can do so." We ask: What enables them to do now what they couldn't do before? What makes the patient want to change? Hirsch complains that "There's something contradictory here. On the one hand, you're conveying what your atmospheric input is, on the other hand you're saying it had nothing to do with people changing."

Wolstein replies that you must assume that the patient energizes something from within and then moves forward. But he does not articulate what that energizing factor is, or how it is specific to psychoanalysis, beyond simply the attainment of more self-awareness and self-understanding. Thus, Wolstein leaves us, as he says he leaves the patient, to find out what we need to know for ourselves. Is this exchange between Wolstein and Hirsch a sample of what Wolstein did with his patients? He gives the expectation of a very idiosyncratic approach to treatment, in which his own self-expression will be very important. But in the end he relies (at least in part) on insight and interpretation, as many of us do.

The clinical implications of Wolstein's insistence on leaving the patient alone to free herself include refraining from both support and confrontation. But how does this work with the requirement of exposing the analyst's thoughts? This would seem to imply an analyst who talks about nothing but his own reactions, thoughts, and feelings. Can this be true? Is it mostly an injunction to abstain? The injunction to abstain brings him close to ego psychologists. Support is implied whenever one agrees with or does not challenge what the patient is presenting. The alternative is to question and ask for clarification or disagree. All of these are confrontations. All alternatives are variants of one or the other.

Wolstein's assertion that there is an unconscious connection between therapist and patient is similar to Isakower's notion of "the analyzing instrument." Wolstein's question about whether the analyst should have an unconscious experience of his own that parallels that of his patient is the same question that Isakower (1992) asked and that Spencer, Balter, and Lothane (1992) grappled with several decades later. For Wolstein, there are three possibilities: (1) deal with the experience as it happens with the patient; (2) deal with it with one's own analyst; or (3) deal with it in self-analysis. It seems to us that these are, in fact, the *only* three -possibilities. Isakower's choice was to use one's unconscious fantasies to gain insight into the patient's unconscious. Both Wolstein and Isakower had the same view of what happens in the analytic situation, but chose to act upon it differently. Isakower says you process silently and instruct the patient about his unconscious. Wolstein seems, at one point, to be saying that you provide a model for the patient by having the courage to talk about your unconscious. But when Hirsch states that as his understanding of Wolstein, Wolstein seems to back off. Are we looking at using two different learning theories here, one didactic and the other demonstrative? If so, which works better? Does one have to choose? Can one use one at one time and the other at another time? Wolstein seems to be saying that you adjust to the patient. He knew how. But for other analysts it may be difficult to decide what to do and when to do it. One of the reasons for theory is to inform the decision-making process.

Now we would like to offer a few comments based on our recent reading of some of Wolstein's books and papers. His oeuvre is substantial: ten books and more than 100 papers, not including the reviews and commentaries listed on the PEP CD-ROM. The papers elaborate in a vivid fashion upon the issues that emerge from the interview, and upon which we have reflected in the first part of this article. We had hoped to be able to make some clinical comparisons, but we were disappointed to find that his published contributions are longer on theory than on clinical illustration. He most often uses clinical examples when writing about supervision, and rarely details his own clinical work. But we did find some unexpected convergences between Wolstein's theorizing and our own. He writes that the distinction of psychology from metapsychology is a fundamental distinction in psychoanalysis "that keeps various levels of inquiry from obstructing or even overrunning each other." In this, he seems to us to be in sync with Waelder's ideas about levels of abstraction in psychoanalytic discourse, which categories—clinical observation, clinical generalization, clinical theory, and metapsychology—we find both helpful and felicitous.

We believe that the failure to recognize these distinctions is very much at the heart of the misunderstanding of contemporary Freudian theory prevalent in the current literature. A case in point is the so-called drive-relational dichotomy, which involves drawing a contrast between Freudian metapsychological concepts (considered experience-distant, biologic, organismic, and impersonal) with relational observational concepts (considered experience-near and interpersonal). It was somewhat surprising to us, given the current interpersonal-relational zeitgeist with regard to this matter, to find that Wolstein is quite comfortable with the concept of "distortion," a term that borders on anathema for other contributors in his tradition. He refers to "Many complex patterns of relatedness and communication organized as personal psychology" which intervene between a hypothesized childhood theme and observable distortions in the experiential field of therapy." In his book *Transference* (1954) he defines distortion as a "repeated form of behavior, a habit of misperception which is observed with an especial frequency and which may be attributed to events in the history of the individual" (p. 39). Of course, we recognize that what we consider Wolstein's wisdom, because it is consistent with our own point of view, might be taken as the opposite by those who emphasize the co-constructed nature of the analytic interaction and abjure the term "distortion" very emphatically. David Wolitzky (in press) discusses this issue in depth. But we think that Wolstein takes a very balanced view when he emphasizes that the distortions of transference are always related "at a particular time and a particular place to a particular psychoanalyst who relates his own countertransference through a particular phase of their inquiry and experience." His bridging spirit is very much in evidence when he writes about a convergence between ego psychology and interpersonal psychoanalysis. "In their respective terminologies," he writes, "whereas both focus new attention on the clinical study of resistance, neither surrenders the biological base of id metapsychology and each extends the new emphasis in social adaptation." In our view, Wolstein in 1971 was way ahead of his time. One of us (A. Richards, 1998) called attention to the convergences between Harry Stack Sullivan and Paul Gray, and between Sheldon Bach and Philip Bromberg, that Spezzano (1998) discusses in that same issue. The distinction between a Freudian theory, which emphasizes endogenous etiological factors, and an interpersonal psychoanalysis, which emphasizes environmental factors, is a specious one. In our view, both traditions are committed to a broad bio-psycho-social model in regard to both theory and clinical practice.

We think that if Wolstein were alive today, he would find a congenial audience for his ideas among contemporary Freudians, and a place in *JAPA* for both his theoretical contributions and his wisdom. We were as impressed with the spirit of his writing as we were with the content. He conveys an open, questioning, nonrigid, and undogmatic attitude, and seems to be open to critical comments from other points of view. We hope that he would have found some interest in our response here, and that it might have served as the basis for an ongoing discussion. Although clearly that is not to be, we do hope that other members of the interpersonal tradition will increasingly join in such conversations. In that spirit, we thank Jay Greenberg for inviting us to be part of this issue.

REFERENCES

Arlow, J. & Beres, D. (1991). FANTASY AND IDENTIFICATION IN EMPATHY. IN: *Psychoanalysis: Clinical Theory and Practice,* ed. J.A. Arlow. Madison, CT: International Universities Press.

BRENNER, C. (1983).. Transference and countertransference. In: The Mind in Conflict. Madison, CT: International Universities Press.

FENICHEL, O. (1941). *Problems of Psychoanalytic Technique.* New York: Psychoanalytic Quarterly.

FONAGY, P. (1999). Memory and Therapeutic Action *International Journal of Psycho-Analysis* 80:215–223.

GOLDBERG, A. (1999). *Of Two Minds.* Hillsdale, NJ: The Analytic Press.

ISAKOWER, O. (1992). The analyzing instrument in the teaching and learning of the analytic process. *Journal of Clinical Psychoanalysis* 1:181–222.

PEYSER, S. (1998). Building Bridges: Negotiation of Paradox in Psychoanalysis. Hillsdale, NJ: Analytic Press.

RACKER, H. (1953). The meanings and uses of countertransference. In: *Transference and Countertransference.* London: Hogarth.

RICHARDS, A.D. (1998). Politics and Paradigms *Jounral of the American Psychoanalytic Association* 46:357–360.

SPENCER, J., BALTER, L. & LOTHANE, Z. (1992). Otto Isakower and the analyzing instrument. *Journal of Clinical Psychoanalysis,* 1:246–260.

SPEZZANO, C. (1998). The Triangle of Clinical Judgment *Jounral of the American Psychoanalytic Association* 46:365–388.

TOWER, L.E. (1956). Countertransference. *Jounral of the American Psychoanalytic Association* 4:224–255

WOLITZKY, D. (2000). The conception of transference. In: *Changing Conceptions of Psychoanalysis: The Legacy of Merton M. Gill.*

Hillsdale, NJ: The Analytic Press.

Wolstein, B. (1954). *Transference: Its Meaning and Function in Psychoanalytic Therapy.* New York: Grune & Stratton.a

V. Contemporary Conflict Theory

Richards and others, in Chapters 14–18, explore their theoretical core: modern conflict theory. In chapter 14 Richards reviews the work of Charles Brenner inclusive of his seminal work "The Mind in Conflict" (1982), through his final contribution "Psychoanalysis or Mind and Meaning" (2005).

● What elements of theory are essential to a Modern Conflict Theorist?
● What method did Brenner use to construct, modify, extend or reject psychoanalytic theory?
● What role does theory play on technique?

In Chapter 15, Richards (with Arlow) spells out "Psychoanalytic Theory" in a way that broadens the frame with contributions from other conflict theorists. The chapter follows seven major areas of psychoanalytic theory: psychoanalysis as a biological science, fundamentals, methodology and therapy, psychic structure, compromise formation, social applications, more recent theoretical formulations:

● What forces mediate the functions of the mind?
● What is the nature and origin of unconscious fantasy?

In chapter 16, Richards (with Lynch) reviews the theoretical roots from ego psychology to contemporary conflict theory in five sections. They ask:

● What are the theoretical influences that shaped Freud's work to the present day?
● How have these influences modified and extended theory?

In chapter 17, Richards (with Lynch) looks at the contributions of Leo Rangell. Rangell, a theorist closely allied to contemporary conflict theory, retained his own identity as a developed Freudian; "one who has retained the enduring insights and formulations of an evolving general psychoanalytic theory and added such new ones as he thinks have earned inclusion" (Rangell, 2004, p. 304). Rangell worked tirelessly to create a unified psychoanalytic theory called the "total composite psychoanalytic theory."

- What are the sequential steps of intrapsychic process?
- How can decision making be, primarily, an unconcsious process?
- How does "total composite psychoanalytic theory" redress the problems created by theoretical pluralism?

In the final chapter of this section, chapter 18, Richards (with Richards) looks at psychoanalytic theory and its consequence on technique. This paper was responded to by a variety of discussants and the authors' response to their respondents is also included. Here the authors ask the question:

- How is technique affected by theory?
- Are all psychoanalytic theories comparable?

To address these questions they summarize the dominant theories, discuss how the theories inform technique and propose a series of potential technical challenges. To provide common ground they present a case to discuss these challenges.

CHAPTER 14

Introduction to *Psychoanalysis: The Science of Mental Conflict: Essays in Honor of Charles Brenner*

[Richards, A.D., (1986) Introduction to: *Psychoanalysis, the Science of Mental Conflict: Essays in Honor of Charles Brenner.* Hillsdale, NJ: Analytic Press.]

What words one uses in constructing one's theories and what their derivatives were is less important, in most instances, than what meaning the words have in terms of the new data and new generalizations about those data that constitute psychoanalytic theory. Words for what is new necessarily derive from what is familiar. This means neither that the words that have been redefined in this way should be retained nor that they should be replaced. Sometimes one course is followed, sometimes the other. Either can be defended or preferred, provided one realizes that it makes no great difference. It is not language that is important. One can think or speak in one language as well as in another. What one says is the important thing, not how one says it [Brenner, 1980, p. 208].

This passage from "Metapsychology and Psychoanalytic Theory" is quintessentially Charles Brenner. Although he penned these remarks in the context of his defense of the language of metapsychology, they stand as eloquent testimony to the values that have guided him throughout a distinguished career as both theorist and practitioner.

This is the credo of a "classical" analyst, disinclined to supplant the language of Freud's discoveries with trendier words that offer no real gain to conceptual understanding or explanatory power. It is at the same time the credo of a classical analyst who understands full well that theory-building is an evolving enterprise and that the words through which the analyst frames his theories must themselves evolve if they are to do justice to the ever growing data base generated by the psychoanalytic method. If for three decades Brenner has been content to innovate by addressing the meaning of traditional psychoanalytic concepts, drive, defense, super-ego, affect, it is because he has never been a revolutionary, intent on demolishing the psychoanalytic edifice bequeathed us by Freud. His appreciation of the fundamental principles that are Freud's legacy has cultivated in him a great respect for the language in which these principles were formulated. It is Brenner's signal strength to have retained the language of classical analysis, all the while showing how the meaning of psychoanalytic concepts must evolve if analysis is to remain a fully adequate science of mind.

Brenner is no psychoanalytic maverick. He has no "school" and seeks no "followers." Yet he has emerged as one of the preeminent theorists of his generation, one whose substantive innovations are masked by the classical terminology he retains and by his modest disclaimers that his theoretical contributions are but clarifications or refinements of traditional thinking. As I hope to demonstrate, however, Brenner's contributions in a variety of areas are far from incremental; they culminate in significant reformulations and bear witness to the continuing ability of classical psychoanalytic discourse to accommodate the growth of psychoanalytic knowledge. And this is perhaps Charles Brenner's greatest contribution as both theoretician and educator, to have shown that the concepts of classical analysis are not frozen in the past but rather are flexible instruments of conceptual and clinical advance. He is a conservative who believes in process, and his work admirably bears out his cautionary reminder that "what one says is the important thing, not how one says it."

PSYCHOANALYSIS AS SCIENCE

Brenner's *Elementary Textbook of Psychoanalysis,* first published in 1955 and revised in 1973, is the most notable explication of psychoanalytic principles in the history of the discipline. It has probably been read by more analysts, psychiatrists, psychologists, physicians, and students than any other work in the field. In its elegance and lucidity, it is matched only by Freud's own Introductory Lectures. It is in this early work that Brenner outlined the principles that guide him in his estimation of psychoanalysis as a natural science. For Brenner, it is Freud's discovery of the psychoanalytic method and his objective attitude toward the data generated by this method that place analysis squarely within the domain of the natural sciences. This distinctive method of data gathering, along with the interrelated hypotheses of psychic determinism and unconscious mental processes, is one of three pillars of the psychoanalytic edifice.

The language of psychoanalytic theory is commensurate with the data obtained by means of the psychoanalytic method. The heuristic test of this language is its clinical explanatory value.

Corollary to this perspective is Brenner's belief that the mere fact that it is possible to reformulate analysis in language compatible with that of other disciplines says nothing about the desirability of such translation. In a contribution published in 1969, he discusss Gardner's attempt to make psychoanalytic terminology dovetail with the language of neurophysiology. Brenner (1969a) observes that Gardiner's integrated strategy is belied by the fact that Gardiner "thinks" in terms of neurophysiology and aims at a unified science in which the concepts of both disciplines become coterminous with those of chemistry and physics. Lost in this intgrative shuffle, however, is the distinctive nature of psychoanalytic data, the complex thought processes issuing in wishes, fantasies, and anxieties. Until the precise relationship between mental representation and, neuronal functions can be stipulated, which neither Gardner nor any of his successors has been able to do, it is idle to judge the admissibility of psychoanalytic concepts in terms of their compatibility with neurophysiology. Analogizing at the level of terminology, which is all Gardner really does, cannot establish conceptual compatibility and can provide no basis for jettisoning the mere metapsychological language commensurate with psychoanalytic data.

Brenner further observes that Gardner's attempt to place a notion of "organismic equilibration" at the heart of psychoanalytic theory is fraught with logical difficulties: "If one follows the line of reasoning which it embodies, one would expect that evolution has eliminated psychosis and severe neurosis altogether or that it will do so in the course of time" (p. 50). Brenner adds that an equilibration model does violence to the data of psychoanalytic observation by ignoring the fact that "the urge to achieve instinctual gratification and to avoid unpleasure dominates mental activity to an extraordinary degree" (p. 51). For Brenner, then, "the pleasure principle is not only central to the psychoanalytic theory of the drives; it is central to the whole of the psychoanalytic theory of mental conflict as well" (p. 51). In supplanting this principle with an organismic "need" to adapt to external stimuli or to achieve a table equilibrium among opposing tendencies of the mind, theorists ignore the facts of mental life as disclosed by the psychoanalytic method: "Such theories may explain very well what the experimenter observes in a psychological laboratory. But they do not explain nor do they fit what the clinician daily observes of the wellsprings of human behavior and the conflict in human life to which they give rise" (p. 51).

Such remarks are central to Brenner's work and highlight the radical disjunction between his approach and that of theorists like George Klein, Heinz Kohut, and John Gedo. The latter all evoke some notion of the "self and its organization in order to supplant the pleasure principle with an updated version of Gardner's organismic equilibration hypothesis.

In "Psychoanalysis and Science/' a paper presented in 1968 and stimulated in part by the New York University Symposium on "Psychoanalysis and Scientific Method" in the fifties, Brenner amplified his response to Gardner. He argues that a science is defined not by the nature of the subject matter under investigation but rather by the approach it adopts toward that subject matter. It is by virtue of the analyst's investigative attitude that psychoanalysis qualifies as a natural science. In adopting this position, Brenner was disputingthe claim, made most forcefully by Kohut in his influential paper of 1959, that analysis departs from the natural sciences by virtue of its reliance on "introspection" in its data gathering.

Brenner maintains, contra Kohut, that introspection is a notoriously unreliable tool for obtaining information about mental phenomena: "An independent and outside observer with the help of the psychoanalytic method can gain a far more accurate and useful and informative view of the mental functioning of the patient's verbal communications, than anyone can from introspection" (p. 689). For Brenner, the introspective tendency to attribute our own thoughts and feelings to others is something "we must unlearn with experience." He agrees that we may reasonably assume that other people's minds are very similar to our own, but adds that "it is risky to go too far in this direction, that too great a reliance on what we call empathy and intuition leads to the undesirable type of activity that we call wild analysis" (p. 690).

In "Psychoanalysis: Philosophy or Science" (1970). a contribution to *Psychoanalysis and Philosophy,* he buttresses his argument by stressing that Freud did not "base his theories on introspective data but on observation—in particular on the close and extended observation of mentally, ill (neurotic) patients who came to him for treatment" (p. 36). Freud's unparalleled achievements, he believes, derive not from his introspective powers but from his ability to evaluate with scientific objectivity "previously unknown and largely unsuspected data derived from the psychoanalytic method" (p. 37). In the guise of self psychology, Kohut's contrary position of 1959 would blossom into the point of view that Freud's greatness derived largely fom disciplined introspection, and that it is *only* through introspection and empathy that the analyst obtains important data about his patients' mental functioning. For Brenner, the pleasure principle and "extrospection" *of* the natural scientist would remain central.

Brenner's most recent contribution on the scientific status of psychoanalysis is the 1980 "Metapsychology and Psychoanalytic Theory." Here, in response to critics such as George Klein and Merton Gill and Roy Schafer, who deem metapsychologyan undesirable, pseudoscientific accretion to the "hermeneutic" core of analysis, Brenner undertakes a careful review of Freud's various uses of the term, beginning with a statement in 1898 in which he construed metapsychology as the bridge connecting the unconscious biological and the conscious psychological. At a later stage in his career, Freud equated metapsychology with the psychology of the unconscious, and still later in his 1915 paper "The Unconscious," he seemed to equate the metapsychological with the economic aspects of mental functioning. But Brenner goes on to adduce fairly compelling evidence that Freud ultimately came to equate metapsychology with psychoanalytic theory in general, rather than simply with the psychoanalytic theory of unconscious mental processes; in Freud's footnote to the title of , "Metapsychological Supplement to the Theory of Dreams" (1915b). "metapsychology" and "psychological system" are used synonymously.

On the basis of this philological judgment, Brenner takes issue with the attempt by Rapaport and Gill (1959) to dissect metapsychology into six discrete assumptions and viewpoints. His argument is that each viewpoint invoked by Rapaport and Gill implicates all the others, so that "so-called structural theory, for example, is not merely a structural point of view. Its propositions are dynamic, genetic, adaptive, economic, and structural propositions" (p. 198). In short, metapsychology as a notational shorthand for psychoanalytic theory cannot be differentiated from the individual viewpoints that jointly comprise it: metapsychology itself *denote* the fact of this mutual implication. Psychoanalytic understanding and the theory that encapsulates it is the confluence of these several viewpoints.

In a related vein, Brenner takes issue with the attempt by Robert Waelder (1962) to divide psychoanalysis into a hierarchy of "levels" based on a putative proximity to the data of observation. Disputing Waelder's judgment that metapsychology is less proximate to the data and hence "far less necessary" to analysis than less abstract levels of explanation, Brenner argues that Waelder's entire classificatory schema is based on a fundamental misconception "of the nature of scientific observation and theory formation":

> In every branch of science even the simplest observations involve ideas of the highest order of abstraction. In physics, for example, such high level abstractions as space and time are data of observation. In psychoanalysis, as in every other branch of science, both theories and observations involve greater numbers of abstractions. What makes a theory useful and dependable has no relation whatever to its abstractedness. A theory is either well supported by a large amount of data that are relevant, or, it is poorly supported by data. The correct basis for a hierarchy of theories of any science is not abstractness or concreteness. It is the degree to which a given theory is supported by the relevant data or, conversely, how speculative it is. "Speculative" is not a synonym for "abstract," nor is "well supported by relevant data" its antonym [p. 200].

Through his defense of metapsychology as a mode of discourse commensurate with psychoanalytic data, Brenner returns to his view that analysis as a natural science takes up an observational stance no different from that of other natural sciences. He disputes the hermeneutic claim that analysis forfeits its claim to scientific status by virtue of its preoccupation with "meaning." For Brenner, the analytic concern with meaning only highlights the fact that analysis is a separate branch of science addressing its particular subject in the manner of any other science:

> The data of psychoanalysis are principally wishes, fears, fantasies, dreams, neurotic symptoms, associative material, etc., expressed in language and gestures that have meaning. In other words, psychoanalysts do deal with meanings as data, which physicists and neurophysiologists, for example, do not. But what psychoanalysts *do* with their data is no different in principle from what any other scientists do with their data. What psychoanalysts do that is of particular importance . . . is that they make inferences with respect to the causes of the wishes, fears, fantasies, dreams, neurotic symptoms, and associative material that constitute their data of obser-

vation. They postulate the same cause and effect relationships with respect to their data as physicists, for example, do with respect to theirs. That is to say, psychoanalysts try to discover or, to be more precise, to infer what it is that causes the normal and pathological mental phenomena they observe. Their discoveries or inferences are what constitute psychoanalytic theory, just as, for example, Newton's inferences, which are more usually called his laws of motion, constitute the theory of celestial and terrestial mechanics that bears his name [p. 205].

It is from this standpoint, and with the data of psychoanalytic observation in mind, that Brenner proceeds to defend the much attacked notion of psychic energy.

Is it justified and useful as a concept and as a term? I believe so, but not because the word, energy, was derived in the first instance from a term and concept of physics. I believe so because I think that drive theory is a valid and useful generalization (theory) about mental functioning and that in that theory there should be some term to designate the concept that drives have the capacity to impel the mind to activity- a capacity that varies in strength from time to time. What that concept is called *matters not at all, any more than it matters whether one speaks English, French, Spanish, or German in discussing it. Call it psychic energy, motivation, impetus, or "abc."The tag is unimportant. It is the concept that matters. If you drop the concept altogether, as many analysts would like to do, you have to discard drive theory as well and* you have to substitute something else for it. Just changing the *name* from "drive" to, say, "motivation" changes nothing in the theory. It makes the theory no more "psychological," no less "mechanistic," no more "human," than it was before [pp. 210–211].

Here, as always, Brenner's concern is not with words but with the theoretical assumptions that underlie them and the implications of these assumptions for psychoanalytic theory-building. To jettison the notion of psychic energy is to abandon drive theory in its common form; it is to make a "real change" in psychoanalytic theory, which has held since Freud that mental life is composed of conscious and unconscious wishes that impinge on the mental apparatus with varying degrees of intensity.

In drawing attent tion both to the assumptions that underlie the abandonment of individual psychoanalytic concepts and to the implications of such a move, Brenner highlights the magnitude of Freud's achievement: the promulgation of a theory of mental life that achieves cohesiveness and explanatory force through the conceptual interweaving of all its major concepts.

THE DRIVES, AGGRESSION, AND STRUCTURAL THEORY

In the second chapter of the *Elementary Textbook,* Brenner (1955) suggests a position on the drives that dovetails in most essentials with that of Freud. The drives, he tells his readers, are "abstractions from the data of experience. They are hypotheses-operational concepts, to use a term which is fashionable nowadays—which we believe enable us to understand and explain our data in as simple and as systematic a way as possible" (p. 20). His contention that there are two kinds of psychic energy, one associated with libido and one with the aggressive drive, implies a basically biological concept of the drives. He departs from Freud only in contesting the validity of the concept of repetition compulsion and the idea that the gratification associated with aggression is beyond the pleasure principle. With respect to the latter point, he is content to cite Hartmann and inform the reader that "the majority of psychoanalysts appear to have accepted this view" (p. 30).

In chapter 2 of *The Mind in Conflict,* written almost 30 years later in 1982, Brenner draws a clearer distinction between his views and those of Freud. At the onset, alluding to Freud's concept of the instinct as a "frontier concept" at the interface of mind and body, he disputes the contention that psychoanalytic data by themselves can never be an adequate basis for a satisfactory theory of the drives. Rather, Brenner argues that a satisfactory theory of drives can derive *only* from psychoanalytic data. In contesting the need to anchor psychoanalytic drive theory in nonanalytic data derived from biology, physiology, animal observation, and the like, Brenner also contests Freud's attempt to "biologize" libido by tracing its origins to particular regions of the body. For Brenner, as for Freud, the connections between libido and the erogenous zones are "indisputable and intimate," but Brenner adds that "this is not the same as saying that libido arises from mouth, anus, genitals, etc." (p. 14). He then cites certain facts that weigh against Freud's conceptualization, including the intensification of libidinal wishes at the time of menopause and the climacteric, and the efflorescense of sexual wishes during the oedipal period. Brenner continues:

> Everyday analytic experience demonstrates, for example, that events occurring in the context of a relationship between patient and analyst, such as impending separation or the commencement of analysis, can powerfully increase, i.e., stimulate, the urgency of libidinal wishes, but no one would conclude from such observation that the relationship between patient and analyst, i.e., the transference, is a source of libido, much less the source of it. In the same way, it is not truly convincing to conclude from the very intimate relationship between erogenous zones and libidinal derivatives that the zones are the *source* of the libidinal drive. That they are intimately linked is certain. That one is the source of the other is less so [pp. 14–15].

In the seemingly fine distinction that concludes this passage, we see Brenner's emancipation from certain mechanistic accoutrements of Freud's approach to motivation. It is tantamount to the espousal of an entirely psychological and "personalized" approach to drive behavior. This attitude carries over to Brenner's discussion of aggression (1971 b). Here he differentiates between the theory of the aggressive drive, which derives from "the accumulation of psychoanalytic evidence," and the theory of the death instinct, through which Freud sought to give the phenomenon of human aggressiveness a transcendent biological meaning. Brenner argues that just as Freud required a somatic source for libido, that is, the excitation of the nerve endings in the erogenous zones, so he required one for aggression. He believed he had located this in "the universal tendency of living matter to die," an idea Brenner finds invalid on grounds both empirical and logical. More important, it cannot be inferred from psychoanalytic data and so has no place in psychoanalytic explanation. Clinical explanations of aggression, including self-destructive behavior, implicate only those aspects of Freud's theory that derive from psychoanalytic data. Through such data we

> explain such behavior in terms of murderous childhood wishes, fears of retribution, fears of loss, and self-punitive trends. None

of these depend on the assumption that a death drive is common to all living matter. It depends essentially on the data furnished by the application of the psychoanalytic method [p. 21].

Brenner's critique of the death instinct as nonpsychological and nonpsychoanalytic paves the way for his redefinition of the drives as "generalizations" about two classes of "wishes" corresponding to two types of motivation. This definition, in turn, leads him to accord pride of place not to the drive itself, but to drive derivatives, the "wish for gratification" that is uniquely individual. It is in his attention to the variousness of drive derivatives as uniquely individual embodiments of the drives that Brenner approaches the position of hermeneuticists like George Klein and Roy Schafer. For Brenner, that is, it is insufficient simply to impute to analysands libidinal or aggressive conflicts stemming from their drives. And it is of little moment to go one step further and categorize the analysand's wishes as oral, anal, or phallic. Rather,

> What is important in respect to each patient is to learn as much as possible about the libidinal ad aggressive drive derivatives which are important at the moment, including their relationship to childhood derivatives and to subsequent experience and development. What is important, in other words, is to learn as much as possible about what a patient wishes, about who is involved in his wishes, about how and why he has just those particular wishes about those particular persons [p. 26].

It is ironic that Brenner, in his sensitivity to the experiential specificity of the analysand's conflicting wishes, adopts a position of nominal agreement with those analysts who, unlike him, seek to dispense entirely with psychoanalytic metapsychology. The essential difference, of course, is that Brenner arrives at his position using the language and conceptual framework of classical analysis. Indeed, his stance is a refinement of classical thinking; it is premised on an entirely psychoanalytic appreciation of the drives and generalizations about wishes. Klein (1976) and Schafer (1976). on the other hand, feel that they can articulate the singularity of the individual's conflicts and wishes and wishful impulses only by supplanting psychoanalytic drive theory, which includes the crucial notion of the drive derivative, with a new vocabulary and a new conceptual framework. Brenner finds such departures gratuitous:

> Critics of the psychoanalytic theory of the drives often charge
> that it is impersonal and mechanistic. The facts do not justify the
> charge. Such critics either ignore or misunderstand the distinc-
> tion between drive and drive derivative. The former is imper-
> sonal and general, the latter is general and specific. Drive theory
> includes both (p. 26).

It is to Brenner's lasting credit to have shown how clarifying emen-
dations to the psychoanalytic theory of the drives, which amount to
Freud's own position refined and shorn of the extraanalytic presuppositions,
culminate in a substantive revision of the structural theory.
Rejecting Freud's speculations about the biological origins of the drives,
Brenner is led to reassess the notion of the id, which Freud envisioned as
the repository of the drives. Freud, and most analysts since him, viewed
the drives as constitutionally determined and present from the very
beginnning of postnatal life. The clear implication is that drives are more
independent of experience than are those aspects of mental functioning
subsumed under the rubric of "ego." Brenner, however, drawing on all
the available psychoanalytic evidence, suggests that drive-related activities, whether libidinal or aggressive, are from birth influenced by experiential factors that gain expression in ego development. In short, clinical
analysis does not sustain the separation of ego development from issues
of drive expression and drive gratification. It follows that a sharp distinction between ego and id, even a sharp *heuristic* distinction, must be
brought into question.

Brenner makes the same point when he notes that what psychoanalytic theory subsumes under ego functions are distinguishable from
drives and drive derivatives only in situations of conflict. Ego functions,
he reminds us, are executants of drives and hence come into opposition
to drives only when drive derivatives evoke unpleasure and defense. For
Brenner, then, conflict is a *sine qua non* of structural theory itself. In *The
Mind in Conflict* (1982a). he supports this point by appealing to Anna
Freud's remark that "in the absence of conflict there is no division among
the mental agencies, or, in other words, no id, ego, or superego" (p. 73).
In a similar vein, he cites David Beres, who remarked that in order to be
consistent, repressed wishes and fantasies must be regarded as belonging
properly in the heading of the ego. In thus stressing the role of the ego in
drive gratification from the very beginning of life, he implicitly departs
from Freud, who was content to situate repressed wishes first in "the

unconscious" of the topographical theory and ultimately in the "id" of structural theory.

Brenner's reformulation of structural theory culminates in the revised estimation of the superego set forth in chapter 8 of *The Mind in Conflict* (1982). In the *Elementary Textbook* (1955) Brenner accepted the traditional view of the superego as one agency in the psychic apparatus. In articles published over the next two decades (1959,1982a). he significantly enlarged our clinical appreciation of this mental agency by drawing attention to the role of both masochism and libidinal gratification in superego formation. By contrast, in *The Mind in Conflict* Brenner offers an entirely new perspective on the superego, construing it as a compromise formation functionally analogous to other compromise formations revealed by psychoanalytic investigation: neurotic symptoms, dreams, delusions, character traits, and so on. Brenner continues to stress that the superego is a "structure" that enters into psychic conflict along with id and ego. But as id and ego are presumably *not* compromise formations, Brenner's recent formulations appear to forego the symmetry of the three intrapsychic agencies of traditional structural theory. This suggests that, implicitly at least, Brenner has arrived at a theoretical juncture where he questions the validity and clinical usefulness of conceptualizing mental-life in terms of three structurally equivalent mental agencies. I will not venture to predict where Brenner's theorizing will lead him, beyond speculating that his forthcoming contributions will offer increasingly nuanced depictions of the interrelated constituents of psychic conflict while simultaneously incorporating certain features of the hermeneutic theorists like Klein and Schafer. Brenner seems to have understood well the aphorism of his friend and colleague, Jacob Arlow, that id, ego, and sperego exist not in the patient but in psychoanalytic textbooks. It is conceivable that Brenner will eventually articulate a model of the mind in conflict in which the interpretation of the elements of conflict is such that the traditional concepts of id, ego, and superego become superfluous.

AFFECTS

For Brenner the problem of affect is coterminous with the problem of anxiety. His earliest publication on the topic, misleadingly entitled "An Addendum to Freud's Theory of Anxiety" (1953). is actually a seminal contribution to affect theory that paves the way for his recent formulations regarding depressive affect. Brenner begins by arguing against

Freud's theories of actual and traumatic neuroses. Here again his point of departure is diametrically opposite that of Kohut, whose early acceptance of the concept of actual neurosis was crucial to his later theorizing (Ornstein, 1978).

With respect to actual neurosis, Brenner critically reviews the data suggesting that anxiety can arise automatically owing to a quantitative flooding of the psychic apparatus. His conclusion is that analysis has not generated any data suggesting that anxiety can emerge independently of a psychical source. Otherwise, he finds no evidence of Freud's claim that neurotic anxiety can arise from simple frustration or sexual strivings. Returning to the traumatic neuroses, Brenner finds that available analytic data contradict Freud: they suggest that the anxiety associated with traumatic states derives from the conflicts evoked by traumautic situations and not from a "rupture of the stimulus barrier, that is, from the sexually quantitative variations in psychic energy or citation" (1953, p. 21).

Brenner considers one final basis for Freud's views on the actual neurosis, a point central to the "addendum" he proceeds to formulate. This concerns the affective state of infants who are separated from their mothers. Brenner suggests that we cannot really know *what* an infant experiences under such circumstances and that it is therefore unwarrantedly adultomorphic to equate the infant's emotion with "anxiety." For Brenner it makes more sense to characterize the emotion of the traumatically distressed infant as "extreme unpleasure rather than specifically as anxiety, although we may reasonably assume that as the infant matures it develops the capacity to be anxious in danger situations." Pursuing this line of reasoning, Brenner offers the following conceptualization:

> Anxiety is an emotion (affect) which the anticipation of danger evokes in the ego. It is not present, as such, from birth or very early infancy. In such very early periods, the infant is aware only of pleasure or unpleasure as far as emotions are concerned. As experience increases and other ego functions develop (e.g., memory and sensory perception). the child becomes able to predict or anticipate that a state of unpleasure (a "traumatic situation") will develop. This drawing ability of a child to react to danger in advance is the beginning of the specific emotion of anxiety, which in the course of further development we propose becomes sharply differentiated from other unpleasant emotions [p. 22].

Brenner's formulation, like Freud's, rests "on the assumption that there is a genetic, relation between anxiety in later life and the emotion of the child in traumatic situations of infancy" (p. 23). But unlike Freud's theory of the actual neurosis, Brenner's alternative explanation "leaves open the possibility that the emotion experienced in the traumatic situation is also related genetically to other unpleasant emotions in later life" (p. 23). In a revealing passage that foreshadows his future theoretical concerns, Brenner adds that his formulation leaves open the possibility that this state of psychic helplessness that we associate with traumatic situations may be "the forebearer of depression as well as anxiety" (p. 23).

The addendum of 1953, an important revision of the psychoanalytic theory of affects, is revealing of how in general Brenner approaches the task of theory-building. He begins with a careful review of Freud's contributions on a topic, locates an aspect of Freud's theory that is not borne out by clinical data, and then offers a clinically based reformulation that serves as a point of departure for subsequent theorizing. In this instance, his differentiation of the infant's reaction to danger and the child's (and the adult's) experience of anxiety ties the latter to the maturation of ego functions and, hence, to psychological referents. As an added benefit, "it avoids the unwelcome necessity of assuming that there are two kinds of anxiety" (p. 22). Finally, in suggesting that affect theory must posit developmental linkages not only between infantile unpleasure and later anxiety, but between such unpleasure and the crystallization of unpleasant affect, it opens an avenue for future theoretical work.

But it was not until twenty years later, in a presentation for the 28th International Psychoanalytic Congress, that Brenner took up the challenge posed by his early paper. He begins "Depression, Anxiety, and Affect Theory" (1974a) by reprising the basic premise of the 1953 "Addendum": "that early in life, before any substantial degree of ego development has taken place, all affects can be divided into pleasurable and unpleasurable" (p. 29). Now, however, he makes this point to highlight the fact that the generic unpleasure associated with the traumatic insults of infancy are the source not only of later experiences of anxiety but of experiences of depression as well: 'These emotions, too, no less than the emotions of anxiety,are genetically related to the unpleasure of the traumatic state; in some ways they develop out of it" (p. 30). Brenner next distinguishes between the unpleasurable affects of anxiety and grief by appealing to their differing ideational content:

Grief, for example, is unpleasure associated with ideas that in general have to do with instinctual frustration, i.e., disappointment, with ideas of inadequacy, inferiority, with ideas of loneliness and often the idea that things will never be any better, that frustration, loneliness, and inferiority will persist, that they are inevitable (p. 30).

Thus Brenner invokes a temporal referent to differentiate the two principal categories of affect: anxiety concerns something bad that will happen in the future, depression something bad that has already happened. The nexus of Brenner's theory of affects, then, is "that psychologically, i.e., subjectively speaking, affects are distinguishable from one another on only two grounds. First, whether they are pleasurable or unpleasurable, and second, what thoughts are connected with them, what their ideational content is" (p. 30).

Brenner systematizes this idea in a companion paper, "On the Nature and Development of Affects, A Unified Theory" (1974b). Here affects are introduced as complex phenomena that include sensations of pleasure, unpleasure, pleasure and unpleasure in varying combinations, and ideas. A pleasurable or unpleasurable sensation together with an associated idea constitutes the mental phenomenon known as an affect. Affects originate early in life, when ideas first become linked to sensations of pleasure and unpleasure. The development of affects, and their differentiation from one another, go hand in hand with subsequent ego and superego development. The advantages of Brenner's unified theory of affects are manifold. Consistent with his innovations in other areas, this theory reformulates what we can know about affects from the data of clinical analysis. In so doing, he dispenses with unwarranted biological inferences that cannot be verified by analysis and with more subjective inferences about the nature of the "emotions" experienced very early in life. At the clinical heuristic level it provides criteria for distinguishing different affects, along with a workable language for explaining these differences.

The clinical yield of Brenner's theory is perhaps more salient with respect to depression. By situating the anlagen of depression in the amorphous unpleasure of early life, he shows how adult depression, no less than adult anxiety, yields to analytic unraveling with respect to its essential structure and meaning. Like symptoms of anxiety, depressive symptoms are crystallizations of complex affect, that is, compromise formations issuing from the various wishes, fears, defenses, self-punitive trends, and environmental pressures brought to bear at a given point in time. Whether or not patients are consciously aware of being depressed, "the affect of a depressed patient has the same complex structure as does any other fantasy, thought, action, or symptom" (1974a, p. 32).

Brenner continues this line of thought in "Affects in Psychic Conflict" (1975). a rich presentation whose accessibility and pragmatic clinical importance belie the nuances of reasoning that inform it. Here Brenner shows how affect theory, in relation to both anxiety and depression, provides a crucial vehicle for discerning the unique constellation of conflicts presented by each analysand. This paper is especially noteworthy for its wealth of clinical examples highlighting the role of depressive affect in conflict formation. In addressing conflict through the vehicle of affect theory, Brenner adopts an approach that is entirely dynamic. Moving toward a position to be spelled out more fully in *The Mind in Conflict,* (1982) he shows how psychoanalytic affect theory can afford the clinician a detailed grasp of the elements of intrapsychic conflict that far surpasses the insights provided by the potentially reifying constructs of traditional structural theory.

In a "Depressive Affect, Anxiety, and Psychic Conflict in the Phallic-Oedipal Phase" (1979a). Brenner elaborates on the phenomenology and dynamic meaning of specifically depressive conflicts. This paper, one of very few in which Brenner advocates a terminological departure from the language of classical analysis, introduces the term "calamity" as a substitute for "danger." The former, it is argued, connotes bad experiences that are either impending or have already happened; it can therefore be linked equally well to anxiety or depressive affect. "Danger," by contrast, has primarily a future orientation and is therefore less suggestive of the past events or circumstances associated specifically with depressive affect. Brenner proceeds to recast the major danger situations of classical theory, loss of object, loss of the object's love, and castration anxiety as the three calamities of childhood. He takes pains to dispel the timeworn belief that each of these correlates neatly with a specific psychosexual stage. He argues, for example, that fear of loss of the object and of the object's love frequently plays an important role even in the phallic-oedipal phase. For Brenner, the calamities are interwoven into a tangible and analyzable whole, so that to segregate them along a time line is to compartmentalize the child's mental life artificially.

With this in mind, Brenner goes on to argue that both depressive affect and anxiety enter castration conflicts regardless of the individual's sex, though the former is predominant in girls and the latter in boys. As always, his theoretical formulations culminate in useful therapeutic precepts: (1) View the unpleasurable affect as a symptom masking unsatisfactory compromise formations; and (2) proceed with the work of analysis by looking for the cause of the particular genre of unpleasure that gains expression in the symptom. These and other clinical insights are eloquently put forth in the third chapter of The *Mind in Conflict,* a distillation of over three decades of thinking and writing about the role of affect in psychoanalytic theory and practice.

DEFENSES

In his presentation of structural theory in the *Elementary Textbook,* Brenner uses the term "ego" in a reified way far removed from the mode of discourse typifying his more recent work. This is particularly true of his explanation of signal anxiety, where he invokes an ego that "produces anxiety as a signal of unpleasure. With the help of the pleasure principle in this way, the ego is able to offer a successful opposition to the emergence of the dangerous impulses" (1955, p. 79). Not so his concept of defense, which even in 1955 has much the same character to be found in his writings of the 1970s and 1980s. To the question, "What defenses does the ego offer against the id?," the *Elementary Textbook* answers as follows:

> The ego can use anything which lies at hand that will serve the purpose. Any ego attitude, any real perception, a change in attention, furtherance of another id impulse which is safer than the dangerous one and will compete with it, a vigorous attempt to neutralize the energy of the dangerous drive, the formation of identifications, or the promotion of fantasy can be used alone or in any combination in a defensive way. In a word, the ego can and does use all of the processes of normal ego formation and ego function for defensive purposes at one time or another [p. 80].

In a series of papers following the *Elementary Textbook,* Brenner develops his view of defensive processes as content-neutral by focusing on repression. In 1957 he ended a scholarly review of Freud's concept of repression by underscoring the status of repression in Freud's final view of defense: Repression is but one of several defense mechanisms the ego may employ against drive derivatives, the latter being the source of anxiety. The target of repression is ordinarily a libidinal drive, but it may be an aggressive drive derivative or superego demand as well. Finally, the mechanism of repression is the establishment of a countercathexis of the ego; it follows that repression becomes possible only after significant ego development has occurred.

In a paper published ten years later, Brenner (1967) explicitly attempted to apply the principle of multiple function to the theory of repression. He was thereupon led to revise Freud's classical concept of repression which he contends has two aspects: (1) the belief that repression is tantamount to barring certain mental elements access to conscious mental life, and (2) the derivative notion that the intrusion of these elements into consciousness betokens the failure of repression or "return of the repressed." Against this, Brenner argues that repression results from an interplay of forces within the mind in which the balance is predominantly in favor of those forces seeking to bar one or several mental representations from consciousness. Since the repressing forces usually achieve but limited success, it follows that repressed mental elements routinely enter conscious mental life, quite apart from those instances in which their return signifies the outright failure of repression. In a similar vein, Brenner calls into question the belief that neurotic symptoms signal a failure of repression and are thus tantamount to the return of the repressed:

> Repression signifies a dynamic equilibrium between forces striving for discharge (e.g., an instinctual derivative) and other opposing forces (defenses, superego prohibition). If something happens to shift the balance among these forces in a direction which is unfavorable to the ego's defenses, there-suit will be an increased emergence into conscious mental life and action of the previously instinctual derivative. If the shift is long continued, and if the emergence of the instinctual derivative is felt to be dangerous (arousing signal anxiety). the compromise which results will be of the nature of a neurotic symptom or character trait. By the same token, a shift in the equilibrium which is favorable to the defensive forces, and which diminishes a patient's tendency to react with anxiety to an instinctual derivative which has given rise to a neu-

rotic symptom, will result in the symptom disappearing or becoming less severe [pp. 398–399].

We might say that for Brenner the vicissitudes of symptomatic behavior and character pathology derive from the continually changing balance between opposing forces within the mind. In a paper of 1981, "Defense and Defense Mechanisms," he elaborates as implicit in this viewpoint a "major, even a radical revision of this part of conflict theory" (p. 558). He now states boldly that discrete defense "mechanisms" simply do not exist.

Rather, "defense is an aspect of mental functioning that is definable only in terms of its consequences, reduction of unpleasure associated with the drive derivative, i.e., with the instinctual wish, or with superego functioning" (p. 559). It follows for Brenner that the very aspects of mental functioning which in certain contexts function as defenses against drive derivatives can in other contexts facilitate gratification of the same derivatives. Since the mental mechanisms traditionally equated with defenses serve nondefensive purposes as well, it is erroneous to characterize them, as intrinsically defense related.

The argument that there are no ego functions exclusively subserving defense implies a radically broadened concept of ego. Brenner's revision here does not parallel that of Hartmann (1939). who assigned certain aspects of ego functioning to an entirely "conflict-free" sphere. Rather, in contending that no ego function can be assigned a priori to a particular sphere of functioning, Brenner adopts a viewpoint that is nonmechanistic and nonreductionistic, and, as such, "faithful to the facts of life" (p. 563).

The language in which he casts his insights into the reversibility of defensive and drive-related purposes is action-oriented, dovetailing in certain respects with the "action language" proposed by Schafer (1976). Consider Brenner's characterization of a defense as a "say no to whatever is the target of defense" (p. 562). Consider as well how he describes the mind at work:

> When unpleasure is aroused or threatens to be aroused, one does whatever one can to avoid and reduce it. When one desires ratification and pleasure, one does whatever one can to achieve it. . . . It is the function served by what one does that determines whether it is properly called defense [pp. 564–565].

The ready identifiability of a particular analysand's "repertory of defenses" is another traditional assumption called into question by Brenner's functional estimation of defensive processes. His contention that all aspects of ego functioning are all-purpose, capable of subserving, variously, drive gratification, ego defense, and superego prohibition, militates against the belief that analysands have limited defensive repertories. For Brenner, any repertory of defense necessarily draws on every aspect of ego functioning:

> Thus to speak of a characteristic repertory of defense is really to say only that prominent neurotic symptoms and/or character traits are apt to be persistent in any patient and to require repeated analysis and interpretation in the course of treatment. . . . It is not patients who show a limited repertory of defensive methods; it is one or another symptom, or other compromise formation, which is characterized by a special method or methods of defense [pp. 567–568].

In chapter 5 of *The Mind in Conflict* (1982) Brenner offers additional insights drawn from his estimation of defense. Linking his reconceptualization of defensive processes to his unified theory of affect, he observes that defenses may be directed not only against drive derivatives or affect or superego functioning, but against the anxiety or depressive affect they mobilized. In the latter instance, defense may be directed at the sensation of unpleasure, the ideational correlate of the unpleasure, that is, the real or fantasied calamity, or both. Further, defenses neither disappear during the course of analysis nor become increasingly "normal." Rather, their character and preemptoriness alter as the balance among opposing mental forces changes in response to the analytic work (p. 92).

It is clear that Brenner's reformulation of the concept of defense and the status of defensive processes in mental functioning will not win easy acceptance. In particular, his proposal that we dispense entirely with the notion of defense mechanisms will likely encounter strong resistance in view of the longevity of this concept and its identification with both Freud and his daughter Anna. But here, as elsewhere, Brenner theorizes in a clinically relevant way that enhances our understanding of the analytic process. He is awed neither by traditional concepts nor by their traditional deployment. Rather, he is intent on doing full justice to the data that follow from the use of Freud's psychoanalytic method. Drawing on scientific sensibilities tempered by broad clinical experience, he subjects each psychoanalytic formulation he examines to the tests of clarity, consistency, logical validity, and clinical usefulness. His proposaal that we abandon the concept of defense mechanism is not offered lightly; though it may make case presentations more difficult or simply less facile, it augurs well for our day-to-day clinical work. It aids us in keeping the analysand "as a whole" in the foreground, relegating isolated drive derivatives and defenses to a subordinate role both conceptual and clinical.

TECHNIQUE

The psychoanalytic situation is organized according to the psychoanalytic theory of mental functioning and in keeping with the goals and aims of psychoanalysis as a therapy. Whatever is consonant with the dynamic principles of psychoanalysis and with the goals of psychoanalytic therapy is properly part of the analytic situation. Whatever is in conflict with those principles and goals is not legitimately part of the psychoanalytic situation and should be avoided and discarded [Arlow and Brenner, 1966, p. 43].

In this passage from 'The Psychoanalytic Situation," we encounter again the leitmotif of Brenner's work. The "theory of mental functioning" that "organizes" the psychoanalytic part of the analyst's task is to understand the nature and origins of his patient's mental conflicts" (Brenner 1976, p. 33). Issues of technique can be addressed only from the standpoint of the analyst's comprehension of the analysand's psychic conflicts. Brenner's work in this area has a twofold intent: (1) to show how specific aspects of technique subserve psychoanalytic conflict theory, and (2) to see to it that no single element of technique, and no single explanation or justification of an element of technique, achieves a weight disproportionate to its status within this theory of mental functioning. Brenner repeatedly cautions his psychoanalytic colleages regarding the pitfalls, theoretical and clinical, of overvaluing specific aspects of technique, or specific rationales for technique, currently in vogue. In the Arlow-Brenner (1966) paper, the cautionary note centers on the view of the "psychoanalytic situation" popularized by Leo Stone, Rene Spitz, Elizabeth Zetzel, and others in the early 1960s. These authors invoke an "*a priori* assumption that the psychoanalytic situation re-creates the relationship between mother and infant during the earliest months of life"

(1966, p. 23). They hold as a corollary that analytic termination is invariably an "experience that parallels that of weaning" (p. 24). Arlow and Brenner counter that "while this is doubtless true in many instances, it seems unlikely that it is invariably the case" (p. 23). They warn here against what Hartmann (1939) called a genetic fallacy: 'The fact that the first situation is dependence in the life of every individual, his relationship with his mother," they write, "does not prove that every subsequent relationship of dependence produces the prototype" (Arlow and Brenner, 1966, p. 26). They offer case examples that run counter to the then current estimation of the analytic situation: a patient who did not react to termination with separation anxiety and another, for whom the "basis of the transference was not the patient's early tie to her mother, but her later relationship with her father" (p. 28).

Arlow and Brenner's approach in this paper illustrates the empirical open mindedness, the receptivity to the yield of psychoanalytic inquiry that will guide Brenner through a succession of works on technique: "The meaning of the psychoanalytic situation is not the same for every patient . . . analytic data are the only basis on which one can validate the unconscious significance which the analytic situation holds for a particular patient" (p. 43). Brenner's determination to examine and justify elements of technique with respect to the dynamic principles of analysis is expressed in his reconsideration of dream interpretation. In the chapter on dream psychology in *Psychoanalytic Concepts and the Structural Theory* (Arlow and Brenner, 1964). Brenner recasts the analytic understanding of dreaming from the standpoint of structural theory. Brenner goes beyond Freud's formulations in *The Interpretation of Dreams* (1900) by reconceptualizing dreams as the product of the interplay of id, ego, and superego; as such, they are compromise formations. The technical consequence of this structural reappraisal is, ironically, the dethroning of dream interpretation from its privileged position in clinical work. As but one example of compromise formation, the dream is hardly unique in affording the analyst a view of the analysand's unconscious conflicts. This position is articulated with great force in a paper, "Dreams in Clinical Psychoanalytic Practice" (1969b):

> It is not only the case with dreams that they are a compromise formation among instinctual id wishes, defenses motivated by anxiety or guilt and superego demands or prohibitions. The same is true of neurotic symptoms, parapraxes, slips, jokes, many charac-

ter traits, one's choice of a profession, one's sexual practices and preferences, daydreams, conscious childhood memories, including screen memories, one's reaction to a play, film or book, one's social habits and activities in general, and above all, in every patient's so-called free associations [p. 336].

In his Brill Lecture of 1966, "Some Comments on Technical Precepts in Psychoanalysis" (1969c). Brenner uses his view of dreams as situated on a continuum of compromise formations to reconsider two standard technical precepts: (1) Never interpret a patient's first dream, and (2) dream interpretation is the "royal road to the unconscious." Brenner argues that technical precepts, these included, are not universal truths applicable to all analysands regardless of time and place; rather, technical strategies can be justified only in terms of the requirements of specific psychoanalytic situations, which subsume the cognitive style and interpretive orientation of a particular analyst. The first precept he appraises as follows: "A first dream may and should be used like any other analytic material: in a way that is appropriate to the circumstances of the analytic situation at the time. No single rule-of-thumb can suffice to cover all the various possibilities" (p. 342). As for the "royal road," here Brenner is equally pragmatic. Dreams are valuable grist for the analytic mill, to be sure, but they enjoy no privileged status. Certain analysts may be especially drawn to them in elucidating the analysand's conflicts, but other analysts, with different cognitive styles and interpretive orientations, may focus more profitably on other kinds of interpretable phenomena. In either case, analysis may proceed to a satisfactory conclusion:

> Whether the one view and the practical consequences which appear to be associated with it has any substantial advantage over the others is not possible to decide at present. All that one can say at present with any degree of assurance is this: There is no convincing evidence that dream interpretation still offers the quickest and easiest road to knowledge of the hidden workings of the mind at the present time as it doubtless did 65 years ago [p. 345].

Brenner similarly demystifies some long-held assumptions regarding transference analysis. In the same paper, he judges anachronistic the traditional dictum that transference should be interpreted only when it constitutes a resistance. Rooted in Freud's initial belief that "the pervasive effect of a strongly positive transference" is central to the analytic treatment (p. 336). this dictum and its rationale are undercut by the theoretical reformulations undertaken by Freud conceptualized the therapeutic action of analysis in terms of overcoming resistances and observed that positive transference could as easily serve resistance as could the negative variety. This theoretical shift anticipated what we have learned in the decades following: *all* transference must be analyzed, as one simply cannot tell in advance whether a transference is in the service of defense.

As for the traditional belief that transference acting out necessarily impedes analysis, here again Brenner avoids categorical injunctions in favor of a more measured appreciation of the vicissitudes of different psychoanalytic situations:

> In other words, acting out in the transference is sometimes readily analyzable, sometimes analyzable only slowly and with difficulty, and sometimes not at all, at least for the time being. It is not always especially accessible to analysis, as our precept would have it. It is not necessarily an impediment or danger to analysis which must be forestalled in some nonanalytic way [1969c, p. 31].

Finally, as for the dictum that every interpretation must be a transference interpretation if it is to be effective (p. 347). Brenner presents counterinstances demonstrating that this precept too yields to the requirements of specific transactions. Take, for example, the patient who comes to an analytic session upset because of the sudden death or illness of a close relative. The transferential aspects of his reaction are certainly important. But one is not thereby "justified in following the maxim to the extent of ignoring and failing to interpret to the patient other aspects of his reaction to the situation which are important to recognize and understand" (p. 348).

The prudent correctives are elaborated in Brenner's *Psychoanalytic Technique and Psychic Conflict* (1976). Here Brenner stresses that transference, understood as the valence of the past in the relationships of the present, is hardly unique to the analytic situation. On the contrary, it is ubiquitous in everyday life. It follows, then, that the distinguishing characteristic of the analytic relationship is not transference per se, but rather "its place in the relationship, i.e., the analyst's attitude toward the transference and the use he makes of it. It is the analytic attitude that is the hallmark of analysis, not the phenomenon subsumed under the heading of transference" (p. 112).

Since it is the analytic attitude toward transference manifestations, not a preoccupation with transference analysis, that is constitutive of psychoanalysis, summary pronouncements about the tatter's preeminence in analytic treatment are misleading. Rather, the requirements of specific analyses will determine the role of transference interpretation relative to other types. Consistent with his technical revisions (1969c). Brenner insists that "transference should be neither ignored nor focused on to the exclusion of all else; it should be neither excluded from analytic work nor dragged in by the heels" (1976, p. 128).

This attitude toward transference is central to the argument of the important 1979 paper, "Working Alliance, Therapeutic Alliance, and Transference." Here in the same questioning spirit in which he contested Stone's (1961) characterization of the analytic situation in 1966, Brenner confronts the widely accepted notion, first formulated by Zetzel (1965) and Ralph Greenson (1965). of a therapeutic or working alliance distinct from transference and exempt from interpretation. Examining the data invoked by Zetzel and Greenson in support of the concept's clinical usefulness, he concludes that the evidence does not justify a position of an extratransferential and uninterpretable dimension oi the analytic relationship. He also questions whether the working alliance, however conceived, can be promoted by anything other than accurate and well-timed interpretations. For Brenner, the analyst's humanistic bearing toward the patient is neither constitutes an analytic relationship nor is sufficient to insure a successful analytic outcome. Implicit in the working alliance paper is the belief that the analyst's attitude toward the analysand, no less than that of theanalysand toward the analyst, is a compromise formation. In a more recent publication, "Countertransference and Compromise Formation" (1985). Brenner expands on this formulation. Earlier (1979b). he asserted that all aspects of the analysand's relationship with the analyst, including the desire to cooperate, are interpretable. In 1985 he makes the same point with regard to the analyst, whose countertransferential attitude toward the analysand is invariably a compromise formation and consequently is understandable in terms of the components of conflict, affect states, defenses, self-punitive trends, drive derivatives, and the like.

The working alliance and countertransference papers are in a sense complementary. Jointly they offer a broad perspective on issues of technique. Adopting this perspective, we can no longer make easy correlations of specific affects or clinical syndromes with individual drive derivatives; for example, depression cannot be equated with problems in the oral phase. Similarly, particular therapeutic reactions are not easily associated with individual agencies within the psychic apparatus; negative therapeutic reactions cannot be equated with superego problems. In each case Brenner obliges us to look at both sides of the explanatory coin —at the issues of drive gratification and drive-related prohibitions that codetermine every symptom, behavior, and character trait. Like his theoretical contributions, his contributions to technique achieve their explanatory force through terminological clarification. In the paper on the "working alliance" (1979b). Brenner steers us away from a seductive terminological innovation simply by reminding us of the universality of transference. In the counter-transference paper (1985). he offers new insights into the analyst's relation to the analysand by showing us the "explanatory reach of the concept of compromise formation" first used by Freud in the 1890s.

In his contributions to technique, as in all his work, Brenner is keenly aware of the interdependency of theory and practice. His illuminating commentaries on technical issues often have the serendipitous side effect of clarifying the theoretical status of the concept under review. For example, Brenner's cautionary remarks regarding transference analysis contribute to our understanding of the status of transference within analytic theory. Inn the chapter on defense analysis in *Psychoanalytic Technique and Psychic Conflict* (1976). his technical arguments against the dictum that defenses should invariably be analyzed before the instinctual derivatives they ward off add to our understanding of the concept of defense. In the course of arguing that drive, affect, defense, and the like should be interpreted as they appear in the patient's associations "and not according to some schematic formula" (p. 64). he observes that analysis cannot alleviate defensive operations, but can only alter the structure and adaptive adequacy of compromise formations: "Defenses are never abolished as such, not even the 'pathogenic' or 'infantile' ones" (p. 74). Likewise, his commentary on free association in relation to technique is theoretically enlightening as a critique of the suitability of this term to characterize what actually occurs in analysis:

> Free association is a bad term to apply to the psychoanalytic method. . . . It obscures the fact that an analytic patient is often

asked to associate to a specific conscious stimulus. And second and more important, it obscures the fact that Freud's great discovery, the discovery that became the very cornerstone of psychoanalytic technique, was that associations are never free. They are, on the contrary, always caused by some psychic stimuli or other [p. 190].

Similarly, Brenner's paper on the "working alliance" is not only a storehouse of information on the relative dosages of frustration and gratification that should typify the analytic situation, but a persuasive demonstration of the fact that such issues cannot be dissociated from understanding *of* the theoretical status of transference. Brenner's most recent contribution to technique, soon to be published in *The Psychoanalytic Quarterly,* also enriches theory. This reassessment of working through not only examines the clinical development we customarily associate with this concept but also questions whether the term is clinically useful as a characterization of such development.

The five foregoing synopses hardly constitute a comprehensive presentation of Brenner's contributions to psychoanalysis. At best they provide a helpful overview of certain broad areas to which he has given continuing attention over the course of his analytic career. Although synopses cannot capture the subtlety of Brenner's expositions, their usefulness exceeds the summary of "content" they provide. Taken together, they highlight the interrelationships between Brenner's contributions to the various topics and convey a clear sense of the unity of his psychoanalytic outlook. By this I mean that all of Brenner's contributions to theory and practice are grounded on a consistent and clear-sighted estimation of what psychoanalysis *is* and what it is that psychoanalysts do. His conception of analysis as a science of mental conflict based on data obtained in the analytic situation informs all his contributions to theory. Similarly, his belief in the interpretability of the myriad of symptomatic, behavioral, and characterological compromise formations through which psychic conflict is expressed informs all his contributions to the technique of psychoanalysis.

His specific reappraisals of affect, defense, instinct theory, structural theory, and principles of technique follow from these essential principles of his psychoanalytic *Weltanschauung.*

In recent years Brenner has done much to keep the dialogue among analysts of different theoretical persuasions on track by explicating these topics in terms of the basic principles of the psychoanalytic view of mental life. Whether we consider his questioning of a technical assumption (e.g., the primacy of dream interpretation in analysis). his critique of recent terminological innovations (e.g., therapeutic alliance). or his reaffirmation and amplification of a basic theoretical precept (e.g., the role of compromise formation). it is these superordinate principles that are both the points of departure and the conceptual testing ground for his proposals.

Through his emphasis on the principles that guide theory and practice, Brenner has emerged as one of the outstanding teachers of his generation, a teacher whose pedagogical message transcends the specific content of his books and papers. One may say that Brenner is an analyst whose deep commitment to Freudian principles has sharpened his probing revaluations of the concepts and explanatory perspectives that Freud himself developed. And this is perhaps Brenner's greatest contribution as a theorist and as a teacher—his work demonstrates that an analysis can retain both the vitality and the innovativeness that will take it beyond Freud's legacy only by adhering to the principles of mental functioning fundamental to Freud's science of the mind.

The next work to consider is Brenner's final statement about his work. Richards reviews this book as a continued statement of Brenner's contribution.

Psychoanalysis or Mind and Meaning, by Charles Brenner, is a book not to be reviewed so much as appreciated. Brenner tells us that he has spent two years collecting in one place all the conclusions about the way the mind works that he has arrived at over his more than fifty years as an analyst. He reached these conclusions by proceeding as all scientists proceed, developing hypotheses or theories, collecting data, and then determining whether or not the data support or contradict those hypotheses and theories. And on more than one occasion, he has framed a new conclusion to replace his earlier conclusions or the conclusions of others, including Freud's. For example, he is most convincing when he marshals the data against Freud's conclusion that there is a principle of mental activity that is beyond the pleasure principle.

By way of a historical aside, he tell us that, while he was still a candidate at New York Psychoanalytic Institute, he attended a session in which the question was raised of whether or not psychoanalytic theories had factual evidence to support them. He summarizes the facts that Freud had marshaled in support of the repetition compulsion. Although he does not say so directly, the reader is likely to conclude from Brenner's discussion of the repetition compulsion that, in this instance, he agreed with Freud's method but not with Freud's conclusion.

Brenner acknowledges that Freud also had doubts about the data, that conscious unpleasure can cover over unconscious pleasure, that pain can gratify a masochistic wish or a need for punishment. But Freud, not letting it go at that, postulated a death drive that "offers strong evidence in favor of the view that repetition is more important in mental life than are the attempts to gain pleasure and avoid unpleasure" (p. 16). Brenner notes. He points out that Freud's evidence here is not psychological in nature. Arguments about the tendency of all protoplasm to die have "nothing to do with observations made by using the psychoanalytic method of investigation" (p. 16).

In 1964, Brenner (along with Jacob Arlow) argued—persuasively, for many—against the priority of the economic and topographical metapsychological points of view in Freud's theorizing, and made the case for the structural model in a stronger fashion than even Freud did in 1926.[1] But Brenner has also gone on more recently to modify his own views and move from a model of psychic structure with potentially reifiable structures—id, ego, and superego—to more functional categories and processes. The ego becomes the person, drive becomes wish, and the superego becomes a compromise formation, as I wrote in my introduction to a festschrift for Brenner,[2] anticipating by a decade the direction he was taking:

It is conceivable that Brenner will eventually articulate a model of the mind in conflict in which the interpretations of the elements of conflict is such that the traditional concepts of id, ego and superego become superfluous. What Brenner offers us is an ego which is not a fully integrated agency informed by the primary process but is dynamically indistinguishable from a neurotic symptom: a language of persons and individuals instead of a one of hypothetical mental structure: a view of the child motivated above all by the need to win his or her parents' love. [p. 11]

For me, the most powerful concept that Brenner champions is that of compromise formation. It can be found early in Freud, but was never

---

[1]Arlow, J.A. & Brenner, C. (1964). *Psychoanalytic Concepts and the Structural Theory.* New York: Internatinoal Universities Press.
[2]Richards, A.D. & Willick, M.S., eds. (1986). *Psychoanalysis: The Science of Mental Conflict, Essays in Honor of Charles Brenner.* New York: Analytic Press.

given the pride of place by Freud that Brenner gives it. The concept of compromise is based on facts, the observation of the components of mental conflict—wish, defense, affect, guilt, and adaptations, as well as, in particular symptoms, behaviors, inhibitions, and personality traits—in short, of everything that is part of mental life. The concept of compromise formation is the algebra of how the mind works and the path to the essential task of psychoanalysis in determining meaning.

Chapter 4 of Brenner's book is the best primer on how to conduct an analysis that I have read. In twenty-three pages, he presents an approach to psychoanalytic technique that both the beginning candidate and the seasoned practitioner will find useful. He also makes the important point that psychoanalysis is not defined by position or furniture, lying on a couch or sitting in a chair, or by the number of weekly visits. It is defined by an analytic attitude— the search for meaning, the effort to understand, the conviction that everything a patient says or does is a potentially useful source of information about the patient's conflicts and compromise formations.

Earlier, Brenner wrote: "What words one uses in constructing one's theories [are] ... less important, in most instances, than what meaning the words have in terms of the new data and new generalizations about those data that constitute psychoanalytic theory" (p. 208). [3] This statement reflects his disinclination to supplant the language of Freud's discoveries with trendier terms (*self-object, container, projective identification,* and *intrasubjectivity* come to mind) that offer no real gain in conceptual understanding or explanatory power.

This volume demonstrates that Brenner is not a revolutionary, but a modifier, to use Bergmann's term.[4] He is an extender who innovates by addressing the meaning of traditional psychoanalytic concepts—drive, defense, superego, affect, transference, countertransference, and regression. But this book, perhaps a final statement from Brenner, demonstrates that his contributions culminate in significant reformulations that are part of a process by which Freudian thinking in psychoanalytic discourse accommodates the growth of psychoanalytic knowledge.

Brenner's book can also be read as a challenge to alternative schools to provide a comprehensive and coherent presentation of their funda-

---

[3]Brenner, C. (1980). Metapsychology and psychoanalytic theory. *Psychoanal. Q.*, 49:189–214.
[4]Bergmann, M. S. (1997). The historical roots of psychoanalytic orthodoxy. *Int. J. Psychoanal. Psychother.*, 78:69–86.

mental principles and concepts; thus, he also challenges the notion of psychoanalytic pluralism. Brenner is offering us his total composite theory,[5] whose principles I and many of my colleagues find persuasive; these principles should continue to be studied by the broader psychoanalytic community.

REFERENCES

ARLOW, J.A. & BRENNER, C. (1964). *Psychoanalytic Concepts and the Structural Theory.* New York: International Universities Press.

——— (1966). The psychoanalytic situation. In: *Psychoanalysis in the Americas,* ed. R.E. Litman. New York: International Universities Press, pp. 23–43.

BRENNER, C. (1953). An addendum to Freud's theory of anxiety. *International Journal of Psycho-Analysis* 34:18–24.

——— (1955). *An Elementary Textbook of Psychoanalysis,* 2nd ed. New York: International Universities Press, 1973.

——— (1957). The nature and development of the concept of repression in Freud's writings. *The Psychoanalytic Study of the Child* 12:19–46. New York: International Universities Press.

——— (1959). The masochistic character: Genesis and treatment. *Journal of the American Psychoanalytic Association* 7:197–226.

——— (1967). The mechanisms of repression. In: *Psychoanalysis— A General Psychology: Essays in Honor of Heinz Hartmann,* ed. R.M. Lowenstein, D. Newman, D. Schur, & D. Solnit. New York: International Universities Press, pp. 390–399.

——— (1969a). Discussion of Gardner: Organismic equilibration and the energy-structure. Duality in psychoanalytic theory: An attempt at theoretical refinement. *Journal of the American Psychoanalytic Association* 17:41–53.

——— (1969b). Dreams in clinical psychoanalytic practice. *Journal of Nervous and Mental Disease* 149:122–132.

——— (1969c). Some comments on technical precepts in psychoanalysis. *Journal of the American Psychoanalytic Association* 17:333–352.

——— (1970). Psychoanalysis: Philosophy or science. In: Psychoanalysis and *Philosophy,* ed. C. Hanly & M. Lazerowitz. New York: International Universities Press, pp. 35–45.

——— (1971a). Some problems in the psychoanalytic theory of the instinctual drives. In: *Currents in Psychoanalysis,* ed. M. Marcos. New York: International Universities Press, pp. 216–230.

---

[5]See also: Rangell, L. (2007). The Road to Unity in Psychoanalytic Theory. Lanham, MD: Aronson

———— (1971b). The psychoanalytic concept of aggression. *International Journal of Psycho-Analysis* 52:137–144.

———— (1974a). Depression, anxiety, and affect theory. *International Journal of Psycho-Analysis* 55:25–32.

———— (1974b). On the nature and development of affect: A unified theory. *Psychoanalytic Quarterly* 43:532–556.

———— (1975). Affects and psychic conflict. *Psychoanalytic Quarterly* 44:5–28.

———— (1976). *Psychoanalytic Technique and Psychic Conflict.* New York: International Universities Press.

———— (1979a). Depressive affect, anxiety, and psychic conflict in the phallic-oedipal phase. *Psychoanalytic Quarterly* 48:177–197.

———— (1979b). Working alliance, therapeutic alliance, and transference. *Journal of the American Psychoanalytic Association* 27:137–158.

———— (1980). Metapsychology and psychoanalytic theory. *Psychoanalytic Quarterly* 49:189–214.

———— (1981). Defense and defense mechanisms. *Psychoanalytic Quarterly* 50:557–569.

———— (1982a). *The Mind in Conflict* New York: International Universities Press.

————(1982b). The concept of the superego: A reformulation. *Psychoanalytic Quarterly* 51:501–525.

————(1985). Countertransference as compromise formation. *Psychoanalytic Quarterly* 54:155–163.

———— (in press). On working through. *Psychoanalytic Quarterly*

FREUD, S. (1887–1902). *The Origins of Psycho-Analysis. Letters* to *Wilhelm Fliess, Drafts and Notes: 1887–1902,* ed. M. Bonaparte, A. Freud, & E. Kris. New York: Basic Books, 1954.

———— (1900). The interpretation of dreams. *Standard Edition,* 4 & 5.

———— (1915e). The unconscious. *Standard Edition,* 14:161–215.

———— (1917). A metapsychological supplement to the theory of dreams. *Standard Edition,* 14:222–235.

———— (1926). Inhibitions, symptoms and anxiety, *Standard Edition,* 29:87–172. London: Hogarth Press, 1959.

GREENSON, R.R. (1965). The working alliance and the transference neurosis. *Psychoanal. Quart,* 34:155–181.

HARTMANN, H. (1939). *Ego Psychology and the Problem of Adaptation.* New York: International Universities Press, 1958.

KLEIN, G.S. (1976). *Psychoanalytic Theory: An Exploration of Essentials.* New York: International Universities Press.

KOHUT, H. (1959). Introspection, empathy, and psychoanalysis. *Journal of the American Psychoanalytic Association* 7:459–483.

ORNSTEIN, P. (1978). *The Search for the Self, Selected Writings of Heinz*

Kohut, 1959–1978, Vol. 1. New York: International Universities Press.
RAPAPORT, D., & GILL, M.M. (1959). The point of view and assumptions of metapsychology. *International Journal of Psycho-Analysis* 40:153–162.
SCHAFER, R. (1976). *A New* Language *for Psychoanalysis.* New Haven: Yale University Press.
STONE, L. (1961). *The Psychoanalytic Situation: An Examination of its Development and Essential Nature.* New York: International Universities Press.
WAELDER, R. (1962). Psychoanalysis, scientific method and philosophy J. *Amer. Psychoanal. Assn.,* 10:617–637.
ZETZEL, E.R. (1965). The theory of therapy in relation to a developmental model of the psychic apparatus. *International Journal of Psycho-Analysis* 46:39–52.

CHAPTER 15

Psychoanalytic Theory

[Arlow, J.A. & Richards, A.D. (1991). in Encyclopedia of Human Biology, vol. 6:Pi–Se. R. Dulbecco, Ed, San Diego, CA: Academic Press.]

PSYCHOANALYSIS has a threefold character. It is a method for studying the function of the human mind, a means of treating certain psychological disorders, and a body of knowledge derived from psychoanalytic investigation. Mental activity reflects the function of the brain. It constitutes the result of the dynamic interaction of conflicting psychological forces operating within and beyond the scope of consciousness. The nature of an individual's intrapsychic conflicts and the various compromise formations instituted in an attempt to resolve conflicts are deeply influenced by the vicissitudes of individual development.

I. PSYCHOANALYSIS AS A BIOLOGICAL SCIENCE

Psychoanalysis takes its place among the biological sciences as a naturalistic discipline deriving conclusions from observations within a standard setting. Psychoanalysis views the functioning of the mind as a direct expression of the activity of the brain. This activity reflects the experience of the total organism and operates according to certain inherent biological principles. A primary principle is the tendency of the human organism to seek pleasure and to avoid pain or unpleasure. Clearly, this principle must have had survival value in the course of evolution since painful sensations are likely to be noxious in nature (i.e., threatening the integrity of the organism) while pleasurable sensations are usually associated with gratification of biological needs, with security, and safety.

This last point is especially pertinent because of the helpless, immature state of the human infant at birth. The newborn child is totally incapable of fending for itself. Without the nurturing and protective care of adults, it would soon perish. Furthermore, this state of dependency continues for a long time, longer than in the case of other mammals. The consequences of this fact for the development of the human psyche are profound. It underlies the importance of the "others" upon whom the individual depends. Perforce, man is destined to become a social animal, keenly aware of the distinction between himself and others, as well as his relations to others. Recent studies of infant development have demonstrated certain features of preadaptation to socialization in the form of inherent patterns of behavior, patterns that serve to stimulate pleasurable reactions in the mother and dispose the infant in turn to respond to the mother's expressions. Human communication begins in the context of the *pleasure-unpleasure principle.*

At the beginning of life, it would appear that the quest for complete and instantaneous gratification is the paramount principle of mental activity. The exigencies of human existence, however, are such that attaining endless, unalloyed pleasure is impossible. Pleasurable sensations disappear as new needs arise. Tensions rise when needs are not immediately met and new experiences do not correspond fully with memories of lost pleasures. Thus, in pursuit of pleasure, gratification of needs must be postponed and some activity relating to the external world must be instituted. Help must be enlisted and substitute gratifications accepted.

The capacity for pleasure is biologically rooted. It is related to the physiology of the body and ordinarily seems to follow a consistent course of maturation and development. During the earliest months of life, the pleasurable sensations connected with feeding seem to be the most important ones. These include not only the alleviation of hunger but also the concomitant sensations associated with the experience-bodily contact, warmth, the mother's gaze, the sound of her voice. The central need of the child is to be nourished and the mother is the object that satisfies the need. Wishes emanating from this phase are called the *oral phase* and remain active throughout life in one form or another, even though augmented and modified by subsequent wishes and events. During the second year of life, other interests come to the fore. The child becomes aware of himself as an independent entity. He begins to assert his independence from his mother and he begins to appreciate developing capacities and a sense of mastery. The biological sources of pleasure now center about digestive and excretory functions, the mastery of one's body and its content. The child tests his ability to manipulate his body contents in fact and in fantasy and observes how these activities influence others. This period, roughly covering the age span from two to four, is referred to as the *anal phase.*

Perhaps the most crucial period for psychological development begins about the age of three to three-and-a-half and culminates between the ages of five-and-a-half to six. During this period the child is intensely preoccupied with the activity of his genitals and their potential for pleasure. He begins to contemplate such fundamental issues as the differences between the sexes, the mysteries of conception and birth, the powers and privileges of the adult, and the puzzle of death. Sexual urges become very strong and become manifest in speech and play or covertly in fantasies and dreams. Since, in both sexes, the possession of a phallus becomes a central issue and because of the fact that, at the same time, sexual wishes are often directed towards the parents, this phase has been called the *phallic-oedipal period*. Sexual wishes appear in the content of fantasies accompanying masturbation, a practice common during this phase.

From the study of sexual perversions, observations of children, the psychology of dreams, and the structure of neurotic symptoms, as well as many aspects of normal sexual experience, Freud concluded that these biologically based pleasure-seeking activities of childhood represented constituent elements of the sexual impulse, which attains its final genitally dominated character only towards the end of adolescence.

II. FUNDAMENTALS OF PSYCHOANALYTIC PSYCHOLOGY

Several other principles are fundamental to psychoanalytic theory. Foremost among these is the concept of *determinism*. Mental life is not random or chaotic. Psychological experiences demonstrate the persistent effects of significant antecedent events in the life of the individual. What happens in mental life is part of an ongoing historical process that gives form and meaning to what the individual thinks and feels. Both nature and nurture contribute to developmental sequences of mental functioning, resulting in a patterning of experience that is clearly motivated and in which events are causally related.

Psychoanalysis, furthermore, is a *dynamic* psychology. It conceptualizes mental functioning in terms of an apparatus that performs work, an apparatus that is propelled into motion, driven to action by inner urges consciously experienced as wishes. Some of these urges, as indicated above, are clearly biological in nature. They stem from the physiological functioning of the organs of the body. This is clearly true in the case of the sexual drives. Other dynamic forces in the mind are less clearly linked to specific physical zones or bodily functions, but they are equally important. Foremost among these are the propelling drives toward aggression, hatred, and destructiveness. Unlike the sexual drive, evidence suggesting the operation of a persistent urge towards aggression has no clear base in biology. The evidence for this concept is psychological in nature. Psychoanalysts differ as to whether other motivational forces, such as safety, security, self-esteem, integrity, and mastery should be considered primary drives or should be subsumed in some way under the broader categories of the *sexual and aggressive drives.*

A note on the history of terminology must be inserted here. Freud used the German world "trieb" to indicate the dynamic, driving forces acting upon the mind. Unfortunately, the term was mistranslated into English as "instinct" and it is in this form that the term for the concept has persisted in the literature, sometimes expressed as instinctual drive. The term "drive" conveys the precise meaning of the concept.

The drive concept, of course, is an abstraction. In practice, what one observes are mental representations of the drives. They take the form of specific, concrete wishes and are designated drive derivatives. As the individual develops and matures, the manifest forms of the *drive derivatives* undergo change and transformation. This occurs in keeping with the pleasure principle, with the tendency to avoid or mitigate the potential experiencing of unpleasant or painful affects.

Certain specific fears play a leading role in the transformation of the drive derivatives. The first is the danger that the organismic distress the infant experiences in situations of unfulfilled needs might assume devastating proportions. At a later stage of cognitive functioning, with a beginning appreciation of the perception that the mother's face signals impending relief, the failure of the mother to reappear melds into a fear of separation from her. This combination of events becomes a danger situation, fraught with the possible evolution of intense unpleasure or pain. At a still more advanced level of interaction with the mother and a fuller appreciation of her as an independent object, the child comes to face another set of potential dangers. He feels threatened by situations that may lead to the loss of the mother's love. Somewhat later, the child perceives another set of threatening situations, the all pervasive fear of punishment, specifically by means of physical mutilation of the genitals. Subsequently, as the individual conscience begins to develop, a new source of danger comes into being, namely, the painful affects connected with self-condemnation, the sense of guilt, and the need for punishment. The latter constitute an example of self-directed aggression. It is important to note at this juncture that the drives, sexual and aggressive, operate towards the self and one's own body just as they do towards other objects. An individual may feel love and hate for himself even at the same time, very much as he may experience these feelings towards others. The urge to punish one's self evokes unpleasant affects, which the individual perceives as a signal of impending unpleasure or pain.

These considerations lead us to another fundamental principle of psychoanalysis. Psychoanalysis is a psychology of *conflict*, a psychology of dynamic forces in opposition to each other. Intrapsychic conflict is ubiquitous and never-ending. The forces in conflict are multiple and diverse. They bespeak the contradiction among wishes and fears, threats and warnings, hopes and anticipations for the future, regrets of the past. Freud formulated his final theory of the structure of the psychic apparatus according to the role that each mental element played in intrapsychic conflict. Thus, the persistent wishes of the past, operating as continuous stimuli to the mind and giving rise to innumerable, repetitive, relatively predictable patterns of mental representations, collectively constitute a structure of the mind, a system of the psychic apparatus designated as the *id*. The term *id* derives from the Latin word for *it*, and the choice of the term reflects how alien and unacceptable some of its derivative manifestations are when presented to consciousness. The id is the vast reservoir of motivational dynamic. It consists of sexual and aggressive wishes, primitive in nature, self-centered and often antisocial.

Another source of motivational dynamic consists of the ideal aspirations, the moral and behavioral imperatives, the judgment of right and wrong. This group of relatively stable functions of the mind Freud called the *superego,* in recognition of the fact, as he thought, that it developed later in the life of the mind, but also from its function as an observer and critic, seeming to stand above and beyond the self, passing judgment on it. Frequently, but by no means always, impulses emanating from the superego oppose the demands of the id. Moral considerations are repetitive and relatively predictable but, like the id, the superego is full of internal contradictions.

The third structural component of the psychic apparatus is made up of those functions that serve to integrate and to mediate the complementary or contradictory aims of the other agencies of the mind. At the same time it takes into account the nature of the objective, realistic situation in which the individual finds himself. Freud called this set of functions the *ego*. It comprises activities that identify it as the executant for all the agencies of the mind. It is the mediator between the internal and the external world, between the world of thoughts and feelings on one hand, and the world of perception and objects on the other.

The concept of psychic structure should not be taken too rigidly. The essential criterion that applies to any mental representation is the role it plays in intrapsychic conflict. Id, ego, and superego constitute only abstract conceptualizations of the patterning of the forces in conflict within the mind. In the clinical setting, situations of intense conflict delineate most clearly the boundaries of the constituent structures of the psychic apparatus. Under more harmonious psychological circumstances, the contributions of the component systems tend to fuse. It is the function of the ego to integrate and to resolve intrapsychic conflicts in order to avoid the danger of unpleasant affects, particularly depressive affect and anxiety. The end products of the ego's efforts, so to speak, represent compromise formations, which is to say that all the various participants in the internal conflict find at least some representation of their dynamism in the final mental product. The compromise formations effected by the ego may be successful ones in the sense that they ward off or circumvent the appearance of pain or unpleasure or they may fail in the sense that the final product of the process is fraught with a greater or lesser component of pain or brings the individual into conflict with the environment and actual danger to his person. Various affects, anxiety in particular, serve as signals, warning that a danger situation of one of the several types mentioned earlier may be developing. The potential danger may be actual or imagined, real or fantasy. The functioning of the mind is an endless exercise in adaptation, reconciliation, and integration. Needless to say, this effort is not always successful.

The ego has at its disposal many different methods for dealing with danger situations. For example, certain mental processes signaling danger, from whatever source, may be rendered nonexistent, which is to say they are promptly forgotten and cannot be recalled to mind. They no longer are available to consciousness. The individual is not aware of them and, as far as he is concerned, they never happened. Such mental processes are said to have been *repressed*. In a definitive act of repression, the repressed element leaves no traces, which is to say it ceases to function as a driving force stimulating the psychic apparatus into action.

Psychically it has become nonexistent. It is only when the process of repression is incomplete, when the element excluded from consciousness continues to exert some dynamic impetus, as evidenced by the appearance of derivative representations, that one may infer the presence of a repressed element, of an unconscious mental process. Unconscious mental processes are not apprehended directly. They are inferred from an examination of the data of observation, utilizing criteria of interpretation applicable to any form of communication.

The ubiquitous influence of unconscious processes on conscious mental functioning is a major principle of psychoanalytic theory. The role of unconscious processes in mental functioning follows inexorably from the dynamic principle in psychoanalysis, from the theory of forces activating the mental apparatus. Deriving from the metaphorical use of surface for conscious and depth for unconscious, psychoanalysis has come to be considered a depth psychology." While the concept of surfaces or layering is hardly appropriate, it has nonetheless served as the basis for a term applied to this aspect of psychoanalytic theory, namely, the *topographic principle,* the relationship between conscious and unconscious mental processes.

One of the empirical findings of psychoanalysis is the persistent and powerful influence of early child-hood experience. Although the events and wishes of the years before the age of six seem to fade from memory and very little of them can be recalled in later years, these events nonetheless affect psychological development and personality structure in the most profound ways. For ages, educators have appreciated this principle intuitively. Freud reached the conclusion empirically. Ethologists have confirmed the principle experimentally.

The human mind develops as the interplay between the maturation of inherent, biologically determined capacities and the vicissitudes of experience. In the transformation of the newborn infant into a mature human being, every stage of development presents the individual with a specific set of problems, with fresh goals to be achieved. How problems are solved at one stage will influence the ability of the individual to negotiate the next set of developmental challenges. The specific needs, achievements, and conflicts of one phase are superseded but not displaced or eliminated in the next phase. As a rule, but not always, the successful resolution of developmental challenges of earlier phases seems to facilitate successful resolution of later developmental challenges. On the other hand, accidents of fate, such as severe illness, inborn physical or psychological deficits, cruel treatment, negligent care, or abandonment may all have adverse effects upon individual development, causing pathological development immediately or rendering the individual incapable of mastering subsequent developmental challenges. Such events or influences constitute psychological trauma when they overwhelm the ego's capacity to master the terrifying and painful dangers that may occur at all periods of life. This is the beginning of the process of pathogenesis, which may lead to inhibitions, symptoms, perversions, and character deformations. Emphasis on the importance of childhood events for normal and pathological development constitutes the *genetic principle* in psychoanalysis. It is an empirical finding, not a derivative hypothesis.

Before considering the form that the persistent wishes of childhood take, it is necessary to appreciate the nature of children's thinking. The child's wishes are urgent, imperious, and uncompromising. His interests are self-centered. The distinction between objective perception and inner wishful thinking is not firmly established. Fantasies of the magical power of thought, of omnipotence and destructiveness are taken very seriously. The child's grasp of reality and causality take a long time to develop. In many ways, infantile notions of magic persist in the minds of many adults. Evidence for this fact is readily available in the prevalence of superstitious beliefs, etc.

It is against this background that the child tries to formulate answers to fundamental existential problems. He must confront the inevitability of frustrations of his needs and wants, the limitations of his control over his own body, and the discrepancy between himself and adults. Issues of procreation, life and death, sex and violence, the different roles of men and women-the challenges are universal, true for children all over the world, no matter the cultural level of the environment in which they are being raised. Each child attempts to answer these questions with the limited intellectual resources at his command. The assistance that he gets from grownups is not always cognitively useful or affectively satisfying.

The child creates his own fantasy solutions to these problems and these fantasies serve as vehicles for the powerful driving wishes, fears, and self-punitive notions typical for that period of development. Originally, it may be presumed, such fantasies are exclusively or primarily imagined representations of wishes fulfilled but, as the child becomes aware of the dangers connected with the emergence or the expression of such wishes, even their fantasy expressions are modified by the process of compromise formation. Because the more primitive expressions of these wishes prove to be dangerous, they are repressed and forgotten. As an adult, the individual is not at all aware that he ever harbored such notions. Such repressions, however, are rarely definitive. Although the wishes remain unconscious, they continue to exert a dynamic role, making their effects discernible in derivative forms. Some of these derivative forms emerge as fantasies, watered-down versions, symbolically altered, less threatening representations of the original wishes. Derivative, acted-out forms of the same wishes may take the shape of habits, character traits, special interests, choice of profession, and a wide range of psychopathological formations. In summary, the unacceptable wishes of childhood take the form of persistent unconscious fantasies, exerting a continuous stimulus to the mind, eventuating in compromise formations. Some of these compromise formations are adaptive and are considered normal. Others are maladaptive-"abnormal."

Just how early in life the ability to create fantasy emerges is difficult to say. The process is certainly facilitated by the acquisition of language, but the ability to fantasize seems to antedate the appearance of language to some degree. This occurs probably in the second year of life. The complex fantasy life that certain observers believe to characterize the psychological activity of infants even as far back as the first six months of life does not seem to be a tenable proposition. Fantasy thinking is metaphoric in nature and makes extensive use of symbolism. This is an inevitable outcome of the fact that human thought is inherently metaphoric. Fundamentally, perceptual experience is processed according to the criteria of pleasant or unpleasant, familiar or unfamiliar. Memories of perceptual experiences are stored, organized, and patterned in keeping when these principles. The facile transfer of meaning from one mental element to another on the basis of similarity or difference, of association in memory or experience leads quite directly to metaphoric thinking and symbolism.

While the nature of the unconscious fantasies remains constant, their derivative manifestations evolve and are transformed in the course of time. They change with the advancing cognitive capabilities, with the appreciation of the real environment, and with the consolidation of moral values. The fundamental plot of the fantasies, however, remains the same. The characters and the settings change and "grow up" with time. There is good evidence to suppose that unconscious fantasying goes on all the time we are awake and a good deal of the time we are asleep. Every individual harbors a set of unconscious fantasies typical for him. They represent the special way in which that individual integrated the major experiences and relationships, the important traumata and drive conflicts of his childhood years. The persistent unconscious fantasies serve as a mental set against which the sensory data are perceived, interpreted, and responded to. Furthermore, specific perceptions of events in the external world may resonate with elements in the individual's unconscious fantasy system and may evoke conscious representations of unconscious fantasy wishes. The derivatives consist of compromise formations that may be adaptive or maladaptive. The emergence of maladaptive compromise formations of unconscious fantasy wishes marks the beginning of the process of pathogenesis.

III. PSYCHOANALYTIC METHODOLOGY AND THERAPY

The fundamental operational principles of psychoanalysis-determinism, dynamic conflict, and the role of unconscious mental elements-all enter into the organization of the standard mode of psychoanalytic investigation. This is known as the psychoanalytic situation. The patient reclines on the couch, looking away from the analyst. He is asked, as far as possible, to report with complete candor whatever thoughts or feelings present themselves to consciousness. In effect, he is asked to function as a nonjudgmental reporter of his own mental functioning. No consideration justifies the exclusion of any element that occurs to the analysand's mind. This technique of reporting is called *free association*. Its aim is to obtain a dynamic record of the analysand's mode of mental functioning, reflecting an endogenously determined flow of the individual's thought. External influences are reduced to a minimum. When external influences do intrude upon the analysand's awareness, they are examined from the point of view of the dynamic, evocative power they exert upon the stream of the analysand's associations, on his mode of mental functioning. During the analytic session, external intrusions may take many forms. The siren of a passing fire engine, the perception of a change in the decor or furniture arrangement in the analyst's office, the odor of flowers in the room, and, most important of all, whatever the analyst does or says. In any event, the approach to each of these perceptual experiences remains the same. What the analyst studies is the dynamic, evocative effect of the perceptual experience upon the nature of the analysand's thoughts.

The analyst has a dual role in this procedure. He is an observer of how the patient's mind works. At the same time, however, through the things that he says and does, he becomes a participant in the process. Functioning as a participant observer, the analyst pays special attention to the effects his interventions produce in the stream of the analysand's associations. It is for this reason that the analyst must pursue rigorously a stance of nonjudgmental neutrality regarding the analysand's realistic decisions, moral dilemmas, or partisan conflicts. The fundamental concern of the analyst is to observe and to understand how the patient's mind works. The analyst's opinions and prejudices are irrelevant to this work and, in fact, introducing them may be counterproductive. Such efforts would be suggestive and educational in nature, subtly directing the analysand away from trends in his own thinking that he would consider to be counter to the analyst's point of view or interests. The technical aim of the analyst is to supply understanding and insight, not to furnish a set of directives or to act as a model for the analysand to emulate. This conjoint investigation of the workings of a person's mind has no parallel in any other form of human communication.

From the point of view of theory, the results of this inquiry may be examined from several hierarchically related levels of abstraction. From the fundamental, experiential level of *clinical observation,* the analyst gets to know things not available to other observers. More than that, he becomes aware of the form and content in which thoughts appear, the patterning and configurations they assume, the repetition of certain themes, the irrelevant or unexpected intrusions of ideas and actions, the struggle of the patient to hide some elements or to minimize or repudiate their significance.

The next level is that of *clinical interpretation.* As in any form of communication or dialogue, more meaning is conveyed than is contained in the explicit verbal or motor expressions alone. The context in which ideas occur, the relationship to contiguous elements, the position of the idea in a sequential series of thoughts, the similarity to antecedent mental presentations or their persistence and repetition-all of these, augmented, to be sure, by the nature of the quality of the analysand's speech, the affective mood that is projected, and the motor concomitants of communication, enable the analyst to make connections that are not immediately apparent in the manifest text of the analysand's productions. In this respect, he is aided by the analysand's use of figurative speech, especially metaphor and symbol. Their use enhances and extends the communicative significance of the analysand's productions. At this level of the analytic work, what the analyst does is to make connections among the analysand's thoughts, connections that the analysand has been unable or unwilling to acknowledge on his own. From the stream of the analysand's associations, the analyst infers meanings and motives unknown to the analysand, which he communicates to him.

How is it possible for the analyst to learn something about another person's thinking, something of which the latter is himself not at all aware? In the genesis of interpretation, a number of important processes take place in the mind of the analyst. First is the experience of *empathy.* The analyst identifies with the patient, that is, he puts himself in the patient's position psychologically but is aware at the same time that the moods and thoughts that occur to him represent his reflections and reactions to what the patient has been telling him. The second process is *intuition,* according to which the analyst organizes the patient's productions and integrates them with what he has learned about the analysand previously, but it is a process that takes place outside the scope of the analyst's awareness. The end result of this integrative working over of the patient's productions into a meaningful hypothesis presents itself to consciousness through the process of *introspection.* The thought thus formed may be incomplete, incorrect, or usually only a step in the direction of the proper apprehension of the meaning of the analysand's associations. A more accurate interpretation comes about when the results of this intrapsychic communication to the analyst are consciously and cognitively examined in the light of the criteria already mentioned. Meaning derives from context, contiguity, sequence, similarity, figurative language, especially metaphor and symbolism, and other elements which, in general, hold sway in communication.

An interpretation is actually an hypothesis offered to the analysand. Interpretations vary in the amount of data they attempt to comprehend. There are interpretations concerning minute sequences of mental processes, ranging to comprehensive formulations concerning the meaning, origin, and purpose of lifelong patterns of behavior, thought, and feeling. Like any hypothesis, an interpretation must be consistent with the data of observation and it must be coherent. Furthermore, a psychoanalytic interpretation is not proffered in the course of analytic investigation merely as a summary of the relationship among observable data. The dynamic impact of a particular intervention called interpretation is what is important. An immediate acceptance or rejection of the interpretation by the analysand can be totally misleading and is actually beside the point. The effect of the intervention on the subject's flow of thought, the new material that it brings to light these are of paramount significance. In effect, each interpretation the analyst makes constitutes a sort of experimental intervention. From the experience of clinical observation and interpretation, certain *clinical generalizations* become possible. Such generalizations may apply to the meaning of repetitive, diverse, but related patterns of mental activity or syndromes articulating similar compromise formations. They may be observed repetitively in the individual; they may be recapitulated from patient to patient. In a compulsion neurosis, for example, the compulsive symptom generally protects the individual against unpleasant affects resulting from conflicts over murderous impulses. For the fetishist, the presence of the fetish is an essential condition for making sexual pleasure possible by presenting the individual with an actualization of an unconscious fantasy of a female phallus, a concept necessary in the case of the fetishist, to deny the possibility of genital mutilation.

From clinical interpretations and clinical generalizations, it becomes possible to formulate certain theoretical concepts that flow logically from the interpretations and to which the interpretations may lead. Most of the basic, operational, theoretical concepts of psychoanalysis belong to this category. Among these, for example, are the concepts of repression, defense, unconscious fantasy, compromise formation, etc. This is the level of clinical theory.

Finally, there are those abstract theoretical concepts not directly derived from clinical observational experience. Accordingly, this level of abstraction is referred to as *metapsychology,* i.e., beyond psychology. Metapsychology concerns such issues as the compulsion to repeat, the nature and origin of mental energy, the relationship of quantitative changes in drive energy to the experience of pleasure and pain, or whether repression takes place because a mental element is divested of its drive energy or is opposed by countervailing drive force supplied by the ego. Most of these concepts Freud borrowed from physics and biology. Waelder, who delineated the levels of psychoanalytic propositions just mentioned, said that these levels are not of equal importance for psychoanalysis. The data of observation and clinical interpretation are entirely indispensable, not only for the practice of psychoanalysis but for an appreciation of the empirical basis upon which psychoanalytic propositions are founded. Clinical generalizations and clinical theory are necessary too, though perhaps not to the same degree. Studying the record of free associations in context, a person may be able to understand a situation, a symptom, or a dream with little knowledge of clinical theory. Metapsychological abstractions, however, bear little relevance to the interpretations of the observational data and to the generalizations drawn from them. In actual therapeutic experience, metapsychological theories play hardly any role in the formulation of psychoanalytic conclusions.

IV. PSYCHIC STRUCTURE

Psychoanalytic theory is not static nor unchanging. It has been the subject of continuing revision, sometimes radical in nature, in keeping with new insights and fresh discoveries. The current division of mental organization according to the specific function that each psychological element plays in intrapsychic conflict has been designated the *structural hypothesis*. Persistent patterns of functioning, repetitive in nature, more or less predictable in 'function, are grouped together as a component structure of the mind. This theory replaces an earlier concept of mental organization that Freud enunciated, the topographic theory. According to that theory, accessibility to consciousness was the paramount criterion of mental organization. Repressed elements collectively constituted the system *unconscious,* usually designated *ucs,* and the elements it contained shared certain characteristic modes of functioning. They were primarily instinctual wishes, driving impulsively towards gratification. The wishes were basically primitive in nature and operated in complete disregard for logic or the fixed categories of mental concepts, functioning indifferently to realistic considerations. Freud abandoned this theory when his observational data indicated that forces opposed to the drives, fixed mental concepts, defensive activities, and adaptive mechanisms also operated outside of the individual's awareness. The system ucs contained more than representations of repressed ·drives. According to structural theory, portions of the ego, the id, and the superego, that is to say, parts of all of the psychic structures, function outside of consciousness and exert a significant influence on conscious mental activity.

The delimitations of the structural components of the psyche are not as sharp as one might think. In a manner reminiscent of behavior in political organizations, there are shifting alliances among the component psychic systems and there are even contradictions within the component parts of each system. Severe intrapsychic conflict lays bare most clearly the outlines of the different psychic agencies. Typically, in the hysterias, the ego must deal with a sharp conflict between the wishes of the id for forbidden gratifications and the countervailing condemnation of the superego. In severe depressions, the id and superego impulses join forces in a murderous assault upon the self. In certain forms of psychopathy, an alliance is made between the id and the ego. In asceticism, superego and ego combine against the pleasure-seeking impulses of the id. To be sure, these formulations represent extreme simplifications but they serve to illustrate the clinical conceptualization of intrapsychic conflict within the structural theory.

Pursuing its function of attempting to reconcile the conflicting demands made upon it, the ego has available to it a wide range of mental mechanisms. The mechanism of repression has already been mentioned, but there are many others in addition. A drive impulse may be diverted from its primary object onto other objects, objects less important and less threatening. Or the impulse may be transformed into or displaced by a different impulse, even an opposite one, e.g., hatred into love, or vice versa. The existence of the disturbing impulse may be acknowledged, but it may be mistakenly perceived as being present in someone else. These mechanisms rarely function in isolation in regard to a particular conflict. Because they were first described as modes of ego functioning, serving the common purpose of fending off an impending danger, these operations were referred to as mechanisms of defense. Closer examination, however, reveals that the ego makes use of such operations for many purposes other than defense. Fundamentally, these are mechanisms of the mind, serving the process of adaptation in the broadest sense of the word.

The unconscious defensive displacement of fantasy wishes from the original or primary object onto others is a constant feature of psychological life. Unconsciously, the individual may transfer these persistent wishes onto other objects who in some way become associated with the original object of the individual's drives. It is as if the individual foists a preconceived scenario onto people and events, a process that endows a unifying pattern upon the course of the individual's life. This process of transferring fantasy wishes onto other persons, called *transference,* plays an important role in psychoanalytic treatment. In contrast to other people in the course of everyday life, the analyst does not respond to the transferred wishes the patient directs towards him. Accordingly, derivatives of the patient's fantasy life and experiences of the past emerge with special clarity in the course of the analytic relationship.

Analyzing the transference enables the analyst to demonstrate to the patient how the unconscious wishes of childhood have persisted in the patient's life, causing him to confuse fantasy with reality, past and present. Analysis of the transference is a particularly effective instrument to demonstrate to the analysand how the past is embedded in the present.

In addition to the formative role played by gratification and/or frustration of the drives, there are other aspects of the interrelationship with the "others" that play a crucial role in developing psychic structure. The term used for the interaction with other individuals is *object relations*. The term distinguishes between self and object, but it probably owes its origin to earlier concepts in the history of psychoanalysis. Freud used the term originally to apply to the mental representation that was the object of an instinctual drive. Strictly speaking, the term ''object'' could refer to the self, to a portion of one's body or to representations of other individuals. In actual practice, it has come to apply almost exclusively to other persons. The term *narcissism* applies when the self is taken as the object of the erotic drive.

From his interaction with objects in his immediate world, the individual acquires a wide catalog of methods for coping with difficult situations, preferred solutions to conflicts, skills to master, ideals to aspire to, etc. Basically, these acquisitions result from an identification that the individual effects with certain objects. The individual remodels himself after the object and takes over some aspect of the personality of the other. Identification, however, is never complete; one person is never a psychological clone of another. Nor is it possible to predict in advance with which aspect of an object an individual will identify. Affective considerations play an important role in this process. Nor is it essential for one to have direct experience with an object in order to identify with him. Fantasy objects, individuals from literature, history, or religious teaching may become models from whom the individual acquires modes of thinking and acting. While the personality of the individual is shaped greatly by the identifications effected with primary objects during childhood, it is a fact that identification is possible later in life, especially during adolescence. In many instances, such late identifications help to give the final stamp of character upon the personality.

Identifications the individual makes in childhood tend to be primitive, highly idealized, and invested with grandiose illusions. Furthermore they are self-centered, that is to say, narcissistic. Part of the process of attaining maturity consists of replacing the exaggerated, grandiose, ideal aspirations of childhood with more realistic, obtainable goals, as well as developing a more objective evaluation of the primary object and of one's objects and of one's self. Some residues of early ideal formation persist in everyone and they serve as a standard against which the individual measures his self-worth. The feeling of self-esteem depends, to a large extent, upon how he judges himself in terms of the distance between his actual situation and the ideals and standards he has set for himself. According to the conclusions reached, he will either like or dislike himself. Some individuals, however, continue to harbor the grandiose ego ideals of childhood. They are impelled towards impossible goals and exaggerated expectations, all of which are doomed to failure and disillusionment. Such issues become central in the psychology of narcissistic persons. They require endless supplies of narcissistic gratification in order to feel worthwhile. When successful in the pursuit of their goals, they are elated; when unsuccessful, they become depressed and even suicidal.

V. COMPROMISE FORMATION

The turbulent conflicts of childhood come to a head during the phallic-oedipal phase. Powerful though his wishes are, the child ultimately recognizes that they can never be fulfilled. He dare not risk the loss of his parents nor can he master the fear of retaliation. In a sense, his own wishes come to represent a source of great danger to him. Either he renounces his wishes or masters them by modifying them. Injury to the genitals, the so-called castration anxiety, is the danger typical for this period. How the child resolves the conflicts of this period has fateful consequences for the development of his personality and the course of his life. The manner in which such conflicts are resolved varies from individual to individual. The inherent drive endowment of the individual, the nature of the relationships with his parents and other significant figures, the specific events in his life and other experiential and maturational factors all play a role in shaping the final outcome of the conflicts of the oedipal phase. Certain forms of the wishes may be renounced entirely; others may be repressed but only incompletely. Taking the form of persistent unconscious fantasies, such wishes may exert a continuing influence upon mental functioning for the rest of the individual's life.

The turmoil of the oedipal phase is followed by a period of relative quiescence. This is known as the latency period and it lasts until the onset of adolescence. The intensity of conflicts abates and the individual becomes socialized and educable. But, while the conflicts have become relatively quiescent, they are hardly extinct. The turmoil of adolescence represents a secondary, more sophisticated attempt to resolve the conflicts of the oedipal phase at a higher level. A certain degree of restructuralization of the psychic apparatus occurs, out of which emerge the individual's sexual identity, his social and professional roles, and his inner moral commitments. Whether the secondary recapitulation of the conflicts of the oedipal phase during adolescence is primarily the result of biological or sociological factors is impossible to ascertain.

How the individual resolves the inevitable conflicts of life decides the issues of normality or pathology, of health or illness. Largely, this is a question of degree, since it is impossible for all compromise formations instituted by the ego to be equally effective under all circumstances. Some individuals, for example, seem never to have been able to master their childhood fears. They continue to suffer from irrational inhibitions, fears, and compulsions throughout latency and adolescence and into adult life. In other cases, pathology originates when some event in life upsets the balance of compromises that the ego has managed to maintain. This situation activates a latent conflict from childhood, and the individual responds to fantasied dangers articulating the effects of persistent unconscious childhood wishes. The reactivation of such latent unconscious conflicts is called *regression*. The responses to the inherent dangers are automatic, that is to say, outside of the individual's control. In addition, they are maladaptive and may be painful. The goal of psychoanalytic therapy is to give the patient insight into the nature of his fears and to demonstrate to him the automatic, inappropriate, largely unconscious measures he has undertaken to cope with his irrational anxieties. As the patient comes to recognize how the past is operative in his functioning in the here and now, he becomes able to organize more effective, less conflictual compromise formations to manage the effects of his persistent conflicts.

VI. SOCIAL APPLICATIONS

By applying some of the principles derived from the knowledge of the psychology of individuals, psychoanalysis has been able to afford some measure of insight into social and group phenomena. Certain group phenomena appear to replicate *en masse* some of the themes and psychological mechanisms observable in individuals. Themes and modes of expression common to myths, fairy tales, literary works, and religious traditions and rituals often repeat, sometimes in minute detail, the derivative expressions of unconscious conflicts observed in individuals. They prove appealing to the individual because, like fantasies and dreams, they represent disguised representations of repressed wishes. In large measure, the fantasy life of each individual represents a secret rebellion against the need to grow up and to renounce the gratification of his drives. In a very specific sense, it constitutes rebellion against society and certain of the strictures that civilization imposes upon the individual. In the process of mythopoesis and literary creation, the poet and the mythmaker transform their private daydreams into creations compatible with the ideals of the community, capable of giving pleasure and conveying at the same time disguised, transformed expressions of forbidden wishes that other members of the community share in common with them.

In the myth or the work of art, an individual may find in the external world a projected representation of his own unformed and unexpressed wishes. By identifying with the principal characters in a work of fiction or with the hero of the historical or religious myth, the individual attains some measure of gratification of his repressed, unconscious wishes, impulses that are ordinarily forbidden. Those who participate in this process, the audience or the members of a cult, constitute a group by virtue of sharing with each other disguised indulgence in forbidden wishes. In doing so, they exculpate each other by the knowledge that they have all participated, however transiently, in the pleasure of an unconscious fantasy shared in common. As Sachs said, everybody's guilt is nobody's guilt.

An unconscious fantasy shared in common serves as the bridge from individual conflict to mass participation. The capacity of the political or religious leader to evoke unconscious fantasies shared by large numbers of the population has played a significant role in many of the mass movements of this century. Mass movements are often organized around a central charismatic figure, who is intuitively perceived as the hero of a latent or manifest group mythology and who comes to represent the ego ideal of the members of the group. Because of the inherent methodological problems, however, validation of psychoanalytic insights into mass phenomena remains problematic.

VII. MORE RECENT THEORETICAL FORMULATIONS

Many new developments have occurred in psychoanalytic theory during the past few decades. Some may be considered extensions or elaborations of the basic concepts of the drive-conflict-compromise formulation with renewed emphasis on certain vicissitudes of development. Other approaches are clearly revisionary in nature. Foremost among these are object relations theory, attachment theory, and self-psychology. Some of these have coalesced into identifiable orientations or schools of thought, but none so far has achieved preeminence. Whether these newer theoretical formulations expand the internal consistency or explanatory power of the more traditional Freudian theory remains to be seen.

Modern object relations theories challenge the motivational importance of biologically grounded drives in human experience, including the role of the drives in establishing the infant-mother bond. Instead, they emphasize that drive-related strivings gain expression and are really understandable only in terms of the early experiential interactions with gratifying or nongratifying objects. The early patterns of self-object relations are internalized and repressed but they exercise a dynamic power upon the mind, leading the individual to repeat earlier patterns of interaction with significant objects. Thus, from these perspectives, it is not the derivatives of conflictual childhood wishes *per se* that are repudiated but the direct relational constellations through which these wishes came into being. It is the tendency to repeat earlier pathological patterns of interaction with significant objects that brings about pathology. Proponents of this approach believe that object relations formulations are especially relevant to the understanding of more disturbed patients, patients often referred to as borderline or narcissistic. Characteristic of such patients is a tendency to split the mental representation of the primary objects into two parts, one entirely good and the other entirely bad. This primitive defense of splitting, it is maintained, is more germane to the psychopathology of such patients and their regressive reactivation of unconscious fantasy wishes typical for neurotics.

A variant of the object relations approach, one that is somewhat closer to the conflict concept in psychoanalytic theory, is the separation-individuation paradigm proposed by Margaret Mahler. Based upon observations of infants and toddlers, she conceptualized a series of stages through which the individual achieves psychological as well as physical separation from the mother. Successful separation culminates in subjective feelings of autonomy and the emergence of the individuality that become the foundations of the self, of psychological personhood. From this standpoint, pathology results from an inability to negotiate successfully the psychological challenges of the separation-individuation process. In such instances, the individual finds it difficult to engage and resolve the conflicts of the oedipal period. Psychotic pathology reflects the failure to emerge from the state of symbiotic fusion with the mother; neurotic pathology would point to an inability to reach that stage of autonomy in which the object is firmly conceptualized as an independent and constant one. While Mahler's research concentrated on the neonate's dependence on the mother, more recent studies by infant researchers have stressed the infant's inborn perceptual preferences, experiences of perceptual unity, and programmed capacity to interact with the environment. Evidence of the infant's ability to order and differentiate a variety of stimuli and, by inference, to experience the process of emerging organization has led some researchers to postulate a series of different senses of selfhood present from birth on. The findings of such investigations present a direct challenge to some of Freud's earlier metapsychological theories, such as the notion of "primary narcissism," a theory which assumed that, at the beginning of life, all pleasurable drive tendencies are vested in the self.

Theories that delineate successive senses of self-experience during the first two years of life, based upon direct observations of neonates, parallel certain psychological theories of the self introduced by other psychoanalysts in recent decades. These theories elevate the concept of the self to a· superordinate position in explaining mental development, psychopathology, and psychoanalytic treatment.

Such theories hope to replace explanations framed in terms of Freud's structural hypothesis and the concepts of intrapsychic conflict. Theories of the self claim to address two types of deficiencies they discern in traditional psychoanalytic therapy. They assert their explanations of clinical phenomena to be closer to actual experience than those explanations framed in terms of the traditional model, which they regard as mechanistic, experience-distant, and wed to a metapsychology based on dated neurobiological and energic concepts. Second, they claim superior insight into the more disturbed patients, particularly those with severe character pathology. According to them, the pathology of the more disturbed patients is based not on the conflicts associated with the oedipal phase of development but on what they call "archaic," "preoedipal," "narcissistic," or "self object" transferences that characterize the object relations of such patients. Conflicts concerning mothering and nurturing become central in treatment. The classic conflicts of the oedipal phase, conflicts concerning envy, rivalry, hostility, and fear, are held to be of secondary importance. Self psychologists see their patients relating to them in primitive ways that correspond to the modes in which infants and young children use and depend upon their parents, especially their mothers. For such analysands, the analyst becomes an object who promotes their development by mirroring and fostering emergent feelings of adequacy and self worth. The analyst becomes an object for idealization, someone who calms and soothes the patient, thus aiding the· patient in the regulation of his inner tensions.

Unlike most object relations theories, these theories of the self tend to understand early development in terms of the programmed unfolding of a constellation of functions that collectively constitute the self. The self in its regulatory, mediating, integrating, and initiative-taking activities thus supplants the ego in Freud's structural theory. Whether in the guise of a "self schema," a "self organization" or a ''bipolar nuclear self,'' such theories understand mental health as the adequate realization of certain maturational potentials inherent in the self. Correlatively, pathology is viewed as a derailment of this biopsychological program at some point in early life. Thus, some self theories, construing early development in terms of successive stages or phases to be transversed, are led to view psychopathology from the standpoint of a deficit psychology, whereby pathology is seen to intrude when an individual fails to negotiate particular developmental challenges. Proponents of these theories trace psychological difficulties back to developmental arrests, nodal points in early life from which the self was unable to proceed with its programmed agenda. This position stands in contrast to the conflict psychology through which psychoanalysis has traditionally approached psychopathology and psychotherapy. The relationship between deficit and conflict psychologies, as is also the question of whether the self has explanatory or heuristic power greater than that of the Freudian ego, is a subject of ongoing debate within contemporary psychoanalysis. According to some self psychologists, pathology is a consequence of a failure to achieve a vital, cohesive, "nuclear" self, a failure generally rooted in unempathic, unresponsive mothering that has not mirrored or reinforced the early feelings of grandiosity that, under conditions nearer optimal, can blossom into healthy feelings of vitality and self-worth. While self psychology is offered as a rival theory to the conflict-danger-compromise approach, it may be that actually it only adds a further danger situation to the four typical dangers mentioned previously, namely, the danger of loss of self. Among recent theoretical developments, biological formulations of psychoanalytic concepts deserve special mention, but with a proviso. Descriptions of neurobiological mechanisms have not as yet been shown capable, and indeed may never supplant psychological propositions. The most productive work in neurobiology involves work on the neuroanatomical structures and the neurophysiological processes that subtend psychoanalytic concepts. Rather than modifying its understanding of mental functioning on the basis of neurobiological findings, psychoanalysis has pointed neurobiology in the direction of particularly promising conceptual and experimental endeavors. Thus we now have a body of ·literature that addresses topics of analytic concern: neurophysiological demonstrations of unconscious mental processes, e.g., between right brain and left brain, that relate to Freud's notions of primary and secondary processes; research on the neurophysiological pathways of affective expression; and research on the impact of perceptual environmental experiences on neurological development. Notions of "neuroplasticity" (the notion of critical periods during which certain experiences are necessary for optimal brain development) and of a "neurorepresentational system" have been proposed as bridge concepts linking neurobiological functioning to mental activity, including unconscious mental processes. A recent study equates the Freudian unconscious with biogenetically ancient mechanisms that involve REM sleep and are located in the prefrontal cortex and associated structures. Research that seeks to elaborate a neurobiological substrate to psychoanalytic concepts provides the same useful function as research into the psychological processes associated with neurobiological events. In the case of neurobiology and psychoanalysis, benefit is derived from reporting research in coordinate rather than in casual terms so that, in the words of Smith and Ballinger, "For the neurobiologist, psychological events are markers of neurobiological processes and for the psychologist, neurobiological events as markers of psychological processes."

REFERENCES

BLUM, H., KRAMER, Y., RICHARDS, A.K., & RICHARDS, A.D., eds. (1988). *Fantasy, Myth, and Reality: Essays in Honor of Jacob A. Arlow.* International Universities Press, Madison, CT.

EAGLE, M.N. (1984). *Recent Developments in Psychoanalysis: A Critical Evaluation.* McGraw-Hill, New York.

EDELSON, M. (1988). "Psychoanalysis: A Theory in Cri sis." University of Chicago Press, Chicago and London.

KERNBERG, O.F. (1984). *Severe Personality Disorders: Psychotherapeutic Strategies.* Yale University Press, New Haven, CT.

KOHUT, H. (1984). *How Does Analysis Cure?* University of Chicago Press, Chicago.

PINE, F. (1985). *Developmental Theory and Clinical Process.* Yale University Press, New Haven.

REISER, M.F. (1984). *Mind, Brain, Body: Toward a Convergence of Psychoanalysis and Neurobiology.* Basic Books, New York.

RICHARDS, A.D., & WILLICK, M., eds. (1986). *Psychoanalysis, the Science of Mental Conflict: Essays in Honor of Charles Brenner.* The Analytic Press, Hillsdale, NJ.

SMITH, J.H., & BALLINGER, J.C. (1981). Psychology and neurobiology, *Psychoanalysis and Contemporary Thought* 4(3), 407–421.

STERN, D.N. (1985). *The Interpersonal World of the Infant.* Basic Books, New York.

WALLERSTEIN, R.S. (1986). *Forty-Two Lives in Treatment: A Study of Psychoanalysis and Psychotherapy.* The Guilford Press, New York.

CHAPTER 16

From Ego Psychology to Contemporary Conflict Theory: A Historical Overview

[Richards, A.D. & Lynch, A.A. (1998). In *The Modern Freudians: Contemporary Psychoanalytic Technique* by C. Ellman; S. Grand, M. Silvan & S. Ellman (eds.) Northvale, NJ: Jason Aronson]

Ego psychology is rooted in the third and final phase of Freud's theorizing (Rapaport's [1959a] classification and takes "The Ego and the Id" (1923a) and "Inhibitions, Symptoms and Anxiety" (1926a) as its foundational works. More specifically, it grows out of Freud's final model of the mind, the structural hypothesis of id, ego, and superego. Levy and Inderbitzen (1996) aptly define ego psychology in terms of the underlying assumptions of Freud's structural hypothesis: "Ego psychology is . . . a systematic and coordinated conceptualization of various mental activities grouped together by virtue of their similar aims and behavioral manifestations especially associated with delay or control of instinctual discharge, on the one hand, and adaptation to reality opportunities and danger on the other" (p.412).

In "The Ego and the Id," Freud explained why the structural hypothesis was preferable to the earlier topographic point of view, which used the property of consciousness to characterize mental activity. A more balanced approach to psychic functioning, the new model with its three structural agencies allows for both environmental and biological determinants, for both purpose and drive, and for both the reality and the pleasure principles. In "Inhibitions, Symptoms and Anxiety," Freud considered the clinical implications of his earlier partitioning of the human mind. He began by identifying an error in the prestructural theory: the formulation that repression causes anxiety. He then shifted from an energic model to a meaning model, the central idea being that childhood wishes are associated with childhood dangers related to loss. These dangers are loss of the object (a significant person), loss of the object's love, loss or injury to the genital (castration), and fear of punishment (guilt). On this model, a threatening wish seeking expression in consciousness signals danger to the ego, which occasions anxiety. In Freud's monograph, the ego is at the center of exploration, but the primary importance of relationships, internal and external, real and fantastic, is also brought into focus. This emphasis on the relational or interpersonal was anticipated in "Group Psychology and the Analysis of the Ego" (1921), where Freud wrote: "In the individual's mental life someone else is invariably involved, as a model, as an object, as a helper, as an opponent; and so from the very first individual psychology, in this extended but entirely justifiable sense of the words, is at the same time social psychology as well" (p. 69).

Arlow personal communication) has noted that the clinical material that informed the structural hypothesis is to be found in a number of cases Freud published around the same time. These include "Some Character-Types Met with in Psycho-analytic Work" (1916), "Mourning and Melancholia" (1917), "A Child Is Being Beaten" (1919), "Associations of a Four-year-old Child"" (1920a), The Psychogenesis of a Case of Homosexuality in a Woman" (1920b), and "Some Neurotic Mechanisms in Jealousy, Paranoia and Homosexuality" (1922).

Modern ego psychology begins with the contributions of Richard Sterba, James Strachey, and Anna Freud. It took shape in the 1930s, as analytic theorists probed further the clinical and, especially, the technical implications of the structural hypothesis. Many contributions were made during this era by such theorists as Wilhelm Reich, Hermann Nunberg, Karl Abraham, and Paul Federn, and many more were made in ensuing years by theorists like Edward Glover, René Spitz, Erik Erikson, and Annie Reich. The most important contributors, however, were Anna Freud, Heinz Hartmann, Rudolf Loewenstein, Ernst Kris, Phyllis Greenacre, Otto Fenichel, and Edith Jacobson, all of whom, in varying degrees, extended or modified Freud's theory.

Two crucial papers of 1934, Sterba's "The Fate of the Ego in Analytic Therapy" and Strachey's "The Nature of the Therapeutic Action of Psychoanalysis," laid the groundwork for the technical modifications that arose in the aftermath of the structural hypothesis by offering two contrasting visions of the theory of therapeutic action. Sterba described a therapeutic split in the patient resulting in an experiencing ego and an observing ego. The analyst was to side with the latter, helping patients to incorporate the analyst's observing function in order to strengthen their own. Strachey stressed incorporation from the side of the superego rather than the ego. The analyst was to help patients diminish the harsh, judgmental character of their conscience by offering for identification and incorporation a greater tolerance for drive expression. These contrasting viewpoints came to the fore in two pivotal events of 1936. In the Marienbad symposium of that year, Strachey's emphasis on the patient's introjection of the analyst's superego and on the importance of the resulting superego alliance seemed to carry the day, though not without dissent (Friedman 1988). Nonetheless, Anna Freud's *The Ego and the Mechanisms of Defense,* (1936) published that same year, echoed Sterba's concern with the technical importance of strengthening the patient's observing ego in order to achieve mastery over the experiencing ego. Anna Freud's clinical contribution to this task was to single out the ego's unconscious defensive operations as perhaps the most important set of ego activities entering the treatment.

Many later contributions to the theory of pathology, technique, and development owed a debt to Anna Freud's *The Ego and the Mechanisms of Defense.* Following its publication, the history of psychoanalytic technique, from a ego psychologically standpoint, can be seen to revolve around a single issue: the clinical role of the analysis of conflict and defense, as opposed to the analysis of unconscious mental content. The position taken on this key issue by the major contributors to the theory of technique provides a basis for their differentiation. The issue is central to the differences between Anna Freud and Melanie Klein, and also serves to distinguish the technical recommendations of Sterba, Strachey, Nunberg, Fenichel, and Hartmann, Kris, and Loewenstein.

Levy and Inderbitzen (1996) note how Anna Freud's reframing of the technical issue of the analyst's attitude complemented an attentiveness to the patient's observing ego. This latter emphasis is the ego-psychological tributary flowing from Sterba's influential paper of 1934. As Levy and Inderbitzen remark,

> Her recommendation that the analyst listen from a point equidistant from id, ego and superego emphasized the importance of neutrally observing the influence of all three psychic institutions. However, the analyst's activity (interventions) always begins with and is directed toward the ego and in this sense the analyst is actually nearer to the ego than to the id or superego. The ego wards off not only derivatives of instinctual drives but also affects that are intimately connected with the drives. She advocated that

priority be given to the interpretation of defenses against affects as well as defenses against instinctual drives. [p. 414]

Anna Freud's egopsychological rationale for Freud's technical requirement of analyst neutrality, an issue that has generated controversy to the present day, was influential during this period. Greenacre's advocacy of the blank screen with no disclosure or social contact (1954) stood at one extreme, while a middle position was taken by Leo Stone (1961), who recommended benign neutrality and physicianliness. Other staked out a position in the middle by advocating the role of the real relationship as a therapeutic and curative factor. Ralph Greenson (1965) wrote of the working alliance, Elizabeth Zetzel (1956b) of the therapeutic alliance, and Hans Loewald (1960, 1971) of the role of the relationship. At the other extreme stood Sandor Ferenczi's (1920) active therapy (1920), Franz Alexander's (1956) corrective emotional experience and Harry Stack Sullivan's outright disregard of the transference. Theorists at this more active end of the spectrum believed that the analyst's more direct involvement in the patient's treatment was necessary for a lasting thera

Within psychoanalytic ego psychology, Sterba's concern with the fate of the ego has been more influential than Strachey's attentiveness to a therapeutic partnership between the superegos of analyst and analysand. The Strachey line is continued in the Kleinian, object relations, and self psychological schools, whereas the Sterba–Anna Freud line extends to the development of American ego psychology in the 1940s and 1950s. This was also the period when analysts who had lived and worked in Central Europe in the 1930s and emigrated to the United States later that decade and in the 1940s continued Freud's 1920s exploration of the structure and functioning of the ego. This cohort included Nunberg, Erikson, Fenichel, Jacobson, Anna Freud (who emigrated to England), David Rapaport, and Margaret Mahler, Robert Waelder, Ernst Simmel, Siegfried Bernfeld, and the triumvirate of Hartmann, Kris, and Loewenstein.

The Hartmann Era

What was the ego psychological paradigm that grew out of the collective efforts of these emigré theorists? Whereas the ego of Freud's topographical theory was conceptualized mainly in opposition to the id, the pioneer ego psychologists took a much larger purview. For them the ego was a complex structure, emerging, as Freud had noted, out of the perceptual apparatus and functioning as an executive forging compromises among id, superego, and external reality.

Hartmann, Kris, and Loewenstein, proposed revisions to the Freudian models of mind, development, pathogenesis, and technique. They understood survival as a primary motivating force and adaptation to the environment as essential to this end. The reality and pleasure principles were reconceptualized in line with this insight. One result of this effort was the transmuting of psychoanalysis into a general psychology of the human condition, ranging from the normal to the pathogenic.

Hartmann's 1939 monograph, *Ego Psychology and the Problem of Adaptation,* is in the spirit of Freud's lifelong project of creating a biopsychosocial model. Hartmann emphasized that the individual is born with innate psychic structures (the primary autonomous ego functions of perception, memory, thought, and motility) into an average expectable environment, and that the individual's personality is molded by this social surround. The child growing up in a familial and societal world learns to fit in with or adapt to the environment. The alternatives are to change the environment (alloplastic adaptation), to change oneself (autoplastic adaptation), or to leave the environment. Hartmann, Kris, and Loewenstein, like Freud, stressed that psychoanalysis does not claim to explain human behavior only as a result of drives and fantasies; human behavior is directed toward a world of men and things" (Hartman and Kris 1945, p. 23). The child in interaction with the environment, they believed, acquires secondary autonomous ego functions and develops a sense of self and other, while mental equilibrium is promoted by an ego that mediates inner and outer imperatives, fitting them together. The adaptative viewpoint emphasized the role of the environment in the shaping of conflicts and added the interpersonal dimension to the psychoanalytic intrapsychic emphasis. It should be recognized that during the forties and fifties both ego psychologists and the interpersonal school were exploring the influence of relationships and the environment on the individual.

A second thrust of Hartmann's theoretical project was to widen the categories of motivation from the more confined aims of libidinal pleasure and destruction, or love and hate, proposed by Freud. Hartmann retained Freud's energic model and language but offered the concept of neutralization as a way out of Freud's narrow and experience-distant drive/energy/instinct box. Neutralized libido came to include a range of experiences from lust, sensuousness, and intimacy to friendliness, warmth, and affection. Neutralized aggression likewise subsumed a spectrum of experience, from self-assertion and competitive strivings to hate and destructiveness. Each had its place in the individual's panoply of affects.

Hartmann, Kris, and Loewenstein's work(1946, 1949) provided the rationale and impetus for observational research on infants and children. The thrust was to study how mother-child interactions affected the developing ego and the sense of self and other. Hartmann (1950b) wrote: "[While] the development of object relations is co-determined by the ego, object relations are also one of the main factors that determine the development of the ego" (p.105). Contemporaries of Hartmann joined this object relations conversation. Anna Freud (1965) elaborated the concept of developmental line, Edith Jacobson (1964) investigated the self and object worlds, and Margaret Mahler (1963; Mahler et al. 1975) provided the classic formulations of separation-individuation. Attention was directed to the impact of the preoedipal period of childhood on later development, as well as to the ways in which external controls, deriving in part from the child's transactions with the parents, are internalized. These various strands were woven into an ego psychological / object relations fabric.

Jacobson's contributions deserve special mention. She postulated an undifferentiated instinctual energy at birth which, "under the influence of external stimulations" (1964, p. 13), develop into libidinal and aggressive drives. Frustration and gratification, laid down as memory traces of the ambivalent conflicts of childhood, organize affective experience. Jacobson's work figured in debates over the concept of identity in the 1950s and 1960s. Erikson took one position and Greenacre, Mahler, and Jacobson another. For Erikson (1956) identity was like a beach; it remaims the same yet changes with the tide: "The term identity . . . connotes both a persistent sameness within oneself . . . and a persistent sharing of some kind of essential character with others" (p. 57). Erikson acknowledged the importance of childhood development, but maintained that a lasting and stable identity is not formed until the close of adolescence. He placed considerable emphasis on social role, values, and ideals. Jacobson took exception to Erikson's formulations. She felt that his theory overemphasized social descriptive aspects and lacked a clear metapsychological presentation of identity formation. Further, his focus on processes of late adolescence and early adulthood gave short shrift to the immense influence of early childhood. For Jacobson (1964), identity was equated with self-feeling or self-awareness, qualities that emerged in the process of self and object differentiation: "I would prefer to understand by identity formation a process that builds up the ability to preserve the whole psychic organization—despite its growing structuralization, differentiation and complexity—as a continuity at any stage of human development" (p. 27).

In regard to psychopathology, ego psychologists did not limit their purview to neurosis. In a paper on schizophrenia, Hartmann (1953) described, as the most significant etiological factor in the development of this psychosis, the failure of the capacity to neutralize aggressive energy and thereby build adequate defensive structures. Arlow and Brenner (1964) presented in essence the same thesis but without the economic/energic language. The ego psychological purview extended also to the investigation of character and personality disorders, including the oral character (Glover 1925), the anal character (Abraham 1923), the phallic-narcissistic character (W. Reich 1933), the hysterical character (Marmor 1953), the masochistic character (Stein 1956), the as-if personality (Deutsch 1934), the impostor (Abraham 1935) and the perverse character (Arlow 1971). Jacobson (1964) noted that from the clinical standpoint "serious identity problems appear to be limited to neurotics with specific narcissistic conflicts, and to borderline and psychotic patients" (p. 29). This expansion in diagnostic categories eventuated in clinical recognition both of the widening scope of psychoanalysis (Stone 1954), and of the need for careful empirical studies for example the Menninger Research Project a long term followup of forty two patients and the Hampstead Index an in depth study of the psychoanalytic case material of a two-year-old child.

Clinical Implications of Ego Psychoogy

Many of the contributions to the theory of ego psychology had general implications for psychoanalytic technique. Anna Freud (1936) shifted the technical emphasis of observation to the ego. She noted that it was only through the patient's ego that the analyst could observe the presentations of the id, ego, and superego with equal attention. Hence, she concluded, the ego is the agency through which analysis occurs. Hartmann's work broadened the scope of understanding beyond the individual's psychopathology to include the total personality, where both nonconflictual functioning and ego autonomy play important roles. Hartmann described how autonomous functions can facilitate free association (e.g., through self-observation and verbalization) or inhibit it (e.g., through purposive thinking).. Loewenstein (1972) noted "that if the main though not exclusive interest of psychoanalysis is the study of conflict in man, the *tools* of this study are the autonomous functions" (pp. 213–214). Nevertheless, these functions may at times come serve resistance and become objects of the analysis. Hartmann (1939)called this unexpected occurrence a "change of function." Loewenstein (1963) moved the understanding of resistance beyond the basic rule by calling attention to the distinction between resistances mobilized to address core conflicts and those mobilized that are against the emergence of a particular feeling or thought.

Neutralized energy was regarded as a reservoir by which the ego could to support its aims and functions independently of drive pressure. Likewise, neutralized energy fueled the ego's defenses against drive demands. Clinically, Hartmann's theoretical concepts provided the impetus for ego psychology to explore such concepts as reality testing, sublimation, altruism, modes of internalization, ideal formation, and self-esteem regulation. These contributions provided a "shift in emphasis [that led to] significant consequences" (Loewenstein 1954, p. 189) without changing the basic psychoanalytic technique. These ranged from considering the effects on interpretations of speech, timing, and direction to redefining the main therapeutic goals from recovering repressed material to modifying the ego's mode of functioning. Nunberg (1955) concisely captured the clinical outcome and goals of ego psychology in noting that "the changes which are achieved through treatment in the ideal case involve the entire personality and are as follows: the energies of the id become more mobile, the superego becomes more tolerant, the ego is freer from anxiety and the synthetic function is restored" (p. 360).

Interpretation and Clinical Process

Ego psychology shifted the emphasis in technique from the recovery of the repressed to the modification of the patient's ego, including the alteration of automatic defensive functions. Interpretation, though not the only mode of intervention, is the major intervention resulting in insight (Kris 1956a), the critical element in lasting personality and behavioral change. Loewenstein (1951, 1957, 1958) saw interpretation as a continuous effort aimed at broadening the patient's understanding of how the past remains dynamically integral to current experiences. Loewenstein (1958) argued for a view of interpretation as a process that respects the unique personalities of analysand and analyst, both as individuals and in the therapeutic interaction. Kris (1951) also noted the analyst's role as participant-observer, a dynamic presence in the analytic situation. Loewenstein provided a framework to guide the analyst in the work of discovering the unconscious meanings that underlie the patient's communications. The analyst makes conjectures and then gathers evidence for them in the patient's verbal and nonverbal communication. This careful approach placed a new emphasis on the role of speech (Hartmann 1951; Loewenstein, 1956, 1961), and the person was not lost sight of in the treatment process. "Interpretations deal with the individual experiences of a human being,"Loewenstein (1951) wrote."They aim at widening the conscious knowledge of the individual about himself and should therefore deal with the psychological realities of the individual" (p. 5). This aspect of ego psychology is often missed by critics who view it as impersonal and mechanistic.

Kris (1956b) in his paper on the personal myth elaborated how a person's unique history infuses the self-image with an important early fantasy. The personal myth is preserved as a "treasured possession," and the person reenacts the repressed fantasy in various aspects of life. The personal myth serves multiple functions, acting as a defense and as a pattern of life. Its interpretation of the personal myth fosters the analysand reintegration. "The unacceptable wishes of childhood," we have noted (Bachant, Lynch, and Richards 1995b), "are part of the persistent unconscious fantasies that seek resolution in the present through compromise formation. As we develop, these fantasies mature and shape our special interests and character traits, determine our behavior, and produce our neurotic symptoms. The essential plot or narrative of unconscious wishes and fears endures even as their manifestations are transformed. (p. 75).

Transference and Countertransference

We have also noted (Lynch, Richards, and Bachant 1997) that Freud's definition of transference in 1905(a) laid the groundwork for the recognition of the therapeutic value of the interactive aspects of the transference: he characterized that transference phenomena as

> . . . new editions or facsimiles of the impulses and phantasies which are aroused and made conscious during the progress of the analysis; . . . they replace some earlier person by the person of the physician. To put it in another way: a whole series of psychological experiences are revived, not as belonging to the

past, but as applying to the person of the physician at the present moment [p. 116].

Freud (1912a, 1915c) went on to note that transference is found in every adult relationship, a point emphasized by Loewenstein (1969), Brenner (1982), and Bird (1972). According to Brenner, what distinguishes the therapeutic relationship from the ordinary adult relationship is not the presence of transference but its use by the analyst to analyze psychic conflict (Bachant et al.1995b).

The concept of countertransference did not become a subject for close investigation until the 1950s, when discussions of the concept burgeoned in the literature. The most systematic papers of this time were written by Annie Reich (1951, 1960, 1966), who followed in the ego psychological tradition. Like other contemporary contributors, Reich chose a definition of countertransference broader than Freud's, but one that stopped short of embracing the analyst's total response to the analysand.

> Countertransference comprises the effects of the analyst's own unconscious needs and conflicts on his understanding or technique. In such instances the patient represents for the analyst an object of the past onto whom past feelings and wishes are projected, just as it happens in the patient's transference situation with the analyst. The provoking factor for such an occurrence may be something in the patient's personality or material or something in the analytic situation as such [1951, pp. 138–139].

Loewenstein (1957) highlighted the difference between, on the one hand, reactions in the analyst that are induced by the analysand and, on the other, true countertransferential feelings and responses. The former were to be understood as an expression of activity in the analytic relationship. Regarding the distinction between countertransference and the analyst's total response to the analysand, Annie Reich (1960) noted that the analysand is responded to not only as an object for unconscious strivings but as an object in reality as well. To achieve empathy, she maintained, the analyst must have some object libidinal investment in the analysand. Countertransference occurs only when unconscious infantile strivings are expressed in intense and inappropriate feelings, responses, or actions. Thus, she wrote, "If, for private reasons, the analyst . . . is too charged with his private problems, too many conflicts will be mobilized, too many inner resistances stirred up, or some instinctual impulses too near to breakthrough will threaten" (p. 352). It is the intensity of these conflicts that blocks understanding, interferes with technique, and leads to a breakdown of the analytic task. Within contemporary conflict theory, Arlow (1979, 1985a), Boesky (1982), Brenner (1976, 1982, 1985), Jacobs (1983, 1986a), McLaughlin (1981, 1988), and Silverman (1985) are among those who have contributed to the expansion and modification of the current clinical status of countertransference.

Initiating a different line of thought, Paula Heimann (1950) and Margaret Little (1951) advocated broadening countertransference to include the total response of the analyst. Maxwell Gitelson (1952) and M.B. Cohen (1952) identified the place of interactions between analyst and analysand; Heimann (1950) stressed that the analyst's emotional response is important for empathy and that countertransference is a creation of the analysand as well as of the analyst. This body of work by ego psychologists and object relations theorists provided the grounding for contemporary debates about transference actualization and enactment. Contributors to these debates include Abend (1989), Boesky (1982), Chused (1991) Jacobs (1993), McLaughlin (1991), Ogden (1982, 1983), Schwaber (1983), Sandler (1976a,b,) Sandler and Sandler (1978). Various subtexts of these debates have galvanized discussion (Lynch, et al. 1997): the place of philosophical relativism and social constructivism, the clinical valorization of the here and now, the status of the real relationship, the impact of the analysand on the analyst, and the role of the analyst's self-revelation and self-disclosure.

Contemporary Psychoanalytic Conflict Theory

The ego psychological tradition has also come to fruition in the theoretical viewpoint commonly referred to as modern structural theory, although contemporary conflict theory is perhaps a more apt designation and is one that we prefer. This viewpoint was developed primarily by a group of American analysts who trained in the late 1940s and early 1950s and were analyzed and supervised, for the most part, by emigre analysts from Central Europe. Jacob Arlow, David Beres, Charles Brenner, Martin Wangh, and Leo Rangell were members of this original group; all but Rangell attended the New York Psychoanalytic Institute. After completing their training, Arlow, Beres, Brenner, and Wangh met together—and subsequently with their teachers and supervisors (Hartmann, Kris, Lewin, Loewenstein, et al.)—to examine critically the received psychoanalytic wisdom of their time. Out of this examination, which focused on the concepts of anxiety, repression, defense, and symptom formation, the modern structural viewpoint emerged.

What precisely is the relationship between ego psychology and contemporary conflict theory? The latter is an outgrowth of the former, inasmuch as it devotes "considerable attention to the role, function, and characteristics of the ego" (Arlow 1963). Yet, as Boesky (1988) has observed, the two are not synonymous, as contemporary conflict theory focuses on the essential interrelatedness of id, ego, and superego (Boesky 1988). Indeed, Rangell (1988) suggested "id/ego/superego psychology" as a more appropriate designation for the theory, which embraces the central presupposition of Freud's structural hypothesis: that psychoanalysis is primarily a psychology of conflict. Contemporary conflict theory approaches mental life and all psychic phenomena as the expression of intrapsychic forces in conflict and the resulting compromises. The thrust of contemporary conflict theory has been to refine and amend Freud's hypothesis in order to achieve a fuller appreciation of the range and scope of conflicts and compromise formations in mental life and to develop a more powerful psychoanalytic treatment approach.

Initially, this approach led to the espousal of structural concepts as more useful clinically than concepts associated with Freud's topographic model. Even within the structural model, moreover, the dynamic and genetic viewpoints were given precedence over the economic/energic. Arlow and Brenner's *Psychoanalytic Concepts and the Structural Theory,*(1964) is an important articulation of this viewpoint. Its verdict has been underscored by Boesky (1988), who observes that Freud's concepts of psychic energy are no longer accepted by those espousing contemporary conflict theory.

Along with this selective use of structural concepts come a trend toward loosening the dependence of a conflict theory on Freud's model of the three psychic agencies. Beres gave voice to this trend in "Structure and Function in Psychoanalysis" (1965), as did Hartmann in "Concept Formation in Psychoanalysis (1964). Beres argued that Freud always understood the psychic structures as "functional groups" and that his emphasis was always on issues of organization and process. Sharing Arlow and Brenner's belief that theoretical concepts are ways of organizing clinical phenomena, Beres urged analysts to follow the functional direction of Freud's theorizing, an approach that viewed the structural entities of id, ego, and superego as metaphorical rather than concrete.

Beres's cautionary advice has generated a range of theoretical responses. One set of responses, associated with the work of Arlow and Brenner, has been to dissociate contemporary conflict theory from the metapsychological propositions that Freud imported into his structural theory. Arlow, Brenner, Beres, and Boesky all argue for the jettisoning of economic concepts, such as cathexis and decathexis, that are far removed from clinical observation. The modern structural emphasis on unconscious fantasy as an ego function, an emphasis growing out of an influential body of work by Arlow (1969a) and Beres (1962), is consonant with this trend.

The progressive loosening of contemporary conflict theory from Freud's formulations of id, ego, and superego has resulted in a more clinically based focus on the components of psychic conflict, a development accompanied by a widening of the experiential and dynamic realm of conflict. The shift in emphasis is from id, ego, and superego as components of conflict, to the dynamic constellations closest to the data of observation.

The common frame of reference of modern conflict theorists has not precluded their espousal of different clinical emphases. Two major variations, both legacies of ego psychology, focus on the interpretation of conflict and compromise formation in the context of unconscious fantasy (Arlow, Brenner, Abend, Boesky, Rangell, Rothstein) and on the patient's resistance to awareness of the operation of defenses (Busch 1995, Gray 1994;). The latter perspective is cautious about interpreting unconscious content, emphasizing instead an analytic partnership that facilitates the patient's self-discovery and emerging capacity for self-analysis. Busch links therapeutic success to the extent to which, during analysis, "the patient's unbypassed ego functions have been involved in a consciously and increasingly voluntary partnership with the analyst.

An important controversy among proponents of contemporary conflict theory concerns the technical role of the patient-analyst relationship. At issue is the active use of the relationship, as opposed to a greater emphasis on its interpretation. This attachment/interpretation dialectic has been a major theme of egopsychological discourse since the 1930s. It was a subject of dispute at the Marienbad symposium of 1936, where Sterba held that attachment was preliminary to understanding, whereas Strachey contended that it was the vehicle of structural change. The debate was continued at the Edinburgh symposium of 1962, where Gitelson, arguing in the spirit of Strachey, held that attachment was "a restructuring experience in itself, operating on the entire psychic apparatus and not just the ego or the superego" (Friedman, 1988, p. 51). The next installment of this debate, occurring in the 1960s and 1970s, revolved around the concept of the therapeutic alliance. Zetzel and Greenson, the proponents of this concept, saw it as redressing the inadequate attention to the real relationship that typified the reigning egopsychological approach. Their position was opposed by Brenner (1979b), who considered the concept superfluous and even countertherapeutic, and by Martin Stein, whose "The Unobjectionable Part of the Transference" (1981), offers the clearest statement of the way in which positive transference can be enlisted by patient and analyst together in the service of resistance. It is fair to say that the egopsychological tradition, from Sterba through Fenichel and Kris to Arlow and Brenner, has been cautious about using the analytic relationship as a lever of treatment. Yet contemporary analysts trained in the egopsychological tradition—e.g., James McLaughlin, Owen Renik, Theodore Jacobs, and Judith Chused— are among those who have alerted us to the importance of the analyst's subjective experience as a guide to understanding the patient. These analysts propound a range of different positions regarding the nature and extent of the analyst's participation in the therapeutic process, but they share an appreciation of the analyst's subjectivity and find value in the enactments that occur inevitably in analytic treatment. Contemporary conflict theory, building on the foundations of ego psychology and a spectrum of psychoanalytic theories is an evolutionary, (as opposed to revolutionary) viewpoint, since it takes Freud's conflict psychology as a conceptually and clinically adequate perspective. To be sure, it is a perspective subject to ongoing emendation (as in the work of Arlow, Brenner, and Rangell) and expansion (as in the work of Renik, Jacobs, McLaughlin, and Chused). It is noteworthy that Brenner, in his most recent writings (1993, 1994a), has dispensed entirely with Freud's model of id, ego, and superego in expounding conflict and compromise formation. And Arlow, for his part, has long argued against the clinical explanatory importance of a structural model with reified psychic agencies: "Id, ego, and superego," he has remarked, "exist not in the patient but in psychoanalytic textbooks" (personal communication). Still, other prominent contemporary structuralists continue to believe that the tripartite model remains the most illuminating and clinically useful way to understand conflict and compromise. Clearly there is no "last word" in contemporary conflict theory, and future decades will witness continuing advances in our understanding of, and clinical approaches to, "the mind in conflict" (Brenner 1982).

Having attempted to elucidate the influences and controversies along specific lines of inquiry in psychoanalytic history, we end with a disclaimer: it is not possible to neatly divide psychoanalysis into independent schools with disparate theories and techniques. Rather, psychoanalytic history bears witness to an ongoing process of accommodation and mutual. influence. There is a central core of theory from Freud to the present, with many diverse elaborations. Often, seemingly radical differences among theories diminish their clinical presentation. Like any science, psychoanalysis will continue to generate diverse and conflicting positions; it will continue also to be influenced by contributions from the social and natural sciences. Amid these currents of change, a firm grasp of our collective history and scientific influences will help us to avoid the partisan squabbles and irrational battles that too often have plagued our field.

REFERENCES

ABEND, S. (1979).Unconscious fantasy and theories of cure. *Journal of the American Psychoanalytic Association* 27:579–596
———— (1989). Countertransference and psychoanalytic technique. *Psychoanalytic Quarterly* 58:374–395.
ABRAHAM, K., (1921). Contributions to the theory of the anal character. *International Journal Psycho-Analysis* 4:400–418.
———— (1925).The history of an impostor in the light of psycho-analytical knowledge. *Psychoanalytic Quarterly* 4:570–587, 1935.
ALEXANDER, F. (1956). *Psychoanalysis and Psychotherapy.* New York: Norton.
ARLOW, J.A. (1963a). The supervisory situation. *Journal of the American Psychoanalytic Association* 11: 576–594.
———— (1969a). Fantasy, memory, and reality testing. *Psychoanalytic Quarterly* 38: 28–51.
———— (1969b). Unconscious Fantasy and Disturbances of Conscious Experience. *Psychoanalytic Quarterly* 38:1–27.
———— (1971). Character perversion. In *Currents in Psychoanalysis,* ed. I. M. Marcus. New York: International Universities Press, pp. 317–336.
———— (1985a). Some technical problems of countertransference. *Psychoanalytic Quarterly* 54:164–174.
ARLOW J.A., & BRENNER, C. (1964). *Psychoanalytic Concepts and the Structural Theory.* New York: International Universities Press.
BACHANT, J.L., LYNCH, A.A., & RICHARDS, A.D. (1995a), Relational models in psychoanalytic theory. *Psychoanalytic Psychology,* 12: 71–87.

BACHANT, J.L., LYNCH, A.A., & RICHARDS, A.D. (1995B). The evolution of drive theory: A response to Merton Gill. *Psychoanalytic Psychology* 12:565–573

BERES, D., (1962). The unconscious fantasy. *Psychoanalytic Quarterly* 31:309–328.

——— (1965).Structure and function in psycho-analysis. *International Journal of Psycho-Analysis* 46:53–53 .

BIRD, B. (1957). A specific peculiarity of acting out. *Journal of the American Psychoanalytic Association* 5:630–647.

——— (1972). Notes on transference: Universal phenomenon and hardest part of analysis. *Journal of the American Psychoanalytic Association* 20:267–301.

BOESKY, D. (1982). Acting out: A reconsideration of the concept. *International Journal of . Psycho-Analysis* 63:39–55.

——— (1988). Comments on the structural theory of technique. *International Journal Psycho-Analysis* 69:303–316 .

BRENNER, C. (1976). *Psychoanalytic Technique and Psychic Conflict.* New York: International Universities Press.

——— (1979b). Working alliance, therapeutic alliance and transference. *Journal of the American Psychoanalytic Association* 27:137–158.

——— (1982a). *The mind in conflict.* New York: International Universities Press.

——— (1985). Countertransference as compromise formation. *Psychoanalytic Quarterly* 54:155–163.

——— (1994). Mind as conflict and compromise formation. *Journal of Clinical Psychoanalysis* 3:473–488.

——— (1995). Some remarks on psychoanalytic technique. *Journal of Clinical Psychoanalysis* 4:413–428.

BUSCH, F. (1995). *The Ego at the Center of Clinical Technique.* Northvale, NJ: Jason Aronson.

CHUSED, J.F. (1991). The evocative power of enactments. *Journal of the American Psychoanalytic Association* 39:615–640.

COHEN, M.B. (1952). Countertransference and anxiety. *Psychiatry* 15:231–243.

DEUTSCH, H., (1942).Some forms of emotional disturbance and their relationship to schizophrenia. *Psychoanalytic Quarterly* 11:301–32.

ERIKSON, E.H., (1956). The problem of ego identity. *Journal of the American Psychoanalytic Association* 4:56–121.

FERENCZI, S. (1920). The further development of an active therapy in psychoanalysis. In *Further Contributions to the Theory and Technique of Psychoanalysis.* New York: Brunner/Mazel, Publishers.

FREUD, A. (1936). *The Ego and the Mechanisms of Defense.* New York: International Universities Press, 1946.

——— (1965). Normality and pathology in childhood: Assessment of development. *Collected Papers* Volume 6 New York: International Universities Press.

FREUD, S. (1905e). Fragment of an analysis of a case of hysteria. *Standard Edition* 7:112–122.

——— (1912a). The dynamics of transference. *Standard Edition* 12:97–108.

——— (1915a). Observations on transference-love. *Standard Edition* 12:157–171.

——— (1916d).Some character types met with in psychoanalytic work *Standard Edition* 14:309–336).

——— (1917e). Mourning and melancholia. *Standard Edition* 14:237–258.

——— (1919e). A child is being beaten. *Standard Edition* 17:175–204.

——— (1920d). Associations of a four-year-old child. *Standard Edition* 18:266.

——— (1920a). The psychogenesis of a case of homosexuality in a woman. *Standard Edition* 18:146–172.

——— (1922b). Some neurotic mechanisms in jealousy, paranoia and homosexuality. *Standard Edition* 18:221.

——— (1921c). Group psychology and the analysis of the ego. *Standard Edition* 18:65–144.

——— (1923b). The Ego and the Id. *Standard Edition* 19:1–66.

——— (1926d). Inhibitions, symptoms and anxieties. *Standard Edition*

——— (1937). Analysis terminable and interminable. *Standard Edition* 23:209–254.

FRIEDMAN, L., (1988a). *The Anatomy of Psychotherapy.* Hillsdale, NJ: The Analytic Press.

GITELSON, M. (1952). The emotional position of the analyst in the psychoanalytic situation. *International Journal of Psycho-Analysis* 33:1–10.

GLOVER, E. (1925). Notes on oral character formation. *International Journal of Psycho-Analysis* 6:131.

GRAY, P. (1994). *The Ego and Analysis of Defense.* Northvale, NJ: Jason Aronson, Inc.

GREENACRE, P. (1954). The role of transference—practical considerations in relation to psychoanalytic therapy. *Journal of the American Psychoanalytic Association* 2:671–684.

GREENSON, R.R. (1965). The working alliance and the transference neurosis. *Psychoanalytic Quarterly* 34:155–181.

HARTMANN, H. (1939). *Ego Psychology and the Problem of Adaptation.* New York: International Universities Press.

——— (1950b). Psychoanalysis and developmental psychology. In *Essays on Ego Psychology: Selected Problems in Psychoanalytic Theory.* New York: International Universities, 1964, pp. 108–109.

——— (1951). Technical implications of ego psychology. In *Essays on Ego Psychology: Selected Problems in Psychoanalytic Theory.* New York: International Universities Press, 1964, pp. 142–154.

——— (1953). Contribution to the metapsychology of schizophrenia. In *Essays on Ego Psychology: Selected Problems in Psychoanalytic Theory.* New York: International Universities Press, 1964, pp. 182–206.

——— & Kris, E., (1945). The genetic approach in psychoanalysis. *The*

Psychoanalytic Study of the Child 1.11–30.

——— ——— & Loewenstein, R.M. (1946). Comments on the formation of psychic structure. *The Psychoanalytic of the Study of the Child* 2.11–38.

——— ——— ——— (1949). Notes on the theory of aggression. *The Psychoanalytic Study of the Child* 3/4, 9–36.

HEIMANN, P. (1950). On Countertransference. *International Journal of Pyscho-Analysis* 31:81–84.

JACOBS, T. (1983). The analyst's and the patient's object world: Notes on an aspect of countertransference. *International Journal of Psycho-Analysis* 31:619–642.

——— (1986a). On countertransference enactments. *Journal of the American Psychoanalytic Association* 34:289–307.

——— (1991). *The Use of the Self.* Madison, CT: International Universities Press.

JACOBSON, E. (1964). *The Self and the Object World.* New York: International Universities Press.

KRIS, E. (1951). Ego psychology and interpretation in psychoanalytic therapy. *Psychoanalytic Quarterly* 20:15–30.

——— (1956a). On some vicissitudes of insight in psychoanalysis. *International Journal of Psycho-Analysis* 37:445–455.

——— (1956b). The personal myth. *Journal of the American Psychoanalytic Association* 4:653–681.

LEVY, & INDERBITZEN, (1996). Ego Psychology and Modern Structural Theory: consolidation of Ego Psychology pp 412–413. In *Tasman, Kay and Lieberman editors Psychiatry Volume 1.* W.B. Saunders Cpmpany, Philadelphia, Pa.

LITTLE, M. (1951). Countertransference and the Patient's Response to It. *International Journal Journal of Psycho-Analysis* 32:32–40.

LOEWALD, H.W. (1960). On the therapeutic action of psycho-analysis. *International Journal of Psycho-Analysis* 43:16–33.

——— (1971). Some considerations on repetition and repetition compulsion. *International Journal of Psychoanalysis* 52:59–66.

LOEWENSTEIN, R. M. (1951). The problem of interpretation. *Psychoanalytic Quarterly* 20:1–14.

——— (1954). Some remarks on defenses, autonomous ego, and psychoanalytic technique. *International Journal of Psycho-Analysis* 35:188–193.

——— (1956). Some remarks on the role of speech in psychoanalytic technique. *International Journal of Psycho-Analysis* 37:460–468.

——— (1957). Some thoughts on interpretation in the theory and practice of psychoanalysis. *Psychoanalytic Study of the Child* 12:127–150.

——— (1958). Remarks on some variations in psychoanalytic technique. *International Journal of Psycho-Analysis* 39:202–210.

——— (1961). Introduction to panel: The silent patient. *Journal of the American Psychoanalytic Association* 9:2–6.

——— (1963). Some considerations on free association. *Journal of the American Psychoanalytic Association* 11:451–473.

——— (1969). Developments in the theory of transference in the last fifty years. International Journal of Psycho-Analysis 50:583–588.

——— (1972). Ego autonomy and psychoanalytic technique. In *Practice and Precept in Psychoanalytic Technique: Selected Papers of Rudolph M. Loewenstein.* New Haven: Yale University Press, pp. 211–228.

LYNCH, A.A., RICHARDS, A.D., & BACHANT, J.L. (1997). Interaction in the transference. countertransference continuum. Presented at the 40th International Psychoanalytic Association Conference, Barcelona, Spain.

McLaughlin, J.T. (1981). Transference, psychic reality and countertransference. *Psychoanalytic Quarterly* 50:639–664

——— (1988). The Analyst's Insights. *Psychoanalytic Quarterly* 57:370–388.

——— (1991). Clinical and theoretical aspects of enactment. *Journal of the American Psychoanalytic Association* 39:595–614.

——— & Johan, M., (1992). Enactments in psychoanalysis. *Journal of the American Psychoanalytic Association* 40:827–841.

Mahler, M.S., (1963). Thoughts about development and individuation. *Psychoanalytic Study of the Child* 18:307–324.

——— Pine, F., & Bergman, A., (1975). *The Psychological Birth of the Human Infant: Symbiosis and Individuation.* New York: Basic Books.

MARMOR, J., (1953.). Orality in the hysterical personality. *Journal of the American Psychoanalytic Association* 1:656–671.

NUNBERG, H., (1931). The synthetic function of the ego. *International Journal of Psycho-Analysis* 12:123–140.

——— (1955). *Principles of Psychoanalysis.* New York: International Universities Press.

Ogden, T.H. (1982). *Projective Identification and Psychotherapeutic Technique.* New York: Jason Aronson.

——— (1983). The concept of internal object relations. *International Journal of Psycho-Analysis* 64:227–241.

RANGELL, L. (1988).The future of psychoanalysis:The scientific crossroads. *Psychoanalytic Quarterly* 57:313–340.

RAPAPORT, D (1959a).A historical survey of psychoanalytic egp psychology: A generalization In Psychological Issues, Vol 1, No 1, ed. G.S. Klein, New York: International Universities Press, pp. 5–17.

REICH, A. (1951). *On countertransference. Annie Reich: Psychoanalytic Contributions.* pp. 136–154 New York: International Universities Press.

——— (1960). *Further Remarks On Countertransference. Annie Reich: Psychoanalytic Contributions.* pp. 271–287 New York: International Universities Press, 271–287.

——— (1966). *Empathy and Countertransference. Annie Reich: Psycho-analytic Contributions.* New York: International Universities Press, 344–360.

REICH, W., (1933). *Character Analysis.* New York: Orgone Institute Press.

RENIK, O. (1993). Analytic interaction: conceptualizing technique in light of the analyst's irreducible subjectivity. *Psychoanalytic Quarterly* 57:553–571.

SANDLER, J. (1976a). Actualization and object relationships. *Journal of the*

Philadelphia Association .for Psychoanalysis 3:59–70.

———— (1976b). Countertransference and role-responsiveness. *International Review of Psychoanalysis* 3:43–47.

———— & SANDLER, A., (1978). On the development of object relationships and affects. *International Journal of Psycho-Analysis* 59:285–296.

SCHWABER, E. (1983). Psychoanalytic listening and psychic reality. *International Review of Psychoanalysis* 10:379–392.

SILVERMAN, M. (1985). Countertransference and the myth of the perfectly analyzed analyst. *Psychoanalytic Quarterly* 54:175.

STEIN, M.H., (1956). The problem of masochism in the theory and technique of psychoanalysis. *Journal of American Psychoanalytic Association* 4:526.

———— (1981).The unobjectionable part of the transference. *Journal of the American Psychoanalytic Association* 29:869.

STERBA, R. (1934). The fate of the ego in analytic therapy. *International Journal of Psycho-Analysis* 15:117–126.

STONE, L. (1954). The widening scope of indications for psychoanalysis. *Journal of the American Psychoanalytic Association* 2:567–594.

———— (1961). *The Psychoanalytic Situation.* New York: International Universities Press.

STRACHEY, J. (1934). The nature of the therapeutic action of psychoanalysis. *International Journal of Psychoanalysis* 15:127–159.

ZETZEL, E., (1956a). Current concepts of transference. *International Journal of Psycho-Analysis* 37:369–376.

CHAPTER 17

Leo Rangell: The Journey of a Developed Freudian

[Lynch, A.A., & Richards, A.D. (2010). *Psychoanalytic Review* 97:361–391.]

Throughout his career Leo Rangell has been a major contributor to the scholarly corpus of psychoanalysis. He has been a strong advocate for an important theme—the unification of psychoanalytic theory. He has been a man on a mission—the development of what he calls "total composite psychoanalytic theory." He has added significantly to our understanding of clinical and theoretical issues and provided us with wise input on complex group, organizational, and political dilemmas. His ideas have matured and deepened over the years as they have been refined by the inclusion of new data. His work has focused on how intrapsychic events lead to action as they affect and are affected by the varieties of human experience. The body of his work includes over 450 articles and eight books, and he continues to write and contribute to our science. He is often engaged in a dialogue with the profession about the significant issues of the day—original but always anchored in sound psychoanalytic theory, grounded in the works of Freud and his successors, chief among them Heinz Hartmann, Otto Fenichel, David Rapaport, Anna Freud, and Edith Jacobson. He writes from a position of psychoanalytic leadership: twice President of the International Psychoanalytic Association, twice President of the American Psychoanalytic Association, and three times President of his local Society. Dr. Rangell is currently Honorary President of the International Psychoanalytic Association. Throughout his professional career he has been at the center of the psychoanalytic world and from that vantage point he has witnessed and contributed to the great debates for more than half a century. In this paper, our aim is to present an overview and a more detailed account of the development of Rangell's work.

The Human Core

Rangell began his efforts to unify psychoanalytic theory by looking at the problem of anxiety and then considered four additional concepts.

In an early Alexander lecture, Rangell (1967) placed unconscious intrapsychic conflicts at the center of what he identified as "the human core." In subsequent papers which elaborate on this concept (Rangell, 1990, 2001a), he discussed interconnected and contiguous psychic phenomena, anxiety, the "intrapsychic process," a new ego function of unconscious decision making, the syndrome of the compromise of integrity, and the exercise of free will as an aspect of ego autonomy.

Anxiety

Rangell (1955a, 1968a) began his unifying efforts by addressing Freud's problem of anxiety. Freud had two theories of anxiety: The first viewed anxiety as the direct transformation of libido (actual-neurosis) (1894, 1895); in the second theory, anxiety was a signal (1926). Freud's first theory was a somatic formulation:Anxiety was the painful consequence of repression (defense) that interfered with the discharge of libido. This painful affect was experienced passively by the ego.

Freud's (1926) second model became more universally accepted and was in part a consequence of his adding the structural point of view to the topographical one. The second model was psychological rather than somatic: Anxiety was a signal of danger, and thought was an experimental action. Freud (1926) was uncertain about the compatibility of the two theories, ending his monograph *Inhibitions, Symptoms and Anxiety* with the phrase "non liquet," that is, they do not flow together. Rangell proposed a "Unitary Theory" that contained the critical elements of both theories along a spectrum of the "intrapsychic process." With this understanding, Rangell felt anxiety was "now liquet."

Freud did not abandon his first theory of anxiety although he believed that his newer signal anxiety theory was better suited for the understanding of specific clinical phenomena. Freud, Rangell noted, continued to distinguish his two types of anxiety. Freud (1926), in his most definitive work on the subject, noted: "In these two aspects, as an automatic phenomenon and as a rescuing signal, anxiety is seen to be a product of the infant's mental helplessness which is a natural counterpart of its biological helplessness" (Freud, 1926, p. 137). Rangell maintained that this broader view is necessary to account for the phenomena of early traumatic anxiety. But he also agreed with Kris (Rangell, 1955a) that the basis for trauma was not sexual frustration.

Drawing on the findings of the day (Bibring, 1953; Brenner, 1953; Greenacre, 1945; Kubie, 1941; Schur, 1953; Spitz, 1950) Rangell elaborated a developmental perspective and traced the origins of anxiety to the first pleasure-unpleasure sensations in infancy. Spitz's (1950) empirical work with early infants found that anxiety began around the third quarter of the first year of life. This left the question open as to whether or not anxiety existed before there was an ego, when only ego precursors exists.

Greenacre (1941a, 1941b) believed that the organic components of anxiety were increased when distress, danger, or threat was present in fetal or early postnatal life. These painful moments were experienced prior to the capacity for organized psychological content or defense functioning. She suggested that the negative consequence of these painful situations led to an increase in faulty reality testing and pathological narcissism, and promoted the predisposition for severe neurosis and borderline states. Building on these ideas, Rangell proposed his unitary theory of anxiety, which included the concept of the new "signal" theory but also applied to the whole gamut of anxiety reactions.

The theory rested on three propositions: (1) Actual neurosis is indeed a valid and demonstrable entity; (2) the idea of "automatic" anxiety without ego participation does not necessarily follow; and, (3) a dual theory of anxiety is not necessary or desirable. Rangell followed Fenichel (1945), who believed that "actual-neurotic symptoms form the nucleus of all psychoneuroses" (p. 192, quoted in Rangell, 1955a, pp. 396–397). In other words, the dread or distress set down by trauma in early development, before the organization of thought or the functions of defense, is at the heart of all pathology.

Following Greenacre (1941a, 1941b) and Fenichel (1945), Rangell stressed that during the course of development the ego emerged and acted to continuously integrate internal and external stimuli, while seeking maximum satisfaction. With this developmental progression, the individual moves from experiencinghelplessness as an all-or-nothing response to attaining a more modulated reaction with the ability to anticipate—a signal anxiety. The traumatic situation and all its associational elements provide an anticipatory or signal quality that alerts one to a sense of danger. These identified or tagged elements herald a future state of impending helplessness or danger. At times, when the ego's control weakens, it becomes incapable of anticipating and signaling. Then regression follows, and internal and external factors converge as a traumatic situation converts signal anxiety into traumatic anxiety. The regression produces motor and psychichelplessness. In this state of fear, the ego does not have sufficient resources to master the intensity of the painful affect and "an anticipation of being overrun by stimuli" (Rangell, 1955a, p. 391) occurs.[1] It is the unpleasant affect, not anxiety, that occurs automatically, but depending on circumstance unpleasant affect may not mean that there is an absence of ego involvement. Anxiety is always a reaction to the danger that either "the helpless state will get worse, and/or it will continue and never stop" (Rangell, 1955a, p. 396). The fear the ego faces, Rangell noted, has been given various descriptions: the "dread of the strength of the instincts" (Anna Freud, 1936, p. 63, quoted in Rangell, 1955a, p. 397);[2] trauma based on a primary model of passivity (Rapaport, 1954, quoted in Rangell, 1955a, p. 397); the notion of being abandoned to one's fate or as a presage to annihilation (Fenichel, 1945, quoted in Rangell, 1955a, p. 398); the nature of "an overthrow or extinction" (Freud, 1923, quoted in Rangell, 1955a, p. 398); and a view of the destruction or submergence of the ego (Wäelder, 1936, quoted in Rangell, 1955a, p. 398). Melanie Klein (1946), Rangell noted, was more specific in her belief that the danger was destruction of the ego by the force of instinctual aggression.

Rangell next described the signal process used for testing for the presence or absence of anxiety. The ego experimentally permits a small, controlled discharge of instinctual tension, which tests associated memory traces for the possibility of mastery or the onset of a small, trial traumatic reaction. The ego samples the results of this experimental conflict, searching for either safety or a small signal anxiety at the onset of a controlled and incipient traumatic state. The ego judges the potential outcome of further discharge by comparison of the induced traumatic state with the memory of previous traumata. The discharge is an active process, while the anxiety signal is automatic, impinging experimental-trauma upon the ego. It is through this testing that the ego, through the anxiety signal, becomes aware of danger. Over time this will lead to the automatic signaling of anxiety. In a later paper on intrapsychic conflict, Rangell (1963a) distinguished this process as a testing for either anxiety

---

[1]Earlier, Rangell (1954a) had studied the dynamics of similar states, for example, the state of being flustered, where the unexpectedness of the moment seizes the ego unaware and a mild, and transitory, state of helplessness ensues. The ego recovers, in most cases, fairly quickly and the helplessness subsides.

[2]Anna Freud's (1936) formulation offered a broader revision which included (1) loss of love, with separation from the source of narcissistic supply; (2) castration; (3) alienation of the superego; and (4) instinctual flooding (pp. 58–64). Given the nature of intense states of unpleasure Rangell also felt this more accurately reflected the childhood dangers.

or safety. Moore (1988) also noted the ego's use of such trial discharges and that fantasy may be central to this process.

Rangell believed that in his unitary theory of anxiety, the formulations of the actual neurotic state and signal anxiety are compatible and supports the view thatanxiety is always a response to danger. Rangell's (1955a) first anxiety paper demonstrated that the actual neurosis of Freud's first theory also results in the signal anxiety of the later theory, while his (Rangell, 1968a) second paper showed the reverse, that signal anxiety is preceded by an actual neurotic phase. This is in accord with the views of Kubie (1941), Spitz (1950), Schur (1953), Greenacre (1945), and others. Rangell, however, disagreed with Brenner (1953), Strachey (1959), and Wäelder (1936, 1967), who felt that Freud's first theory has been discarded. Rangell fused the two theories, as did Fenichel (1945). Although this line of research has not remained prominent in our field, it has foreshadowed the work of others. Rangell's approach is compatible with the psychoanalytic advances in understanding persons suffering from schizophrenia and borderline organizations (Abend, Porter, & Willick, 1983, 1988; Arlow, 1963; Bellak & Goldsmith, 1984; Bellak, Hurvich, & Gediman, 1973; Kernberg, 1967, 1975, 1984, 1986, 1992, 2003; Willick, 1990, 1993, 1994, 2001, 2002). Rangell's model is also compatible with recent neuroscience approaches. LeDoux (1996) identified the role of the amygdala in initiating the emotional fearful response, which is then elaborated and contextualized in the prefrontal cortex. There are efforts in the literature (Goldman, 2000; Marsh et al., 2008) to account for the conversion of more contextualized/organized/cognitive signal anxiety[3] into a more emotional disorganized traumatic anxiety. Rangell's model, following Greenacre (1941a, 1941b), maintains the belief that very early life experiences can shape behavior and can be stored in the brain in adulthood. One can make the case that Rangell's unitary model of anxiety has presaged the growing body of literature relating increased risk of psychopathology (e.g., ADHD, schizophrenia) to children of mothers exposed to severe stress or toxins during the first trimester of pregnancy (Kimhy, et al., 2006; Malaspina et al., 2008; Perrin et al., 2007; Richardson, Zorrilla, Mandyam, & Rivier, 2006; Weinstock, 2005).

---

[3]A neuroscience explanation might account for this regression as "amygdala overactivity."

From Intrapsychic Conflict to Intrapsychic Process

Rangell continued his effort to develop a total composite theory in a series of papers detailing the specific mental activities, which incrementally take place inthe unconscious, starting with the original stimulus and going on to the final psychic outcome. His ongoing elaboration of the unitary theory of anxiety (Rangell,1968a, 1978) parallels and supports his research into the sequential steps of intrapsychic conflict, which is ultimately expanded to the entire intrapsychic process.

Hartmann (1950) and Hartmann and Loewenstein (1962) had argued for the significance of intrasystemic conflicts. In a 1962 panel on the "significance ofintrapsychic conflict," Rangell and Arlow suggested the concept needed to be qualified (see Nemiah, 1963), and Rangell began to spell out the scope (1963a) and structural problems (1963b) of intrapsychic conflict.

Rangell (1963a) charted the progression of an unconscious conflict from the initiation of the precipitating stimulus to some final resolution. He (Rangell, 1989a, 1990) mapped out a model, or "microscopic view," of twelve steps that outline the process. To paraphrase these steps:

1. The ego samples reactions from the external world and superego by discharging a small amount of instinctual impulses, which are both tentative and experimental. The ego does this from an inactive and homeostatic state.
2. The ego automatically scans memories associatively connected to the intended actions.
3. The ego receives a danger signal accompanied by the affect of anxiety, or a signal of safety and freedom from anxiety.
4. The ego pursues the direct external activities when it receives the signal of safety.
5. The signal of anxiety signifies to the ego that there is a conflict.
6. If anxiety is mild and controllable the ego can pursue external activities (e.g., thought, affect, or action) similar to the processes it follows when it gets a safety signal.
7. Defense is instituted when anxiety crosses a quantitative threshold or is of a certain unbearable quality of unpleasure.
8. An intrapsychic state of poise develops when the psychic forces between ego and id find a balance.
9. If stability is lost and the id becomes stronger than the ego's capacity to contain it psychic tension builds.

10. This state is accompanied by anxiety rooted in the fear of traumatic helplessness.

11. Following receipt of the signal of anxiety, the ego is confronted with a choice or dilemma type of conflict, as to what to do next.

12. The variety of potential outcomes of ego action constitutes the great multiplicity of clinical phenomenology.

To reprise, the ego initially tests for the signal of anxiety. The ego initiates a series of trial actions. The ego then appraises the reactions from the superego and the external world to determine if either the signal of anxiety or of safety appears. If there is an anxiety signal, conflict has ensued. If there is not an anxiety signal, the ego indicates safety in movement toward the intended acts. This sequence mapping project by Rangell continued well into the 1980s. The sequence he outlined moves from dilemma/choice conflicts to oppositional conflicts and back again to dilemma/choice types with choices and compromise formation outcomes at different stages. His microscopic view contrasts with the "macroscopic view" of the clinical material seen in the therapeutic situation, where the manifest surface reflects derivatives of the underlying intrapsychic process.

Rangell (1967) defined the domain of psychoanalysis as the area of unconscious intrapsychic conflict. Studying this process is what separates it from the otherbehavioral sciences. He (Rangell, 1969b) later expanded the notion of unconscious intrapsychic conflict to the broader and more comprehensive concept of "the intrapsychic process." This more extensive view of mental functioning includes the outcomes of trial actions, which do not result in conflict. This is in harmony with both Hartmann's (1939) work on adaptation and the conflict-free sphere of ego functioning, and Rapaport's (1951, 1958) contributions on autonomy.

As Rangell continued to explore the unconscious process, he became more focused on the ego as agent, as the principle mediator that provided direction for life in the social and physical surround. He turned his attention to the final common pathway for the expression of action: "the unconscious decision-making function of the ego" (Rangell, 1986a, p. 102). This function is needed to resolve intrapsychic choice or dilemma conflicts. Unconscious decision making is involved in most aspects of psychic life. It is, Rangell notes, like "the psychological sea or air around us" (p. 426).

Rangell proposed that making choices and carrying out decisions among competitive alternatives is a key and essential unconscious function found in bothconflict and nonconflict spheres, such as, problem-solving activities which make "explicit 'a decision-making function of the ego' among the inventory of ego functions" (Rangell, 1969a, p. 599). This unconscious function of the ego must choose whether or not to institute defense or some other measure to deal with theanxiety once the danger has been perceived. When the signal of anxiety or safety has been estab-lished, the ego proceeds to unconscious decision making, which leads to an outcome: resolution of conflict, choice between alternatives (Rangell, 1969a, 1971), or compromise formations, which includes choice of com-promise, autonomous acts, or adaptive responses. The individual's per-sonal history of previous internal "solutions" determines the facilitating pathways that guide future alternatives so that these choices seem, at times, to be automatic or seamless. Over time choices are incorporated into durable character traits and fixed expectations from the individual. Rangell emphasizes that unconsciouschoice and the function of decision making are not always or automatically followed by compromise formations, even though this may be a major psychic outcome.Other possible outcomes may involve choice between alternatives (for example, the choice of one arm of a conflict over another), or instinctual discharge or denial. Rangell feels that both methods are operative, with countless variations of external psychic outcomes possible. Differing from Brenner (1982, 2006), Rangell points out that not every outcome of conflict is, or necessitates, or even can be a compromise.[4]

Both Rangell and Brenner (1982) would agree that aspects of drive derivatives, unpleasurable affects, defense, superego manifestations, and environmental influence all affect behavior. Brenner argues that com-promise formation is the basic unit of the mind. Rangell argues that uncon-

---

4 Rangell's finding on Unconscious decision making has found some support in the psychoanalytic literature (e.g., Bush, 1978; Druss, 1976; Gehl, 1973; Holzman & Aronson, 1992;Meissner, 1994; Power, 2000; Weiss, 1995); however, no studies or theoretical perspectives have deepened this work with new findings. Decision mak-ing continues to be of enormous interest to many fields including medicine, law, eco-nomics (e.g., behavioral economics and management theories), cognitive sciences, neuroscience, and political science. Unconscious decision making in the non psycho-analytic literature has also blossomed. We see evidence of the pursuit of this concept in economics (Simonson, 2005; Simonson & Nowlis, 2000; Zhou, Vohs, & Baumeister, 2009), cognitive neuroscience (Bechara, Damasio, & Damasio, 2000; Dijksterhuis, 2004; Dijksterhuis, Bos, Nordgren, & van Baaren, 2006; Soon, Brass, Heinze, & Haynes, 2008; Wilson, 2002). It is significant that the studies we reviewed in the nonpsychoanalytic literature did not reference Rangell's work. Our assumption is that psychoanalysis is still viewed by most disciplines as dealing primarily with the unconscious and have not caught up with theory development.

scious choice is a critical factor neglected by Brenner and most other psychoanalysts. He also emphasizes that unconscious choice and decision making are not limited to individuals without psychopathology. Whether behavior is pathological or not, outcome choice is made during the intrapsychic event sequence: "... filtering, scanning, judging, then deciding, choosing—whether defense, or adaptation, motility, etc." (Rangell, 1963b, p. 124). Symptoms, for Rangell, are as much an unconscious choice as normal behavioral outcomes. He notes that while we speak freely of choice of symptoms, we do not as readily acknowledge the unconscious choice to have symptoms at all.

This brings up the problem of "free will." Rangell (1986b, 1989a) differentiates free will from both the instinctual wish (the wish of early psychoanalytic theory) and from a superego demand or requirement. Free will is an ego faculty, a directing capacity that takes into account motivations from the id, superego, external reality, and the goals and intentions of the ego itself. For Rangell (1986b, 1989a), the extent of the presence of freedom of the will is a measure of the degree to which there is ego autonomy. Free will is not absolute but is on a spectrum that includes psychic determinism. Free will and psychic determinism define a complementary series in which there are no absolutes. Psychic determinism is derived from the instinctual wish; free will is the result of the active, directing, executive function of the unconscious ego that shapes intention and purpose and creates action. The operation of "relatively free will" is firmly rooted in unconscious intrapsychic activity. Relatively free will (relative autonomy) shares the psychic stage with determinism. For Rangell, there are forces that impinge on the person in daily life, from within and without. Rangell (1986b) concludes, "Human history, individual and collective, results from a combination of determinism, random occurrences, and the guided event" (p. 30). From the perspectives of psychic determinism, and degrees of ego freedom, he states that: "Life is a combination of what has to be, and what we make of that" (Rangell, 2004, p. 314).

Addressing the matter of mental functioning in social and political life, Rangell (1974) introduced the "syndrome of the compromise of integrity" (1974,1976, 1980, 2000c) as on par with neurosis in human affairs. Integrity, Rangell (2004) observed, relies upon a necessary willingness to live by superego values, and "where ego interests are high enough, the effectiveness of superego control lessens" (p. 198). The compromise of integrity is ubiquitous: It ranges from being ego syntonic to ego alien and falls on a continuum of psychopathology from mild to severe. While neuroses arise from conflicts between the ego and the id, the syndrome of the compromise of integrity is the outcome of conflicts between the ego and the superego. "Narcissism unbridled," he notes, "is the enemy of integrity" (Rangell, 1974, p. 8). These moral and ethical conflicts, like the subclinical neuroses, are built into ordinary human conduct and play a part in the psychopathology of everyday life. The syndrome of the compromise of integrity is to sociopathy and crime as the neurosis is to psychosis. The two sets of dynamics are not mutually exclusive, nor is either excluded from general intrapsychic dynamics. Rangell points out that ambition, power, and opportunism in the service of the ego are desired qualities sought after in our culture. These traits can become excessive in direct proportion to the reward wished for or expected, and any of these traits may be a prodrome for the pathological syndrome of integrity. Clinically, we see these excesses in greed and envy. Therapeutically, one addresses these conflicts as any other conflict, through analysis, with the analytic aim of "turning out an honest man," "one as much free of C. of I. [compromise of integrity] as neurosis, which is not complete in either case" (Rangell, 1974, p. 10). Here Rangell highlights the continuous pull from the interaction of the analytic relationship. This is not a cold, sterile engagement void of any genuine relationship. Instead, it is a fusion of empathy with objectivity. The advantage for the analyst lies in the relentless incorruptibility of the analytic attitude. In Rangell's (1974) words: "The scientific attitude of psychoanalysis is carried to the patient by a caring human. The capacity to achieve the proper blend between the two is one of the most difficult but necessary goals for training to impart" (p. 11).

This concludes our tracing of Rangell's expansion of theory on the model of the mind. The line of thought has taken us from anxiety, to active unconsciousdecision making, to breaches of integrity, and to questions of personal responsibility and accountability. In reviewing his own contributions, Rangell (2004)concludes that "man is both less responsible and more responsible than he thinks. Psychoanalysis has always exposed contradictions" (p. 202). Next we explore Rangell's contributions to the psychoanalytic process.

The Psychoanalytic Process

While Rangell wrestled with the complex functions of the ego he was also a practical clinician and believed that the final test of any idea was in the clinical realm. When assessing the range of Rangell's clinical contributions one must be cognizant of two distinct types of contributions: those related to the psychoanalytic core (1954b, 1968c, 1969b, 1975, 1979, 1981a, 1985b, 1989d, 1992, 1995, 1996, 2001b), and others written about specific clinical problem in the applications of technique (1954a, 1955b, 1959, 1966, 1968b, 1972, 1978, 1981b, 1982a, 1983, 1987, 1989a, 1989b, 1989c, 1991).

A Psychoanalytic Core

Contributions made to the psychoanalytic core concentrate on the technical procedure. This topic is part of the fabric of Rangell's "total composite theory." For Rangell (1992, 1995, 1996, 2001b), psychoanalytic change comes from strengthening the ego's control over anxiety,defense, trauma, and symptom formation. This psychoanalytic process is the psychoanalytic core.

Rangell (1954b, 1981b) first defined the ever-changing border between psychotherapy and psychoanalysis. In a 1953 panel (O'Neil & Rangell, 1954; Rangell, 1954b), "On Similarities and Differences between Psychoanalysis and Dynamic Psychotherapy," he focused on defining the borders of psychoanalysis as well as how to extend the borders, establishing a wider province, without losing the center. In 1953, he asserted that there are sharp demarcations between psychoanalysis and dynamic psychotherapy, and offered the following definition of psychoanalysis.

> Psychoanalysis is a method of therapy whereby conditions are brought about favorable for the development of a transference neurosis, in which the past is restored in the present, in order that, through a systematic interpretative attack on the resistances which oppose it, there occurs a resolution of that neurosis (transference and infantile) to the end of bringing about structural changes in the mental apparatus of the patient to make the latter capable of optimum adaptation to life (Rangell, 1954b, pp. 739–740).

There were crucial differences between psychoanalysis and dynamic psychotherapy. "One method is neither better nor worse, more or less praiseworthy than the others. There are indications and contraindications for each which must be applied on rational grounds. There is a spectrum of patients who require one or the othermethod and a spectrum of therapists able to do one or both" (Rangell, 1990, p. 484). The difference between psychoanalysis and psychotherapy is not based on differences in the basic views or conceptualization of psychopathology nor on a model of how the mind works. Rangell (1990) believed that both technical methods needed to rely on "a single correct estimation of psychodynamics and pathogenesis" (p. 478); both methods must "spring from the same rational and correct evaluation of the origins of mental disease, rather than on basically opposed or contrasting systems" (p. 478); and "the validity of the basic theories is certainly open to contest or revision which should be derived from endless clinical and experimental studies for whatever extensions or modifications are seen to hold true must then be applied equally to both disciplines" (p. 478). As early as 1953, Rangell took the position that there is a body ofknowledge, a science of psychoanalysis, that best explains the facts but that could change with new facts.

By 1979, the participants from the 1953 panel had undergone an apparent transitions. Rangell (1981b) was more comfortable with the essential aspects of treatments. He was less concerned with formal and logistic considerations—the number of times per week and the posture of the patient—than with the words and attitudes of the analyst. He had become more technically flexible, willing to see patients sitting up as well as lying down, conducted sessions on the telephone, sessions back-to-back, in regular schedules, and so on. For Rangell (1990), these 25 years had underscored the point that "the therapeutic process was determined not by outer mechanical but inner processes" (p. 488).

In his second paper on the distinction between the psychoanalysis and psychotherapy, Rangell (1981b) considered the divisive issues of the day and tried to demonstrate the unity between many of these discordant theoretical positions (e.g., transference vs. reconstruction, oedipal versus pre-oedipal or postoedipal, the cognitive-affective duality), as well as considering the negative therapeutic reaction and the fate of signal anxiety in the patient during the process of change. One of the problems with the emphasis on transference is that it can be overdone, obscuring the rest of the analytic process. Rangell (1981b) challenged the trend bytransference purists, those for whom "the centrality of transference has acquired almost a moral tone" (p. 675). He pointed out how this was a problem in the work of Gill (1979a, 1984) where "transference neurosis becomes the neurosis, that antecedents and genetic roots are not only out of reach but more and more become unnecessary" (Rangell, 1990, p. 549; also Rangell, 1979). Contrasting his position with Gill's, Rangell maintained, like Bird (1972), Gray (1973), and Stone (1981a, 1981b), that transference was the most difficult and subtle part of analysis. He (Rangell, 1990) highlighted the excessive dependence and the absence of working through. "Patients treated with excessive, even compulsive concentration on transference can emerge looking and feeling analyzed but with a pathetic and clone like quality of dependence. They cling to the analyst, can become devotees or even benefactors of analysis, but with a shallow defensiveness through which the opposite can break through" (p. 551). The same poor end result, he stated, can come from too little as from too much interpretation of transference, and countertransference can lead equally in either direction. Rangell offered three additional thoughts about the inherent limitations in transference and its relationship to other critical elements of the clinical method. The transference is not sufficient to capture the complex development of a neurosis (Rangell, 1981b, pp. 675, 676); transference was more likely to demonstrate issues of separation anxiety than castration anxiety or negative oedipal phenomena; and transference was not the best vehicle to reveal the patient's aggression.

Rangell (1981b) offers us a revised perspective of the transference, noting that new approaches tend to downplay the crucial role of insight in psychoanalysis: "Transference facilitates the approach to certain important aspects of neurosis without being able to recapitulate them in depth" (p. 677). He believed that all elements in an analysis (e.g., dreams, symptoms, character traits, material from the hour, the neurosis, and the analysis as a whole) required an understanding of the present, past, and transference, without an excessive attachment to any one. By highlighting that stress in a patient's life was not limited to the time of the original traumas but continues throughout life, he altered our perspective and revealed the broader scope of the analytic task. Transference became "a necessary but not sufficient condition to see an analysis through to its goal" (Rangell, 1981b, p. 675).

Rangell (1981b) evaluated other clinical phenomena (e.g., oedipal/pre-oedipal, cognitive/affective, and the complex nature of the therapeutic reaction) and concludes that most alternative schools contain within their systems important individual contributions that could have been supplemental to the total theory but that instead usually are immersed in "more global substitutes which detract and obscure, rather than clarify and expand" (p. 684). Their interests got stuck in one or more areas. In this regard, he referred to Erikson's ego identity, the self-object of Kohut and separately Kernberg, the self schema as a unit in George Klein's formulations, the whole person responsible for action in Schafer's work, and Green's emphasis on the defenses of splitting and decathexis. All could be seen as contributions to the larger theory. In later works, Rangell continued this train of thought, extending it to the nature of the self (1982b) and the object (1985a). Rangell (1990) asserted the self had always been part of the structural theory and that narcissism "does not delineate a specific segment of psychopathology but is as central as anxiety and as much to be dealt with in all patients" (pp. 504–505). He found similar problems with Kernberg's (1975) insistence on the predominance of the defenses of splitting and projective identification in borderline states, and with Green's (1975) replacement of separation and castration anxieties with the existential fear of death and/or fear of madness.

This highlights one of the values of Rangell's total composite theory. It allows one to follow the historical developments, the various points of view and various differences in psychoanalysis as they unfold. The two examples we have outlined so far are the differences between psychoanalysis and psychotherapy and the role of interpretation of the transference. Rangell tries to show how fateful certain definitions or definitional positions can be for the development of a psychoanalytic theoretician's thinking, for example, Kohut's distinction between narcissistic and object libido. In summary, Rangell (like Arlow, 1979, 2002; Jacobs [see Beland & Bergman, 2002]; and Stone, 1981a, 1981b) rejects privileging of any technical aspect of the psychoanalytic process until it is clinically called for. Transferenceanalysis has clearly been privileged by many analysts, in many different schools, as has defense analysis. He views the unfolding of the psychoanalytic process as immersing oneself in an understanding of the analysand's life. This process is facilitated technically by working with material closest to consciousness, with an understanding of its multidetermined derivatives and functions. For Rangell it is not frequency or furniture that make the difference between psychoanalysis anddynamic psychotherapy. The analysand might be seen on a four times a week basis and be on the couch, yet remain in intensive therapy. What distinguishes psychoanalysis from psychoanalytic psychotherapy, for Rangell, was the process that goes on between analyst and analysand. Where there is not a psychoanalytic process, there is not analysis. The condition of seeing a patient four times a week on the couch facilitates the process but does not define it.

The term "composite," which was later (Rangell, 1985a) be broadened to the "total composite theory," was introduced by Rangell (1969b) in his plenary address to the International Psychoanalytic Congress in Rome. The theme of this Congress was "Recent Developments in Psychoanalysis." In that paper, after presenting his views on the "human core," Rangell (1969b) showed how the intrapsychic process moves from the core to the periphery and back. This interactive process situated clinical practice closer to external action and had a specific impact on technique, as well as on research and current social issues. Clinically, he(Rangell, 1990) noted, "one is confronted by a composite mass, an aggregate consisting of diverse elements" (p. 518). Technically, the task is to deconstruct, to "decompose, de-stratify, analyze, break up the agglutinated whole into its component parts, and set the latter into their proper order, into their logical syntactical relationships, according to cause and effect" (Rangell, 1990, p. 518). Here Rangell noted aphoristically, "the psychoanalytic process is the intrapsychic process under supervision" (1990, p. 519; also 1969b). In that vein, he offered some thoughts on the concept of the therapeutic alliance popular at the time. "The therapeutic alliance in analysis is, in my opinion, between the analyzing function of the analyst and the observing, critical and judging functions of the ego of the patient, i.e., between the analyst and the healthy part of the patient's ego" (Rangell, 1990, p. 523). Rangell pointed out the commonality of his views with those of Bibring (1937) and Arlow and Brenner (1966), and this led to another clinical contribution—the psychoanalytic process (Rangell, 1968c).

Rangell (1990) offers an interesting account of what happened in psychoanalysis: "Only in psychoanalysis, under the protection of the analytic situation, is the patient motivated and willing to produce voluntary psychic disequilibria in a regressive path toward such original nuclear etiological situations" (pp. 540–541).

Rangell (1990) emphasizes the analyst as a "stabilizing, predictable, and unswerving object around which the patient's regressions and undulations can safely occur if they are to have the possibility of coming back" (p. 543). Here Rangell emphasized that symptom analysis, although important, plays only a small part in psychoanalysis. The analytic process for Rangell takes place in the patient, as the patient identifies with the analyst's analytic functions, (i.e., the analyst's rational, observing, understanding, objective, scientific views). The core of this process, that is, self analysis, outlives the analysis in the postanalytic phase.

Psychoanalysis: Critical Conversations . . . Arnold D. Richards

Applications

Specific clinical issues in the applications of technique include the components at the core of psychoanalytic treatment, in the process of change. Here Rangell returns from the more abstract and moves closer to the experience-near. In "On Defense and Resistance," Rangell (1983) looked at the present status of these subjects fifty years after Anna Freud's classic book on the topic. In "On Understanding and Treating Anxiety," Rangell (1978) followed anxiety from its theoretical centrality to its role throughout the clinical treatment situation. Other papers examine the nature of structural change (1989a, 1989c), the core of the treatment process (1987), the phases of insight and after insight (1980–1981), and the termination phase (1966, 1982a).

In the contribution, "Defense and Resistance in Psychoanalysis and Life," Rangell (1983) described what he believed was a very common characteristic of Freud's thinking and of the thinking of some of his successors as well, including Anna Freud, namely, the tendency to divide larger categories into their componentparts: "The principle followed was the same. In regard to the understanding of larger groups as composed of smaller ones" (p. 154). Rangell observed that there was also an opposition and resistance to distinguish part processes within the whole, as if it "does violence to the subjective integrity of the individual" (p. 155). He cites the work of Rogers, Horney, Sullivan, and, more recently, Kohut, Klein, and Gedo as examples and stated: "A common motivation for the followers of these theories is the feeling that scientific decomposition of the mental apparatus is somehow accompanied by psychological fragmentation of the person or personality or in the latest theory ofthe self (p. 155). Rangell, however, believed that mainstream psychoanalytic theoretical development retained the importance of integration as "a parallel process and principle alongside the process of differentiation" (p. 156). Relevant here is the ego's "synthetic function," described by Nunberg (1931); the "organizing, integrating function" described by Hartmann (1950); and, of course, the "unconscious ego decision-making executive function" described by Rangell (1969a,1971). "The road to healthy integration in analysis is differentiation and reintegration, by destratification of clinical aggregates and their resynthesis into more stable and adaptive wholes" (Rangell, 1983, p. 161).

Rangell (1989c), leaning on the work of Spitz, Anna Freud, Brazelton, and Stern, as well as Greenacre, noted the continued importance of preoedipal issues throughout psychoanalytic literature. He warned, however, against the overuse of some concepts and gave as an illustration Mahler's "rapprochement crisis." Rangell was concerned about its overuse as a specific etiological determinant of pathology. He pointed to Socarides and the Tysons for their primary reliance on the concept to explain the etiology of perversion and pseudonarcissistic personality. Rangell (1989c) writes that the term rapprochement should take "its place alongside all such universal tools of insight. But its enlistment as a distinct memory or as a developmental year or few months of specifically experienced anxiety, trauma ordepression cannot be automatically pointed to, or taken for granted from universal knowledge, as an individually exposed and remembered event or condition or series of experiences (p. 28). He concluded, "Psychopathology stands on a base, not a point" (p. 28).

It is in remarks such as this that Rangell, who so often is taken as the representative of an outdated and ossified classical Freudian theory, demonstrates an outlook that preempts the criticisms of would-be revisionists. In these papers, he has elaborated the developed body of Freudian thought in a way that highlights its long-standing attention to both wholes and parts. While he rejects any easy dichotomy that would identify a psychology of the whole as humanistic and a psychology of the parts as mechanistic, he (1990) insists that "the self, and the object, as whole entities, have always had a firm place in central unified psychoanalytic theory" (p. 6). That theory is not ego psychology but a total composite psychoanalytic theory, embracing id, ego, and superego, as well as the external world. Pluralism is not an option for Rangell. Borrowing from Fenichel's axiom, Rangell believes, "There are many ways to treat neuroses but there is only one way to understand them" (quoted in Rangell, 2004, p. 52). Resisting the widespread tendency to characterize the classical position narrowly as drive theory or ego psychology or structural theory, Rangell presents an approach whose aim is to render unnecessary a plurality of competing theories.

Models of Theory

Rangell believes that the main problem for psychoanalysis today is the current state of theoretical pluralism. He has repeatedly outlined (1988, 1997, 2000a, 2000b, 2000c, 2002b, 2002c, 2004, 2006, 2007a, 2007b, 2008) his view of how pluralism has cumulatively been the most erosive force to psychoanalysis leaving it fragmented and deadlocked. Ultimately the problem of pluralism shakes the confidence of the psychoanalytic consumer and inspires doubt and insecurity. "Is it acceptable" Rangell (2007b) asks, "that a patient should turn out to have an Oedipal conflict or a problem with self-cohesion depending on which analyst he is with?" (p. 7). Tracing the array of pertinent historical players and incidents Rangell (2004) outlined the development of pluralism beginning with Freud. Here he proposed that the early fractures with Jung, Adler, and Rank, which resulted in their official separation from the field, fashioned the prototype models for future splits. Rangell (1982c) detailed how a powerful dynamic leadership could become a negative force in theory development, due to a phenomenon he calls "transference to theory." After the first split, Rangell identified the second series of splits beginning with Horney, Sullivan, and Fromm as they attempted to show how political, economic, and interpersonal forces affect the individual. Next were the splits after the war that cut across ideological lines between Otto Fenichel and Franz Alexander on the topic of the analytic attitude and its technical implications. This contributed to the organizational splits in Los Angeles, New York, Philadelphia, and Washington-Baltimore. The 1960s saw further fragmentation with the arrival of Melanie Klein's work to the United States and the advocacy of "two theories" by George Klein and his colleagues Gill, Holt, Schafer, and others. This was quickly followed by Kohut in the 1970s and the organization of Self Psychology. Finally, Rangell believed that pluralism was given a quasi-official sanction by Wallerstein (1988, 1991) in his 1987 Presidential Address of the International Psychoanalytic Association (IPA). This last finding was challenged by Wallerstein and led to an interesting discussion between these two theorists (Rangell, 2006, 2007a; Wallerstein, 2007).

Rangell (2004, 2007b) showed how the various stages in the emergence of pluralism were fostered by four basic fallacies. The first is the replacement of a preexisting set of observations or parts of explanatory theory by another when both new and old are valid. The second is the pathogenic fallacy—"pars pro toto"—a selection of a part and its replacement for the whole. Parallel to this is the simple discarding of necessary elements within the whole. The third illogical position is when knowledge and insight gained in one sphere are not aptly applied to related relevant situations. Finally, the fourth logical flaw is the failure to follow up one's thought or actions with the consequences that could be expected from new discoveries or insights. This treatment of theory construction has led to a drifting of the theory with no real efforts at "retention of consistency or intellectual unity" (Rangell, 2007b,

p. 99). Instead, we have the current state of theoretical pluralism and its consequential fragmentation.

Paralleling these splits, the evolving character of the total composite theory is traced by Rangell. He sees the first total composite theory beginning with Freud's five metapsychological points of view: topographic, economic, dynamic, genetic, and structural. The second phase of the total composite theory includes all that is encompassed under the condensed title of Ego Psychology. This not only adds the adaptive point of view, outlined by Hartmann, to the original metapsychology, but ushers in a major transition in the technique with the focus on defense analysis begun by Freud and carried on by Anna Freud. It also accounts for much of the advances in the genetic perspective introduced during this time (e.g., works by Anna Freud, Phyllis Green-acre, Edith Jacobson, Margaret Mahler, Rene Spitz, and Donald Winnicott).

Rangell worked to separate the consequence of what, he noted, Richards (1999) had identified as the "politics of exclusion," which Richards felt has contributed to both the disenfranchised state of lay analysts and the proliferation of alternative theories. Rangell agrees with the first claim but not the latter. He believes that these two important issues are temporally entangled but must be teased apart and treated separately. Ultimately, where the law may be relevant to the issue of lay analysis, it is "hardly the arbiter in science" (Rangell, 2007b, p. 52). Rangell further teased out some historical antecedents, located psychoanalysis in psychology via Freud (1926), and underscored the importance but not primacy of neurology and medicine in general. Like Freud, Rangell is advocating for a biopsychosocial model where the clinical findings are core and feed other ancillary applications.

How then does pluralism affect technique? Rangell answers this question by observing that small innovations in technique have become exaggerated into major dimensions of treatment. He notes that this is not only a prime example of pars pro toto (i.e., ascension of the part to the whole) but often the result of atransference to theory. Rangell (2007b) reviewed the leading themes of self-disclosure, enactment, and intersubjectivity and concluded that "these [are] irrational incursions into the analytic instrument itself, and through that into the analytic process, which need to be recognized and corrected. . . . It is as though laxity and lapses, which may be unavoidable, are regarded instead as flexibility, which is desirable" (p. 83).

To correct this view, Rangell follows Fenichel's adage that "treatment is through the rational ego" and that technique "must be arranged according to rational criteria" (Fenichel, 1941, p. 13, quoted in Rangell, 2007b, p. 83). This does not imply technical rigidity, but highlights the aim of explaining the irrational by the rational. Yet the technical "variations . . . challenging clinical phenomena in a general psychoanalytic practice are as infinite as people are" (Rangell, 2007b, p. 83).

Rangell (1988, 1997, 2000b, 2004, 2006, 2007b) proposes a single "total composite psychoanalytic theory," a theory that is cohesive and cumulative, aiming at "completeness with parsimony" (Rangell, 2007b, p. 116): *"total"*—containing all nonexpendable elements; *"composite"*— a blend of all valid discoveries; and *"psychoanalytic"*—fulfilling the criteria of psychoanalysis (Rangell, 2007b, p. 85). The total composite psychoanalytic theory continues to develop alongside of the alternative partial theories growing as new clinical evidence is established. This is the third wave of such a total composite theory. What is accepted into the theory is decided by both the collective and the individual. For Rangell this includes every viable contribution, including Freud's five meta-psychological points of view and the sixth added by Rapaport and Gill (1959), the adaptive point of view. Contributions converge from many directions and all follow the principle of the complementary series: attachment and separation, conflict and adaptation, neutrality and empathy, drive and object, tragic and guilty man, historical and narrativetruth. Referring to the work of Reed and Baudry (1997), Rangell (2007b) believes that three basic questions are crucial to the debate about divergent theories: "What clinical observations make the innovations necessary? Is the revision independent or does it link to or depend on some unrecognized aspect of previous theory? Does the new theory contradict some aspect of previous theory on which it silently depends?" (p. 101). Following Freud, Rangell envisions the field as an overall science of man. The mind develops and is cultivated by its physical and social environment and is studied accordingly.

Considering himself not a contemporary Freudian but "a developed Freudian," Rangell believes that a unitary theory remains elusive for reasons that are overdetermined. First, there is a cultural influence that stems from the deep and pervasive affective pull toward diversity and away from unity. Rangell identifies this as particularly relevant to our society, highlighted in the concept of the "rugged individual." It was also noted by Freud (1926): "It is remarkable that, little as men are able to exist in isolation, they should nevertheless feel as a heavy burden the sacrifices which civilization expects of them in order to make a communal life possible" (p. 6). Next, there is a developmental pull to separate and attach. Then there is a group pull in which people refuse to go along with convention but dread being different. As noted earlier, there is also a pull from the transference to theory and, perhaps the ultimate influence, there is identification with theory. "An analyst becomes 'a self psychologist,' 'a classicist,' or 'a Kleinian,' not one who simply thinks that way" (Rangell, 2007b, p. 94).

In a recent work, Rangell (2007b) makes a strong appeal for unity and internal reconciliation. Rangell, and from another perspective Brenner (2006), hold out the ideal of a scientific psychoanalytic theory. To reach this ideal, clinical data will need to continue to be gathered in a variety of ways within diverse clinical contexts. When emerging theoretical constructs are left to their domains of origin, however, they remain categorical in nature and nonintegrated. Here we find the "ferocity of the emotions involved in the controversies" that Bergmann (2004) spoke of (p. 263), but it is also where all too often we find stagnation. As these concepts are shared by the various domains their integral nature emerges and a chance for integration appears. We have seen this recently in the literature on actualizations and enactments (Lynch, Bachant, & Richards, 2008). This maybe one subtle characteristic of theory change that does not require a new scientific paradigm shift. At the same time, several theorists (Boesky, 2008; Reeder, 2002; Richards, 2003; Richards & Lynch, 2008; Summers, 2008; Willock, 2007) are attempting to create comparative models or methods to more rigorously assess the contributions of the various schools.[5]

---

[5]We (Richards & Lynch, 2008) see the value of understanding psychoanalysis as a natural science, as put forth by Rangell (2007b) and Brenner (2006). In this view, science is a way of looking at the world guided by facts. Facts are not immutable truths (Brenner, 2006) but amenable to pragmatic confirmation or denial. Freud (1893) recognized this, frequently quoting Charcot's aphorism: "Theory is good; but it doesn't prevent things from existing" (p. 13). The scientific point of view requires that theory be the best explanation that one can give to the facts. In this way, science remains an ideal for psychoanalysis. How do we arrive at this ideal state of science? Clinical evidence progresses toward scientific evidence as it moves on a continuum of substantiation: from discovery through a hermeneutic practice, to the continuous repetition and validation of the findings, to the ultimate creation of testable hypotheses from internal and external sources. In our current pluralistic world, contributions come from many perspectives. These diverse perspectives should continue to be nurtured, contributed to, and substantiated. Welcoming these contributions is the organization of theory. This can only be done by productive communication and discourse. Every advocate must be given the opportunity to present her or his position as clearly and forcefully as possible, to the widest audience available.

In his journey to become a "developed Freudian," Rangell has made an enormous contribution to the literature and to the field. Arlow (1988) best summed this up in his appreciation to Rangell: He "has made an indelible mark on the development of psychoanalysis in our time, not only in the United States but in the rest of the world as well." Whether you agree with Rangell or not, the breadth and depth of his work reminds us just how complex our work is. To this end he has succeeded brilliantly.

REFERENCES

ABEND, S.M., PORDER, M.S., & WILLICK, M.S. (1983). Borderline patients: Psychoanalytic Perspectives Kris Study Group, New York Psychoanal. Institute, Monogr. 7. New York: International Universities Press.
——————— (1988). A Response. *Psychoanalytic Inquiry* 8:438–455.
ARLOW, J.A. (1963). Conflict, regression and symptom formation. *International Journal of Psychoanalysis* 44:12–22.
——— (1979). The genesis of interpretation. *Journal of the American Psychoanalytic Association* 27(Suppl.):193–206.
——— (1988). Leo Rangell: An appreciation. *Psychoanalytic Quarterly* 57:297–301.
——— (2002). Transference as defense. *Journal of the American Psychoanalytic Association* 50:1139–1150.
——— & Brenner, C. (1966). The psychoanalytic situation. In P. E. Litman, ed., *Psychoanalysis in the Americas* (pp. 23–43). New York: International Universities Press.
BECHARA, A., DAMASIO, H., & DAMASIO, A.R. (2000). emotion, decision making and the orbitofrontal cortex. *Cerebral Cortex*, 10(3):295–307.
BELAND, H., & BERGMAN, A. (2002). Changing psychoanalytic psychotherapy into psychoanalysis. *International Journal of Psychoanalysis* 83:245–247.
BELLAK, L. & GOLDSMITH, L., Eds. (1984). *The Broad Scope of Ego Function Assessment.* New York: Wiley.
——— ——— HURVICH, M & GEDIMAN, H. (1973). *Ego Functions in Schizophrenics, Neurotics and Normals.* New York: Wiley.
BERGMANN, M. (2004). *Understanding Dissidence and, Controversy in the History of Psychoanalysis.* New York: Other Press.
BIBRING, E. (1937). Therapeutic results of psychoanalysis. *International Journal of Psychoanalysis* 18:170–189.
——— (1953). The mechanism of depression. In P. Greenacre, ed., *Affective Disorders* (pp. 13–48). New York: International Universities Press.
BIRD, B. (1972). Notes on transference: Universal phenomenon and hardest

part of analysis. *Journal of the American Psychoanalytic Association* 20:267–301.

BOESKY, D. (2008). *Psychoanalytic Disagreements in Context.* New York: Aronson.

BRENNER, C. (1953). An addendum to Freud's theory of anxiety. *International Journal of Psychoanalysis* 34:18–24.

———— (1982). *The Mind in Conflict.* New York: International Universities Press.

———— (2006). *Psychoanalysis or Mind and Meaning. Psychoanalytic Quarterly Monograph.* New York: Psychoanalytic Quarterly.

BUSH, M. (1978). Preliminary considerations for a psychoanalytic theory of insight: Historical perspective. *International Reviwe of Psycho-Analysis*5:1–13.

DIJKSTERHUIS, A. (2004). Think different: The merits of unconscious thought in preference development and decision making. *Journal of Personality and Social Psychology* 87:586–598.

———— BOS, M.W., NORDGREN, L.F., & VAN BAAREN, R.B. (2006). On making the right choice: The deliberation-without-attention effect. *Science,* 311(5763):1005–1007.

DRUSS, R.G. (1976). Indecision and orality. *International Reviwe of Psycho-Analysis*3:203–207.

FENICHEL, O. (1941). *Problems of Psychoanalytic Technique. Psychoanalytic Quarterly Monograph.*New York: Psychoanalytic Quarterly.

———— (1945). The psychoanalytic theory of neurosis. New York: Norton.

FREUD, A. (1936). *The Ego and the Mechanisms of Defense.* New York: International Universities Press, 1946.

FREUD, S. (1893). Charcot. *Standard Edition* 3:7–23.

———— (1894). The neuro-psychoses of defence. *Standard Edition* 3: 41–61.

———— (1895). On the grounds for detaching a particular syndrome from neurasthenia under the description "anxiety neurosis." *Standard Edition* 3:85–115.

———— (1923). The ego and the id. *Standard Edition* 19:3–66.

———— (1959). Inhibitions, symptoms, and anxiety. *Standard Edition* 20:75–175.

GEHL, R.H. (1973). Indecision and claustrophobia. *International Journal of Psychoanalysis* 54:47–59.

GILL, M.M. (1979a). The analysis of the transference. *Journal of the American Psychoanalytic Association* 27S:263–288.

———— (1984). Psychoanalysis and psychotherapy: A revision. *International Review of Psycho-Analysis* 161–179.

GOLDMAN, D.S. (2000). Application of Ledoux's neurobiological findings in treating anxiety disorders. *Journal of the American Academy of*

Psychoanalysis and Dynamic Psychiatry 28:701–716.

GRAY, P. (1973). Psychoanalytic technique and the ego's capacity for viewing intrapsychic activity. *Journal of the American Psychoanalytic Association* 21:474–494.

GREEN, A. (1975). The analyst, symbolization and absence in the analytic setting: On changes in analytic practice and analytic experience. *International Journal of Psychoanalysis* 56:1–22.

GREENACRE, P. (1941a). The predisposition to anxiety (Part 1). *Psychoanalytic Quarterly* 10:66–94.

———— (1941b). The predisposition to anxiety (Part 2). *Psychoanalytic Quarterly* 10:66–94.

———— (1945). The biological economy of birth. In *Psychoanalytic Study of the Child* 1:31–51.

HARTMANN, H. (1939). Ego psychology and the problem of adaptation New York: International Universities Press, 1958.

———— (1950). Comments on the psychoanalytic theory of the ego. *Psychoanal. St. Child*, 5:74–96.

———— & LOEWENSTEIN, R.M. (1962). Notes on the superego. *Psychoanalytic Study of the Child* 17:42–81.

HOLZMAN, P.S., & ARONSON, G. (1992). Psychoanalysis and its neighboring sciences: Paradigms and opportunities. *Journal of the American Psychoanalytic Association* 40:63–88.

KERNBERG, O. (1967). Borderline personality organization. *Journal of the American Psychoanalytic Association* 15:641–685.

———— (1975). Borderline conditions and pathological narcissism. New York: Aronson.

———— (1984). Severe personality disorders. New Haven, Conn.: Yale University Press.

———— (1986). Identification and its vicissitudes as observed in psychosis. *International Journal of Psychoanalysis* 67:147–158.

———— (1992), Aggression in personality disorders and perversions. New Haven, Conn.: Yale University Press.

———— (2003). The management of affect storms in the psychoanalytic psychotherapy of borderline patients. *Journal of the American Psychoanalytic Association* 51:517–544.

KIMHY, D., HARLAP, S., FENNIG, S., DEUTSCH, L., DRAIMAN, B.G., CORCORAN, C., GOETZ, D., NAHON, D., & MALASPINA, D. (2006). Maternal household crowding during pregnancy and the offspring's risk of schizophrenia. *Schizophrenia Res.*, 86(1–3):23–29.

KLEIN, M. (1946). Notes on some schizoid mechanisms *International Journal of Psychoanalysis* 27:99–110.

KUBIE, L.S. (1941). A physiological approach to the concept of anxiety.

Psychosomatic Medicine 3:263–276.

LeDoux, J. (1996). *The Emotional Brain: the Mysterious Underpinnings of Emotional Life.* New York: Simon & Shuster.

Lynch, A.A., Bachant, J.L., & Richards, A.D. (2008). Erotic transference and the spectrum of interaction. Online at: http://internationalpsychoanalysis.net/wp-content/uploads/2008/03/bachantlynchpresentation15.pdf

Malaspina, D., Corcoran, C., Kleinhaus, K.R., Perrin, M. C., Fennig, S., Nahon, D., Friedeander, Y., & Harlap, S. (2008). Acute maternal stress in pregnancy and schizophrenia in offspring: A cohort prospective study. *BMC Psychiatry* 8:71.

Marsh, A. A., Finger, E. C., Mitchell, D. G., Reid, M. E., Sims, C., Kosson, D. S., Towbin, K. E., Leibenluft, E., Pine, D. S., & Blair, R.J.R. (2008). Reduced amygdala response to fearful expressions in children and adolescents with callous-unemotional traits and disruptive behavior disorders. *Am. J. Psychiatry*, 165:712–720.

Meissner, W. W. (1994). Psychoanalysis and ethics: Beyond the pleasure principle. *Contermporary Psychoanalysis* 30:453–472.

Moore, B.E. (1988). On affects: Biological and developmental perspectives. In H. P. Blum, Y. Kramer, A. K. Richards, & A. D. Richards, eds., Fantasy, Myth, and Reality: Essays in honor of Jacob A. Arlow (pp. 401–419). Madison, Conn: International Universities Press.

Nemiah, J.C. (1963). The significance of intrapsychic conflict. *Journal of the American Psychoanalytic Association* 11:619–627.

Nunberg, H. (1931). The synthetic function of the ego. *International Journal of Psychoanalysis* 12:123–140.

O'Neil, M., & Rangell, L. (1954). Panel Reports—Annual Meeting, 1953: I. Psychoanalysis and dynamic psychotherapy: Similarities and differences. *Journal of the American Psychoanalytic Association* 2:152–166.

Perrin, M. C., Opler, M. G., Harlap, S., Harkavy-Eriedman, J., Kleinhaus, K., Nahon, D., Fennig, S., Susser, E. S., & Malaspina, D. (2007). Tetrachloroethylene exposure and risk of schizophrenia: Offspring of dry cleaners in a population birth cohort, preliminary findings. *Schizophrenia Res.*, 90(1–3):251–254.

Power, D. G. (2000). On trying something new: Effort and practice in psychoanalytic change. *Psychoanalytic Quarterly* 69(3):493–526.

Rangell, L. (1954a). The psychology of poise, with a special elaboration on the psychic significance of the snout or perioral region. *International Journal of Psychoanalysis* 35:313–332.

——— (1954b). Similarities and differences between psychoanalysis and dynamic psychotherapy. *Journal of the American Psychoanalytic Association* 2:734–744.

———— (1955a). On the psychoanalytic theory of anxiety: A statement of a unitary theory. *Journal of the American Psychoanalytic Association* 3:389–414.

———— (1955b). The role of the parent in the Oedipus complex. *Bulletin of the Menninger Clinic* 19:9–15.

———— (1959). The nature of conversion. *Journal of the American Psychoanalytic Association* 7:632–662.

———— (1963a). The scope of intrapsychic conflict: Microscopic and macroscopic considerations. *Psychoanal. St. Child*, 18:75–102.

———— (1963b). Structural problems in intrapsychic conflict. *Psychoanal. St. Child*, 18:103–138.

———— (1966). An overview of the ending of an analysis. In R.E. Litman, ed., *Psychoanalysis in the Americas* (pp. 141–165). New York: International Universities Press.

———— (1967). Psychoanalysis, affects, and the "human core": On the relationship of psychoanalysis to the behavioral sciences. *Psychoanalytic Quarterly* 36:172–202.

———— (1968a). A further attempt to resolve the "problem of anxiety." *Journal of the American Psychoanalytic Association* 16:371–404.

———— (1968b). A point of view on acting out. *International Journal of Psychoanalysis* 49:195–201.

———— (1968c). The psychoanalytic process. *International Journal of Psychoanalysis* 49:19–26.

———— (1969a). Choice-conflict and the decision-making function of the ego: A psychoanalytic contribution to decision theory. *International Journal of Psychoanalysis* 50:599–602.

———— (1969b). The intrapsychic process and its analysis: A recent line of thought and its current implications. *International Journal of Psychoanalysis* 50:65–77.

———— (1971). The decision-making process: A contribution from psychoanalysis. *Psychoanal. St. Child*, 26:425–452.

———— (1972). Aggression, Oedipus and historical perspective. *International Journal of Psychoanalysis* 53:3–22.

———— (1974). A psychoanalytic perspective leading currently to the syndrome of the compromise of integrity. *International Journal of Psychoanalysis* 55:3–12.

———— (1975). Psychoanalysis and the process of change: An essay on the past, present and future. *International Journal of Psychoanalysis* 56:87–98.

———— (1976). Lessons from Watergate: A derivative for psychoanalysis. *Psychoanalytic Quarterly* 45:37–61.

———— (1978). On understanding and treating anxiety and its derivatives.

International Journal of Psychoanalysis 59:229–236.

—— (1979). Contemporary issues in the theory of therapy. *Journal of the American Psychoanalytic Association* (Suppl.), 27:81–112.

—— (1980). The mind of Watergate. New York: Norton.

—— (1980–1981). Some notes on the post analytic phase. *International Journal of Psychoanalytic Psychotherapy* 8:165–170.

—— (1981a). From insight to change. *Journal of the American Psychoanalytic Association* 29:119–141.

—— (1980–1981). Some notes on the post analytic phase. *International Journal of Psychoanalytic Psychotherapy* 8:165–170.

—— (1981b). Psychoanalysis and dynamic psychotherapy: Similarities and differences twenty-five years later. *Psychoanalytic Quarterly* 50:665–693.

—— (1982a). Some thoughts on termination. *Psychoanalytic Inquiry* 2:367–392.

—— (1982b). This self in psychoanalytic theory. *Journal of the American Psychoanalytic Association* 30:863–892.

—— (1982c). Transference to theory: The relationship of psychoanalytic education to the analyst's relationship to psychoanalysis. *Annu. Psychoanal.*, 10:29–56.

—— (1983). Defense and resistance in psychoanalysis and Life. *Journal of the American Psychoanalytic Association* 31:147–174.

—— (1985a). The object in psychoanalytic theory. *Journal of the American Psychoanalytic Association* 33:301–334.

—— (1985b). On the theory of theory in psychoanalysis and the relationship of theory to psychoanalytic therapy. *Journal of the American Psychoanalytic Association* 33:167–185.

—— (1986a). The enduring armature of psychoanalytic theory and method. In A. D. Richards & M. Willick, eds., Psychoanalysis, the Science of Mental Conflict (pp. 89–106). Hillsdale, N.J.: Analytic Press.

—— (1986b). The executive functions of the ego: An extension of the concept of ego autonomy. *Psychoanalytic Study of the Child* 41:1–37.

—— (1987). A core process in psychoanalytic treatment. *Psychoanalytic Quarterly* 56:222–249.

—— (1988). The future of psychoanalysis: The scientific crossroads. *Psychoanalytic Quarterly* 57:313–340.

—— (1989a). Action theory within the structural view. *International Journal of Psychoanalysis* 70:189–203.

—— (1989b). The analysis of defense: The ego and the mechanisms of defense revisited. By Joseph Sandler with Anna Freud [Book review]. *Journal of the American Psychoanalytic Association* 37:245–251.

—— (1989c). Rapprochement and other crises: The specific and nonspecific in analytic reconstruction. *Psychoanal. St. Child* 44:19–39.

———— (1989d). Structural and interstructural change in psychoanalytic treatment. *Psychoanalytic Inquiry* 9:45–66.

———— (1990). The Human Core: the Intrapsychic Base of Behavior, 2 vols. Madison, Conn.: International Universities Press.

———— (1991). Castration. *Journal of the American Psychoanalytic Association* 39:3–23.

———— (1992). The psychoanalytic theory of change. *International Journal of Psychoanalysis* 73:415–428.

———— (1995). Psychoanalytic realities and the analytic goal. *International Journal of Psychoanalysis* 76:15–18.

———— (1996). The "analytic" in psychoanalytic treatment: How analysis works. *Psychoanalytic Inquiry* 16(2):140–166.

———— (1997). Into the second psychoanalytic century: One psychoanalysis or many? The unitary theory of Leo Rangell, MD. *Journal of Clinical Psychoanalysis* 6:451–612.

———— (2000a). Psyche and soma: Leaps and continuities. *Journal of Clinical Psychoanalysis* 9:173–200.

———— (2000b). Psychoanalysis at the millennium: A unitary theory. *Psychoanal. Psychol.*, 17:451–466.

———— (2000c). A psychoanalytic view of the impeachment process: The psychoanalysis of hypocrisy. *Psychoanal Dial.*, 10(2):309–313.

———— (2001a). Affects and power. *Psychoanal. Psychol.*, 18:656–666.

———— (2001b). Psychoanalytic psychotherapy: The enduring legacy of psychoanalysis. *Psychoanal. Rev.*, 88:1–14.

———— (2002a). Discussion of Brenner's "Reflections on Psychoanalysis"— and parallel reflections.*Journal of Clinical Psychoanalysis*11:96–114.

———— (2002b). Mind, body, and psychoanalysis: The science of psychotherapy. *Psychoanal. Psychol.*, 19:634–650.

———— (2002c). The theory of psychoanalysis: Vicissitudes of its evolution. *Journal of the American Psychoanalytic Association* 50:1109–1137.

———— (2004). My life in theory. New York: Other Press.

———— (2006). An analysis of the course of psychoanalysis: The case for a unitary theory. *Psychoanal. Psychol.*, 23(2): 217–238.

———— (2007a). Response to Dr. Wallerstein: Part 1. *Psychoanal. Psychol.*, 24(3):510–514.

———— (2007b). The road to unity in psychoanalytic theory. New York: Aronson.

———— (2008). Reconciliation: The continuing role of theory. *Journal of the American Academy of Psychoanalysis and Dynamic Psychiatry* 36(2):217–235.

RAPAPORT, D. (1951). The autonomy of the ego. *Bulletin of the Menninger*

Clinic 15:113–123.

———— (1954, March 5). Activity and passivity. Paper presented at the meeting of the Los Angeles Psychoanalytic Society.

———— (1958). The theory of ego autonomy: A generalization. *Bulletin of the Menninger Clinic* 22:15–35.

———— (1954, March 5). Activity and passivity. Paper presented at the meeting of the Los Angeles Psychoanalytic Society.

———— & Gill, M.M. (1959). The points of view and assumptions of metapsychology. *International Journal of Psychoanalysis* 40:153–162.

REED, G S., & BAUDRY, F. (1997). The logic of controversy: Susan Isaacs and Anna Freud on f(ph)antasy. *Journal of the American Psychoanalytic Association* 45:465–490.

REEDER, J. (2002). Reflecting psychoanalysis: Narrative and resolve in the psychoanalytic experience. New York: Karnac.

RICHARDS, A.D. (1999). A. A. Brill and the politics of exclusion. *Journal of the American Psychoanalytic Association* 47:9–28.

———— 2003). Psychoanalytic discourse at the turn of our century: A plea for a measure of humility. *Journal of the American Psychoanalytic Association* 51S:(S) 73–89.

———— & LYNCH, A.A. (2008). The identity of psychoanalysis and psychoanalysts. *Psychoanal. Psychol.*, 25:203–219.

RICHARDSON, H.N., ZORRILLA, E.P., MANDYAM, C.D., & RIVIER, C.L. (2006). Exposure to repetitive versus varied stress during prenatal development generates two distinct anxiogenic and neuroendocrine profiles in adulthood. *Endocrinology* 147:2506–2517.

SCHUR, M. (1953). The ego in anxiety. In R. M. Loewenstein, ed., Drives, affects, behavior (pp. 67–103). New York: International Universities Press.

SIMONSON, I. (2005). In defense of consciousness: The role of conscious and unconscious inputs in consumer choice. *Journal of Consumer Psychology* 115(3):211–218.

SIMONSON, I. & NOWLIS, S.M. (2000, June). The role of explanations and need for uniqueness in consumer decision making: Unconventional choices based on reasons. *Journal of Consumer Research* 27:49–68.

SOON, C.S., BRASS, M., HEINZE, H.J., & HAYNES, J.D. (2008). Unconscious determinants of free decisions in the human brain. *Nature Neuroscience* 11:543–545.

SPITZ, R.A. (1950). Anxiety in infancy: A study of its manifestations in the first year of life. *International Journal of Psychoanalysis* 31:138–143.

STONE, L. (1981a). Notes on the noninterpretive elements in the psychoanalytic situation and process. *Journal of the American Psychoanalytic Association* 29:89–118.

———— (1981b). Some thoughts on the "here and now" in psychoanalytic technique and process. *Psychoanalytic Quarterly* 50:709–733.

STRACHEY, J. (1959). Editor's introduction to "Inhibitions, symptoms and anxiety." In J. Strachey, ed. and trans., The standard edition of the complete psychological works of Sigmund Freud, 24 vols. London: Hogarth Press, 20:77–86.

SUMMERS, F. (2008). Theoretical insularity and the crisis of psychoanalysis. *Psychoanalytic Psychology* 25:413–424.

WÄELDER, R. (1929). Hemmung, Symptom und Angst: By Sigm. Freud. Vienna: Internationaler Psychoanalytischer. Reprinted *International Journal of Psychoanalysis* 1929, 10:103–111.

———— (1936). The principle of multiple function. *Psychoanalytic Quarterly* 5:45–62.

———— (1967). Inhibitions, symptoms and anxiety: Forty years later. *Psychoanalytic Quarterly* 36:1–36.

WALLERSTEIN, R.S. (1988). One psychoanalysis or many? *International Journal of Psychoanalysis* 69:5–21.

———— (1991). *The Common Ground of Psychoanalysis*. Northvale, NJ: Aronson.

———— (2007). Leo Rangell and I: Where Do We Differ? *Psychoanalytic Psychology* 24:507–509.

WEINSTOCK, M. (2005). The potential influence of maternal stress hormones on development and mental health of the offspring. *Brain, Behavior, Immunity*, 19:296–308.

WEISS, J. (1995). Bernfeld's "The facts of observation in psychoanalysis": A response from psychoanalytic research. *Psychoanalytic Quarterly* 64:699–716.

WILLICK, M.S. (1990). Psychoanalytic concepts of the etiology of severe mental illness. *Journal of the American Psychoanalytic Association* 38:1049–1081.

———— (1993). The deficit syndrome in schizophrenia: Psychoanalytic and neurobiological perspectives. *Journal of the American Psychoanalytic Association* 41:1135–1157.

———— (2001). Psychoanalysis and schizophrenia: A cautionary tale. *Journal of the American Psychoanalytic Association* 49:27–56.

———— (2002). Martin S. Willick replies. *Journal of the American Psychoanalytic Association* 50:316–319.

WILLOCK, B. (2007). Comparative-integrative psychoanalysis: A relational perspective for the discipline's second century. New York: Analytic Press.

Wilson, T.D. (2002). Strangers to ourselves: Discovering the adaptive unconscious. Cambridge, Mass.: Harvard University Press.

ZHOU, X., VOHS, K., & BAUMEISTER, R. (2009). The symbolic power of money: Reminders of money alter social distress and physical pain. *Psychological Science* 20(6):700–706.

CHAPTER 18

Notes on Psychoanalytic Theory and Its Consequences for Technique (plus "A Response to Our Respondents"[1])

[Richards, A.D. & Richards, A.K. (1995). *Journal of Clinical Psychoanalysis* 4:429–456.]

In this paper we will explore the relationship between psychoanalytic theory and psychoanalytic technique. We are interested in pursuing two questions: (1) Does theory have technical consequences? If so, what are they? (2) Can theories be compared? We are mindful of the state of our field and the nature of current psychoanalytic debates about theoretical pluralism versus common ground, paradigm competition versus paradigm integration, and theory evolution versus theory revolution.

We will begin with a clinical example which we will use to show that our technique has been determined by our informing theory. Critics have called this theory Freudian theory, drive theory, one person psychology, classical or orthodox psychoanalysis, or the theory of the isolated mind. Other characterizations refer to a nonrelational, noninteractionist, and nonconstructivist and positivist approach. They add that it is noninterpersonal, neutral rather than empathic, asymmetrical rather than symmetrical, authoritarian rather than democratic, and conflict-centered versus deficit-centered. They also point out that it is focused on internal psychic reality rather than on real trauma, real events, and the here-and-now. In addition, this theory is said to view transference as a distortion rather than as a response to the real qualities and actions of the analyst.

We characterize our approach as modern conflict theory. Our key theoretical constructs are conflict, compromise formation, and unconscious fantasy. When we designate these ideas we mean to invoke the names of many contributors, and we rely on the reader's familiarity with

---

[1]For the full text of the commentaries to which the authors are responding (by Frances Baudry, Robert Caper, Elizabeth de Bianchedi, James Fosshage, Paul Ornstein, Irving Steingart, Robert Stolorow, and Robert Wallerstein) see the *Journal of Clinical Psychoanalysis* (1995) volume 4.

them to help locate our approach. These contributors include Annie Reich, Margaret Brenman, Charles Brenner, Jacob Arlow, Leo Rangell, Dale Boesky, Sander Abend, Arnold Rothstein, Harold Blum, Marianne Goldberger, and Allan Compton.

A patient in her second year of treatment reported that she had been fired from her job. She had come into treatment for a general malaise. Depressed and hopeless, she had been working at temporary jobs which were far below her educational level and which she found profoundly unsatisfying. She came from a family of high achievement. Her mother had been the widow of an important political figure before marrying the patient's quiet, shy father. The patient was among several people fired in a general cutback; she had been among the last hired.

Common sense would say that this is an external problem, not an intrapsychic one. But this incident was part of a larger context: the patient had complained that the woman she had recently been assigned to work for didn't answer her phone messages. When callers complained, she blamed the patient for not bringing the calls to her attention, even though the patient was not her secretary. The incident happened in the context of another aspect of the patient's current life: her analysis had been dealing with her resentment of her roommate's cats. They came into her bedroom all the time, even though they were supposed to be confined to her roommate's bedroom or the kitchen. The incident of the firing took place in a longitudinal context as well: the intrusion reminded her of her mother's constant attempts to intrude on her reading when she was a child. She had been complaining that her mother would come into her room, adjust the lamps, offer her juice, ask her what book she was reading, and so on. The firing also took place in the context of the analytic situation: she had been coming late to her sessions and not talking about why this happened. When the analyst inquired about her lateness, she blamed the bus system and seemed annoyed to be asked. The analyst felt intrusive. Months later, the patient was exasperated with the analyst for "not having noticed" that she got fired from that job because she could not tolerate her boss.

The patient believed that her mother loved the active, achieving children of her first marriage more than she loved the patient. She also believed that her mother had loved her first husband more than she did the patient's father. Therefore she was very disappointed that her father was devoted to her mother and seemed to the patient to prefer her mother to herself. Her fantasy of being a second-rate Cinderella had eventuated in her impoverished life. In the course of her treatment, she recalled that when she was younger, she had adopted the Cinderella posture in hopes that Prince Charming would then come to rescue her. As this fantasy was traced to the patient's many current troubles, she became better at getting and keeping jobs that led her along a career path more consonant with her abilities than her previous work had been.

The analyst used a stance that evolved from the "classical" analysis of Freud, ego psychology of the 1930s through 1960s, structuralism of the 1960s and 1970s, and poststructuralism of the 1980s and 1990s. She was searching for the unconscious fantasy that would make the patient's apparently self-defeating behavior understandable and allow the patient to give it up. Understanding the patient's unconscious fantasy was facilitated by attending to the analyst's experience. The analyst had been feeling uncomfortable. She thought that if she asked questions, she would be intrusive. If she didn't ask questions she would be ineffectual. By putting together similarities between the patients' interactions with people in her current life (e.g., her roommate and her coworker), and with people in her past (e.g., her mother), analyst and patient together came to the conclusion that the patient's fear that her analyst must be either intrusive or ineffectual reflected her idea that women are helpless to protect her unless they intrude on her.

This idea served many functions. At this juncture it was primarily a defensive operation, protecting the patient from the fear that her mother could not protect her. Over many months, we related her fantasy of a phallic, intrusive mother to her fear and wish to be intruded on by her parents, her longing to keep her mother's love when her mother was tending to one of her siblings or her father, and her fear that she would destroy herself or one of her rivals for mother's attentions unless she was restrained.

When the patient came to see that she had provoked the firing, it was not as a result of the analyst telling her that she had done that. It felt to her like a spontaneous realization. It seemed to the analyst to be the result of the step-by-step identification of the contextual regularities and repetitions of patterns of relating, the emphases, omissions, and inconsistencies which occurred in the examination of her feelings, wishes, and prohibitions that constituted the analytic work.

Getting fired represented many things to this patient, including her desire to reject the mother who used her for protection instead of protecting her. To deal with her alternative fear, that of provoking a mother to attack her, the patient propelled herself from job to job and from living arrangement to living arrangement. The unconscious fantasy of a phallic, protective mother had been structuring the patient's reality. She had been fighting against the wish even as she had been unknowingly enacting it in her life.

By looking at her own affect and that of the patient, the analyst was using a key aspect of the theory of compromise formation. The patient was understood to be struggling with fear of loss of the object, evidenced by her inability to tolerate her mother's vulnerability. Fear of loss of her mother's love, a conclusion based on her inability to tolerate sharing her mother's attentions with other family members, was seen as an additional dimension of this compromise formation. The intolerable fear of her mother's vulnerability reverberated in this patient as a fear of loss of her own (phallic) competence based on identification with a castrated mother. Guilt over her wishes to annihilate all rivals for her mother's love was interpreted. The analyst hypothesized that she felt guilty about her wish to destroy her rivals. Working within the framework of compromise formation led to hypotheses about the patient's affects, wishes, fears, and moral dilemmas.

Thinking in terms of the unconscious fantasy led to a more experience specific and explicitly narrative hypothesis, with the story of the unconscious fantasy fleshing out the bones of the compromise formation. The unconscious fantasy elaborates and specifies what the compromise formation outlines. Unconscious fantasy can be thought of as a synthetic, integrative concept whereas compromise formation is an algebra of the mind, enabling the analyst to tease apart separate strands of thought and feeling.

Both unconscious fantasy and compromise formation inform technique as the analyst uses them to impart to patients new knowledge about their thoughts and feelings. These concepts rest on the assumption that much of what goes on in the human mind is not directly accessible to the subject. Unconscious fantasy is inferred from behavior, symptoms, dreams, slips of the tongue, and similar unintended manifestations. It requires analytic thinking to tease it out of what may appear to be rational, goal-directed activity or externally determined events. By using the concepts of unconscious fantasy and compromise formation, the analyst asks analysands to give up the idea that they are conscious of all their thoughts and feelings and that these are within their control.

According to some theorists, analysis is painful because it exposes analysands to the repeated, humiliating vulnerability of having someone else know more about them than they know about themselves. We believe that three new theoretical approaches to psychoanalysis were formulated at least in part by an attempt to provide alternative techniques to create what their proponents believe to be a more effective and less injurious analytic process. As Arlow (1994) pointed out, there is no evidence that analytic interventions are painful because they expose the patient to the experience of someone else knowing more about him or her than the patient knows. What is painful is the uncovering of disagreeable disavowed wishes and thoughts. For example, Arlow says, the patient who learns that she has characterological generosity or rescue fantasies will not be humiliated. The patient who is told that he lives for the pleasure of seeing his father dead will feel hurt by that knowledge.

Theories which claim to protect the patient from painful revelations are based on alternative theories of motivation and pathogenesis. With their concern about the patient's injury, these theories have moved away from the centrality of unconscious conflict rooted in childhood and toward that of deficit inducing developmental traumas. The conflict—deficit distinction is most important for self psychology, while the opposition of a relational perspective to the putative endogenous drive emphasis of classical psychoanalysis is central to relational and intersubjective theories. A central tenet of self and relational theories of technique is validation of the patient's perceptions, past and present. By contrast, in Kleinian theory, as in Brenner's (1983) formulation, the mind is in conflict, and interpretation of unconscious fantasy rather than validation of the patient's perceptions is therapeutic.

The literature relating theory to technique is very sparse, although the topic is implicit in all psychoanalytic writing. In 1924 Freud offered a prize for the best paper on the relationship between theory and technique. Rank and Ferenczi (1924) responded with their book on the development of psychoanalysis, but they did not get the prize because their contribution was not directly addressed to the subject. The literature of more recent decades includes several papers and one book, a volume written by Louis Berger (1987). He stresses the concept of "logical entailment," arguing that if it were so, change in theory should lead by deductive steps to more effective treatment. Berger concludes that this kind of synchronist progress has not typified psychoanalysis in the past and is not occurring now. Can we agree? A problem in the relationship between psychoanalytic theory and technique is that theory is not unitary. In fact it is a set of discrete yet interrelated theories: a theory of development, a theory of pathogenesis and symptom formation, a theory of the therapeutic process and cure, and a theory of how the mind works. Therefore the relationship between theory and practice is more complicated than Berger imagines. There are theories and there are theories, and some are more technically consequential than others. For example, psychoanalysis as a general psychology includes concerns not directly related to psychopathology. Changes in those domains would not occasion changes in technique. In some respects, technique leads a life of its own and technical advances may be made apart from any change in theory.

In the United States, the ego psychology of the 1940s and 1950s entailed significant changes in the conduct of psychoanalysis. It led to a new emphasis on defense and adaptation, a technical turn which has been elaborated by a whole generation of Freudian psychoanalysts, Arlow (1991a), Brenner (1983), Weinshel (1992), Gray (1994), Boesky (Panel1995), and Rangell (1990) among them. The recommendation that analysis of defense precede the analysis of content follows from theoretical principles if not directly deducible.

In their exploration of the relation between theory and technique, analysts of the 1930s and 1940s generally affirmed the pragmatic adaptability of Freud's technique. In the 1940s Edward Glover (1940) and C.P. Oberndorf (1943), working separately, queried colleagues about the relation of their theoretical commitments to their technique. Concerned with the differences between Kleinian and Freudian theory, the two sides converged in the finding that in Oberndorf's (1943) words, "the psychoanalytic method can have no fixed application" (p. 113). Drawing on Glover's survey results, and the Marienbad Symposium of 1936, Sandor Lorand (1948) reaffirmed the loose relationship between theory and technique, and cautioned against too great a reliance on theory as a guide to clinical work. Lorand argued that "we must wait for material from the patient which will tell us whether or not we have been correct in our hypothesis" (p. 43). Lorand here writes as a positivist, revealing a belief that theory-free observation is possible. This puts him at odds with the postmodern deconstructionists. Lorand wrote, "The technique should be adapted to the patient, not the patient to the technique" (p. 43). Lorand has in mind a single set of fundamental rules (subject to revision) and their different applications (subject, of course, to error). By contrast, the relationalists and others propose one set of rules for one patient category (neurotics) and another for a second category (borderlines).

We are now living in a world of psychoanalytic theoretical pluralism. Contemporary Freudian psychoanalysis, self psychology, relational psychoanalysis, Kleinianism, and relational psychoanalysis are models in competition, vying for ascendancy.

Self Psychology

Self psychology is the most comprehensive psychoanalytic theory developed to date as an alternative to the standard Freudian model, which still remains within the Freudian movement. Kohut and his collaborators and successors offer us a theory of pathogenesis, a theory of development, a theory of therapeutic action and cure, and a theory of mind. No other current approach is as disjunctive and at the same time as comprehensive. Relational psychoanalysis may be as disjunctive, but is not as comprehensive. Kleinian psychoanalysis is both less disjunctive and less comprehensive. Self psychology is a set of nomothetically related concepts. Its new language includes the concepts of the selfobject, idealizing and mirror transferences, transmuting internalization, and the self state dream. The self is proposed as the superordinate structure of the mind. Empathy and vicarious introspection are the central means of gathering data in the analytic situation. Parental empathic failure is the primary pathogen, and the identification and repair of empathic rupture is the road to cure.

Self psychology began as a contrast to what Kohut experienced as the coldness and clinical detachment of ego psychology. He presented this contrast in "The Two Analyses of Mr. Z" (1979). Comparing the first analysis in which there was much interpretation of the young man's inordinate and insistent needs, with the second treatment in which the analyst consistently refrained from interpretation and attempted to understand the world through the patient's eyes, Kohut concluded that the latter was the more therapeutic. Technically, therefore, the analyst was to use "empathy" to foster the development of a "mirror transference" (in which the patient uses the analyst as a mirror in which to see the self reflected) or an "idealizing transference" (in which the analyst is used as an image with which the patient may bolster his self-esteem through association). Either way, the analyst functions as a selfobject, used to repair and glue together an otherwise fragmented self. What are the potential technical problems with this approach? One is the perhaps insuperable difficulty of one human being giving him- or herself entirely over to the world view of another; another is the difficulty the analyst must have in listening to an unrealistically idealized image of him- or herself being praised and revered day after day.

Viewed from the perspective of classical theory, the concepts of the idealizing and mirroring transferences which are crucial to the technique of self psychology relabel manifest content while adding little to our understanding of the particulars of an analysand's mental processes (Richards, 1984b). In his final book Kohut (1984) himself says that the classical analyst interprets specific "active mechanisms," while the self psychologist reconstructs general "chronic attitudes." Empathy and vicarious introspection are to self psychology what free association and observation of behavior are to traditional psychoanalytic methodology. Thus self psychology advances a technical approach that offers explanations about the whole person and the person's fluctuating and content-free self states at the expense of the details of thought and behavior and adaptive functions.

Traditional analysts, Kohut believes, are engaged in a continual battle with their patients, attempting to break through or overcome resistance. His theory entails the analyst's accepting, understanding, and explaining resistance as a response to psychological dangers mobilized by the analytic process. But classical analysis already highlights the adaptive functions of compromise formations. Adaptation entails seeing patients as doing their best to mediate between conflictual wishes, fears, and prohibitions while attending to the constraints of the environment. Kohut's focus can be seen as a restriction of the complexity of that model. He draws self-esteem issues into sharp focus while blurring out desire, rage, terror, and their vicissitudes.

In stressing the technical primacy of empathy and vicarious introspection, self psychology enters perilous conceptual waters (Spencer and Balter, 1990). Transference, resistance, the unconscious, and the theory of mind they constitute are the bedrock of psychoanalysis. To dispense with transference and resistance as Kohut seems to have done (Kohut, 1979, p. 308) is to become at best incompletely analytic. Marcia Cavell (1993) points out that "empathy" cannot be a matter of my getting outside my own mind and into yours (vicarious introspection) but rests rather on widening our common shared experiential base. I exercise my imagination in regard to your beliefs and desires, those which make your behavior seem more or less reasonable to you. We need to account, she says, "neither for our knowledge of other minds [at the general epistemological level] nor for that of a real shared material world since such knowledge is a condition of mind itself (p. 233). Empathy is an "instrument of observation," on an equal footing with the senses, but which, it would seem to be the case for Kohutians, becomes an occult faculty, hard to understand or put to use. Taken in the more modest sense described by Cavell, it becomes a natural attitude toward patients as fellow human beings. It is a precondition for good analysis. But stripping empathy of its mysterious power leaves the self psychologist depending on the same powers of observation and understanding available to any analyst. Reed (1987) asserts that self psychologists are more exhortative in treatment than is the classical norm and that by privileging the patient's self understanding they restrict themselves to the manifest level interpretations. These technical strategies differ from those that aim at decoding unconscious fantasies and components of compromise formations.

Can we elucidate the differences between our technique and that of a self psychologist by looking at a clinical example from both points of view? Goldberg (1990) has said that this is impossible because a self psychologist would not have gotten to the same place with the patient. He insists that in order for a nonself-psychologist to evaluate the usefulness of the approach, he or she would have to first accept the system, immerse himself or herself in it, and then apply it with full belief in its efficacy. For Goldberg, then, there can be no nonparticipant evaluator, no objective observer. But the scientific method requires replicability by the noncommitted observer. Let us first look at what Goldberg would allow as evidence; what the noncommitted observer might say about the self psychological interpretation of an example generated by a self psychologist.

A recent paper in self psychology (Ornstein and Ornstein, 1994) showed a clinical case in detail in order to illustrate the curative process as it is envisioned by current self psychologists. The case stirred discussion at a conference sponsored by the *International Journal of Psychoanalysis* at West Point, New York. Most participants followed Freudian or Kleinian points of view. The discussants objected to the language of the patient which sounded to them as if he were a student of self psychology. For example, the patient is quoted as associating to his dream as follows:

Developmentally, the dream is from late adolescence. Hopefully, it means that I brought the difficulties through to a later developmental level. Construction: the image of a structure that could be rebuilt; work is done to make a stable format: concrete or steel; fundamentally stable internal structure. It is the accomplishment of the dream that it can express that. The dream says: still incomplete and unable to function and is dependent—but there is construction going on. How to find the beatific presence in the midst of that construction process? [What are you referring to?] The character in me in the construction with the hard hat goes around freely and performs the tasks without vulnerability and exposure. My entry today was out of sync with my feelings in the dream; the presence for this process was not on the same level as the dream. How to be present here is still a struggle. Your role for the analysis is neutral, like being a gardener. Clear human participation is required for me to be able to be present. To acknowledge the achievement of the dream and the significance of the dream is on the wrong side of the line for you. You don't want to put value on it. I got more trouble with that than you do. Because you won't put value on it, I won't; then you won't, then I won't. I am dependent on you valuing me and what I am doing during the process, then I can fully participate [p. 991].

For a Freudian, this illustrates the way in which the patient and the analyst are engaged in assessing the state of the self rather than listening for fantasies or conflicts. There are no surprising connections, no tentative hypotheses, no room for puzzle solving. Here patient and analyst are immersed in the system just as Goldberg advocated for the analyst. We are not asserting that some of this does not go on in every other theoretical system, our point is that in other systems it is an adjunct, whereas in self psychology it is the method. It seems that self psychologists are less concerned with finding correctives for their own biases than are the proponents of other systems. Is this an inevitable consequence of the comprehensiveness of the theory? Could it be that the more comprehensive a theory, the more closed it is?

It may be instructive, even though Goldberg might not agree that it is fair, to look at our example of a classical treatment through the lens of self psychology. A self psychologist dealing with the patient who lost her job might have focused on the injury she sustained in being fired from her job, and her expectation that the analyst would think less of her because she got fired. The patient would be thought to be using the analyst to maintain her self cohesion by seeing the analyst as all-powerful and as accepting of her. Because of the need to avoid further injury, it would be important to avoid seeming to blame the patient by looking for what she might have done to cause the disaster. The issue of her roommate's cats might have been taken as an assault of her self, and her autonomy within her own space which paralleled her mother's unempathic intrusions into her room when she was a child. The analyst, by contrast, would be respecting her space by not inquiring into her privacy. The self psychologist could have made much of the patient's feelings of being blamed by her boss for the boss's own shortcomings, seeing this as intolerable to the patient because her mother had been similarly denigrating of her activities by interrupting them. Thus, self psychology would lead to a different technical stance than would ego psychology. Because it would not confront the patient with any ideas different from those which she herself expressed, it would not teach her anything new. We believe that this technical consequence makes self psychology nothing more than friendly comfort.

Relational/Intersubjective Schools

The principles of relational psychoanalysis have been set forth by Stephen Mitchell (1988) as follows:

1. Mind consists of "transactional patterns and internal structures derived from an interactive and interpersonal field" (p. 17).
2. These patterns are derived from a tendency to preserve continuity, connections, and familiarity.
3. Sexuality is a response rather than an internal pressure.
4. The human concern is to maintain a sense of identity, to achieve authentic personal meaning.
5. What appears to be the influence of early experience is the manifestation of patterns of relating repeated in different forms throughout development.

The problem with discussing the technical consequences of these theories is that they bash classical technique rather than presenting their ideas as a coherent system. According to these theories, classical analytic technique is cold and painful because it exposes analysands to the repeated humiliation of having someone else know more about them than they know about themselves. Technical modifications are therefore introduced to make analysis less demanding and painful. The analyst must acknowledge the analysand's privileged understanding of his own experience and the analyst's own subjectivity as a codeterminant of the treatment process. The analyst is advised to work against the asymmetry inherent in any doctor-patient relationship. Technique, these new theories hold, should foster a sense of mutuality—of feeling understood, of being accepted—that will gratify the analysand in the treatment. Technique also aims to further the construction and elucidation of new relational or inter-subjective meanings that focus on the analyst-analysand interaction as seen through the eyes of the latter. This is very different from the classical analytic view of the analyst as someone who listens neutrally but with an expectation borne of experience that the analyst will be able to infer unconscious meanings from the patient's symptoms, free associations, interactions with people, and other behavioral descriptions. Richards (1992) discussed this in detail in regard to a case.

Do the technical modifications that follow from these new theories represent genuine advances? Stolorow, Brandchaft, and Atwood (1987) fault the classical theorist for "invoking the concept of objective reality and distortion" (p. 135), for tending to "view pathology in terms of processes and mechanisms located solely in the patient" (p. 3), and for failing "to decenter from the structure of experience into which he has been assimilating his patient's communications" (p. 143). They believe that only the intersubjectivists can comprehend the patient's "psychic reality" and formulate interpretations guided by timing, tact, and compassion.

For Greenberg (1991) an important aspect of technical consequentiality is the relational analyst's use of countertransference. Sharing the viewpoints of Gill, Hoffman, Mitchell, Aron, and others, he argues that analysands often have accurate perceptions of their analyst (including their analyst's countertransferences), and that a significant analytic task is finding out how analysts perceive and think about their analysands. This task furthers the understanding of the relational matrix in which analysis occurs and the achievement of new meanings, understood as jointly arrived at meanings incorporating the subjectivities of analysand and analyst alike. Greenberg is concerned with blind spots that develop in response to the patient's more-or-less accurate perception of the analyst, including those perceptions that form the nucleus of the transference. Greenberg contends that Freud's emphasis on psychic reality and on transference as distortion has systematically directed our attention away from an important source of transference: those observations that patients, like anyone else, continually make in the course of being with other people. Is Greenberg correct about classical analysis? Boesky (Panel, in press) notes that the argument that the analyst's actual intervention is so often misperceived does not prove that correct perceptions by the patient can be secondary or irrelevant. If they were, he reasons, why would interpretations have any effect?

Relationists like Greenberg and Mitchell argue that analysts can "catch on" to patients' feelings and moods because they resonate with something in the analyst's own personal experience. Boesky, writing from the standpoint of the conflict-structural model, speaks of the need to view certain behaviors of the analyst which actually join in the creation of a useful resistance as a creative contribution which is necessary only for the analyst to make and would not be necessary for another analyst. Boesky recognizes that the manifest form of a resistance is . . . sometimes unconsciously negotiated by . . . patient and analyst.

Greenberg (1991) has argued that theorizing within the relational-conflict model of the mind shifts the balance away from Freud's emphasis on endogenous instinctual forces and toward interpersonal experience. He says that interpersonal experience includes such contemporary constructs as pathogenic beliefs, danger situations, and the representational world. It should be noted, however, that the concept of danger situations has long been central to the work of Boesky, Brenner, Arlow, and many others who do not disparage Freud's theoretical model.

There is disagreement between the classical idea that the patient's fantasies shape the patient's perceptions of the analyst's behavior, and the interactional idea that the analyst's actions shape the patient's fantasies. For classicists, resistance is the most meaningful emotional engagement between analyst and analysand; for relationalists, resistance signals a failure of the analyst's engagement or a failure of empathy. The absence of tension between analyst and analysand leads classicists to suspect collusion rather than a fruitful working relationship.

The relationalist allegation that ego psychology injures the patient by making it obvious that someone else knows more about what is going on inside the patient than the patient knows about himself or herself, is clearly incorrect. As Arlow pointed out (1994) the patient comes to an analyst precisely to get special expertise. Evidence that the analyst knows something that the patient does not know is welcome to most patients. If it were not, why would anyone pay for analysis? Freud dealt with this issue in his paper "On Negation" (1925). He recognized that patients would need to say no to that which they had been keeping out of awareness for exactly the same reason they had pushed the unwelcome knowledge or ideas away in the first place. He cautioned analysts to take into account the patient's need to become aware of painful thoughts and feelings gradually rather than try to insist that a patient who was not ready to accept something must do so immediately.

Concern for interpreting in a way that would allow patients to hear the analyst without needing to reject what was said because it was painful, has been a concern of ego psychologists. Ego psychologists established the idea of an order of interpretation. Kaiser (1976) believed that interpretations of resistance were the only necessary and appropriate interventions in analysis. Interpreting the defense before the id wish, the negative transference before the positive transference, and surface before depth, became shibboleths in ego psychology. Poland (1975) linked timing with tact. Putting off an interpretation until the patient is able to accept it, using indirection, waiting for the previous interpretation to be assimilated, are all aspects of tact. He also cautioned against the pseudo-tact of avoiding all confrontation. This avoidance of aggression on both sides, Poland observes, leads to mutual admiration and failure to analyze.

Tact may also involve prefacing a potentially humiliating interpretation with a disclaimer. Such phrases as, "I could be wrong, but here is what I think . . ." or, "I may be off the mark here, but . . ." give the patient the idea that he or she is free to disagree. They provide a model of openness and hypothesis testing on the part of the analyst. In this way, they invite ego functions such as judgment and self observation to be brought to bear by the analysand. Why is it necessary to develop a whole new relational theory to do something that analysts have been aware needed to be done from very early on?

The relationalists might have reacted to the patient who lost her job by examining the analyst's feelings in this situation. The analyst was keenly aware of the patient's unwillingness to see herself as at fault. She understood her patient to be extremely self-punitive already. Thus, she might have been advised to inquire about the patient's experience of the analyst's subjectivity, asking the patient if she had any thoughts about the analyst's experience. During this inquiry, the revelation that the analysand was uncomfortable about discussing the firing with her, afraid that she might be blaming her for something that was clearly not her fault, could be put on the analytic table.

Additional issues such as the way the job loss threatened the treatment should be brought into the treatment as well. The analyst couldn't be doing such a good job if her patient had not become sufficiently aware of what was going on in her interaction with her boss to avoid getting fired. The analyst's self-esteem was threatened by her patient's loss. Thus, the relationalist would advise this analyst to discuss the here-and-now interchange in the room and include more of how she herself was contributing to the construction of the analytic situation. It is just on the question of how much the analyst should tell about herself that relational and intersubjectivists differ from the classical ego psychological stance this analyst used. A thoughtful patient would tell such an analyst that she did not come into treatment to find out about the analyst's fears and wishes, but to learn things about herself that she could use in her life outside the sessions. Relational and intersubjective ideas would appear to have an important and, from our perspective, deleterious, effect on technique.

Modern Kleinian Theory

Attempting to clarify the theoretical differences between Klein and Freud, we looked at the record of a series of meetings arranged by members of the British Psychoanalytical Society in the years immediately after Freud went to London (King and Steiner, 1991). The differences can be summarized as: (1) For Freud, libido is primary both developmentally and in its importance in psychopathology; for Klein, aggression is primary in both senses. (2) For Freud, the oedipal constellation is crucial for later psychopathology; for Klein the first year of life is decisive. (3) For Freud, the early years of life, especially the preverbal years, are forever shrouded in the mists of later development; for Klein, envy dating to the first year of life is a central motivator. (4) For Klein the characteristics of early objects are crucial, for Freud characteristics of the objects of the oedipal phase are secondary to their roles in the oedipal drama. (5) For Freud, defenses such as repression and isolation are characteristic of neurotic patterns; for Klein projection, introjection, and projective identification are central to ubiquitous psychotic aspects of the personality.

While there long appeared to be vast differences in theory between Kleinian and classical views, Greenson (1974), believing that the differences were not irreconcilable, began a process of contrast, comparison, and reconciliation of the two schools of thought. This process has been carried on since by Kleinians in Britain (King, 1983), Israel, South America, and North America, and by ego psychologists (Robbins, 1980; Baudry, 1993) in the United States. Baudry studied the Freud—Klein controversies and concluded that very little attention was paid to the theory of the method of cure, while much attention was devoted to the nature of the first year of life, a topic he considered irrelevant to technique. He believed that the two sides were motivated by political differences.

One issue that divided Kleinians from ego psychologists was the number and depth of interpretations thought appropriate for an hour (King and Steiner, 1991). At that time, Kleinians gave many more than the followers of Anna Freud. Levine (1992) reported a discussion in which modern Kleinians Segal and Etchegoyen give no more interpretations in an hour than the modern ego psychologist Weinshel. But not all modern Kleinians are agreed on this point. Racker (1968) has taken Klein's idea that interpretations must be offered at the point of urgency to mean that more is better. Etchegoyen (1991) has taken it to mean that interpretations are useful only when they become urgent.

A second focus of debate within the Kleinian school is whether interpretations or relationships are essential carriers of analytic change. The Barangers (1964) believe that patient and analyst construct a mutual fantasy which constitutes the bipersonal field. An impasse in the analytic progress pushes the patient to create a "bulwark" in response to the analyst's limitations. The analytic couple defines the dialectic between stereotype and mobility of the field. Insight is a function of the couple rather than an intrapsychic event. Etchegoyen (1991) points out that in their emphasis on interaction, the Barangers agree with Weinshel and Loewald. Among those who have developed the interactional point of view are the relationalists as noted extensively above. Other Kleinian analysts (Bleger, 1971; Zac, 1973) emphasize the difference between analyst and patient in that the patient's feelings and thoughts are the focus of the analytic work. These analysts are closer to the idea of how analysis works as described by Brenner, Arlow, and Stein. Both interpretations and the relationship are aspects of the more inclusive theory mentioned earlier of which current thinkers emphasize only one side.

A third point of debate in the Kleinian perspective is the issue of when pathology develops. The Barangers believe that a life event becomes significant for the patient when it is reactivated in analysis. They see the analyst as essentially paternal in intervening to break up the mother infant dyadic fantasy. In this, they are like Blum, Mahler, and others who emphasize preoedipal issues of closeness and distance. By contrast, Etchegoyen sees analytic impasse as most often due to erotic transference fantasies. While Weinshel is one of those thought to believe that oedipal issues are crucial, he clearly stated (Levine, 1992), "that in the course of an analysis, he typically spends more time with preoedipal matters than with phallic-oedipal ones" (p. 813). Brenner, Abend, and others of the American ego psychological school do regard oedipal pathology as central.

The fourth issue of debate seems more relevant as an issue between ego psychologists and the Kleinian school than within the Kleinian perspective. This issue is the relative importance of the real events in the life of the developing child as compared with the fantasy life of the child. In their actual clinical work, both Weinshel and Segal took both fantasy and real events into account. Weinshel noted that it was difficult to decide whether differences between his work and that of Segal were due to theoretical differences between their schools of thought or differences in personal style.

Recent Kleinian contributions (Bianchedi, Boschan, Cortiñas, and Piccolo, 1988; Stein, 1990) have emphasized the role of affect in the clinical application of theory. Bianchedi and her colleagues conclude that both anxiety and libido are foci of mental life, with anxiety developmentally primary for Klein, and libido primary for Freud. Stein emphasized the role of affect in Klein's theory in this way: "Klein's Envy and Gratitude (1975) is a prime example of a treatise on one single emotion which bears various combinations of feelings. Very different feelings are shown to be linked with one emotion (i.e., envy), a variety of feelings which perhaps would have been unthinkable without this delving, as Klein did, into the world of one emotion" (p. 503).

Stein says the "ever-present strife between feelings, this very basic ambivalence, is in the Kleinian world-view, the essence of psychic reality" (p. 506). This implies a meticulous investigation of affect in the analytic hour, an investigation implied equally by Brenner's (1983) attention to affect as the clinical key to compromise formation. For Brenner, a leader in the development of ego psychology, affect theory has taken a central place in clinical psychoanalysis, replacing structural concepts of id, ego, and superego. Thus, his work converges on that of Klein in a surprising and, to those who have taken great pains to learn the structural concepts he and Arlow adumbrated, discomfiting way.

To continue the comparison of ego psychological and Kleinian viewpoints, it may be instructive to compare the statements of Arlow, a classicist, with those of Susan Isaacs, a Kleinian, in order to see where they converge and diverge. Both have written about the central importance of unconscious organizations of mind. Arlow calls these fantasies and attributes their centrality to their role in the consolidation of the mind in the oedipal period. Isaacs speaks of phantasy and places it in the very earliest period of development.

When it comes to technique, however, are these crucial theoretical differences salient? For Isaacs (1948) the analytic method consists of observation:

> These three ways of obtaining evidence of mental process from observation of behavior—that of noting the context, observing details and approaching any particular data as a part of a developmental process—are essential aspects of the work of psychoanalysis and most fully exemplified there. They are, indeed, its breath of life. They serve to elucidate the nature and function of phantasy, as well as of other mental phenomena [p. 76].

She goes on to elaborate what these three ways mean in the analytic situation. The analyst observes detail and context together. She listens for: (1) what is included and what is left out; (2) emphasis; (3) repetition; (4) changes in the analysand's account of events or persons and how they are referred to; (5) idiosyncracies of speech; (6) metaphors and verbal style generally; (7) selection of facts; (8) denials of previous statements, of affect appropriate to what is being said, of things in the consulting room, of facts in the patient's life, and the world around, and of knowledge of facts about the analyst's life; (9) the patient's manner, behavior, gesture, and tone of voice; (10) any variations or deviations from routine in these or other behaviors.

The third principle, genetic continuity, refers to the understanding of all of this in terms of the developmental process. By this, Isaacs means the theory that the relationship with the analyst is determined by the analysand's earliest experiences.

For Arlow (1993), the analytic method consists of intuitive attunement to the analysand followed by rational observation of behavior. He believes that analytic listening is guided by criteria that elucidate the underlying, meaningful structure of the patient's associations. These criteria are: context, contiguity, repetition, similarities and differences, figurative speech, especially metaphor, unusual words and images, and convergence of data into a comprehensible hypothesis.

Both Arlow and Isaacs flag certain aspects of the patient's productions as conveying special meaning and hence being worthy of analytic attention. Both privilege what is repeated, what is unexpected, what is contiguous with a statement, and what is metaphoric. Most of all, both value context as making meaning. The analysand of either Arlow or Isaacs would become aware of these cues as the most important avenues to self-understanding as the analyst demonstrates their usefulness by basing interpretations on them. It is our hypothesis that herein may lie the mutative efficacy of psychoanalysis. If this is true, it would account for the relatively good results claimed by practitioners who use different theories. The salient issue would then be not oedipal versus preoedipal, deficit versus conflict, or holding environment versus interpretation, but rather the learning of what might be called a third signal system, a language of affect that allows analysands to attend to and understand their own affects.

What would Kleinians say about the patient with whom we began this discussion? Modern Kleinians might emphasize the aggressive aspects of the patient's job loss. They might see her actions as pushing the analyst away so that she would not have to deal with her envy of the analyst's success. They might focus more on the maternal transference, seeing the patient as needing to enact her fantasy that the analyst is a bad provider. Early Kleinians were known for their early, deep interpretations. Modern Kleinians would not be likely to interpret at greater depth this early in the treatment. They would believe that the fantasy was analogous to the "bad breast." But they would be listening for the repetitions, omissions, contextual clues and metaphoric meanings rather than for evidence to back up the concept of the "bad breast."

American Object Relations

Influenced by Winnicott, Balint, and other British object relations theorists, some analysts in the United States formulate theory to account for their treatment of patients who would not have been able to tolerate the rigors of analytic treatment as practiced by ego psychologists. Steingart (1983) understands acting out as similar to what children do in play therapy, rather than as a regressive substitute for expressing thoughts and feelings in words. He believes that for a borderline patient enactment may be the only way to gain access to preoedipal pathology. Allowing enactment may permit later verbalization and interpretation. Bach (1985) writes about narcissistic character disorders and other severe pathologies. He points out that such patients cannot keep in mind that the same events may be viewed differently by different people. This inability shows up in their transference experience of being unable to see that the analyst's point of view and their own can both have reality and legitimacy. He believes that the patient can develop this capacity when allowed to handle anxieties, depressions, and feelings of emptiness in a better way than with earlier objects, and develops the ability to regulate affects and thinking. Difficulties with separateness and constancy are analyzed in the interaction with a separate and constant object: the analyst. Be cause defects of evocative constancy lead to defects of symbolism and awareness, these patients often communicate by enactment. Bach emphasizes the use of the therapeutic object relationship, therapeutic enactment, and understanding as preludes to the eventual interpretation. This sequence of interventions is designed to raise enactments to the level of symbolism and to stabilize the representational world so that a classical interpretive stance becomes possible.

An example of how Bach's theory works in practice in tandem with a compromise formation (Brenner, 1983) view is the following:

L has not been able to pray without feeling compelled to "curse God." He is ashamed to say the obscene words that come to him. When he was praying, he mouthed them as "a compromise between saying them and not saving them." The analyst says that he did well to do that. He challenges the analyst:

P: What was so good about that?

T: It worked. Like if you build a bridge and it stays up, you must have done it right.

P: But it was wrong to do that. Wrong to curse God.

T: You talk as if it was the crime. I think it was the punishment.

P: Why do you think that?

T: When you were doing it, you were suffering.

P: That's true. But what was the crime?

T: Your fellowship. You think of it as a crime because it makes you able to live without your father's support.

P: What I get, I know it's against him. But I don't get it, when I say those things you aren't supposed to say against God. Is there anybody else like this? Is this known?

T: Is it too scary if it is not known before?

P: What good are you if you don't know? I better give up. But if you know . . .

T: Then I shouldn't hold out on you. Yes. There was a person Freud wrote about. He's known as the Rat Man. He worried about cursing his father. But his father was dead.

P: I know about father and God. But that still isn't it. Maybe.

T: The thing is you punish yourself by mouthing the words. But that is still a compromise. You don't find it as bad as saying them aloud.

P: Well you say it's a punishment. But it is a bad thing to do.

T: There are two ways to look at it and I keep seeing the punishment part while you keep seeing the crime part. It's like those pictures where you can see it as a vase or two faces in profile. Just depends on how you look at it.

P: Oh. That's possible.

As long as the analyst was imposing her way of looking at this pathological compromise formation on the patient, he resisted seeing it. But when he was reminded of the possibility that there could be more than one way to see what he was talking about, a potential space opened in which he could allow the idea to be put into play. Technically, American object relations fits effortlessly into the ego psychology model that Breen (1993) characterizes as a cognitive psychology which evolved from Hartmann.

Conclusion

The Kleinian mode of thought was alien to ego psychologists in the United States for decades. Ego psychologists believed that they had nothing in common with the Kleinians. Arlow (1981) recalled Loewenstein's (1969) critique of Kleinian technique as blurring distinctions between "past and present, reality and fantasy, between the values of genetic and dynamic interpretations and reconstructions" (p. 586). In the past decade, interest in Klein's theories has been picking up until it is almost a vogue. Why should this happen now? One answer is that the self psychologists taught a generation of analysts to avoid aggression rather than confronting it. This left the Kleinian view to reintroduce an appropriate place for interpretations of aggressive components of the character and personality of analysands. Another reason seems to us to have been given less attention. Ego psychologists in the United States have been paying much attention to female psychology since Blum's (1976) reopening of discussion on this issue. In the course of this discussion penis envy has been removed from its position as the bedrock of female psychology. If not all envy is attributable to penis envy, Klein's work on envy becomes much more valuable and illuminating of clinical evidence than it was before.

Modern Kleinian thought and modern ego psychology are drawing closer to one another. At the same time, modern Kleinian analysts are divided along many of the same issues as the ego psychologists of North America. The differences within the groups are at least as great as the differences between them. This observation, if it holds up, leads to the conclusion that broad theory cannot long hold out against the corrective of clinical experience. Self psychologists differ from ego psychologists and Kleinians in that they do not privilege the unconscious or fantasy life, but focus on the real relationship with the parents and the real relationship with the analyst. Relationalists and interpersonalists narrow the analytic lens still further in that they do not focus on the real relationship with the parent, but on the here-and-now relationship with the analyst who is seen as an equal in the interaction and equally responsible for providing conscious thought as material for discussion in the hour.

The three new theories base their claims of technical superiority largely on the myth that Freudian theory is unitary, and its technical consequence is a set of narrow formulae about how to conduct an analysis. For example, recent presentations by "relational analysts," contrast their two-person interactive approach with what they characterize as the one-person intrapsychic approach of classical analysis. This dichotomous view is a straw man. Even Freud, who in his technical papers paid little systematic attention to the technical implications of the analyst-analysand interaction, was pragmatic, participatory, and responsive to his patients' needs in his clinical work (Lipton, 1977).

Robert Wallerstein (1990) has made the claim that there are fewer differences in technique than in theory among the different schools of analytic thought. We agree that differences in theory do not always translate into differences in technique. Fenichel's (1941) dictum of interpreting affect first, Gill's (1980) emphasis on transference awareness, and Brenner's attention to affect seem to bear out Wallerstein's point; they suggest that analytic technique is best viewed as coterminous with analytic process, a proposition offered by Brenner and Arlow in 1990.

Our brief review of contemporary Kleinianism also supports Wallerstein's position. The differences among Kleinians and the differences among ego psychologists are easily as great as the broad differences between these groups. Ego psychologists and Kleinians share a common understanding of unconscious mental organization. We listen to our analytic patients in like manner and formulate interpretations according to broadly similar criteria. It should be predictable that theoretical differences between these two schools of analytic thought will not long hold out against the corrective of clinical experience. It is more difficult to adhere to this integrationist position in regard to self psychological, relational, intersubjective, and interpersonalist schools. Their concern for the supposed injury inflicted by what they call classical technique has been addressed by the ego psychology of the 1940s and by their descendants.

Self psychology, relational and intersubjective schools ignore these developments in what they take to be the "classical" position. They set up a straw man using obsolete formulations and label it "classical." They differ from the ego psychological and Kleinian schools in basic ways. They begin with fundamentally different conceptions of mind and mental life and propose different theories of development, pathogenesis, and therapeutic action. Each uses a different therapeutic agenda to reach a different treatment goal. They differ in their interpretive criteria and in the meanings they attach to interpretation are different as well. Only the future will tell whether the net of common clinical experience is cast wide enough to effect a convergence among schools of thought whose divergent world and treatment views sustain fundamentally divergent approaches to psychoanalytic technique. When Wallerstein planned the Rome Congress on common ground, he selected an ego psychologist, a Kleinian, and a representative of the British Middle School to demonstrate his position. He did not invite a self psychologist or an adherent of the relational or intersubjective psychoanalytic schools. It is our contention that had he done so the comparison would not have supported his case for common analytic ground.

REFERENCES

ARLOW, J. (1981). Theories of pathogenesis. *Psychoanalytic Quarterly* 50:488–514.
——— (1991a). Methodology and reconstruction. *Psychoanalytic Quarterly* 60:539–563.
——— (1991b). Conflict, trauma and deficit. In: *Conflict and Compromise Formation,* ed. S. Dowling. Madison, CT: International Universities Press.
——— (1991c). *Psychoanalysis: Clinical Theory and Practice.* Madison, CT.: International Universities Press.
——— (1993). Changing perspectives in psychoanalytic technique. Paper

presented at Annual Meeting of the New York Freudian Society. December 12.

———— (1994). Discussion of "Notes on Psychoanalytic Theory and Its Consequences for Technique." Presented at the Scientific Meeting of the New York Freudian Society, February 1, 1994.

———— Brenner, C. (1990). The psychoanalytic process. *Psychoanalytic Quarterly* 59:678–692.

BACH, S. (1985). *Narcissistic States and the Therapeutic Process.* New York: Aronson.

BARANGER, M., & BARANGER, W. (1964). Insight in the analytic situation. In: *Psychoanalysis in the Americas,* ed. R.E. Litman. New York: International Universities Press, 1966.

BAUDRY, F. (1993). Discussion of the Freud-Klein controversies at the meet the author series, American Psychoanalytic Association Meetings, December 17.

BERGER, L. (1987). *Psychoanalytic Theory and Clinical Relevance: What Makes Theory Consequential for Practice.* Hillsdale, NJ: Analytic Press.

BLEGER, J. (1971). La entrevista psicologica: Su empleo en el diagnostico y la investigacion. In: Temas de psicologia: Entrevistas y grupos. Buenos Aires: Nueva Vision.

BLUM, H. (1976). Masochism, the ego ideal and the psychology of women. *Journal of the American Psychoanalytic Association* 24:157–192.

BREEN, D. (1993). General introduction. In: *The Gender Conundrum,* ed. D. Breen. London: Routledge.

Brenner, C. (1979). Working alliance, therapeutic alliance and transference. *Journal of the American Psychoanalytic Association* 27:137–158.

———— (1983). *The Mind in Conflict.* New York: International Universities PRESS.

BREUER, J., & FREUD, S. (1893–1895). Studies on Hysteria. *Standard Edition.*

CAVELL, M. (1993). *The Psychoanalytic Mind.* Cambridge, MA: Harvard University Press.

DE BIANCHEDI, E.T., SCALOZUB DE BOSCHAN, L., de Cortiñas, L.P. & de Piccolo, E.G. (1988). Theories on anxiety in Freud and Melanie Klein. Their metapsychological status. *International Journal of Psycho-Analysis* 69:359–368.

ETCHEGOYEN, H. (1991). *The Fundamentals of Psychoanalytic Technique.* London: Karnac Books.

FENICHEL, O. (1941). *Problems of Psychoanalytic Technique.* New York: Psychoanalytic Quarterly Press.

FRIEDMAN, L. (1991). A reading of Freud's papers on technique. *Psychoanalytic Quarterly* 60:564–595.

FREUD, S. (1910). Observations on "wild" psychoanalysis. *Standard Edition* 11:219–227.

———— (1912). The employment of dream interpretation in psychoanalysis. *Standard Edition* 12:89–96.

——— (1914). Further recommendations: Recollection, repetition and working through. *Standard Edition* 12:145–156.

——— (1915). Observations on transference love. *Standard Edition* 12:159–171.

——— (1919). Lines of advance in psychoanalytic therapy. *Standard Edition* 17:157–168.

——— (1925). On negation. Standard Edition, 19:235–239. London: Hogarth Press, 1961.

GILL, M. (1980). The analysis of transference. *Journal of the American Psychoanalytic Association* 27(Suppl.): 263–288.

GLOVER, E. (1940). *An Investigation of the Technique of Psychoanalysis.* London: Baillière, Tindall & Cox.

GOLDBERG, A. (1980). Letter to the editor. *International Journal of Psycho-Analysis* 61:91–93.

——— (1990). *The Prisonhouse of Psychoanalysis.* Hillsdale, NJ: Analytic Press.

GRAY, P. (1994). *The Ego and Analysis of Defense.* Northvale, NJ: Aronson.

GREENBERG, J. (1991). *Oedipus and Beyond.* Cambridge, MA: Harvard University Press.

GREENSON, R. (1965). The working alliance and the transference neurosis. *Psychoanalytic Quarterly* 34:155–181.

ISAACS, S. (1948). The nature and function of phantasy. *International Journal of Psycho-Analysis* 29:73–97.

JACOBS, T. (1991). *The Use of the Self.* Madison, CT.: International Universities Press.

KAISER, H. (1976). Concerning the theory of psychoanalytic technique. In: *The Evolution of Psychoanalytic Technique,* ed. M. Bergmann & F. Hartman. New York: Basic Books, pp. 448–465.

KING, P. (1983). The life and work of Melanie Klein in the British Psychoanalytical Society. *International Journal of Psycho-Analysis* 64:251–260.

——— Steiner, R., Eds. (1991). *The Freud-Klein Controversies 1941–1945.* London: Tavistock / Routledge.

KOHUT, H. (1971). *The Analysis of the Self.* New York: International Universities Press.

——— (1979). The two analyses of Mr. Z. *International Forum of Psychoanalysis* 60:3–27.

——— (1984). *How Does Analysis Cure?* Chicago: University of Chicago Press.

LEVINE, H. (1992). Freudian and Kleinian theory. *Journal of the American Psychoanalytic Association* 40:801–826.

LIPTON, S. (1977). Freud's technique as shown in his analysis of the Rat Man. *International Journal of Psycho-Analysis* 58:255–274.

LOEWENSTEIN, R. (1969). Development in the theory of transference in the last fifty years. *International Journal of Psycho-Analysis* 50:583–588.

LORAND, S. (1948). Comments on the correlation of theory and technique.

Psychoanalytic Quarterly 17:32–50.

MITCHELL, S. (1988). *Relational Concepts in Psychoanalysis.* Cambridge, MA: Harvard University Press.

NEW YORK PSYCHOANALYTIC INSTITUTE (1963). Minutes of faculty meeting. November 20. Unpublished.

OBERNDORF, C. P. (1943). Results of psychoanalytic therapy. *International Journal of Psycho-Analysis* 24:107–114.

ORNSTEIN, P., & ORNSTEIN, A. (1994). On the conceptualisation of clinical facts in psychoanalysis. *International Journal of Psycho-Analysis* 75:977–994.

HURST, D.M.(1995). Panel: Toward a definition of the termand concept of interaction. *Journal of the American Psychoanalytic Association* 43:521–537.

POLAND, W. (1975). Tact as a psychoanalytic function. Int. J. Psycho-Anal., 56:155–162.

———— W. (1985). At work. In: Analysts at Work: Practice, Principles and Techniques, ed. J. Reppen. Hillsdale, NJ: Analytic Press.

RACKER, H. (1968). Transference and Countertransference. London: Karnac, 1982.

RANGELL, L. (1990). The Human Core. Madison, CT: International Universities Press.

RANK, O., & FERENCZI, S. (1924). The Development of Psychoanalysis. Washington, DC: Nervous and Medical Disease Publishing Co., 1925.

REED, G. (1987). Rules of clinical understanding in classical psychoanalysis and in self psychology. *Journal of the American Psychoanalytic Association* 35:421–455.

RICHARDS, A.D. (1984a). Transference analysis: Means or end? *Psychoanalytic Quarterly* 4:355–366.

———— (1984b). The relationship between psychoanalytic theory and psychoanalytic technique. *Journal of the American Psychoanalytic Association* 32:587–602.

———— (1992). Commentary on Trop and Stolorow's "Defense analysis in self psychology." Psychoanal. Dial., 2:455–453.

ROBBINS, M. (1980). Current controversy in object relations theory. *International Journal of Psycho-Analysis* 61:477–492.

SPENCER, J., & BALTER, L. (1990). Psychoanalytic observation. *Journal of the American Psychoanalytic Association* 38:393–420.

STEIN, R. (1990). Anew look at the theory of Melanie Klein. *International Journal of Psycho-Analysis* 71:499–510.

STEINGART, I. (1983). *Pathological Play in Borderline and Narcissistic Personalities.* New York: S.P. Medical & Scientific/Spectrum.

STOLOROW, R., BRANDCHAFT, B., & ATWOOD, G. (1987). Psychoanalytic Treatment: An Intersubjective Approach. Hillsdale, NJ: Analytic Press.

WALLERSTEIN, R. (1990). Psychoanalysis: The common ground. *International Journal of Psycho-Analysis* 71:3–20.

———— (1992). *The Common Ground of Psychoanalysis.* Northvale, NJ:

Aronson, pp. 203–242.

WEINSHEL, E. (1992). Therapeutic technique in psychoanalysis and psychoanalytic psychotherapy. J. Amer. Psychoanal. Assn., 40:327–348.

ZAC, J. (1973). Psicopatia. Buenos Aires: Kargieman.

A RESPONSE TO OUR RESPONDENTS

[Richards, A.D. & Richards, A.K. (1995). *Journal of Clinical Psychoanalysis* 4:543–564.]

Our paper can be read in two different ways. First, as a discussion of the relation or lack of relation between theory and technique. Second, as an attempt at comparative psychoanalysis. Using a clinical case vignette discussed by ourselves and then explicated from different theoretical points of view, we undertook a kind of psychoanalytic thought experiment in which we imagined what analysts from different schools of thought would say.

We recognized that this design was flawed from the start because it used data already shaped by the theoretical approach of the presenters. As Ornstein puts it in his commentary: "This database may be unsuitable for a comparative assessment because it was obtained with a different observational and treatment method guided by a different theory" (p. 494). Nevertheless, we hoped that responses to our clinical thought experiment by contributors from other schools would sharpen the fundamental differences in theory and technique. We have long believed that the discussions on comparative psychoanalysis in the literature suffer from a lack of conceptual and definitional clarity. The emphasis usually is on different theorists responding to detailed clinical material without focusing on their fundamental premises and the relationship between these premises and technique.

Fosshage faults us for not having representatives of each theory explicate their viewpoint and address detailed clinical material. This format was followed in two issues of *Psychoanalytic Inquiry,* one based on a case by Martin Silverman and the other on a case by Fosshage himself. Our sense was that in both these PI issues discussion of fundamental concepts got lost in the wealth of clinical detail. We hoped to give theoretical issues a better platform in the debate.

It should be apparent that there are, indeed, several ways of looking at the basic issue. One is that the various theories are essentially the same; they are minor variations on the broad theme of psychoanalysis.

They may differ at the level of metapsychology, as Wallerstein proposes, but they converge clinically and hence technically. We can arrive at this verdict from several different directions, one of which is Wallerstein's "common ground."

A second approach views psychoanalytic theory as a developing theoretical corpus that has evolved to the point that the modern-day version of psychoanalytic theory, different from Freud's original conception—what Leo Rangell refers to as "total composite theory"—is broad enough to deal successfully with all the issues and problems that the other theories claim to be better able to address. A variant of this argument, put facetiously, is that what is right is not new and what is new is not right.

A third approach, or position, is that the current landscape of theoretical diversity does indeed involve different theoretical approaches. These approaches share certain basic principles, but their varying foci (i.e., what they propose is figure and what is ground) and emphases (i.e., what is more important and what is less important), are indeed distinguishable. Inherent in this latter point of view is the belief that the different theories lead to different techniques or at least to different technical emphases involving issues of timing and tact.

To summarize, the possibilities are (1) that the theories are the same and the techniques are the same; (2) that the theories are different but the techniques are the same; or (3) that the theories are different and the techniques are different.

Another problem with these assessments concerns what we take to be the "gold standard," as Ornstein calls it, against which the magnitude of theoretical deviation is to be measured. Too often the assumption is that the gold standard for some people is classical psychoanalysis, which is often equated with an earlier version of the theory promulgated by Freud. This viewpoint tends not to take into account the way in which Freud moved the theory along during his lifetime; nor does it consider the way in which the next generations of psychoanalysts developed the theory in an evolutionary fashion.

The strawman which seems to play such a prominent place in this discussion is often an antiquated view of psychoanalysis: psychoanalysis of the drive/discharge model, the blank screen, the surgically neutral analyst, and so forth. New theories frequently proffer their superiority by presenting their concepts side by side with early Freud; the Rosetta Stone then becomes the ancient version of psychoanalysis. This tendency is exemplified by Stolorow's definition of classical psychoanalysis as the model of the isolated mental apparatus or Mitchell's use of metaphors like the "seething cauldron" and the "baby as beast" to characterize non-relational drive psychology. These approaches are based on the idea that Freud's instinctual drive/energic model is fundamental to the theory and has to be dragged into all later versions. There seems to be a great reluctance to recognize the extent to which the so-called modern classical analysts, Charles Brenner and Jacob Arlow, for example, have moved away from Freud's economic point of view and developed a theoretical structure which is, in important ways, antimetapsychological and even converging with the antimetapsychological critique of such eminent Rapaport students as Holt, Klein, Schafer, and Gill.

The thrust of our argument is that no one of the possibilities enumerated above really encompass the entire theoretical landscape. We believe that the new theories vary to the extent to which that they are theoretically disjunctive and to which they lead to disjunctive technical approaches.

Kleinian Psychoanalysis

We are grateful to Robert Caper (as we are to Elizabeth de Bianchedi) for his clarification of the basic tenets of Melanie Klein's theoretical approach. But our sense is that some of the points that we may have misunderstood are not very relevant to issues of technique. Thus, they do not militate against our basic position: that the convergence of modern structural theory and Kleinian theory is based on a common commitment to a conflict model and the notion of unconscious fantasy, including the latter's operational application to the work of psychoanalysis.

Robert Caper has redefined the Kleinian view very fruitfully. He wants us to see Kleinian theory as much closer to Freudian ideas than had been thought in the past. He emphasizes anxiety rather than aggression as the primary motivator in Kleinian theory. His second point is that the depressive struggle is similar to, and can be seen as a precursor of, the oedipal complex. Here he implicitly argues that, with the addition of depressive affect as a motivator (Brenner, 1983), modern classical theory has drawn closer to the Kleinian view. His third point is that reconstructions of greed and envy in the earliest years of life are similar to reconstructions of oedipal wishes and fears.

Caper's fourth point deals with an issue where Kleinian theory and modern classical theory basically agree, over and against the self psychologists, interpersonalists, and intersubjectivists. This is the issue of the real mother as a person. Kleinians believe that the internal object is different from the person one can observe in the real world. Modern classical theorists agree. For the self psychologists and all the "inter" theories, on the other hand, there seems to be no distinction. Caper uses the clinical vignette to elucidate the difference between self psychology and the classical/Kleinian clinical work. Whereas classical and Kleinian analysts would learn something about the patient from the analyst's experience of feeling intrusive, self psychologists presumably assume that the analyst was intrusive. We believe that the latter was not the case: The analyst inquired about the lateness in the service of understanding what the patient was thinking that caused her self-defeating behavior of being late. This inquiry was clearly in the patient's interest. It would have been more pleasant for the analyst to be a benign figure who waited patiently until the patient felt like coming. But the work obligated the analyst to understand this behavior as self-defeating and to analyze it, even though her queries aroused the patient's anger. Both Kleinians and modern classicists regard arousing anger in such a situation as a good thing, not a mistake in technique.

We believe that Caper's argument addresses Stolorow's position equally well. The problem, as Caper and we see it, exists in the patient, not in the space between the patient and her "internalized objects." Therefore, both Caper and we conclude that there is a difference in technique, and not just a difference in theory, between ourselves and the self psychologists.

Caper concurs with our position about the divergence of self psychology from both Freudian and Kleinian practice. We acknowledge, however, that self psychologists too maintain that their data come from the transference—countertransference situation; for example, an idealizing transference that the analyst may be unable to tolerate (countertransference). And, the self psychological mirror transference-countertransference constellation may also be retranslated into Kleinian terms: the patient denying the analyst his analyzing function to avoid the envy which would follow from the analyst being able to be helpful through interpretation. But Caper is correct, we believe, in pointing to the difficulty of formulating exactly how environmental failure experienced by the patient gets expressed in the transference. How, for example, does the patient know how to miss something that was never experienced?

Theory must have an effect on technique. As de Bianchedi, underscoring Hanly, points out, a theory which posits coherence as the ultimate criterion of psychic truth necessarily implies constructions as the means to reach that truth. Likewise, a theory which states that psychic reality corresponds with what happened in the past will use a hypothesis-testing model for interpretations and reconstructions. We agree with Bianchedi that technique and theory are in constant interaction.

Bianchedi believes that the theoretical difference between Bionian theory and the classical one used in our example is that Bionian theory encompasses very primitive fantasies and thoughts that fall outside the purview of classical theory. Thus, a Bionian like herself would include interpretations about wanting to make the analyst wrong, of feeling like an angry baby who cannot stand mother's serenity or patience, or of "behaving like a little girl who thinks mommy prefers her other children . . . or daddy." Bianchedi would underline the hypothetical nature of her remarks by using a special nurserylike language, while a classical theorist would use a more prosaic language but would emphasize the feelings that underlie the behavior. The differences here seem to be small, the similarities large.

Interpersonalists and Object Relations

We are grateful to Dr. Robert Stolorow for participating in this discussion. The most important aspect of Stolorow's critique is his conclusion that he has learned nothing new from reading our paper.

Everything in it was either already known or false. He sees "some limited validity" in our "charge" that he simplifies earlier theories in order to contrast them with his own theory, which he believes to be superior to all previous and all contemporaneous ones. When Stolorow asserts that all analytic theories are the products of the theorist's own psychological histories and current psychopathology, is he then to be included among those theorists? Are we to understand him as implying that he himself is the product of an unattuned mother? Does he mean that he is trying to work out his own troubles in the form of a theory that he wishes to impose on others? Does he have trouble tuning in to other people's affects and needs? If so, we can only commiserate. But if he believes that some people can create compromise formations in which their own pathology plays a part, then he must also concede that the child is not a tabula rasa on which the mother's pathology is inscribed forever, but a separate other who, from the beginning, has a part in his own mental life and is the source of at least some of his own dreams, wishes, and, yes, fantasies. This infant, born with his own unique capacities, potentialities, and limitations is the infant of, dare we say it, Freudian theory. If Stolorow is willing to go so far as to see even the infant as having power in the interpersonal world, then he cannot continue to assert that the caregiver is all. His technique will then bear the marks of a theory of the personal unconscious. And if he proceeds to this point, then we are truly on common ground.

From his discussion, it is clear that Stolorow is uncomfortable with any implication of common ground between his point of view and that of modern Freudians. For Stolorow there is a sharp distinction between the Freudian myth of an isolated mind and his notion of intersubjectivity. The Freudian isolated mind is the strawman that is always the starting point for Stolorow's critique and reformulation. We contend, contra Stolorow, that a theory in which the ambivalence conflicts of childhood and the family drama—parent and children in intense interactions in relation to their needs, wishes, fears, anxieties—is hardly a model of minds in isolation. The Oedipus complex is certainly a depiction of minds in interaction.

Stolorow's reference to "instinctual viciousness" is judgmental and pejorative in the manner of Mitchell's "baby as beast." We are reminded of a line from a Nichols and May skit—"aggression need not be hostile"—mouthed by a Freudian psychoanalyst.

Stolorow states that a major problem with the classical approach is its adherence to positivistic philosophy. We have already expressed our belief that the positivistic/relativistic philosophical debate is not very useful in explicating the theoretical and clinical issues of psychoanalytic practice. It serves in our view to obfuscate rather than illuminate. Space does not permit further discussion of intersubjectivity theory. We would refer the reader to A. D. Richards' discussion of the case presentation of Stolorow and Trop in Psychoanalytic Dialogues and Stolorow's response. Stephen Mitchell also contributes a response that further illuminates the differences in theory between modern conflict theory and relational psychoanalysis/intersubjectivity theory.

Self Psychology

The most controversial part of our paper is our discussion of self psychology. We assert that this theory is different from contemporary classical psychoanalytic theory. Kohut and his disciples are modifiers rather than extenders of classical theory.

Fosshage faults us for not adopting the approach of "having representatives of each orientation present their theories and address detailed
clinical material." As noted above, we elected to forego this strategy in
the knowledge that it had been done in two issues of *Psychoanalytic
Inquiry.* We sought an alternative approach that would concentrate more
on theoretical premises and their relationship to technique.

Although we believe that modern conflict theory is a "comprehensive theory," we did not intend to "prove" that it was the best theory,
or, to use Ornstein's phrase, the Rosetta Stone. We are more concerned
with demonstrating similarities and differences in technique and examining whether those differences followed from theory and, if so, how
they followed.

Fosshage's discussion sets up false dichotomies in defending his
point of view. The dyadic nature of the analytic situation (the dyad) is
axiomatic in the modern conflict approach just as it is in self psychology. We have also a problem with the antithesis that we find so often in
the literature—subjectivity versus objectivity or relativism versus positivism. In this contest, subjectivity and relativism always win over objectivity and positivism. Fosshage's postmodern position covers over a multiplicity of epistemological sins, among them faulty reasoning and argument by fiat. His insistence that the classical view of the analytic situation is nondyadic is logically no different from Stolorow's equally summary assertion that modern conflict theory is founded in the principle of
the "isolated mind."

We are puzzled by Fosshage's insistence that there should not be any
imposition of an outside observer's orientation into the material. He
would then, it seems, deny the subjectivity of the analyst. How can we
have dialogue among different schools if dialogue requires all nonself
psychologists to divest themselves of the concepts that are their tools for
thinking about analytic material?

Fosshage faults us for not providing in our paper a deep enough
explication of a single case. We did not intend to write a paper in which
we provided in-depth explication of an individual case by various points
of view. Our intention with the vignette was to provide an anchoring
point for a discussion of different theoretical principles and their derivative clinical approaches. Fosshage's comment about the difficulty for any
analyst of one orientation fully to comprehend another psychoanalytic
orientation raises some interesting questions. It would appear that Kohut
and his followers had no difficulty in fully comprehending the modern

Freudian orientation and finding it wanting. Relational psychoanalysis in its various forms begins from the conviction that classical theory is deficient in a specific way. Proponents of all manner of "new approaches" have no trouble understanding classical theory even though they insist that a classical theorist cannot understand their theories. We are puzzled that Fosshage faults Arlow for expanding the term unconscious fantasy to include relational and interpersonal aspects from all levels of development simply because Arlow's use is central to the modern conflict approach and was articulated in 1969, before self psychology was born. Fosshage implies that Arlow should not integrate such a usage with the presuppositions of conflict theory, as if self psychology and relational psychoanalysis have "cornered the market" on the use of this concept in a particular way.

On the other hand if what Fosshage is pointing to is a convergence between Kohut and Arlow, we find this an interesting point worthy of further discussion. Further, Fosshage's approval of our clinical approach and his pointing to it as an illustration of a "common ground" among analysts is appreciatively noted. However, for us this only provides further support for our view that the fundamental principles of modern Freudian theory are foundational and comprehensive in the main. The problem, perhaps, is that the development of theoretical pluralism begins with a brief against common ground. Kohut, among others, asserts the absence of common ground between his view and that of modern conflict theorists (Arlow, Brenner, et al.).

The implication of Fosshage's discussion about validation is that there is a distinction to be made between a "bad" authoritarian classical approach and a "good" empathic self psychological/relational approach. This "straw person" figures in many discussions these days; he or she is the cold, authoritarian, blank screen, surgical analyst, trained at the New York Psychoanalytic Institute. We are uncomfortable with theory building which is based on such personal assessments. All good psychoanalysts are sensitive and empathic. The issue then becomes to what extent one can base a theory, a therapeutic approach, and a mechanism of therapeutic action on empathy (Shapiro, T., 1981, A. D. Richards, 1982).

We do not think the empathy/perspective dichotomy is a substantive theoretical issue. However, when Fosshage refers to structure building focused on reparation of self and selfobject ruptures, we do approach a fundamental issue and a potentially profound difference in approach. We believe that transference means something different in self psychology than it does in classical theory. The self psychological concept of transference is a part of a theory of "thwarted development." In this theory infantile needs rather than wishes are transferred. The interpretation of self states addressing such needs would not seem to rely on free association in the same way that Freudian and Kleinian praxis do.

Self state dream interpretation relies on manifest content; it is similar to the interpretation of dreams by symbols. According to Freud, the latter was the interpretative approach of last resort, to be used only when interpretation by free association failed. But in self psychology, the manifest content seems to be the interpretation of first resort. It is as if there were a self psychology dream book, with rules of translation of visual images of the dreamer into representations of the state of the self: anchored, floating, fragmented, integrated and so forth.

Fosshage fails to understand the point we are trying to make about the self psychological concepts of idealizing transference and mirror transference. They are part of a deficit theory of pathogenesis and therapeutic action. We prefer a theory that integrates conflict and deficit variables and sees them as interactive. It is interesting to note that this critique of self psychology, as eschewing conflict in favor of deficit is also held by Mitchell and Stolorow, neither of whom is a classical analyst. Mitchell has referred to this problematic aspect of self psychology as the "developmental tilt" (Greenberg and Mitchell, 1983).

Fosshage stresses the idea that the classical view of resistance sets up an adversarial situation between analyst and analysand and produces resistance iatrogenetically. Frank Lachmann (1986) also makes this point, while suggesting that the adversarial relationship can be therapeutic in itself; the patient, that is, can benefit from battling with a strong opponent.

Fosshage is right in faulting us for not searching carefully enough through the self psychological literature to see the diversity of points of view and the extent to which modern self psychologists (Lichten-berg, Fosshage, et al.) have departed from Kohut. Perhaps this is comparable to the process by which modern conflict theorists (Arlow, Brenner, Boesky, Rangell) have departed from Freud. But our point is that the latter are not moving toward a radical reformulation of basic psychoanalytic theory. They still use classical ideas based on Freud's foundational concepts, among them transference, defense, resistance, unconscious fantasy, and conflicts of ambivalence.

Paul Ornstein

Ornstein begins his detailed response to our paper by considering the methodologic difficulties of our approach. He proposes that a sine qua non for useful discussion in a comparative psychoanalytic effort is for the discussant to "enter into the theoretical framework of the presenting analyst and, more importantly, to enter into the analytic process itself" (p. 493). Commentators should "put themselves imaginatively into the patient's or the analyst's place in order to find out what each of them is experiencing in the analytic relationship." They must "assume an observational vantage point from the inside," as it were, "by attempting to conduct an analysis according to the theory and treatment principles studied" (p. 493).

Ornstein recognizes this is not only enormously difficult but likely impossible, a position he shares with Goldberg, so he in effect leaves us hanging: He acknowledges that it may be impossible to do what he thinks must be done, but then does not offer a way out of the dilemma. His position seemingly precludes any meaningful exercise in comparative psychoanalysis. Our own position is different. We agree that imaginative immersion in another analyst's (or patient's) place is impossible to achieve, but we do not agree that it is a precondition for a meaningful discussion of differences in theory and technique.

We would cite as one case example the discussion by one of us (Arnold Richards, 1992), of Stolorow and Trop's "Defense Analysis in Self Psychology: A Developmental View," published in Psychoanalytic Dialogues, and Frank Lachmann's discussion of Arnold Richards' paper "Self Theory, Conflict Theory and the Problem of Hypochondriasis," published in Psychoanalytic Psychology. The second example is of interest because what Lachmann does is reframe Richards' therapeutic interventions in self psychological terms to account for their positive effects. So here we have the idea that different theories can yield divergent techniques that tend to the same outcome. This example certainly adds to the complexity of the theoretical/technical landscape. In the first example, Richards argues that a divergent technical principle informed the work of Stolorow and Trop, namely, the central role of validation in the form of the analyst's validation of the patient's experience. Richards tried to show that this approach, while linked to the positive therapeutic results, may have foreclosed other avenues of investigation and made for a divergent treatment approach.

In considering methodological difficulties, Ornstein voices agreement with our claim that theory determines technique. Of course, this fact complicates any effort at comparative psychoanalysis. Ornstein submits that we cannot get out of this synchretist dilemma—in that what we see is determined by what we believe, and what happens in the analytic situation is determined by our theoretical outlook—by, in effect, running a controlled experiment. Once we go down one theoretical path, that is, we cannot backtrack and pursue another approach with the same patient and the same analyst. As an aside we might consider Kohut's efforts in his analysis of Mr. Z, presented as a situation in which he looked at the same patient from two different theoretical perspectives; we leave aside for the moment the consequences of the intriguing suggestion that in the second case analyst and patient were the same.

In any case, Ornstein's way out of this dilemma is to press for detailed verbatim process notes, which would enable the outsider "to enter the analytic process and alternatingly empathize with the patient as well as the analyst" (p. 493). We second Ornstein's plea to listen to someone else's work with an open mind. We would contend, however, that all of us tried to do just that and that self psychologists do not have a claim to more inherent open-mindedness than analysts of other theoretical persuasions.

In our own case, our assessments and judgments about the central concepts of self psychology and their consequences for technique are based on an in-depth reading of Kohut and many other self psychologists with an openness to being persuaded of the value of this new approach. Ornstein's methodological concerns are most salient when the purpose of comparative psychoanalysis is to compare different theoretical approaches and make judgments about which is better and which is worse. We are the first to acknowledge that any such judgments would necessarily rest on very shaky ground. But, the methodological problems tend to fall away when the emphasis shifts from a ranking of different theories to an assessment of differences per se. The focus is then on whether differences exist, and whether, and in what ways, such differences are technically consequential. The point of our paper was simply that Kleinian and classical analysis are more convergent than divergent, whereas relational and self psychological treatment are more divergent than convergent with both the classical and Kleinian traditions.

We are pleased to note that our "thumbnail sketch of self psychology aroused full assent" (Ornstein). We note with interest his distinction between empathy and vicarious introspection, namely, that empathy is vicarious introspection in contrast with introspection proper. Empathy, then, is not vicarious introspection in relation to the others, introspection is introspection in relation to the self. Ornstein corrects our assessment of the fundamental shifts in Kohut's points of view when he passed over from classical analysis to becoming a self psychologist. Central to the shift, according to Ornstein, was Kohut's effort "to understand the world through the patient's eyes."

This seems to be the recurrent theme in Ornstein's presentation. That he describes it as a "shift" in Kohut's approach implies that classical analysts then and now do not attempt to see the world as the patient sees it. We are hard-pressed to identify any theoretical postulate of classical analysis that precludes the analyst's effort to do just that. We submit that this is part of any successful therapeutic interaction; it is part of the process that goes on in the analyst's mind as he listens to the patient. In saying this, we must ask ourselves whether, in proposing that the self psychologist's basic methodological approach is not disjunctive from the classical analyst's, we are in effect making a case for Wallerstein's thesis of common technical ground among analysts who espouse different theories.

With regard to the importance of interpreting and understanding from the patient's perspective, we note that this point of view is not limited to self psychology. Evelyne Schwaber (1990) certainly stresses this requirement in her examination of therapeutic intersubjectivity. It does seem to be an implied assumption of this emphasis that the analyst cannot move in the direction of acquiring more understanding of the patient's experience simply by listening to what the patient says and, if necessary, asking the patient what he or she is feeling. The emphasis on empathy, introspection, and vicarious introspection seems to suggest that this process is silent and indirect.

We believe that formulating the process in this way makes it at times border on the mystical and the mysterious (see further, Ted Shapiro). Nevertheless, for Ornstein this distinction is crucial. He writes "the analyst's introspective empathic data-gathering stance permits the emergence of these transferences, where the analyst's extrospective data-gathering stance blocks their emergence as it happened in the case of Mr. Z's first analysis" (p. 497). For us this is the heart of one technical matter. We are unwilling to accept that an extrospective data-gathering stance, which means listening to the patient and pursuing lines of investigation that encourage the patient to describe his or her experience with as much detail and emotion as possible, blocks anything.

The implication of Ornstein's formulation is that the fundamental transferences, or the transferences that self psychologists find fundamental—the mirror idealizing and twinship transferences—are not revealed to the classical analyst because they are "blocked by the stance of the classical analyst." For many of us who have pondered "The Two Analyses of Mr. Z.," the problem has more to do with bad analytic technique defined by classical or any other criteria. It is bad technique that is, to adopt an authoritarian stance in which the analyst always knows best and is right. What Kohut invoked, and Ornstein apparently still endorses, is the model of the classical analyst as rigid and authoritarian, and prone to impose his theoretical convictions on the patient and on the patient's free associations.

The most persuasive counter to this point of view are Arlow's papers on "The Genesis of Interpretation" (1979) and "The Process of Validation and Hypothesis Testing in the Analytic Situation" (1994). However, be that as it may, Ornstein in his formulation makes the next self psychological leap by which he understands the self in the analytic situation in terms of selfobject transferences that develop and serve as glue to hold the fragmentation-prone self together. And he follows with the self psychological theory of cure, whereby interpretations repair the disruptions in the selfobject transferences which lead to belated structure building and thereby consolidate the cohesiveness of the self and restore its lost vitality.

At this point, we refer to our concern that selfobject transferences are manifest content rather than defined, explanatory concepts. We are reluctant to proceed down the self psychological road in which the theory of a superordinate self, its development, pathogenesis, and repair are central to the understanding of the human being and crucial to the formulation of therapeutic process in analysis. It is perhaps at this juncture that we arrive at the great analytic divide between self psychology and classical psychoanalysis—and this despite Ornstein's insistence that insight, interpretation, and understanding are part of both approaches.

Ornstein writes that within the self psychological perspective it is not an insuperable difficulty to decenter from one's own world view and immerse oneself in the patient's, all the while knowing where one's world view ends and the patient's begins. To which we ask: What is the specific difference between classical analysts and self psychological analysts, or what is the difference in the theories that enables decentering to occur with one theory and not with the other? It is Ornstein's contention that conflict theory encourages the development of the transference neurosis, just as self psychology forces the development of a selfobject transference. There are two issues here. One is Ornstein's clearly stated position that we are dealing with two fundamentally different stances in the analytic situation. Here we are in agreement. But, given these different stances, we remain unclear as to how they are brought about, how they relate to theory, and so forth.

Ornstein returns to the convention that for the self psychologist the focus of the analysis is the patient's subjective inner world. This, of course, is the battle cry of intersubjectivity theory and relational psychoanalysis as well. The issue is whether, and to what degree, the conflict psychologist focuses on the subjective inner world: If the subjective inner world includes the analysand's world of unconscious fantasy, we again have reached a position of convergence. And the notion that the classical analyst has no interest in, or gateway to, the patient's subjective inner world is for us the setting up of a straw man—a profound misconception. This is the idea, implied by Ornstein, that for the classical analyst the primary unit of experience is a drive or mental mechanism. We submit that this is simply not the case. The concept of compromise formation is concerned with all aspects of a person's experience—drive, defense, anxiety—to which Ornstein replies that the divide between self psychology and classical analysis is that for the self psychologist the intervention is offered from within, for the classical analyst the intervention is offered from without. This is somehow connected with the way Kohut turned things upside down: "What is nonspecific in classical analysis has become specific in self psychology and what is specific in classical analysis has become nonspecific in self psychology."

We are very grateful for Dr. Ornstein's detailed and sensitive explication of our case from his point of view. He has certainly done a better job at playing the self psychologist than we were able to from our classical vantage point. We think Ornstein demonstrates that there is a significant difference between the approach of the self psychologist and the classical analyst, which of course supports the basic thesis of our contribution.

Francis Baudry

Baudry says that our characterization of self psychology is overdrawn. We did not mean to imply that analysis cannot learn from the writings of Kohut and other self psychologists. We were attempting to underscore the fact that the status of concepts like self-esteem, mirroring, and idealization is different to a modern conflict theorist and to a self psychologist—someone who has immersed himself in the theory (as Goldberg insists is necessary), accepted the theory of development, pathogenesis, and change, and embraced the distinction between Tragic Man and Guilty Man that Kohut presented as foundational. Along different lines, Baudry supports our assertion of the convergence of technique between modern Kleinian and modern classical analysis in noting that his presenting of clinical material to a Kleinian and a classical theorist produced very similar comments and similar perspectives on the development of the analytic process.

Baudry seems to evidence some surprise that Arlow should present a patient who had "oral cannibalization" material. I think this reflects on an important misunderstanding of the approach of conflict theorists such as Arlow. There tends to be the view that this group is focused on a specific universe of oedipal fantasies and does not hear "preoedipal fantasies." We strongly believe that the oedipal/preoedipal dichotomy is not a useful organizer of clinical material. It is much more helpful to look for the fantasy themes (implicating orality, anality, death, immortality, merger, separateness, rescue, etc.), that engage each patient. Every individual transverses a developmental track from infancy and adulthood and deals with the wishes, anxieties, and "players" of each stage for better or worse.

Baudry's discussion about the reality of the analysis and its role in shaping the perceptions of the patient and the analyst along with the resulting transference configuration, presents a position with which we are in agreement. It is not clear to us, however, what aspect of Freudian theory would determine that there is no "day residue" for transference, that there is no thread of reality. The emphasis of some analysts on the pathogenic role of unconscious fantasy does not imply a denial of reality, including the real attributes of the analyst.

Irving Steingart

Steingart begins his discussion by adding his voice to those who claim that we have treated Kohut's self psychology unfairly in suggesting that the self psychological approach involves a relabeling of manifest content rather than an exploration of meaning. Of course, we cannot demonstrate that all self psychologists, at all times in their clinical work, operate at the level of manifest content when they invoke categories of idealizing transference, mirror transference, and self state dreams. Steingart seems to imply that we view Kohut's approach as nontheory laden. Of course it is not. In fact, self psychology brings to each clinical situation an elaborate theory of psychic development, framed around the positive and negative influences that have been brought to bear in childhood, and which collectively determine the state of the self.

Perhaps, our choice of the words manifest content is not well taken, because what self psychology connects with is not simply manifest content but a developmental scenario imposed on the manifest content in the analytic session and the manifest content of the dream. Self psychologists, that is, go from manifest content to interpretations, assessments, and attributions based on their theories of pathogenesis, development, and the nature of psychological structures. But this appears to be at the expense of a more or less investigational stance using the technique of free association and making inferences about latent meaning based on language, metaphor, contiguity, sequence, and so forth. For example, when a patient has a dream in which he is in a rowboat in the middle of a lake and the analyst tells him he feels as if his self is unanchored, the self psychologist is following an interpretive technique (line) that is disjunctive from both the modern Freudian and Kleinian approach. Steingart is correct, and we agree that the difference between Freudian and Kohutian praxis is in "method due to theory," but we feel that the technical difference that follows from theory has a profound effect on the analytic process to the point of making self psychology an independent research tradition.

Steingart finds value in Kohut's term self object as descriptive of the state of the child's mind during the anal—rapprochement phase. The problem is that this is not Kohut's primary or even ancillary use of this term; anal rapprochement is not part of Kohut's lexicon. Steingart's comment that compromise formation ignores the idea of a "total ego" is not clear to us. The concept of compromise formation does not obviate the fact that an individual has an "overall psychic organization." Perhaps what is at issue here is the old analytic/synthetic issue. Perhaps it could be said that for a self psychologist, the emphasis is on helping the patient synthesize in the belief the analysis will take care of its self, whereas for the modern Freudian, the approach is to help the patient analyze, in the belief that the synthesis will take care of itself. For us the technical and heuristic value of the concept of compromise formation is that it has both analytic and synthetic qualities and is conducive to understanding the dialectical interplay between the two.

The view that transference and countertransference constitute an organic clinical unit is not quite clear to us, nor are we sure that theories can be distinguished on the basis of whether they hold to this idea. Perhaps we get to the same point by a different route. The fundamental principle is that transference is ubiquitous, so that it must be experienced by both analysand and analyst. The analyst has transference (called countertransferences) to his analysand. This all goes without saying—the issue is the nature and extent of such countertransferences and how they are handled. It is certainly of value to recognize that, just as there is transference regression, there is also countertransference regression. Fantasies and feelings fill the analytic air, flying in directions.

Steingart's use of the term, construal, which he prefers to fantasy, is felicitous. We would also emphasize his point: "this kind of emphasis on a deep expression of an analysand's psychic reality via free association does not mean a Freudian psychoanalysis is not throughout an object relations experience" (p. 510). Again and again, we see in the literature this tendency to dichotomize Freudian psychoanalysis and object relational approaches, to paint Freudian psychoanalysis into a mechanistic, drive discharge, nonhuman, nonobject relational corner.

Common Ground

We are particularly grateful for Dr. Wallerstein's contribution to this project. He introduced the concept of "common ground," and thus set the stage for discussions of theoretical pluralism and diversity. His position holds that the common clinical phenomena of conflict and compromise formation, transference and countertransference, are the basis of common technical practice. Wallerstein believes that these phenomena underlie self psychology, Kleinian psychoanalysis, relational, and intersubjectivity analysis, just as they do ego psychology and modern conflict theory. But each of the divergent theories developed its approach by first asserting that the common ground concepts were flawed or inadequate to account for clinical phenomena and to provide a basis for technique.

Divergent theories either redefine old concepts in accordance with new principles or offer new concepts. Some proponents of these theories emphasize the revolutionary nature of their technique, thereby opposing Wallerstein's brief for common ground. We believe that the responses by Stolorow, Fosshage, and Ornstein bear out their belief that their theories differ from our model and from a Kleinian one as well. We regret that we have no response from a representative of the relational school. Our sense is that proponents of the relational position fall on a spectrum between the poles of self psychology and intersubjectivity on one side and modern Freudian and Kleinian theories on the other. Greenberg, for example, in his Oedipus and Beyond (1991), has stressed the centrality of conflict and a dual-drive motivational system.

We agree with Wallerstein's verdict that self psychology has performed a valuable consciousness-raising function in regard to self-esteem and self-cohesion issues in treatment. Of course, such issues had previously been discussed by Annie Reich, Edith Jacobson, and others, and have occupied the attention of other nonself psychologists since then.

The responses of Ornstein and Fosshage make a compelling case for self psychology as a divergent technique which does not fit into the common ground thesis. Self psychology claims the allegiance of many analysts who identify their approach as different, and who have gone on to organize their own group meetings and publications. Kohut wrote his "Two Analyses of Mr. Z." (1979) in an attempt to demonstrate that there are two different analytic techniques.

Wallerstein faults us for not being clear enough in our designation of relational psychoanalytic theorists. He would include Renik, Boesky, Poland, and Gill. We believe that their contributions rest comfortably under the banner of modern conflict theory and that the first three identify themselves as such. We understand why Wallerstein includes Gill and Hoffman in the relational/interpersonal category. It is not clear whether Wallerstein wants to abolish the theoretical category of relationalists altogether, but, again, we are faced with a group of analysts who define themselves as relationalists and have a journal to espouse their point of view. The relationalists, as a self-designated group, should not be included in common ground unless they choose to be. We do not agree that their differences from other schools are simply metapsychological rather than clinical.

We acknowledge that we may have created a "school" in bringing together Bach and Steingart under the heading "American object relations" theorists. We chose to discuss their contributions because of our familiarity with their work. We see them as more influenced by Loewald than Sullivan, so that their approach is different from that of Levenson, Zucker, Ehrenberg et al. The latter have a different view of pathogenesis and development and place a greater emphasis on the therapeutic role of the experience of, and with, the analyst than on insight.

To turn now to Wallerstein's final point, the selection of presenters at the Rome Congress. Wallerstein tells us that the reason he chose a classical theorist, a Kleinian, and a representative of the British middle school as his representatives of diverse theoretical positions was a political one. He needed to have representatives of the three continents and that constraint prevented him from including interpersonalists, relationalists, or self psychologists. No one would have suggested that his scientific conclusions incorporated political constraints, but he tells us this himself. Does this constitute an excuse, a self-accusation, or a complaint? If his is simply a political theory in scientific dress, it will pass as the political situation changes. If it is actually a scientific theory, why would it not have been possible to share the platform among proponents of all the major scientific positions? Why not have two from each continent? Or three? More panels or shorter presentations on each panel could have made this possible. We believe that a more convincing representation of viewpoints would have been possible in print, if not in the oral presentation. A case and an example of some relationalists or intersubjectivists or middle-school object relationalists and self psychologists agreeing about the essential clinical focus of the technique would be more convincing to us.

Wallerstein believes that theory is separate from technique. To say that theory matches technique is not to imply that theory comes first. Scientific theories are never constructed in the absence of data. Clinical evidence, usually in the form of clinical cases that do not show improvement with the technique in use, are the occasion for new clinical interventions and these interventions are often claimed to lead to changes in theory. Examples from the psychoanalytic literature are Mr. Z., Melanie Klein's child cases, interaction cases, Freud's change from pressure techniques to free association, and so forth.

Precisely because analysis is a scientific discipline, technique changes in an ongoing mutually corrective process with theory. There are two ways in which this happens: technical changes can modify theory and theoretical changes can modify technique. Let us look at examples of each of these processes. First, technique changes in response to clinical observation. The analyst makes an interpretation. Something seems to work with a patient. The analyst wonders what effected the change. She tries a similar interpretation with another patient. Or she tries an interpretation and it doesn't work. So she thinks that another phrasing may work better, or another aspect of the experience needs to be highlighted before the one she highlighted earlier. Such clinical interpretations then lead her to think of theory in a different way. She understands the importance of aggressive wishes where self-esteem had formerly seemed to be primary. This causes her to think that drive theory has more explanatory value and more therapeutic efficiency than she had thought before.

Finally we would like to express our appreciation to all the respondents for their thoughtful discussions of our paper. In this enterprise all of us have covered a lot of ground, common and uncommon. This process has been very illuminating for us. We hope that it will also be thought provoking for the readers of this Journal.

REFERENCES

ARLOW, J.A. (1979). The genesis of interpretation. *Journal of the American Psychoanalytic Association* (Suppl.)27:193–206.

——— (1994). The process of validation and hypothesis testing in the analytic situation. Unpublished.

BAUDRY, F. (1995). The challenge of comparing competing psychoanalytic theories. *Journal of Clinical Psychoanalysis* 4:457–464.

CAPER, R. (1995). Comments on "Notes on psychoanalytic theory and its consequences for technique." *Journal of Clinical Psychoanalysis* 4:465–470.

DE BIANCHEDI, E.T. (1995). Theory and Technique: What is Psychoanalysis? *Journal of Clinical Psychoanalysis* 4:471–482.

GREENBERG, J. (1991). *Oedipus and Beyond: A Clinical Theory.* Cambridge, MA: Harvard University Press.

FOSSHAGE, J.L. (1995). How theory affects technique. *Journal of Clinical Psychoanalysis* 4:483–490.

GREENBERG, J., MITCHELL, S. (1983). *Object Relations in Psychoanalytic Theory.* Cambridge, MA: Harvard University Press.

KOHUT, H. (1979). The two analyses of Mr. Z. *International Journal of Psycho-Analysis* 60:3–27.

LACHMANN, F. (1986). The interpretation of psychic conflict and adversarial relationships: A self psychological perspective. *Psychoanalytic Psychology* 3:341–355.

ORNSTEIN, P.H. (1995). Self psychology is not what you think it is. *Journal of Clinical Psychoanalysis* 4:491–506.

RICHARDS, A.D. (1982). The superordinate self in psychoanalytic theory and in the self psychoanalysis. *Journal of the American Psychoanalytic Association* 30:939–957.

——— (1992). Commentaries on Trop and Stolorow's "Defense Analysis in Self Psychology." *Psychoanalytic Dialogues* 2:455–465.

SCHWABER, E. (1990). Interpretation and the therapeutic action of psycho-analysis. *International Journal of Psycho-Analysis* 71:229–240.

SHAPIRO, T. (1981). Empathy: A critical re-evaluation. *Psychoanalytic Inquiry* 1:423.

STEINGART, I. (1995). Some Notes on psychoanalytic theory and its consequences for technique. *Journal of Clinical Psychoanalysis* 4:507–518.

STOLOROW, R.D, (1995). The strawman cometh. *Journal of Clinical Psychoanalysis* 4:519–526.

WALLERSTEIN, R.S. (1995). The relational theory to technique. *Journal of Clinical Psychoanalysis* 4:527–542.

VI. Epilogue

Section VI, the the Epilogue, concludes volume 1 with "A View from Now." In this chapter Richards offers us his thoughts on a vast and very productive psychoanalaytic career. He talks frankly about "what he wanted, what he expected and what he got" from psychoanalysis. He asks:

- What has happened to Freud's voice in psychoanalysis?
- Why is psychoanalysis growing around the world but diminishing in the United States?

CHAPTER 19

The View from Now

I will begin with the view from then. I believe these contributions and my scholarship are rooted in what I learned from Hutchens, Adler, and later McKeon at the College at the University of Chicago, whose focus was on the philosophy of knowledge, my experience at the Menninger School of Psychiatry in Topeka Kansas, where I was mentored by noted psychiatrists and psychologists great intellects of that time, Konrad Lorenz, S. I. Hayakawa, Aldous Huxley, Ludwig von Bertanffy, and others who were Sloan Visiting Professors, and finally my psychoanalytic training at the New York Psychoanalytic Institute. I was fortunate again because their faculty included psychoanalytic giants from both Europe and the United States. The Europeans included Otto Isakower, Edith Jacobson, Kurt and Ruth Eissler, Andrew Peto, Nick Young, Margaret Mahler, Werner Musterberger, Ana Marie Weil, Heinz and Dora Hartmann and the Americans included Phyllis Greenacre, Jack Arlow, David Beres, Victor Rosen, Martin Stein, et al. The curriculum was Freud, Freud, and more Freud. That is what I wanted, that is what I expected, and that is what I got. No Melanie Klein, no Harry Stack Sullivan, no Erich Fromm, Karen Horney, Otto Rank, Ferenczi or even Theodore Reik.

I wrote a piece, Growing up Orthodox, which is in this volume and the orthodox referred to psychoanalysis as well as Judaism. I think I derived from that—the classroom experience as well as the supervision and my own analysis—a solid sense of security and identity as a Freudian psychoanalyst, which was tempered by a questioning attitude derived from my Chicago and Topeka experiences. This identity was supported by my peer group, Marty Willick, Sandy Abend, Ernie Kafka, Bob Kabcenel, Bill Grossman, Bennett Simon, and Lester Schwartz, fellow candidates, most of whom had trained at Albert Einstein and were indoctrinated Freudians before they even started their analytic training. I consider myself fortunate that I had the Menninger experience before starting at the institute.

After I graduated from the New York Psychoanalytic Society and Institute (NYPSI) I continued my postgraduate education at the Madison

Delicatessen at Madison Avenue and 86th Street in New York City. A group of us met for lunch every Friday: Charlie Brenner, Sandy Abend, Ernie Kafka, Bernie Brodsky, Mervin Peskin, Arthur Schwartz and Arlene Kramer Richards. We schmoozed about psychoanalytic theory and politics and the state of our world. I graduated from NYPSI in 1969. In 1972, Charlie said to me that someone he knew, Heinz Kohut, (they both had been presidents of the American Psychoanalytic Association (APsaA)) had written a book—would I read it and let him know if there way anything worthwhile in it? The book was, of course, *The Analysis of Self* (1971) and it was a challenge to our version of Freudian psychoanalysis which we called Modern Conflict Theory. There was in fact a theoretical divide at the NYPSI (which I was less aware of in my training) between one group, mostly American: Arlow, Brenner, Beres, Calder (the "AB^{2}C") and others who promoted Ego Psychology and the Structural Metapsychological point of view; and the Europeans and their American acolytes who stayed closer to the original Freud and the economic and topographical metapsychological points of view. But in any case, I read the book and reported back to Charlie.

I elaborated my take on the book in two papers: "Self Theory and Conflict Theory and The Problem of Hypochondraisis" and "The Superordinate Self in Psychoanalytic Theory and the Self Psychologies." In the first paper I tried to demonstrate using a case that self theory did not offer a better understanding of the phenomena than conflict theory and I questioned the new theory's clinical usefulness. I have since become more positive about self psychology and I recognize that judging one theory as superior to another is problematic. My view is that self psychology and conflict theory are different—different theories of therapeutic action, development and cure.

In the second paper I argued against the concept of a superordinate self in psychoanalysis and took on John Gedo, George Klein, as well as Heinz Kohut. This set me on a course of reviewing a series of psychoanalytic contributors including Marshall Adelson, Frank Auld and Marvin Hyman, Lewis Aron, Winfred Bion, John Gedo, Merton Gill, Arnold Goldberg, Irwin Hoffman, Tony Kris, Rudolph Lowenstein, Steve Mitchell, Donna Orange, Fred Pine, Leo Rangell, Robert Stolorow, and Michael Stone. These book reviews are not included in this volume but they did earn me the title of the "Mack the Knife" of psychoanalysis.

These reviews were relatively tame. I reserved my stridency for Relational Psychoanalysis, publishing two papers with coauthors Arthur

Lynch and Janet Bachant, who had been my students. They were in a private seminar in which we read Freud cover to cover, all twenty-four volumes. The first paper was in an issue of *Psychoanalytic Psychology* critiquing Relational Psychoanalysis which was referred to as "The Empire Strikes Back." Some of my print and personal exchanges with the relationalists were less than cordial. Not only did I represent the Drive Theory which the relational psychoanalysts were arguing against, I was part of the American psychoanalyst establishment (APsaA) which had excluded psychologists and did not welcome their critical voices.

The crux of our problem with Relational Psychoanalysis in regard to psychoanalytic theory as it is presented in *Object Relations in Psychoanalytic Theory* by Greenberg and Mitchell (1983) was the drive/relational dichotomy. We maintained that this was a false dichotomy and that, in fact, in Freud's psychoanalytic theory, object relations as well as drives were central. In regard to psychoanalytic technique I wrote that Mitchell's characterization of Freudian psychoanalysts as unresponsive and non-interactive was a straw man. My contribution in the Division 39–Section 10 1999 Newsletter, *The Round Robin* ("Squeaky Chairs and Straw Persons") became the focus of a lively exchange that year between myself and other Freudians (Janet Bachant, Frank Summers, Arlene Kramer Richards, and Sheldon Goodman) and Steve Mitchell and other relationalists (Emmanuel Ghent, Sharon Zalusky, Mary Beth Cresci, David S. MacIssac, and Spiros D. Orfanos). It was published on *InternationalPsychoanalysis.net*, and has been the focus of several private seminars and study groups.

But since then I have become much more ecumenical and much more accepting of diverse theoretical points of view. I have looked for common ground as in the paper I wrote with Arlene Kramer Richards (2000) about Wolstein and in our contribution on the relationship between theory and technique (1995). We asserted a convergence of Freudian and Kleinian theory in which both conflict and fantasy were considered. And overall my pleas have been for a measure of humility in regard to the broad psychoanalytic theoretical landscape.

I have been very influenced by the work of the Polish pathologist and philosopher of science Ludwik Fleck (1935), who maintained that scientific contributions are influenced by historical, cultural, political, economic, and personal determinants. His work on the Sociology of Scientific Knowledge was the warrant for my attempting to define a sociology of psychoanalytic knowledge which relates to the historical and political papers to be published in the second volume of my selected papers.

In that vein, Arlene Kramer Richards and I have offered a theory of the theories of psychoanalytic technique. The thesis is that a psychoanalytic theoretician develops a theory of technique to counter his or her anti-therapeutic proclivities. Freud, who was an interventionist, and sometimes did intervene in the life of his patients—as with his patient Frink—stressed abstinence. Kohut's emphasis on empathy as a technical approach countered his own narcissism. And in a different dimension, Aron has written that Mitchell's development of relational psychoanalysis was a response to what he considered the hegemony of APsaA in American psychoanalysis. My interest in Fleck contributed to my ecumenical turn, over the past several years, as did my ten-year stint as editor of the *Journal of hte American Psychoanalytic Association* (*JAPA*). I welcomed and received papers on diverse points of view. The requirements were that they be well-written, well researched and, where relevant, clinically supported.

So where is psychoanalysis and where am I now? Psychoanalysis is growing in the world. The IPA now has 14,000 members. Psychoanalysis is holding its own in the US outside of the American Psychoanalytic Association. APsaA membership is at best in a steady state but, with its aging membership, it can expect a decade of decline. There was a recent infusion of new members from William Alanson White, and there may be another from the American Institute of Psychoanalysis but few other free-standing institutes who may join APsaA in years to come.

The number of candidates in APsaA is declining, I believe, in part because of the rigid regulatory requirements of its the Board of Professional Standards (BoPS). With fewer candidates there will be fewer new members. There is agreement that APsaA is losing market educational share to non APsaA institutes. *JAPA* has a new editor now who is making an effort to restore its level of scholarship to that achieved in previous decades, but I believe there are fewer good submissions which can be designated as having a Freudian voice. I believe the Freudian "thought collective" to use Fleck's term is shrinking. It is not reproducing itself. On the other hand, other thought collectives are growing—Bionion, Winnicotian, and Lacanian and, perhaps less so, Kleinian. The first three have a strong following in Latin American and in some parts of Europe.

On the other hand, Freud sells in China. For the last three years, six other teachers and I, have travelled twice-a-year to Wuhan China to lecture and supervise a group of 140 eager and enthusiastic students. The course now has over 200 enrollees. Our personal experiences in the program in China and with Skype seminars between meetings is that there is a mutual interest in and an ability to grasp fundamental psychoanalytic theoretical principles and apply them in their therapeutic encounters.

We feel that the response to psychoanalysis is similar to what the first psychoanalysts experienced in Vienna, Berlin, and Budapest in the beginning of the 20th Century. There are now analytic institutes sponsored by the IPA in two Chinese cities, Shanghai and Beijing, and after a time there may be a third in Wuhan. This experience makes me optimistic about the long-term survival and future of our psychoanalytic discipline.

REFERENCES

FLECK, L. (1935).*The Genesis and Development of a Scientific Fact,* eds. T.J. Trenn & R.K. Merton, transl. F. Bradley & T.J. Trenn. Chicago: University of Chicago Press, 1979.

GREENBERG, J.R., & MITCHELL, S.A. (1983). *Object Relations in Psychoanalytic Theory.* Cambridge: Harvard University Press

KOHUT, H. (1971). *The Analysis of the Self.* New York: International Universities Press.

RICHARDS, A.D. (1999). Squeaky chairs and straw persons: An intervention in the contemporary psychoanalytic debate. *The Round Robin* XIV(1):1, 6–9.

———— & RICHARDS, A.K. (1995). Notes on psychoanalytic theory and its consequences for technique *Journal of Clinical Psychoanalysis* 4:429–456.]

———— ———— (2000). Benjamin Wolstein and us: Many roads lead to Rome. *Contemporary Psychoanalysis* 36:255–266.

Arnold D. Richards, M.D.

Acknowledgements

This has been a labor of love for many individuals to whom I am very grateful. Arthur Lynch has written a masterful introduction, and I am also grateful for his collaboration on several papers in the volume (Chapters 8, 12, 16, & 17). Art and I, along with Janet Bachant, another collaborator (Chapters 11 & 12), began a journey together almost 30 years ago when we read the 24 volumes of Freud cover to cover Many of the papers in the this volume reflect what we learned from each other.

I am grateful for my mentors and teachers at these institutions: The College of the University of Chicago, the Menninger School of Psychiatry, and the New York Psychoanalytic Society/Institute. My psychoanalytic journey has been taken hand-in-hand with my wife Arlene Kramer Richards who is also a collaborator on papers in this volume (Chapters 13 & 18). Each if us benefitted form the fact that we followed different disciplinary and analytic training paths.

I am grateful to our son Stephen Richards who taught me how to write. My first psychoanalytic publication was a review of *Haven in a Heartless World* by Christopher Lasch. Stephen learned to write from his mother Arlene Kramer Richards who remembers watching her grandfather sitting at his desk writing for hours. It was only later that she learned he was addressing envelopes because he was the secretary of the Chechenover Benevolent Society

This book would not be in print with out the indefatigable efforts of Tamar and Lawrence Schwartz, the mainstays of the IPBooks imprint, who have attended to every detail from inception to final publication. I am also grateful to Rebecca Richards whose support and good judgment benefitted the project

Finally, over the years I've had the good fortune to have the help of some superb editors—Michael Farrin, Eve Golden, Elizabeth Ronis, and Phyllis Stern—all of whom have polished my words and made my sometimes cumbersome thoughts more accessible to the reader.

CPSIA information can be obtained
at www.ICGtesting.com
Printed in the USA
FFOW03n1318090516
23933FF